COMPARING THE STATES AND COMMUNITIES

COMPARING THE STATES AND COMMUNITIES

Politics, Government, and Policy in the United States

NORMAN R. LUTTBEG
Texas A & M University

HarperCollins*Publishers*

Sponsoring Editor: Lauren Silverman
Project Editor: Thomas R. Farrell
Design Supervisor: Stacey Agin
Cover Design: Butler Udell Design
Production Manager/Assistant: Willie Lane/Sunaina Sehwani
Compositor: Publishing Synthesis, Ltd.
Printer and Binder: R. R. Donnelley & Sons Company
Cover Printer: The Lehigh Press, Inc.

Comparing the States and Communities: Politics, Government, and Policy in the United States

Library of Congress Cataloging-in-Publication Data

Luttbeg, Norman R.
    Comparing the states and communities : politics, government, and
  policy in the United States / Norman R. Luttbeg.
      p. cm.
    Includes bibliographical references and index.
    ISBN 0-673-46184-X
    1. State governments—United States. 2. Local government—United
  States.   I. Title.
  JK2408.L88 1992
    320.973—dc20   91-19722
                                                                          CIP

320
L994

91 92 93 94 9 8 7 6 5 4 3 2 1

Contents

Preface

The United States comprises 50 democracies, each with laws enacted to deal with social problems within available resources and shaped by individual politics. That exciting situation motivated this text. The states could be compared to discover why some enacted policies and others did not, as well as whether the enacted policies make the states better or not. Traditionally, textbooks on state and local politics consider the many institutional arrangements among the states, implying that they make a difference. In this textbook the student will consider the questions of whether it genuinely matters if a state has a close balance between Democrats and Republicans in its legislature or if it asks those legislators to meet nearly continually rather than once every two years for a limited time. While there may be reasons to change the format of a state's government or to enact a specific policy, a fundamental assumption throughout this text is that there is no need to make these changes, if in actuality, they offer no improvement. There is another basis for this perspective: There is no agreement that one state has dealt more effectively with crime, has a clearly more efficient government, has genuinely superior government services, or is a better democracy than the others. Why not?

Ironically, this text represents both the beginning of my graduate studies and the fruition of teaching a state and local course for many years at Texas A&M University. The beginning was a seminar by Charles Press on state politics, in which we were charged to compare all states on some dependent measure and to explain the variation noted. I thus began to consider the 50 states as individual examples. Despite having taught state and local courses in many states, my course was a rather conventional consideration of the basic format of our state governments. That worked well with mainly liberal arts or political science majors, but at Texas A&M, as we discuss in Chapter 1, classes are large and include few such majors. Most students are science, agriculture, and engineering majors with little background in political science.

I began to experiment with restructuring the course to get their attention by the appeal that I was presenting only things that worked. I started with differences among the states that I thought might get their attention, such as the fact that some states are quite poor, that Texas looks similar to other southern states but with oil wealth, and that many innovations for improving education are ineffective. I asked students a simple question: If they had job offers from companies in two states, would they consider not only the salaries and opportunities of the job but also the quality of the government of the state in which they would live? Usually, I was answered with blank stares. I then asked whether they felt they *should* consider that issue. While some agreed that they should, most thought not. Ultimately, I decided to take a more constructive stance, seeking to account for why outstanding states are not to be found. All of this resulted in substantial course-note development and data gathering. That in turn served as the basis of this text.

Pointing out the ineffectiveness of policy-making or of institutional changes reflects no particular ideological perspective. But such a perspective might afford the chance for more effective changes. That perspective may alert the student to the reality that policy-making in the United States often reflects half-hearted efforts that are the result of compromise, dealing with the limited revenues that are available, and may not vary regardless of the institutional differences among the states. To argue this, however, is neither to dismiss the problem nor to discourage the use of government to solve it. In short, saying that thus far we have been largely ineffective in coping with social problems does not mean we should stop making the effort. Rather, we should find more effective means to accomplish our goals.

I should say that my normal semester course gives only several weeks to consider state policies, which are covered here in Chapters 12 and 13. I think this is a very important aspect of the course, and I know that many instructors delete the policy chapters as they fall behind near the end of the term. Instructors should try to find room for the materials in Chapters 12 through 14, because those chapters represent more than a superficial coverage of some social problems and policy differences among the states.

In addition to Charles Press, who introduced me to comparative analysis, I should like to thank Keith Hamm, Harvey Tucker, Chuck Wiggins, and a former colleague from way back, Thomas R. Dye, for continually bringing to my attention the benefits of having multiple governments to compare rather than having a sample of only one (as when studying U.S. national government). I was much encouraged by several reviewers who were warmly responsive to my approach, and I thank them. Reviewers who provided useful comments include Alex Aichinger, Northwestern State University; Charles Barrilleaux, Florida State University; Thad L. Beyle, University of North Carolina/Chapel Hill; David L. Cingranelli, State

University of New York/Binghamton; Peter J. Haas, San Jose State University; Keith Hamm, Rice University; Russell L. Hanson, Indiana University; Albert J. Nelson, University of Wisconsin/La Crosse; Joel A. Thompson, Appalachian State University; and Joseph B. Tucker, Ohio University. I should also like to thank my many students who put up with my two favorite and alternative answers to their questions—"it depends on the state" and "it does not make a difference"—I even thought of that as a title for this text. I should also like to thank Samuel Hudson, who was at one time my research assistant. His accurate and exhausting creation of the matrix of information on which this effort depends allowed my confidence in doing the analysis. Caroline Luttbeg read the entire manuscript. She alterted me both to less persuasive arguments and to awkwardness of some presentations. Finally I would like to thank a series of editors at various companies, coming down ultimately to Lauren Silverman at HarperCollins, for being supportive.

NORMAN R. LUTTBEG

COMPARING
THE STATES
AND
COMMUNITIES

Chapter
1

The Nature of Policy-Making

*M*any of the readers of this text are in the state of Texas and are taking a course in state and local politics. If they were asked whether they wanted to be reading this text, I know that most would answer no! Certainly some might answer yes out of an interest in how state and local governments are run. After all, unless you emigrate to another country, you will be subject not only to federal laws but, perhaps more important, to the laws of your state and local governments. Others may just want to be good citizens, who are informed about how their state and local governments run and about how they might influence these governments to enact their personal preferences into policy. If most answer no, why are they reading? They are reading this text and taking this course because they must. But who requires it? Is it the university that they are presently attending, is it their advisor, their major department, or is it the federal government? It is none of these. If you wish to graduate from an institution of higher education in the state of Texas that accepts public funds, you are required to take this course.

A LAW REQUIRING THE STUDY OF STATE GOVERNMENT

The Texas legislature in 1929 required high school students and college students to take a course considering the constitutions of the United States and the state of Texas. In 1967 the requirement for college students was expanded to two courses for the "consideration of the Constitution of the United States and the constitutions of the states, with special emphasis on that of Texas."[1] One can easily avoid taking this required course merely by seeking one's education elsewhere, since no other state has such a requirement. Readers from other states may be required to take a course on U.S. government, or may be required to take this course because of their major.

Why would one state legislature pass such a law when no others do? What could have motivated the Texas legislature? Several explanations come to mind. First, and perhaps facetiously, they might have thought that students lack things to occupy their time. Rather than drinking beer or lying in the sun, they can help fill their days by satisfying this requirement. But such a thought would seem equally likely in the legislatures of the other 49 states, so this explanation cannot account for the unique Texas statute. Second, legislators may have been motivated to employ twice as many political scientists in their universities, making this a sort of "full employment of political scientists" act. Again why would Texas be unique in this? It is true that because of this act many more political scientists are employed in Texas than would otherwise be the case. This result, however, is an unintended one. It is not at all uncommon for laws to have unintended impacts, some desirable and some not.

The normal expectation is that a representative body acts in response to constituent wishes. Some constituents may write to express their opinions, whereas others telephone or even picket. One can just see picketers with signs demanding that "Ignorant students should be helped!" or the establishment of a new organization to "Save Our Students." Or perhaps it could have become an issue during elections. One political party's candidate might pledge to require such a course if elected, whereas the opposition party's candidate vows to preserve students' time for more important courses, such as math or science. No such constituent acts were evident either in 1929 or in 1967. Rather, the bill seems to have drawn little constituent attention, certainly little student protest, and for that matter, little attention from the mass media—radio and television stations and newspapers.

For any government, the best circumstance is for the public to comply voluntarily with the law. Lacking such compliance, governments must coerce compliance, an expensive course of action that requires the employment of police to assure that people comply with the law. Perhaps the Texas legislature envisioned that these courses would focus on the dignity of debate in

_____

1 Vernon's *Civil Statutes*, chap. 298, p. 714, articles 2663b-2, sec. 2.

the Senate, the impressiveness of the Capitol, the responsiveness of those in the legislature, and the state's proud history. They would thus assure voluntary compliance with the law by inculcating respect for government, its acts, and its personnel.

Certainly there are elements in this textbook, as in others, that might be viewed as intended to engender respect for government. Clearly there is compliance among college students in Texas with the law requiring them to take this course. But is it voluntary? It is difficult to say because it is so easy to enforce this statute. You do not graduate unless you have taken the course. Texans, including college students, do not comply with other less easily enforced laws, such as the 55-mile-per-hour speed limit on most roads and the 21-year-old drinking age.

There is little evidence that requiring Texas college students to take this course has resulted in a public that complies with laws more voluntarily. In fact, Texas is among the states whose citizens show the least compliance with these laws. Besides, why would legislators in other states not be equally interested in gaining voluntary compliance? Perhaps the act was a response to the lack of voluntary compliance by Texans that has merely failed to have the intended impact on public behavior. If that was the legislative motivation, there has been a certain inattention to research findings. The better educated tend to be more voluntarily compliant. This would suggest that the course should be required, not in colleges, but in the early school grades, before anyone can drop out.

A related idea is that the course might be used to teach citizenship, or perhaps more accurately, *how to influence government as a citizen*. Instructors might discuss laws concerning how to run for public office in the state, how to find out when public meetings will be held to deal with legislative issues, how to form a political action committee (PAC), how to assume a position of authority in your local political party, and how to get access to important public information on which to base your opinions. Enactment of the statute might thus be expected to result in more public involvement in government; but if so it failed, inasmuch as Texans are among those least involved in government. In the presidential election of 1988, only 44.2 percent of eligible Texans voted for president, as compared with a national turnout of 50.2 percent. Only citizens in Georgia, Hawaii, North Carolina, and South Carolina voted less.[2] Again it is possible that the Texas legislature merely wished to improve this low participation. But then why were the legislators in the other

2 U.S. Bureau of the Census, *Statistical Abstract of the United States, 1989* (Washington, DC: U.S. Government Printing Office), p. 259.

states—especially Georgia, Hawaii, and the Carolinas—not similarly motivated?

One of the functions of this text, which will be evident throughout, is that of critiquing the performance of state governments to suggest which policies work and which do not. Perhaps the legislators intended that professors provide prospective citizens and representatives, as well as present legislators, with *constructive critiques of government performance*. The idea here is that, by way of their research and informed thinking, professors might recommend improvements in the performance of government, including the legislature. It may be cynical, but there is little evidence that legislators welcome criticism by anyone, much less publicly employed professors. Also, nothing about the Texas legislature would suggest that they are more receptive of criticism than other state legislatures.

It might also be that the legislators thought they were important and that they were in effect saying, "We are important, so study us and respect us." Certainly we all would like to be respected for what we do, so such vanity on the part of those able to enact legislation to satisfy it might be expected. But why not in the 49 other states? There is little evidence that Texas legislators are held in higher or lower respect than their counterparts elsewhere.

Finally, Senator Joseph McCarthy of Wisconsin once fueled national anxiety with charges that communism was taking over as a result of its appeal to the better educated. He created what was called the "red scare." The legislature might have enacted the government course requirements in the hopes of stemming the progress of the communist takeover. Certainly no government in Texas has ever been won by communists, so the course requirements might seem to have been successful. Then again, no government anywhere in the United States has ever been taken over by communists. Note that the statutes were not passed in the period of great anxiety, the 1950s. Again there is no explanation why other states did not enact similar requirements.

LAWMAKING IN TEXAS AND ELSEWHERE

In 1967 the Texas House voted 138 yeas versus 3 nays for the law requiring the two courses in political science. The Senate passed the legislation by a voice vote. It is impossible to say what motivated these legislators, but among the motivations we have discussed are those that typically influence legislators. The statute is but an example of the general process of enacting legislation.

First, there must be a *perceived problem* that the legislation seeks to address. The perceived problem in our example above may have been the threat posed to the state by indifference, lack of participation, communism, failure to comply voluntarily with the law, or the like. Next, one or more legislators, someone in the executive branch, or even a political party or an interest group has to conceive of a *plausible legislative solution.* This solution has to have several other properties. It must seem *workable* and *enforceable;* it must *not be too costly;* and it is best if it has only *weak* or even *no opposition.* All too frequently, however, legislators have little evidence to suggest that the legislation will solve the problem. Little or no research underlies the solutions proposed. Moreover, seldom does anyone reconsider legislation afterward to assess its success in coping with the perceived problem.

Certainly the Texas statute requiring the study of states (with an emphasis on Texas) followed this pattern, as do many other national, state, and local laws. Three other laws are of particular interest to college students. They are the 21-year-old drinking age, the 55-mile-per-hour speed limit on most rural highways, and efforts to improve elementary and secondary education in the states.

OTHER EXAMPLES OF LAWMAKING

The 21-Year-Old Drinking Age.   The states used to differ as to the age when an adult was allowed to drink alcoholic beverages, setting the minimum age anywhere between 18 and 21. They are now required by an act of Congress to set that minimum at 21 years. States that fail to enact such a law lose federal highway funds to build and maintain roadways within the state. The perceived problem seen by Congress was an increase in highway fatalities in which the drivers were both intoxicated and below the age of 25 years. The plausible solution was to raise the drinking age to 21 nationally. The reader might well inquire why they did not raise the age to 25 years of age. A better question is why they did not raise the driving age to 25 rather than changing the drinking age. After all, few drunken pedestrians die by losing control, nor do many die in accidents caused by such pedestrians.

The law did appear to be plausible and enforceable. More important, opposition to the law was weak. Those who were opposed were unable to speak out without seeming to favor drunken driving. Also, few persons below this age have lawmaking power as state legislators, and none is eligible to be a member of Congress. Supporters of the law hoped that compliance would be voluntary, but if not the state governments would assure compliance by requiring bars and grocery markets to "card" potential purchasers before selling alcoholic beverages. Little definitive research suggested that the law would reduce driving-while-intoxicated (DWI) fatalities. Nor has there been follow-up research to suggest that the law has had the desired impact. There is, of course, no constitutional requirement that legislative solutions to problems must work or be declared null and void.

The 55-Mile-per-Hour Speed Limit. This congressionally mandated state law resembles that above, in that if a state wishes to retain federal highway funds, it must enact this speed limit. There has been a subsequent revision to allow a 65-mile-per-hour speed limit on certain interstate highways outside urban areas. The original legislation, however, derives from OPEC's embargo of petroleum in 1973 and went unchanged until 1988. The embargo caused a shortage of gasoline in the United States, and Congress felt that the plausible solution was to reduce speeds for more fuel efficiency. There was opposition, including truckers, who argued that, because of their gearing, trucks were less efficient at 55 mph. Although it was plausible that cars and trucks traveling at 55 mph would get better mileage than at 65 or 70 mph, follow-up research has been inconclusive as to whether gasoline was saved.

At any rate, the issue has changed as the 55 mph speed limit has come to be seen as a saver of lives. Fewer people die in accidents if the vehicle is traveling at 55 mph rather than at 70 mph. Despite research that tended to support the lifesaving aspect of the 55-mph speed limit, Congress raised the speed limit on nonurban interstate highways.[3] Preliminary reports suggest that there is no clear pattern to the impact the increase has had on fatalities, which calls into question whether the 55-mph limit was responsible for any decline in highway fatalities. Again, we have policy-making based on plausible, rather than demonstrated, solutions.

Declining Performance in Public Schools. Many states have experienced declining performance by their college-bound students on the Scholastic Aptitude Tests—or SATs, as they are commonly called. These findings are taken as an indication of a problem—namely, the failure on the part of our public schools to provide an education comparable to that provided in the past. There are many plausible solutions to this perceived problem.

---

3 See *Impact and Implementation of the 55-Mile-Per-Hour Speed Limit*, Hearings before the Subcommittee on Surface Transportation of the Committee on Public Works and Transportation House of Representative, March 18 and 19, 1987; *Research Results of the Speed Limit Increase*, Hearings before the Subcommittee on Transportation, Aviation and Materials of the Committee on Science, Space, and Technology, House of Representatives, July 26, 1989; and *55: A Decade of Experience* (Washington, DC: Transportation Research Board, National Research Council, 1984).

Policymakers can improve teachers' salaries to attract better teachers, who presumably are going into better-paying occupations. They can enact so-called "No pass, no play" laws that disqualify student athletes who are failing a single course to put the emphasis in our schools on education rather than athletics. A teacher competency test would weed out incompetent teachers, and stressing the basics at least would give students necessary information and skills. Finally, policymakers could require that students who, in their senior year in high school, cannot pass a minimum competency test would be denied a diploma. However, there is little research, apart from the declining SAT scores, that demonstrates the existence of a problem.[4] Unfortunately, few sound and inexpensive solutions are known.[5]

Figure 1.1 shows the relationship between the average teacher's salary by state and the average SAT scores for those states. Such figures will be common throughout the text. This is a scatter diagram that merely places each state relative to the variables on the horizontal and vertical axes. There are 50 dots shown, each representing a state. Thus Alaska, with an average teacher's salary of $39,800 and an average combined SAT score of just under 950, appears as shown. Additionally, a regression line and equation are given. This line minimizes the distance of the points from the line, giving the best prediction of SAT scores based on the average teacher's salary.

If the relationship were perfect, all points would fall on the line, meaning that salary perfectly predicted SAT scores. The R, or correlation, between the two measures would be 1.00, or rather -1.0 in this instance. The "$y = 1058 - 4.33x$" equation just defines the line shown. The first term, 1058, is the intercept or the SAT value when average teacher salary is zero. If teachers were not paid, SAT scores, at least in the relationship shown here, would reach 1058! Of course few would teach for no pay and no state on average pays less than $15,000 per year. The −4.33 coefficient is the slope of the equation, or the regression coefficient, and is what you multiply average teachers' salaries in thousands of dollars by and add to the intercept to get the best prediction of SAT scores. Thus, given Alaska's $39,800 average teacher salary, we get:

---

4 This statement is not exactly true, inasmuch as increased illiteracy and the incidence of remedial mathematics courses in colleges also suggest declining educational performance in the United States. See: National Commission on Excellence in Education, *A Nation at Risk* (Washington, DC: U.S. Government Printing Office, 1983).

5 *A Nation at Risk*. The research that underlies this controversial and negative report makes no comparison among states with certain programs as to whether they do better in educating their youth than do those without such programs.

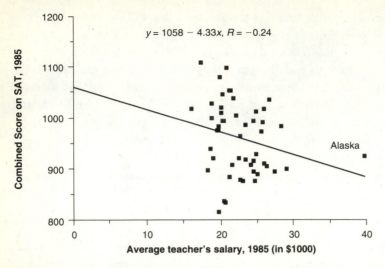

Figure 1.1   SAT combined scores vs. teachers' salaries.

Source: U.S. Bureau of the Census, "Average Teachers' Salaries, 1985," *Statistical Abstract of the United States, 1986,* Washington DC: U.S. Government Printing Office, p. 139; *Scholastic Aptitude Test Scores, 1985,* Princeton, NJ: College Board.

SAT score prediction = 1058 – 4.33 times $39.8 (thousand)

SAT score prediction = 1058 – 172

SAT score prediction = 886

This result is lower than the actual value because the relationship is not perfect. If the states were tightly clustered around the line, the predictions would be more accurate because the relationship would be stronger, or more nearly perfect, and R would be quite close to maximum, or 1.0. If R is close to 0.0, the two variables are unrelated. In this case, this would mean that no difference in the average teacher's salary paid in a state would affect students' performances on the SATs.

Having explained what is shown in Figure 1.1, we can consider what it tells us. Most important, it shows that states with the highest teachers' salaries do not have the highest SAT scores. In fact, although the relationship is weak (R far below 1.0), higher pay is associated with *lower* SAT scores! Is it the case that increasing salaries will result in lower SATs? It seems implausible that higher salaries result in worse teachers who fail to teach their students, resulting in worse performances on the SATs. But there is certainly little reason to believe, given these findings, that raising salaries improves SAT scores, much less education.

Figure 1.2 suggests even more troubling considerations. States with few graduating students taking SATs do better than those with a high percentage of

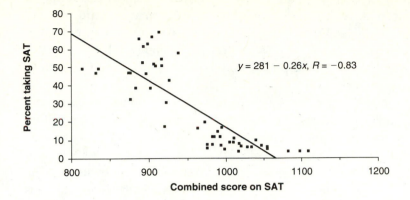

Figure 1.2   Percentage taking SAT vs. combined SAT scores.

Source: Scholastic Aptitude Test Scores, 1985, Princeton, NJ: College Board.

their students taking the SAT. The problem seems to be that more students are taking the SATs to be admitted to college; moreover, as more marginal students take the exams, scores drop. States that use the ACT as their primary entrance test seem to have only their brightest students, who perhaps are eager to go to out-of-state colleges, taking the SAT.[6] To the degree that the decline in SATs defines the problem in education, one simple and effective solution to the problem is to discourage any but the brightest students from taking the SAT. This obviously absurd policy recommendation suggests the difficulties that legislators have in finding solutions to the problems facing society. In this case we do not even know whether we have a problem with education in the United States. Without holding constant the types of students taking the SATs, we cannot know whether the student of 20 years ago was better than today's student.

COMPARING THE STATES AND COMMUNITIES

The reader has now been exposed to the basic approach and thesis of this textbook. The approach is that the 50 states can be used as examples of dif-

---

6 Although data are available for only 28 states, ACT scores show only a modest relationship with SAT scores by state. The equation is ACT score = 12 + 0.01 times SAT scores, with a correlation of 0.28. It should be noted that ACT scores improve with higher teachers' salaries, but modestly, ACT = -4.6 + 1.4 times average teacher's salary in thousands of dollars.

ferent government policies in areas such as education, tax levels, voting in elections, and so forth. The thesis is that there is little to recommend enacting a policy unless other states enacting that policy have found it successful in coping with the problem. If there is no desirable difference between states with and without a particular policy, why bother to enact it other than to humor its proponents?

To elaborate, the states offer a unique laboratory in which we can assess the utility of policies in changing behavior or in confronting problems that affect modern society. Although the 50 states differ in many regards, they share many qualities including a presidential-style government with legislative, executive, and judicial branches.[7] This arrangement contrasts with the more common parliamentary form of democracy, in which the executive is largely indistinguishable from the legislature or parliament. In the parliamentary form of government the idea of checks and balances (formal lawmaking powers that can be used by one branch against the other, such as the veto power of the executive) is not present.

Despite this similarity, however, the states are far from identical, as we shall see. For example, they often enact sharply different policies, such as having the death penalty or banning it, discouraging abortion or saying little about it, substantially underwriting the cost of educating college students out of general tax revenues, or having students pay a more substantial part of the costs of their education. It is certainly possible that the differences in policy have *no* impact. Focusing on the last example above, it is possible that having students pay as little as 7 percent or as much as 50 percent of the cost of their education may have little impact on the numbers seeking an education. It also might not affect the desire of students to remain in the state and make use of their education for society's benefit.

If it were not the case that they had meaningfully different policies, our laboratory of 50 states would not allow us to say much about how to cope with various problems. We could still say that the range of policies in the state is insufficient to judge their impact. The range in teachers' salaries above would appear to be such an example.

States may have differing success in coping with various problems; and by identifying successful policies, we can recommend these policies to the state legislatures that have failed thus far to enact them. Similarly, we can identify ineffective policies that might as well be repealed. Note that we shall be considering the benefits of a broad range of policies. For example we shall

---

7 Since the Massachusetts Constitution of 1780 predates the U.S. Constitution of 1789 and has all of the checks and balances between the executive and legislative branches, perhaps we should speak of our form of government as the "Massachusetts style" of government.

look at policies concerning elections, such as which officials will be elected rather than appointed and how often these elected officials must seek reelection. We shall also look at whether the legislative body is well paid and has support staff to encourage policy production or lacks such pay and staff with the intent to retain the legislature's amateur character. A state's electorate may be encouraged to play an active role in governing and making policy, or it may be discouraged from doing so.

WHY DOES NOTHING WORK?

We have discussed three policies that seem to have had little impact on the problems they were supposed to address. They are the Texas government requirement, the 55-mile-per-hour speed limit, and the 21-year-old minimum drinking age. Ideal legislation works because it is based on knowledge of how to cope with social problems. These policies fail on this test. Unfortunately, society's problems continue. It is not to minimize these problems to argue that few policies meet this expectation. Most policies do not work, but why not?

Many possible explanations can account for this failure. First there is great confidence, at least in U.S. society, that merely passing a law requiring an action or prohibiting it assures compliance and that, if it does not, strict enforcement will work. The 55-mile-per-hour speed limit, prohibition of alcohol and other addictive substances, and extending freedom of expression to include the burning of the American flag are all examples of policies that do not or will not work. Second, and probably related is the oversight of evidence from the social sciences that human behavior is not easily changed. Government is but one of many factors that influence how we behave. It should be noted too that either the social sciences have failed to identify solutions to social problems or those solutions have been ignored by lawmakers. Third, the constitutions of the various states restrict the range of possible laws to cope with social problems. You have to be tried if charged with unlawful behavior, not executed on the spot. Furthermore, if a state were to experiment with some innovative programs, citizens in that state or another might take the state into federal courts for an unconstitutional violation of the "due process and equal protection" clause of the 14th Amendment.

Fourth, all government resources are limited. Greater resources may facilitate a government's ability to act more assertively, and more limited resources may greatly restrict what a government can do. A poor state cannot simply double state aid to education to ensure better education. Fifth, communities and even states are in competition with each other to attract tourists, business, federal money, and even people. A state with high service levels may attract those needing these services and repel businesses because of high taxes to pay for these services. Finally, a successful career in government may depend very little on an individual's contributions to effective public policy. Certainly, many elected officials contribute little more than to appeals to patriotism, hopes, and fears at election time. Unless one or more of these factors change, future policies will be no more successful than those of the past. This subject will be discussed more extensively in the last chapter of this book.

THE PLAN OF THE TEXT

In the next two chapters we shall turn to an exploration of the fundamental ways in which states differ. We shall see that states differ in several quite distinct and relevant ways. This discussion will be followed by a consideration of the history of government in our society, during which certain ideas emerged as to how government is to be run. Next we shall consider one of the foremost concerns of government—the costs of providing services and the sources of revenues required to provide them.

The next two chapters deal with a fundamental concern of political science, the state of democracy in the 50 states, including the role of the governed and those who govern. Voting, political parties, interest groups, and several different perspectives on governing will be considered.

Next we will consider, in four chapters, the basic format of our nonnational governments, from municipal or city governments, school governments, special district governments, county governments, to the governments of the 50 states. Fundamental to our concern will be the process by which policies are enacted into law and variations in government form that are thought to affect those policy decisions.

Finally, we shall seek to make generalizations concerning what seems to matter in terms of producing better state policies. Considering the multitude of changes in U.S. society, it is hoped that we can say something that will aid in developing better future public policy.

CERTAIN RESERVATIONS

The reader may have noticed that most of the statements made in assessing policies' impacts imply a comparative analysis of the states. Although some effort will be made to consider differences among city governments, this analysis will not be as extensive for three reasons. One, the data are not as readily available except for the largest U.S. cities. Second, because municipal governments are considered creations of the states rather than independent governments, their policy prerogatives are sharply limited by statutory restrictions imposed by state governments. There are those who see the prerogatives of even state government sharply limited by Congress under the contemporary federal government. Nevertheless, states still have substantial latitude in dealing with the events and problems of today's society. Third, although there are certainly important ways in which state governments differ, as discussed in the next chapter, municipalities differ even more radically. Comparing New York City and Sopchoppy, Florida affords little insight.

SUMMARY

1. Public policies are intended to solve problems in a society, or at least problems as seen by some in a society.
2. Public policies are plausible, constitutional, enforceable, and hopefully workable solutions that a majority of legislators support and pass into law. Laws are not guaranteed to solve the problems they were intended to solve. And there is no process for removing policies that do not work.
3. Research suggesting whether the policy has worked elsewhere is seldom considered.
4. Comparing states that have a policy with those that do not, if they are otherwise equal, allows us to see whether the policy works.
5. There is little point in recommending solutions, or policies, that do not work.

SUGGESTED READINGS

Henig, Jeffrey R. *Public Policy & Federalism: Issues in State & Local Politics* (New York: St. Martin's, 1985). This basic text focuses on many varied perspectives on how states and local communities make policies.

Stinebrickner, Bruce (ed.). *State and Local Government: Annual Editions* (Guilford, Conn.: Dushkin, 1989). This reader ranges from classics, such as the *Federalist Papers*, to contemporary concerns with state problems.

Chapter 2

Differences Among the States

*I*t is possible to vote with your feet. This phrase is used to suggest that one can move to an area that better reflects one's values or desires in public policy, rather than having to vote into public office those who satisfy one's preferences. For example, if you are reading this book because you are required to do so, you can close it and pursue your education by moving to a state where there is no requirement to take a course in state and local government. Of course, this would be a drastic step and certainly one that would be inconvenient. You would have to leave friends and familiar surroundings and perhaps even take longer to complete your degree. But it is possible.

Similarly, given the many differences among the states on most dimensions, it is possible to pick a state that better fits your political needs or wishes. Few of us, however, will ever do so. Other things—such as a job, resistance to calling oneself a New Yorker, or just inertia—keep us from selecting where we live based on any of the differences among the U.S. states that we are going to discuss. This statement does not imply, however, that no one considers differences among the states or differences among cities in choosing a location. Rand McNally's *Places Rated Almanac* has been popular as a rating of American cities on measures such as culture, job opportunities, and weather. Some who purchase this publication probably act on their readings of those ratings.

ECONOMIC AND SOCIAL CLASS DIFFERENCES

Some states are poor. If governmental services are to be provided, the state government must have a source of revenue to pay for those services. For the most part, revenues available to a state legislature depend on the wealth of the state, which can best be judged by the ability of the public of that state to pay taxes. True, a wealth of resources under the ground, such as oil, coal, or even water, or a desirable climate that will attract tourists, can assure a state other sources of revenue. But a state's wealth is best measured by the wealth of its public.

Table 2.1 shows the total personal income of each state divided by its total population. This gives a measure of income per capita or per person and makes it possible to compare income across states. Connecticut has more than twice the personal income of Mississippi. If both state legislatures passed a personal income tax of 1 percent with no personal exemptions, Connecticut would have $211 in revenue for each man, woman, and child to provide them services. Mississippi, however, would have only $101 per person, which probably means that the state could offer less than half the services provided in Connecticut. If we look at the same data presented on a map, as in Figure 2.1,

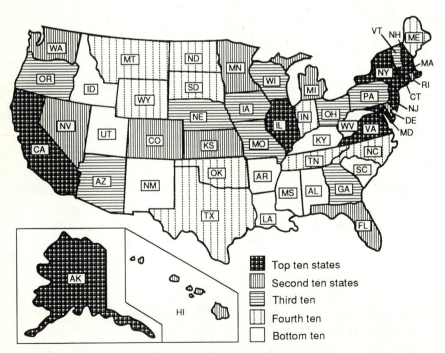

Figure 2.1   Per capita personal income, 1987.

Table 2.1   Per Capita Personal Income in 1987

Rank	State	Income
1	Connecticut	$21082
2	New Jersey	19812
3	Massachusetts	19039
4	New York	18317
5	California	18121
6	Maryland	17717
7	Alaska	17267
8	New Hampshire	16802
9	Illinois	16388
10	Virginia	16257
11	Nevada	16045
12	Minnesota	15956
13	Delaware	15936
14	Colorado	15787
15	Hawaii	15746
16	Washington	15604
17	Rhode Island	15457
18	Florida	15440
19	Kansas	15246
20	Michigan	15145
21	Pennsylvania	15132
22	Wisconsin	14691
23	Ohio	14585
24	Missouri	14490
25	Nebraska	14241
26	Vermont	14168
27	Arizona	14153
28	Georgia	14111
29	Oregon	14012
30	Iowa	13984
31	Indiana	13823
32	Texas	13778
33	Maine	13591
34	North Carolina	13225
35	Wyoming	12829
36	Tennessee	12746
37	Oklahoma	12688
38	North Dakota	12451
39	South Dakota	12310
40	Montana	12239
41	Kentucky	12025
42	Alabama	11957
43	South Carolina	11900
44	New Mexico	11712
45	Idaho	11682
46	Arkansas	11530
47	Louisiana	11452
48	Utah	11391
49	West Virginia	11108
50	Mississippi	10147

Source: State Policy Databook, 1988 (Alexandria, VA: State Policy Research, Inc., 1988), Table B-1.

we can see two bands of poorer states: (1) a group of states extending from West Virginia and North Carolina to New Mexico; and (2) a cluster of western and north central plains states. The wealthier states also form a band from Massachusetts to Illinois and Colorado to California with several breaks. Wealth seems to derive from industrialization. Poorer states lack large metropolitan areas, such as Boston, Chicago, Denver, or Los Angeles, that have high-paying occupations. Obviously, Alaska is an exception to this rule.

Another perspective on the wealth of a state's public can be gained by looking at the percentage of the population surviving in poverty. Table 2.2 shows these rankings. Seven southern states top these rankings; all have 17 percent or more of their population living in poverty. New Hampshire has only 6 percent living in poverty. We might well expect that states with high personal income have few living in poverty. As Figure 2.2 shows, such is the case. Some states, however, have many more poor than might be expected given their personal income. In others poverty is lower than might be expected. States above the diagonal regression line have more living in poverty than we would expect given their personal income. These states include New York, Illinois, and Wisconsin plus many southern states. Those states below the line have fewer poor than would be expected given their per capita personal income; they include Utah, West Virginia, Vermont, and New Hampshire. We shall make further use of this distinction later.

Education.   Table 2.3 shows the percentage of adults with at least a high school education in each state. Education substantially reflects the pattern noted for income. Six of the ten states with the lowest incomes, all southern or border states also have the least educated publics. There are exceptions, such as Utah (which is forty-eighth in income but second in education), and Virginia (which is tenth in income but thirty-ninth in education). Overall the link between income and education among the states is strong, as shown in Figure 2.3.

The regression line in Figure 2.3 shows by how much per capita income would be expected to increase if education were improved. If a state legislature, by investing in education, were able to get 5 percent more of its residents at least a high school education, per capita income could be expected to increase by $540.[1] Typically, such an increase would result in a three- or four-rank jump for such a state. Since state legislatures cannot pass laws demanding a $540 increase in every person's income, improving income by

---

1   If the four central mountain states, Idaho, Montana, Utah, and Wyoming, which have high education but low per capita income were excluded, a 5-percentage-point increase in education would yield an $830 increase.

Table 2.2   Percent of Population in Poverty, 1985

Rank	State	Percent in poverty
1	Mississippi	25.1
2	Arkansas	22.9
3	West Virginia	22.3
4	Alabama	20.6
5	Kentucky	19.4
6	New Mexico	18.5
7	Tennessee	18.1
8	Louisiana	18.1
9	Iowa	18.0
10	Georgia	17.7
11	South Dakota	17.3
12	Montana	16.1
13	Oklahoma	16.1
14	Idaho	16.0
15	North Dakota	15.9
16	Texas	15.9
17	New York	15.8
18	Illinois	15.6
19	North Carolina	15.2
20	South Carolina	15.2
21	Nebraska	14.8
22	Michigan	14.5
23	Nevada	14.4
24	Kansas	13.8
25	Missouri	13.7
26	California	13.6
27	Florida	13.4
28	Ohio	12.8
29	Minnesota	12.6
30	Washington	12.0
31	Wyoming	12.0
32	Indiana	12.0
33	Maine	11.9
34	Oregon	11.9
35	Wisconsin	11.6
36	Delaware	11.4
37	Utah	11.1
38	Hawaii	10.7
39	Arizona	10.7
40	Pennsylvania	10.5
41	Colorado	10.3
42	Virginia	10.0
43	Massachusetts	9.3
44	Vermont	9.2
45	Rhode Island	9.0
46	Alaska	8.8
47	Maryland	8.7
48	New Jersey	8.3
49	Connecticut	7.6
50	New Hampshire	6.0

Source: State Policy Databook, 1988 (Alexandria, VA: State Policy Research, Inc., 1988), Table A-22.

Table 2.3 Percentage with at Least a High School Education, 1980

Rank	State	Percent with high school education
1	Alaska	82.5
2	Utah	80.0
3	Colorado	78.6
4	Wyoming	77.9
5	Washington	77.6
6	Oregon	75.6
7	Nevada	75.5
8	Montana	74.4
9	Hawaii	73.8
10	Idaho	73.7
11	California	73.5
12	Nebraska	73.4
13	Kansas	73.3
14	Minnesota	73.1
15	Arizona	72.4
16	New Hampshire	72.3
17	Massachusetts	72.2
18	Iowa	71.5
19	Vermont	71.0
20	Connecticut	70.3
21	Wisconsin	69.6
22	New Mexico	68.9
23	Maine	68.7
24	Delaware	68.6
25	Michigan	68.0
26	South Dakota	67.9
27	New Jersey	67.4
28	Maryland	67.4
29	Ohio	67.0
30	Florida	66.7
31	Illinois	66.5
32	North Dakota	66.4
33	Indiana	66.4
34	New York	66.3
35	Oklahoma	66.0
36	Pennsylvania	64.7
37	Missouri	63.5
38	Texas	62.6
39	Virginia	62.4
40	Rhode Island	61.1
41	Louisiana	57.7
42	Alabama	56.5
43	Georgia	56.4
44	Tennessee	56.2
45	West Virginia	56.0
46	Arkansas	55.5
47	North Carolina	54.8
48	Mississippi	54.8
49	South Carolina	53.7
50	Kentucky	53.1

Source: U.S. Bureau of the Census, *Statistical Abstract of the United States, 1986* (Washington, DC: U.S. Government Printing Office), p. 134.

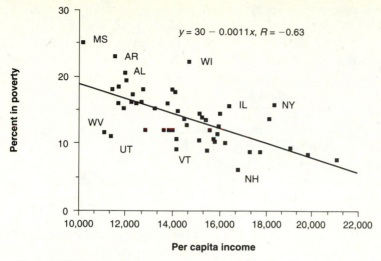

Figure 2.2   Percent in poverty vs. personal income.

improving education is both possible and tempting. A 5 percent improvement in the number of adults with at least a high school education, however, could not be achieved easily.

Traditionally, education is thought to be improved by investing more money in the buildings and facilities as well as in the personnel. This ap-

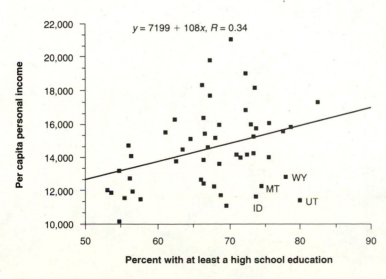

Figure 2.3   Personal income vs. education.

proach is the one commonly used by state governments. A more direct approach might be to require all students to attend high school long enough to obtain a high school diploma. This would be difficult to enforce, would require costly new classroom space, would probably be disruptive in most classrooms, and generally might well prove dysfunctional. Older students with no interest in education might benefit little from a law requiring their attending school.

It is also possible that the states falling below the regression line in Figure 2.3 do so because they emphasize longer attendance in public schools than do other states, even if the students learn little that can be converted into improved per capita income. Perhaps it is difficult to improve education or the percentage with a high school education.

Metropolitan or Urban Living.   As we shall see in Chapter Four, the history of economic growth in the United States is that of industrialization and the concentration of increasing percentages of our population in urban or metropolitan areas. The first industrialized states are still the most metropolitan states, as shown in Figure 2.4. They are in a belt beginning in Massachusetts and extending through Illinois plus Colorado and the Pacific

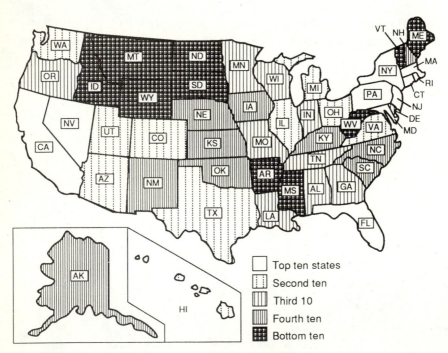

Figure 2.4   Percent living in metropolitan areas, 1986.

Source: See Table A in the appendix to this chapter.

Coast states of California and Washington. The least metropolitan states, not surprisingly, are in the West, northern New England, and several of the southern states, all of which have seen little industrialization.

If the reader were to overlay this map with the personal income map, there would be substantial correspondence. This is also shown in Figure 2.5. Clearly, a substantial part of the wealth available to a state derives from the types of employment available in contemporary metropolitan areas. Unfortunately, as shown in Figure 2.6, so do many problems faced by the states, such as murder and high abortion rates.

State Taxes and Expenditures.   Poor states cannot expect that their residents will be able to pay high taxes. Unfortunately, without such revenues, they can provide fewer services. Tables 2.4 and 2.5 present the top and bottom ten states in terms of per capita general revenues and expenditures. Alaska stands out with better than $10,000 in state general revenue for every man, woman, and child, because of its enormous oil revenues and very small population. Only 11 states have fewer actual dollars of general revenue than Alaska despite this high per capita revenue, but they have to provide services to larger populations.

Apart from Alaska, there are substantial differences in revenue. Wyoming gathers more than three times the revenues per capita collected by either Florida or Tennessee. Among the top states are ones that you might expect to

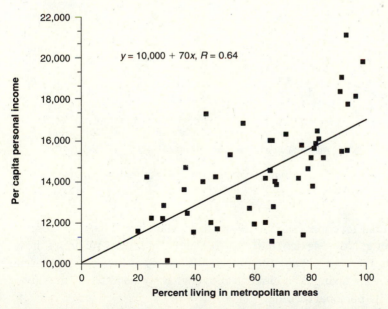

Figure 2.5   The relationship between per capita personal income and percent living in metropolitan areas.

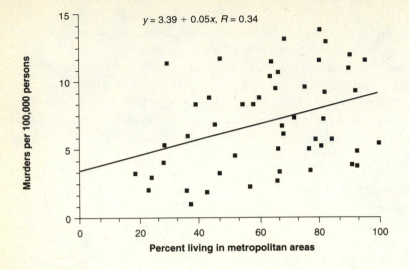

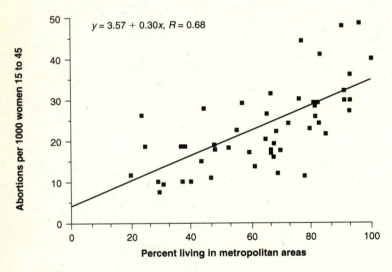

Figure 2.6   Murder and abortion rates vs. percent living in metropolitan areas.

have substantial revenues, such as New York, Massachusetts, and Connecticut. Wyoming, New Mexico, and North Dakota might be surprises, however. None of these are among the "better-off" states as judged by personal incomes. They are taxing their citizens above what seems to be normal given their per capita personal income.

Looking at the bottom states, we again see some expected states and some surprises. Four southern states, as well as Idaho and South Dakota,

Table 2.4   Per Capita State General Revenues, 1986

Top 10			Bottom 10		
Rank	State	Revenues	Rank	State	Revenues
1	Alaska	$10194	41	Nebraska	$1355
2	Wyoming	3416	42	Idaho	1350
3	Delaware	2454	43	Arkansas	1337
4	New York	2303	44	Georgia	1318
5	Hawaii	2288	45	Kansas	1314
6	New Mexico	2285	46	Missouri	1244
7	Massachusetts	2066	47	South Dakota	1226
8	North Dakota	2033	48	New Hampshire	1214
9	Utah	2011	49	Tennessee	1193
10	Connecticut	1996	50	Florida	1141

Source: See Table B in the appendix to this chapter.

form another poor area in the north central part of the United States, are among the bottom ten states. However, New Hampshire, which ranked eighth in personal income, is forty-eighth in revenues. New Hampshire legislators could apparently raise taxes considerably before equaling the tax rates of other states. This idea of considering state revenues as a proportion of income is the basis of considering what is called the "tax effort" or "tax burden" of the state. A wealthy state with low per capita revenues is making little tax effort, whereas a poor state with high revenues per capita is making a great effort. This topic will be discussed more extensively later.

Turning to state expenditures in Table 2.5, we find a very similar pattern. State expenditures are closely related to state revenues. As shown in Figure

Table 2.5   Per Capita State General Expenditures, 1986

Top 10			Bottom 10		
Rank	State	Expenditures	Rank	State	Expenditures
1	Alaska	$7904	41	Kansas	$1431
2	Wyoming	3221	42	Arkansas	1415
3	New York	2427	43	Georgia	1397
4	Hawaii	2328	44	Nebraska	1380
5	North Dakota	2264	45	Indiana	1371
6	Delaware	2236	46	New Hampshire	1313
7	New Mexico	2231	47	Missouri	1279
8	Rhode Island	2223	48	Tennessee	1266
9	Washington	2166	49	Texas	1246
10	Massachusetts	2135	50	Florida	1177

Source: See Table C in the appendix to this chapter.

2.7, expenditures increase by 86 cents for each dollar increase in revenues. States may not gather all the revenues that they might given the wealth of their public, but whatever they gather, they spend. The opposite and equally, if not more, plausible perspective is that whatever they spend, they gather in taxes.

HOMOGENEOUS OR DIVERSE STATES

Thus far we have been assessing differences among the states as though everyone in a state had the same income, education, or contributed the same amount of revenue or received the same governmental services. Some states have such relatively homogeneous populations, where nearly all are employed in agriculture, have very similar incomes, are overwhelmingly white. Others are very diverse, with quite mixed or heterogeneous publics.

In Figure 2.2 we noted that some states have many more living in poverty than might have been anticipated given their per capita income (those states above the line). In other words, these states must have a diverse public with many well-to-do but also many who are very poor. In order for a state to have more people living in poverty given its per capita personal income, there must be many residents who are wealthy, offsetting numerous and quite poor segment of that state's society. Considering both poverty and personal in-

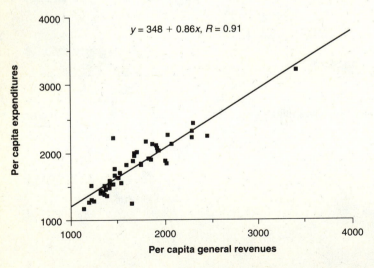

Figure 2.7   The relationship between state per capita expenditures and revenues (Alaska excluded).

Table 2.6   Percentage of Population That Is Black or Hispanic, 1980

Top 10			Bottom 10		
Rank	State	Percent	Rank	State	Percent
1	New Mexico	38.4	41	West Virginia	4.0
2	Mississippi	36.2	42	Oregon	3.9
3	Texas	33.0	43	Iowa	2.3
4	Louisiana	31.8	44	Minnesota	2.1
5	South Carolina	31.5	45	Montana	1.5
6	Georgia	27.9	46	North Dakota	1.0
7	California	26.9	47	New Hampshire	1.0
8	Alabama	26.5	48	South Dakota	0.9
9	Maryland	24.2	49	Vermont	0.8
10	North Carolina	23.4	50	Maine	0.7

Source: U.S. Bureau of the Census, *Statistical Abstract of the United States, 1986* (Washington, DC: U.S. Government Printing Office), p. 29.

come allows us to identify those states that are more mixed in terms of wealth.

A similar measure based on homogeneity in terms of minorities is easier to understand. The absence of minorities, such as blacks and Hispanics, indicates that a state is homogeneous white.[2] Table 2.6 shows that the southern states are the most diverse on this measure, whereas the northern plains, western mountain, and upper New England states tend to be the most homogeneous.

The two measures of diversity are related.[3] Apart from the U.S. South, more rural states tend to lack the diversity of income and race that characterizes overall American society. These homogeneous states are likely to react similarly to events. Their representatives are not likely to hear contradictory demands for policies to deal with social problems. Representing those with similar views is much easier than representing those with different views.

PROBLEM DIFFERENCES AMONG THE STATES

Although there are many differences among the states in terms of resources and social characteristics, the states also differ markedly on many of the so-

2   The Census Bureau allows people to declare whether they are white, black, or other. Therefore, many Hispanics may declare themselves white rather than Hispanic.

3   The slope is 0.12 and the *R* is 0.40.

cial issues being faced by modern society. Some of these differences are more serious than others, and certainly many important issues have been omitted from our consideration. It certainly is not the intent here to be exhaustive, but to make the point that where you live affects the problems your state will be facing and potentially how it will attempt to resolve these problems.

Abortions. There is a continuing dispute between the pro-choice and antiabortion groups concerning abortion and the prospect that state legislatures might be given greater latitude in legislating when and if abortion is allowed. Table 2.7 ranks states by their number of legal abortions per thousand women between the age of 15 and 44. The differences are surprisingly large. California and New York stand apart from the other states, but even Hawaii has more than five times the legal abortion rate of Wyoming. States at the top of the ranking tend to be the more urban states, where we might expect modern life-styles to lead to more abortions. The states at the bottom of the list tend to be southern or upper western states. Even within the limitations imposed by *Roe* v. *Wade*, state legislatures are able to curtail the use of abortion. Part of these differences would seemingly reflect this policy-making ability. If given greater latitude, state legislatures could be expected to enact even more varied policies, resulting in even greater variation from state to state. We shall discuss this issue in much greater detail in a later chapter.

Since these are reports of legal abortion within state boundaries, it is also possible that women might flee more restrictive states to get abortions if they can afford to do so. Pennsylvanians may merely drive to New York with its

Table 2.7   Legal Abortions per 1000 Women Between the Age of 15 and 44, 1985

Top 10			Bottom 10		
Rank	State	Legal abortions	Rank	State	Legal abortions
1	California	47.9	41	South Carolina	13.7
2	New York	47.4	42	Indiana	12.2
3	Hawaii	43.7	43	Utah	11.1
4	Nevada	40.5	44	Idaho	11.1
5	New Jersey	39.6	45	Kentucky	11.0
6	Rhode Island	35.5	46	South Dakota	10.6
7	Florida	31.8	47	West Virginia	10.1
8	Delaware	30.9	48	Arkansas	10.1
9	Arizona	29.9	49	Mississippi	9.7
10	Massachusetts	29.3	50	Wyoming	7.9

Source: See Table D in the appendix to this chapter.

Table 2.8   Murder Rate per 100,000 Population, 1986

	Top 10			Bottom 10	
Rank	State	Murder rate	Rank	State	Murder rate
1	Texas	13.5	41	Idaho	3.2
2	Louisiana	12.8	42	Wisconsin	3.1
3	Nevada	12.6	43	Nebraska	3.1
4	Florida	11.7	44	Montana	2.9
5	New Mexico	11.5	45	Minnesota	2.5
6	Michigan	11.3	46	New Hampshire	2.2
7	California	11.3	47	Vermont	2.0
8	Mississippi	11.2	48	Maine	2.0
9	Georgia	11.2	49	Iowa	1.8
10	New York	10.7	50	North Dakota	1.0

Source: See Table E in the appendix to this chapter.

more permissive abortion environment. It is also possible that illegal abortions replace legal abortions in more restrictive states. Of course, no data are available to assess this possibility.

Crime and Prisoners.   It probably comes as no surprise that crime varies across the United States, but how it varies may not be obvious. For the FBI's eight indexed crimes—murder, assault, arson, larceny, robbery, burglary, rape, and auto theft—we find that Florida ranks first with 823 index crimes per million persons a year. Following Florida are Texas, Arizona, Oregon, Colorado, Washington, California, New Mexico, Michigan, and Nevada. Only California and Michigan are among those typically expected to be high crime states, but missing are New York (number 14) and New Jersey (number 20). West Virginia has the least crime, with only 232 index crimes per million population in 1986. Others at the bottom include North and South Dakota, Kentucky, Pennsylvania (a surprise given that it is a metropolitan state), New Hampshire, Mississippi, Maine, Indiana, and Nebraska.[4]

If we consider just the incidence of murders per 100,000 persons as in Table 2.8, a similar pattern is evident. Texas leads the list, followed by many other unexpectedly dangerous states, although also among the top ten states are Michigan, California, and New York. The states with the lowest murder rates, only about one-fifth as high as those at the top of the list, include states that tend to be rural and nonsouthern. Comparing the map in Figure 2.4 with

---

4   U.S. Bureau of the Census, *Statistical Abstract of the United States, 1988*, p. xx.

Table 2.9   Persons in Jail and Prison per 10,000 Population, 1986

Top 10			Bottom 10		
Rank	State	Persons	Rank	State	Persons
1	Louisiana	71	41	Nebraska	23
2	Nevada	66	42	Maine	20
3	Alaska	66	43	West Virginia	19
4	Georgia	61	44	Massachusetts	19
5	Delaware	56	45	Vermont	18
6	South Carolina	54	46	Rhode Island	17
7	Maryland	53	47	Iowa	17
8	Alabama	53	48	New Hampshire	16
9	Arizona	50	49	Minnesota	14
10	Mississippi	49	50	North Dakota	12

Source: See Table F in the appendix to this chapter.

where murder is least common, we find that five of the states where murder is least common are among the least metropolitan ten states. By contrast, Mississippi, while rural, is among the top ten murder rate states.

Persons incarcerated in jails and prisons, mainly state jails and prisons, are also unevenly distributed across the United States, as shown in Table 2.9. Southern states tend to have the most people held in jails and prisons per 10,000 population, with Louisiana heading the list. The fewest prisoners are found in a mix of metropolitan and rural nonsouthern states. Rankings of states by amount of crime and by the number of prisoners differ substantially. Since the number of prisoners does not reflect the amount of crime (Figure 2.8), we have to assume that other considerations shape the policies of the states regarding who will be put into prison and how long they will stay there.

Traffic Deaths.   We are concentrating on differences among the states that might make a difference to you. These differences would be expected to reflect circumstances in each state as well as policy decisions by that state's legislature. We might expect, when looking at deaths caused by automobiles, that states with more people would lead the list because they have more drivers. We would also expect that those more dependent on their cars, such as Californians, would have more deaths. Apart from these considerations, we might expect that severe winters would increase automotive fatalities, or perhaps that states with more youthful drivers would have more fatalities. Table 2.10 controls for both population and extensive car use by dividing traffic deaths by millions of miles driven. The most dangerous state to drive in is Arizona, with 4.5 deaths per million miles driven. Although other non-

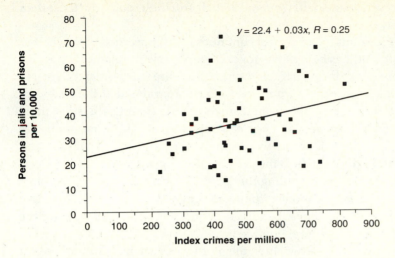

Figure 2.8   Rate of imprisonment vs. crime rate.

southern states, such as New Mexico, Idaho, and Wyoming also top the list, the overall pattern seems to be that of more automotive fatalities in the South. The states with few fatalities have typically one-third as many as those states at the top of the rankings. They range from the far Northeast (Maine) to the far Northwest (Washington), and many have cold and presumably hazardous climates for driving. What accounts for these variations? Certainly all states would claim that they seek to reduce such

Table 2.10   Traffic Deaths per Million Miles Driven, 1986

	Top 10			Bottom 10	
Rank	State	Deaths	Rank	State	Deaths
1	Arizona	4.5	41	Wisconsin	2.0
2	Mississippi	4.0	42	Washington	2.0
3	South Carolina	3.7	43	South Dakota	2.0
4	New Mexico	3.7	44	Rhode Island	1.9
5	Idaho	3.5	45	North Dakota	1.9
6	West Virginia	3.4	46	Connecticut	1.9
7	Arkansas	3.4	47	New Jersey	1.8
8	Wyoming	3.1	48	Minnesota	1.8
9	North Carolina	3.1	49	Massachusetts	1.8
10	Georgia	3.1	50	Hawaii	1.7

Source: See Table G in the appendix to this chapter.

fatalities by keeping unsafe drivers and vehicles off their roads, but these data show that only some succeed.

Welfare Programs.   Our society continues to be concerned with whether too much or too little is being done for the poor. These problems will be discussed in more depth later, but first note that there are substantial differences among the states. There are two major welfare programs that the states administer and into which the federal government channels a substantial amount of money that the state then can supplement. Those programs are Aid for Families with Dependent Children, typically called AFDC, and Medicaid. AFDC gives funds to the poor for dealing with any expenses and Medicaid is dedicated to providing funds for medical expenses, so the same people can and do receive money from both programs. Figure 2.9 shows this relationship. Table 2.11 shows the top and bottom ten states in terms of the percentage of population receiving Medicaid.

States among the top ten include the more industrialized and urbanized states of New York, Michigan, and California, but also many southern states. States with few Medicaid recipients tend to be western plains and mountain states, but two southern states, Texas and Florida, also have many recipients. The differences in percentage of population on Medicaid is substantial, with

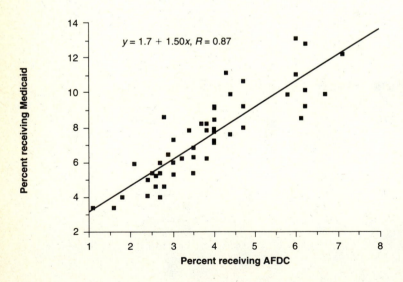

Figure 2.9   Medicaid and AFDC relationship.

Table 2.11   Medicaid Recipients as a Percentage of Population, 1986

Top 10				Bottom 10		
Rank	State	Percent		Rank	State	Percent
1	New York	13.1		41	Kansas	5.3
2	California	12.8		42	South Dakota	5.2
3	Michigan	12.2		43	Florida	5.0
4	Kentucky	11.1		44	Utah	4.6
5	West Virginia	11.0		45	Texas	4.6
6	Maine	10.6		46	Wyoming	4.1
7	Ohio	10.1		47	Idaho	4.0
8	Rhode Island	9.9		48	Colorado	4.0
9	Mississippi	9.9		49	New Hampshire	3.4
10	Louisiana	9.9		50	Nevada	3.4

Source: See Table H in the appendix to this chapter.

the top states having nearly three times more of their population in the program than the bottom states.

Energy Costs.   Does government affect the price of electricity? All states have elected or appointed public utilities commissions with the authority to approve higher utility rates, usually after a request by the utility to raise rates and after public hearings in which consumer representatives have had some say. Table 2.12 shows the cost of an electric bill for 750 kWh across the states. The table demonstrates the effects of inexpensive hydroelectricity in the Pacific Northwest and the need in the Northeast to import oil for electric generation, but there are curious exceptions. Maryland is as dependent on

Table 2.12   Typical Residential Electric Bill for 750 kWh, 1987

Top				Bottom 10		
Rank	State	Dollars		Rank	State	Dollars
1	New Jersey	72.54		41	Minnesota	44.71
2	New York	68.72		42	North Dakota	44.68
3	New Hampshire	68.66		43	Nebraska	43.40
4	Connecticut	67.39		44	Montana	43.02
5	Pennsylvania	65.34		45	Kentucky	42.31
6	Vermont	64.60		46	Tennessee	42.23
7	New Mexico	63.06		47	Wyoming	42.20
8	Alaska	62.40		48	Oregon	35.74
9	Ohio	61.80		49	Idaho	32.38
10	California	61.56		50	Washington	30.74

Source: See Table I in the appendix to this chapter.

Table 2.13   Deaths by Diseases of the Heart per 100,000 Population, 1985

Top 10			Bottom 10		
Rank	State	Deaths	Rank	State	Deaths
1	Pennsylvania	412.5	41	California	262.0
2	New York	403.0	42	Arizona	249.8
3	West Virginia	401.3	43	Texas	245.9
4	Florida	390.7	44	Idaho	243.0
5	Arkansas	383.1	45	Wyoming	208.6
6	Rhode Island	382.5	46	Colorado	198.4
7	Iowa	370.6	47	New Mexico	192.8
8	Maine	369.2	48	Utah	187.4
9	New Jersey	368.8	49	Hawaii	177.8
10	Missouri	367.8	50	Alaska	80.3

Source: See Table J in the appendix to this chapter.

expensive imported oil as the Northeast, but ranks number 33 with a bill of $50.80. New Mexico is seventh at $63.06, whereas its neighbor Texas is number 31 at $51.24. It seems very unlikely that the cost of generating or distributing energy can account fully for the differences in these rates.

Health.   Table 2.13 presents the top and bottom ten states in terms of deaths per 100,000 residents from diseases of the heart. Table 2.14 in turn presents the life expectancy of people living in various states. Both tables show variations that are of some concern. Residents of Pennsylvania, New York, and West Virginia are more than twice as likely to die of diseases of the

Table 2.14   Average Life Expectancy, 1979–1981

Top 10			Bottom 10		
Rank	State	Years	Rank	State	Years
1	Hawaii	77.02	41	Kentucky	73.06
2	Minnesota	76.15	42	North Carolina	72.96
3	Iowa	75.81	43	West Virginia	72.84
4	Utah	75.76	44	Nevada	72.64
5	North Dakota	75.71	45	Alabama	72.53
6	Nebraska	75.49	46	Alaska	72.24
7	Wisconsin	75.35	47	Georgia	72.22
8	Kansas	75.31	48	Mississippi	71.98
9	Colorado	75.30	49	South Carolina	71.85
10	Idaho	75.19	50	Louisiana	71.74

Source: See Table K in the appendix to this chapter.

heart as are those living in Alaska, Hawaii, and Utah. Generally speaking, those living east of the Mississippi River risk more danger to their hearts than do westerners. Southern states fall in the middle of ranking by heart disease deaths. In rankings of life expectancy, however, the South stands out with the lowest life expectancy. Hawaiians live longest, but residents of the upper midwestern and western states live nearly as long.

Government and society can play a role in affecting both of these measures. An unhealthy environment and inadequate health care for the poor can affect disease and life expectancy, and both of these factors are within the influence of government. Although no short-term benefit can be expected from moving from an unwholesome state to one evidencing a healthier public, a lifetime spent in one state rather than another can matter.

CONCLUSION

States differ as to the degree and promptness of political actions taken by legislators or by state executives, such as the governor. Some states are quite poor, although they may seem wealthy in comparison with Third World countries. In trying to provide the quality of life that Americans have become accustomed to, including government services, they cannot provide the level of support available in wealthier states. State legislators in wealthy states can hardly be praised for providing more extensive services. Their more wealthy residents can afford the higher taxes that permit these services. There are, however, policies that legislators would seem able to enact that would improve the wealth of its public, such as investing in improving public education.

Social problems are also not equally distributed across the country. As we have seen, crime and health, just taking two examples, are not the same in all states. Legislators in unhealthy states may be partially responsible for failing to regulate pollution or providing indigent health care. States with high death rates caused by many elderly retiring there cannot be held responsible for aging, however. Metropolitan states seem to have more social problems than do more rural and agricultural states. Fortunately, they have wealthier publics that give them better resources for coping with those problems.

Although states, of course, cannot move, an individual can. If you are wealthy, you might want to move to a state with low taxes, thereby avoiding having your wealth used to provide government services to those less able to provide them for themselves. You may, however, be altruistic and seek out a high-taxing state to distribute wealth better and to provide a quality life for everyone regardless of his or her wealth. Most likely, you will not seriously consider such a move—nor will the poor, who should move to a wealthy state with well-funded government services.

By the same token, few flee metropolitan states because of their high crime rates. Those living in the older central cities of Chicago and St. Louis may, however, move to the suburbs hoping, among other things, to avoid crime. In the next chapter we shall turn to political variables, which are seen as contributing to the effectiveness of states' efforts to cushion residents from social problems.

SUMMARY

1. Some states are wealthy in that people working within their borders earn substantial incomes, which can be taxed. Other states are quite poor because they lack many such individuals. Most of these poor states are concentrated in the South.

2. Better education goes with higher incomes. Although states cannot pass laws demanding that people have higher incomes, they can pass laws that result in better education. Education is the leverage that legislators can use to improve both their economies and the tax potential of their state.

3. Some states remain rural and unindustrialized, thereby avoiding many of this century's social problems by having few people concentrated in large metropolitan areas. Metropolitan states, while having many resources, such as better educated and higher incomed citizens, face many daunting social problems.

4. Many things about the lives we lead vary from one state to the next.

SUGGESTED READINGS

Gray, Virginia. "The Socioeconomic and Political Context of States," in *Politics in the American States*, 5th ed., Virginia Gray, Herbert Jacob, and Robert B. Albritton (eds.) (Glenview, IL: Scott, Foresman, 1990).

Hagstrom, Jerrey. *Beyond Reagan* (New York: Norton, 1988). A descriptive account of state by state differences.

U.S. Bureau of the Census. *Statistical Abstract of the United States, 1990* (Washington, DC: U.S. Government Printing Office, 1990). Although this extensive collection of data on the states offers no interpretations, it is the basis of most comparisons of the states.

Van Horn, Carl E. "The Quiet Revolution" and "The Entrepreneurial States," in *The State of the States*, Carl E. Van Horn (ed.) (Washington, DC: CQ Press, 1989). These chapters are the first and last in an anthology devoted to the revitalization of the states during the 1980s.

APPENDIX

Table A Percent of Population Living in Metropolitan Areas, 1986

Rank	State	Percent
1	New Jersey	100.0
2	California	95.7
3	Maryland	92.9
4	Connecticut	92.6
5	Rhode Island	92.5
6	Florida	90.9
7	Massachusetts	90.8
8	New York	90.5
9	Pennsylvania	84.6
10	Nevada	82.5
11	Illinois	82.4
12	Colorado	81.6
13	Washington	81.0
14	Texas	80.7
15	Michigan	80.2
16	Ohio	78.8
17	Utah	77.0
18	Hawaii	76.9
19	Arizona	75.4
20	Virginia	71.5
21	Louisiana	69.1
22	Indiana	68.0
23	Oregon	67.4
24	Tennessee	66.8
25	Wisconsin	66.5
26	Delaware	66.0
27	Missouri	65.9
28	Minnesota	65.8
29	Georgia	64.3
30	Alabama	64.1
31	South Carolina	60.2
32	Oklahoma	58.5
33	New Hampshire	56.4
34	North Carolina	55.0
35	Kansas	52.0
36	New Mexico	47.6
37	Nebraska	46.9
38	Kentucky	45.5
39	Alaska	44.0
40	Iowa	42.9
41	Arkansas	39.3
42	North Dakota	37.3
43	West Virginia	36.6
44	Maine	36.1
45	Mississippi	30.0
46	Wyoming	28.8
47	South Dakota	28.2
48	Montana	24.4
49	Vermont	23.1
50	Idaho	19.4

Source: U.S. Bureau of the Census, *Statistical Abstract of the United States, 1988* (Washington, DC: U.S. Government Printing Office), p. 27.

Table B   Per Capita State General Revenues, 1986

Rank	State	Revenues
1	Alaska	$10194
2	Wyoming	3416
3	Delaware	2454
4	New York	2303
5	Hawaii	2288
6	New Mexico	2285
7	Massachusetts	2066
8	North Dakota	2033
9	Utah	2011
10	Connecticut	1996
11	Vermont	1938
12	Minnesota	1917
13	New Jersey	1901
14	California	1862
15	Wisconsin	1846
16	Michigan	1816
17	Washington	1795
18	Maryland	1739
19	Maine	1737
20	Montana	1694
21	Nevada	1676
22	Louisiana	1673
23	West Virginia	1652
24	Texas	1638
25	Oregon	1594
26	Kentucky	1531
27	Iowa	1526
28	Oklahoma	1523
29	Pennsylvania	1504
30	Ohio	1470
31	South Carolina	1466
32	Rhode Island	1456
33	Virginia	1453
34	Alabama	1411
35	Illinois	1410
36	North Carolina	1406
37	Colorado	1393
38	Arizona	1388
39	Indiana	1384
40	Mississippi	1366
41	Nebraska	1355
42	Idaho	1350
43	Arkansas	1337
44	Georgia	1318
45	Kansas	1314
46	Missouri	1244
47	South Dakota	1226
48	New Hampshire	1214
49	Tennessee	1193
50	Florida	1141

Source: U.S. Bureau of the Census, *State Government Finances in 1986*, GF86–No. 3 (Washington, DC: U.S. Government Printing Office).

Table C   Per Capita State Expenditures, 1986

Rank	State	Expenditures
1	Alaska	$7904
2	Wyoming	3221
3	New York	2427
4	Hawaii	2328
5	North Dakota	2264
6	Delaware	2236
7	New Mexico	2231
8	Rhode Island	2223
9	Washington	2166
10	Massachusetts	2135
11	California	2126
12	New Jersey	2105
13	Minnesota	2036
14	Vermont	2024
15	Montana	2006
16	Nevada	1990
17	Louisiana	1954
18	Michigan	1920
19	Wisconsin	1907
20	West Virginia	1887
21	Connecticut	1884
22	Utah	1844
23	Maine	1837
24	Oregon	1826
25	Maryland	1822
26	Ohio	1768
27	Oklahoma	1703
28	Iowa	1702
29	South Carolina	1670
30	Pennsylvania	1622
31	Alabama	1588
32	Kentucky	1553
33	Illinois	1543
34	Virginia	1533
35	Arizona	1530
36	South Dakota	1517
37	Colorado	1516
38	Idaho	1512
39	North Carolina	1480
40	Mississippi	1461
41	Kansas	1431
42	Arkansas	1415
43	Georgia	1397
44	Nebraska	1380
45	Indiana	1371
46	New Hampshire	1313
47	Missouri	1279
48	Tennessee	1266
49	Texas	1246
50	Florida	1177

Source: U.S. Bureau of the Census, *State Government Finances in 1986*, GF86–No. 3 (Washington, DC: U.S. Government Printing Office).

Table D   Legal Abortions Per 1000 Women Between the Age of 15 and 44

Rank	State	Legal abortions
1	California	47.9
2	New York	47.4
3	Hawaii	43.7
4	Nevada	40.5
5	New Jersey	39.6
6	Rhode Island	35.5
7	Florida	31.8
8	Delaware	30.9
9	Arizona	29.9
10	Massachusetts	29.3
11	Connecticut	29.3
12	New Hampshire	29.0
13	Colorado	28.8
14	Michigan	28.7
15	Washington	28.0
16	Alaska	27.7
17	Maryland	26.9
18	Vermont	26.2
19	Georgia	26.1
20	Texas	25.5
21	Virginia	24.0
22	Illinois	23.8
23	North Carolina	22.6
24	Ohio	22.4
25	Oregon	22.3
26	Pennsylvania	21.3
27	Alabama	20.2
28	Tennessee	19.1
29	Montana	19.0
30	Maine	18.6
31	North Dakota	18.5
32	Nebraska	18.2
33	Kansas	18.2
34	New Mexico	17.4
35	Louisiana	17.4
36	Missouri	17.3
37	Oklahoma	17.1
38	Minnesota	16.6
39	Wisconsin	15.7
40	Iowa	15.0
41	South Carolina	13.7
42	Indiana	12.2
43	Utah	11.1
44	Idaho	11.1
45	Kentucky	11.0
46	South Dakota	10.6
47	West Virginia	10.1
48	Arkansas	10.1
49	Mississippi	9.7
50	Wyoming	7.9

Source: U.S. Bureau of the Census, *Statistical Abstract of the United States, 1988* (Washington, DC: U.S. Government Printing Office), p. 69.

Table E   Murder Rate per 100,000 Population, 1986

Rank	State	Murder rate
1	Texas	13.5
2	Louisiana	12.8
3	Nevada	12.6
4	Florida	11.7
5	New Mexico	11.5
6	Michigan	11.3
7	California	11.3
8	Mississippi	11.2
9	Georgia	11.2
10	New York	10.7
11	Tennessee	10.4
12	Alabama	10.1
13	Arizona	9.3
14	Missouri	9.2
15	Maryland	9.0
16	Illinois	8.9
17	South Carolina	8.6
18	Alaska	8.6
19	Oklahoma	8.1
20	North Carolina	8.1
21	Arkansas	8.1
22	Virginia	7.1
23	Colorado	7.0
24	Kentucky	6.7
25	Oregon	6.6
26	Indiana	6.0
27	West Virginia	5.9
28	Pennsylvania	5.5
29	Ohio	5.5
30	Wyoming	5.3
31	New Jersey	5.2
32	Washington	5.0
33	Delaware	4.9
34	Hawaii	4.8
35	Connecticut	4.6
36	Kansas	4.4
37	South Dakota	4.0
38	Massachusetts	3.6
39	Rhode Island	3.5
40	Utah	3.2
41	Idaho	3.2
42	Wisconsin	3.1
43	Nebraska	3.1
44	Montana	2.9
45	Minnesota	2.5
46	New Hampshire	2.2
47	Vermont	2.0
48	Maine	2.0
49	Iowa	1.8
50	North Dakota	1.0

Source: U.S. Bureau of the Census, *Statistical Abstract of the United States, 1988* (Washington, DC: U.S. Government Printing Office), p. 159.

Table F   Persons in Jail and Prison per 10,000 Population, 1986

Rank	State	Persons
1	Louisiana	71
2	Alaska	66
3	Nevada	66
4	Georgia	61
5	Delaware	56
6	South Carolina	54
7	Maryland	53
8	Alabama	53
9	Arizona	50
10	Mississippi	49
11	Florida	48
12	California	47
13	North Carolina	45
14	Texas	45
15	Oklahoma	44
16	Virginia	41
17	Michigan	39
18	New York	38
19	Missouri	37
20	Tennessee	37
21	Ohio	36
22	Arkansas	36
23	New Mexico	36
24	Oregon	35
25	Kentucky	35
26	Indiana	34
27	Kansas	33
28	Washington	32
29	Wyoming	32
30	Illinois	32
31	New Jersey	31
32	Idaho	28
33	Hawaii	27
34	Pennsylvania	27
35	Montana	26
36	South Dakota	26
37	Utah	25
38	Connecticut	25
39	Colorado	25
40	Wisconsin	24
41	Nebraska	23
42	Maine	20
43	Massachusetts	19
44	West Virginia	19
45	Vermont	18
46	Iowa	17
47	Rhode Island	17
48	New Hampshire	16
49	Minnesota	14
50	North Dakota	12

Source: U.S. Bureau of the Census, *Statistical Abstract of the United States, 1988* (Washington, DC: U.S. Government Printing Office), p. 176.

Table G   Traffic Deaths Per Million Miles Driven

Rank	State	Deaths
1	Arizona	4.5
2	Mississippi	4.0
3	South Carolina	3.7
4	New Mexico	3.7
5	Idaho	3.5
6	West Virginia	3.4
7	Arkansas	3.4
8	Wyoming	3.1
9	North Carolina	3.1
10	Georgia	3.1
11	Florida	3.1
12	Tennessee	3.0
13	Nevada	3.0
14	Montana	2.9
15	Alabama	2.9
16	Oregon	2.8
17	Missouri	2.7
18	Kentucky	2.7
19	Delaware	2.7
20	Louisiana	2.6
21	Kansas	2.6
22	Indiana	2.6
23	Pennsylvania	2.5
24	Alaska	2.5
25	Utah	2.4
26	Texas	2.4
27	Oklahoma	2.4
28	California	2.4
29	Nebraska	2.3
30	Michigan	2.3
31	Maryland	2.3
32	Iowa	2.3
33	Illinois	2.3
34	Virginia	2.2
35	Vermont	2.2
36	New York	2.2
37	Colorado	2.2
38	Ohio	2.1
39	New Hampshire	2.1
40	Maine	2.1
41	Wisconsin	2.0
42	Washington	2.0
43	South Dakota	2.0
44	Rhode Island	1.9
45	North Dakota	1.9
46	Connecticut	1.9
47	New Jersey	1.8
48	Minnesota	1.8
49	Massachusetts	1.8
50	Hawaii	1.7

Source: Accident Facts, 1987 (Chicago: National Safety Council).

Table H   Medicaid Recipients as a Percentage of Population

Rank	State	Percentage
1	New York	13.1
2	California	12.8
3	Michigan	12.2
4	Kentucky	11.1
5	West Virginia	11.0
6	Maine	10.6
7	Ohio	10.1
8	Rhode Island	9.9
9	Mississippi	9.9
10	Louisiana	9.9
11	Vermont	9.2
12	Pennsylvania	9.2
13	Illinois	9.2
14	Massachusetts	9.1
15	Arkansas	8.6
16	Wisconsin	8.5
17	Hawaii	8.4
18	Tennessee	8.2
19	Minnesota	8.2
20	Washington	8.0
21	Georgia	7.9
22	South Carolina	7.8
23	Iowa	7.8
24	Alabama	7.8
25	New Jersey	7.6
26	Oklahoma	7.3
27	Maryland	7.2
28	Missouri	7.1
29	Connecticut	6.8
30	Nebraska	6.4
31	Montana	6.3
32	New Mexico	6.2
33	Delaware	6.2
34	Oregon	6.0
35	North Carolina	6.0
36	North Dakota	5.9
37	Virginia	5.4
38	Indiana	5.4
39	Alaska	5.4
40	Kansas	5.3
41	South Dakota	5.2
42	Florida	5.0
43	Utah	4.6
44	Texas	4.6
45	Wyoming	4.1
46	Idaho	4.0
47	Colorado	4.0
48	New Hampshire	3.4
49	Nevada	3.4
50	Arizona	NA

Source: U.S. Bureau of the Census, *Statistical Abstract of the United States, 1988* (Washington, DC: U.S. Government Printing Office), p. 348.

Table I Typical Residential Electric Bill for 750 kWh, 1987

Rank	State	Dollars
1	New Jersey	72.54
2	New York	68.72
3	New Hampshire	68.66
4	Connecticut	67.39
5	Pennsylvania	65.34
6	Vermont	64.60
7	New Mexico	63.06
8	Alaska	62.40
9	Ohio	61.80
10	California	61.56
11	Arkansas	61.45
12	Utah	61.18
13	Maine	61.02
14	Arizona	60.13
15	Delaware	59.51
16	Massachusetts	59.40
17	Hawaii	59.37
18	Indiana	58.84
19	North Carolina	58.17
20	Kansas	57.33
21	Rhode Island	57.18
22	Iowa	56.72
23	Florida	56.61
24	South Carolina	55.45
25	Illinois	54.60
26	Virginia	54.00
27	Michigan	51.93
28	Alabama	51.78
29	Oklahoma	51.74
30	Missouri	51.73
31	Texas	51.24
32	Nevada	50.93
33	Maryland	50.80
34	Colorado	50.55
35	South Dakota	49.71
36	Mississippi	48.85
37	West Virginia	48.81
38	Louisiana	47.70
39	Wisconsin	46.53
40	Georgia	46.13
41	Minnesota	44.71
42	North Dakota	44.68
43	Nebraska	43.40
44	Montana	43.02
45	Kentucky	42.31
46	Tennessee	42.23
47	Wyoming	42.20
48	Oregon	35.74
49	Idaho	32.38
50	Washington	30.74

Source: U.S. Department of Energy, *Typical Electric Bills, January 29, 1988* (Washington, DC: U.S. Government Printing Office).

Table J   Deaths by Diseases of the Heart per 100,000 Population, 1985

Rank	State	Deaths
1	Pennsylvania	412.5
2	New York	403.0
3	West Virginia	401.3
4	Florida	390.7
5	Arkansas	383.1
6	Rhode Island	382.5
7	Iowa	370.6
8	Maine	369.2
9	New Jersey	368.8
10	Missouri	367.8
11	South Dakota	364.5
12	Massachusetts	360.9
13	Ohio	355.9
14	Illinois	351.0
15	Kentucky	350.3
16	Nebraska	347.7
17	Oklahoma	339.9
18	Connecticut	338.7
19	Kansas	338.5
20	Wisconsin	337.3
21	Michigan	337.3
22	Mississippi	335.7
23	Delaware	331.2
24	Tennessee	331.0
25	Alabama	325.6
26	Vermont	325.2
27	Indiana	323.2
28	North Dakota	314.5
29	Oregon	308.8
30	North Carolina	304.5
31	New Hampshire	304.4
32	Maryland	298.7
33	Louisiana	293.8
34	Minnesota	290.1
35	South Carolina	285.6
36	Virginia	281.4
37	Georgia	277.1
38	Montana	268.5
39	Washington	267.7
40	Nevada	266.3
41	California	262.0
42	Arizona	249.8
43	Texas	245.9
44	Idaho	243.0
45	Wyoming	208.6
46	Colorado	198.4
47	New Mexico	192.8
48	Utah	187.4
49	Hawaii	177.8
50	Alaska	80.3

Source: U.S. Bureau of the Census, *Statistical Abstract of the United States, 1988* (Washington, DC: U.S. Government Printing Office), p. 79.

Table K Average Lifetime, 1979–1981

Rank	State	Years
1	Hawaii	77.02
2	Minnesota	76.15
3	Iowa	75.81
4	Utah	75.76
5	North Dakota	75.71
6	Nebraska	75.49
7	Wisconsin	75.35
8	Kansas	75.31
9	Colorado	75.30
10	Idaho	75.19
11	Washington	75.13
12	Connecticut	75.12
13	Massachusetts	75.01
14	Oregon	74.99
15	New Hampshire	74.98
16	South Dakota	74.97
17	Vermont	74.79
18	Rhode Island	74.76
19	Maine	74.59
20	California	74.57
21	Arizona	74.30
22	New Mexico	74.01
23	New Jersey	74.00
24	Florida	74.00
25	Montana	73.93
26	Wyoming	73.85
27	Missouri	73.84
28	Indiana	73.84
29	Arkansas	73.72
30	New York	73.70
31	Oklahoma	73.67
32	Michigan	73.67
33	Texas	73.64
34	Pennsylvania	73.58
35	Ohio	73.49
36	Virginia	73.43
37	Illinois	73.37
38	Maryland	73.32
39	Tennessee	73.30
40	Delaware	73.21
41	Kentucky	73.06
42	North Carolina	72.96
43	West Virginia	72.84
44	Nevada	72.64
45	Alabama	72.53
46	Alaska	72.24
47	Georgia	72.22
48	Mississippi	71.98
49	South Carolina	71.85
50	Louisiana	71.74

Source: U.S. Bureau of the Census, *Statistical Abstract of the United States, 1988* (Washington, DC: U.S. Government Printing Office), p. 71.

Chapter 3

Politics Among the States

Before elections in the United States, television commercials, billboards, signs along streets, and bumper stickers widely proclaim that we should vote for candidate Smith for the state legislature, for candidate Doe for governor, and candidate Washington for president. The appeal is always that if they are elected, something will change in the way government does things. Government will be more efficient, taxes will be lower, a specific policy to deal with a problem will be enacted, or greater wisdom and integrity will be applied in dealing with social problems and in the role of government in dealing with those problems.

There are a large number of attributes that political scientists see in how elections happen and in how government performs. For example, we expect that if elections are competitive with two or more candidates vying with nearly equal chances of winning, the importance of the election to what government actions might be will differ from elections in which a single candidate is running with no opposition. Similarly, some states may have a style of politics, such as having little competition in elections and few government services, whereas other states have much competition. We would expect different government actions by states with these differences. We now turn to political differences among the states.

POLITICAL CULTURE DIFFERENCES
AMONG THE STATES

A persistent idea in understanding U.S. politics is that there is a different style
or approach to dealing with social problems as one goes from one state to
another. New York deals with problems differently than Texas, and Oregon
is aggressively concerned with the environment. There is a long-standing
idea that the South is different because of the Civil War, the introduction of
many blacks into those states through slavery, or the poverty and harsh treatment of the area during Reconstruction after the Civil War.[1] Many states
entered the Union after the Civil War. Do they share the approach that might
be characterized as that of northern states, or do they represent a third approach?

Many things have happened since the Civil War. As we have seen, some
states have large industrial cities, some are predominantly of one religious
orientation, and some have many miles between where people live and an
acute shortage of water. All of these elements represent cultural differences
in what residents of the various states expect of their governments, or their
political culture. Political culture is the broadest characterization of how the
states differ politically. Each state, however, is not seen as a unique political
culture; there is sharing among the states of similar approaches to government.

Elazar thought three political cultures and several mixes characterized
the differences he noted among the states.[2] One of the political cultures he
described substantially overlaps the eleven states that seceded and con-
stituted the Confederate States of America, which is the normal definition of
the South.[3] This is the *traditionalistic* political culture, as shown in Figure 3.1.
It reflects an orientation that predates the industrialization and urbanization
of the United States and rests on the "normal" ordering of society going back
to England. Those of wealth and position were expected to rule and to have

1   One research project that has substantially shaped consideration of the American South is
reported in V.O. Key, Jr., *Southern Politics in State and Nation*, A New Edition (Knoxville:
University of Tennessee Press, 1977, originally 1949).

2   Daniel J. Elazar, *Cities of the Prairie: The Metropolitan Frontier and American Politics* (New York:
Basic Books, 1970). He later implied the culture of the state from that which predominated among
its cities; see Daniel J. Elazar, *American Federalism: A View from the States* (New York: Harper &
Row, 1972). Most recently a collection of essays on his ideas has been published: John Kincaid
(ed.), *Political Culture, Public Policy and the American States* (Philadelphia: Institute for the Study
of Human Issues, 1982).

3   Those states are Virginia, North and South Carolina, Georgia, Florida, Tennessee, Alabama,
Mississippi, Louisiana, Arkansas, and Texas. Kentucky and Oklahoma are frequently included
in the South.

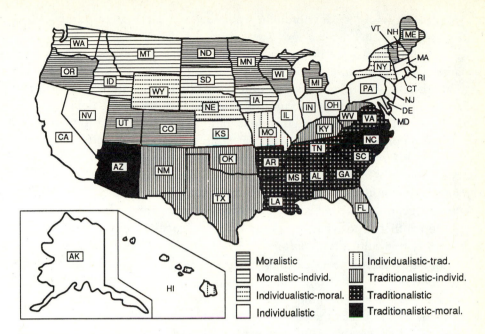

Figure 3.1 Political cultures in the United States in the 1970s.

Source: Daniel Elazar (ed.), *American Federalism: A View from the States*, 2nd ed., New York: Harper & Row, 1972, p. 117.

their property protected by the government from theft by others.[4] The government is expected to play little other role, since that is not traditional. With the exception of Texas, the settlement of the U.S. South, other than its black citizens, was primarily from England, and these ideas were brought with them. Until well after World War II, these states experienced little demand for government action and probably would have been unresponsive to such demands anyway. Probably the best examples of this political culture include South Carolina, Alabama, and Mississippi.

It should be noted that Arizona and New Mexico are nonsouthern traditional political culture states and that all the darker-shaded states in Figure 3.1 have substantial minority populations.[5] It is suggested that poor states with substantial minority populations behave in the manner described as traditionalistic. Perhaps the existence of substantial minorities, rather than the tradition from England, drives this political culture. Perhaps it is a mix-

---

4   Elazar, *American Federalism*, pp. 92–93.

5   Norman R. Luttbeg, "Classifying the American States: An Empirical Attempt to Identify Internal Variation," *Midwest Journal of Political Science* (November 1971).

ture of both, with the ideas brought from England serving the purposes of those with wealth.[6]

Along the northern border in a belt from Maine to Oregon range the *moralistic* political culture states. Good government, promoting the public goods of honesty and selflessness, and government serving God's purpose define the moralistic political culture.[7] Like the traditionalistic political culture, this culture derives from the ideas that whites brought with them, this time from northern Europe, where Protestant religions predominate. In this political culture government is to serve God, either actively or passively, depending on what is morally correct. This attitude might be expected with regard to corruption in public office and the movement to merit in selecting who will get public jobs.[8] Because of relatively homogeneous life-styles, there is little conflict as to what is morally correct. Probably the states that best exemplify this culture are Wisconsin, Minnesota, and the Dakotas.

Finally, there is the *individualistic* political culture, which emphasizes the conception of the democratic order as a marketplace. From this perspective, " . . . a government is instituted for strictly utilitarian reasons, to handle those functions demanded by the people it is created to serve."[9] Again, there is a belt of states included in this culture that runs from Massachusetts through the U.S. industrial heartland. In these states emigrants, employed by the industrial revolution, settled in squalid cities. Conditions made them receptive to the idea of having government provide them necessary services. If those services could only come from organizing to seize government from others who were unwilling to provide such services, then that was acceptable. Government was to be won and to serve those who won it. "To the victor belong the spoils" is the common phrase. It was not limited to what was traditional or to what was moral. Even the ideas of honesty or using government for the public good are less relevant than using government to serve one's purposes.

OTHER POLITICAL DIFFERENCES

A democratic public is supposed to participate in government, at least by voting in elections, and those elections are supposed to be competitive, af-

---

6   V. O. Key thought that race served to keep the numerous poor in the South from defeating the wealthy at the polls; see V.O. Key, Jr. *Southern Politics in State and Nation.*

7   Elazar, *American Federalism*, pp. 89–92.

8   Jody L. Fitzpatrick and Rodney E. Hero, "Political Culture and Political Characteristics of the American States: A Consideration of Some Old and New Questions," *Western Political Quarterly* (January 1987), pp. 145–153.

9   Elazar, *American Federalism*, p. 86.

Table 3.1   Voting Turnout for the Presidential Election of 1984

	Top 10			Bottom 10	
Rank	State	Percent	Rank	State	Percent
1	Minnesota	68.2	41	California	49.6
2	Montana	65.0	42	Tennessee	49.1
3	Maine	64.7	43	Florida	48.2
4	Wisconsin	63.5	44	North Carolina	47.4
5	North Dakota	62.7	45	Texas	47.2
6	South Dakota	62.6	46	Arizona	45.2
7	Iowa	62.2	47	Hawaii	44.3
8	Oregon	61.9	48	Georgia	42.0
9	Utah	61.6	49	Nevada	41.6
10	Connecticut	61.1	50	South Carolina	40.7

Source: See Table A in the appendix to this chapter.

fording voters a choice among candidates. The preferences among voters for certain policies (public opinion) are supposed to be reflected in the policies adopted by elected officials. There are substantial differences among the states on all of these political concepts.

Participation.   For most people the act of voting is their chief act that affects government. Although other possibilities include running for office, peacefully or nonviolently acting against government, or even assassinating political leaders whose acts one opposes, few Americans do anything politically other than vote. However, as shown in Table 3.1, there are substantial differences between the states in voting. Voters in Minnesota voted at a 28 percent higher rate than those in South Carolina. Overall, states in the upper plains and mountain states, with a moralistic political culture, vote most, whereas southern states or the traditional political culture vote least. California, Hawaii, Arizona, and Nevada are also among the bottom ten.

When we turn our attention to the "off-year" elections of 1986, we see much the same pattern in Table 3.2. In these elections, most states elected their state legislatures and governors and all of their representatives to the U.S. Congress. Additionally, one-third of the U.S. Senate was elected. Southern states again tended to be at the bottom of the rankings and the north central states at the top.[10] The correlation between these two measures is 0.63,

---

10   The relationship is not shown, but the equation is 1986 vote = –14 + 0.94 x 1984 vote.

Table 3.2   Voting Turnout for State Elections of Congressmen, 1986

Top 10			Bottom 10		
Rank	State	Percent	Rank	State	Percent
1	North Dakota	58.6	41	New York	29.1
2	South Dakota	56.9	42	Mississippi	28.6
3	Idaho	54.3	43	West Virginia	28.0
4	Montana	54.1	44	New Jersey	26.7
5	Oregon	51.1	45	Texas	25.5
6	Alaska	49.2	46	Georgia	24.0
7	Maine	48.3	47	Virginia	23.8
8	Nebraska	47.4	48	Florida	23.5
9	Vermont	47.0	49	Kentucky	23.1
10	Wyoming	45.4	50	Louisiana	12.4

Source: U.S. Bureau of the Census, *Statistical Abstract of the United States, 1988,* (Washington, DC: U.S. Government Printing Office), p. 251.

indicating that states whose electorates vote in one type of election vote in others.

Liberals and Conservatives.   Both of these terms are used frequently to discuss the preferences of political leaders and of voters. Listed in Table 3.3 are the top and bottom states in terms of voters calling themselves "liberals."[11] Not surprisingly, states with more liberals have fewer conservatives, as shown in Figure 3.2.

The most "liberal" states are sprinkled across the country, as shown in Figure 3.3. They tend to be the more metropolitan or industrialized states, with Montana, Vermont, Oregon, Wyoming, Iowa, and West Virginia being the numerous exceptions. The least "liberal" states include both the South and the less urban states of the northern plains and western mountains.

A comparison between the map of political cultures and that of liberal identification reveals little overlap. The South is both traditionalistic and conservative, but states in other political cultures are equally conservative. The individualistic states tend to be liberal, but so are some moralistic states. There is a clear pattern to the states where the electorate calls itself liberal, but it seems largely unrelated to political culture. Certainly this finding may mean that those who govern hold political attitudes different from those of the general public. The governing few may continue to define the state's political culture. We shall say much more about this subject later.

---

11   Gerald C. Wright, Robert S. Erikson, and John P. McIver, "Measuring State Partisanship and Ideology with Survey Data," *Journal of Politics* 47 (May 1985), pp. 469–489.

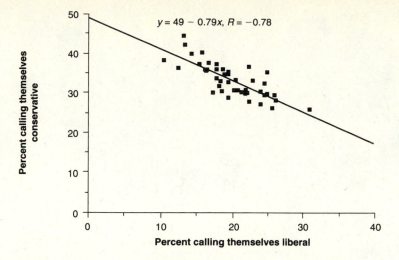

Figure 3.2 The relationship between states with many conservatives and those with many liberals.

Democratic and Republican State Legislatures. Table 3.4 indicates the percentage of representatives in the lower house of each state legislature that was elected as a Democrat. The question of the competitiveness of state politics will be considered more extensively later, but the comparative strengths of the two major political parties in state legislatures has been

Table 3.3 Voters Calling Themselves Liberals, 1976–1982[a]

	Top 10			Bottom 10	
Rank	State	Percent	Rank	State	Percent
1	Nevada	30.8	39	North Carolina	16.4
2	New Jersey	26.2	40	Louisiana	16.3
3	New York	25.9	41	Alabama	16.1
4	Massachusetts	25.5	42	South Carolina	15.7
5	California	24.9	43	Mississippi	15.3
6	Montana	24.8	44	Oklahoma	14.3
7	Connecticut	24.5	45	Idaho	13.4
8	Vermont	24.4	46	Utah	13.2
9	Maryland	24.0	47	South Dakota	12.4
10	Rhode Island	23.9	48	North Dakota	10.5

[a] Figures for Alaska and Hawaii are not available.
Source: See Table B in the appendix to this chapter.

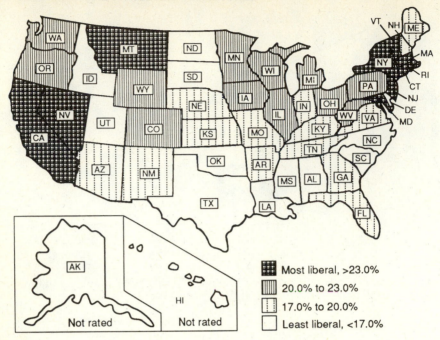

Figure 3.3   Percentage identifying themselves as liberal by state.

central to this consideration since Ranney.[12] The relationship between percentage Democrat in both houses is quite strong, as shown in Figure 3.4. The
Nebraska single-house legislature is excluded because its representatives are
elected on a nonpartisan ballot (political party not listed).

In the 1988 Mississippi legislative session, there were only seven
Republicans in the lower house and 115 Democrats. Although Mississippi is
the most Democratic of states, nine other (mainly southern) states have legislatures that are more than 75 percent Democratic. Only Idaho's lower house
has the reverse composition, with the Republican party predominating.
Generally, the Republican-dominated state legislatures are to be found in the
western mountain and plains states, and in several states throughout the
northeastern part of the country.

Party competition has been considered of primary importance in state
politics since V. O. Key's (1949) ground-breaking study of the U.S. South. By
no measure could politics in the South be called competitive. The legislatures
were overwhelmingly controlled by the Democrats, as were the governor-

---

12 Austin Ranney, "Parties in State Politics," in *Politics in the American States: A Comparative
Analysis,* Herbert Jacob and Kenneth N. Vines (eds.) (Boston: Little Brown, 1965), pp. 61–99.

Table 3.4   Percentage of State Lower House That is Democrat, 1987–1988[a]

Top 10			Bottom 10		
Rank	State	Percent	Rank	State	Percent
1	Mississippi	94.30	40	North Dakota	42.50
2	Arkansas	91.00	41	Kansas	40.80
3	Maryland	87.90	42	Arizona	40.00
4	Georgia	85.00	43	Colorado	38.50
5	Alabama	84.80	44	New Jersey	38.00
6	Rhode Island	80.00	45	Utah	36.00
7	Hawaii	80.00	46	New Hampshire	33.00
8	Massachusetts	79.40	47	South Dakota	31.40
9	Louisiana	78.60	48	Wyoming	31.20
10	West Virginia	78.00	49	Idaho	23.80

[a] Nebraska not included for reasons discussed in text.
Source: See Table C in the appendix to this chapter.

ships, congressional seats, etc. Key also found the South to have a political situation that benefits the "haves" or those that were economically well off. He argued that when there is competition between the political parties, candidates will appeal to the "have-nots" with offers to use government to help them rather than the "haves." This argument apparently holds for the South.

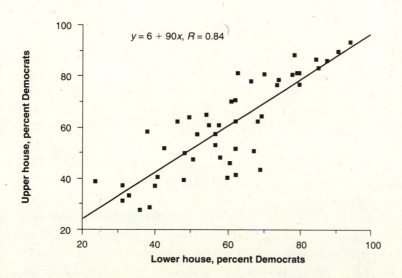

$y = 6 + 90x, R = 0.84$

Figure 3.4   The relationship between percent Democratic in upper and lower houses of the individual states.

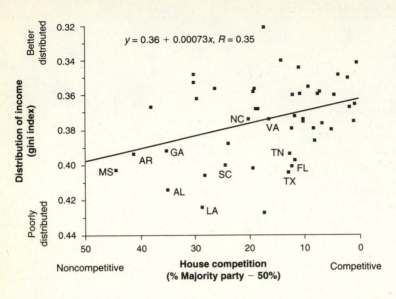

Figure 3.5   The relationship between distribution of income and political party competition.

But political scientists have used this argument to advocate party competition in general, especially for state politics.

Figure 3.5 shows the relationship between competition in the lower house of a state legislature and the distribution of wealth within the state. A state legislature with 50 percent Democrats and 50 percent Republicans would be quite competitive. But Mississippi with 94.3 percent Democrats and Idaho with 76.2 percent Republicans would be uncompetitive. As a measure of such competition, we note how much greater the percentage in the majority party is over the 50 percent truly competitive figure. Thus in the figure, Mississippi is shown at 44.3 percent. Idaho would be 26.2 percent. Vermont and Pennsylvania, with differences of only 0.3 and 0.7 percent respectively, are most competitive states.

Since we have no data on whether a state's policies favor the "haves," we have used overall distribution of wealth as measured by the Gini index. If the top 20 percent of the wealthy had only 20 percent of the wealth and the bottom 20 percent also had 20 percent of the wealth, the Gini index used here would be 0.00, indicating equal distribution of wealth. At the other extreme, a Gini value of 1.00 indicates that all wealth is concentrated in the most wealthy segment of society. States fall in a range between about 0.43 and 0.32, which would indicate that wealth tends to be concentrated among the wealthy but far short of the most wealthy having all of the wealth.

Government can greatly redistribute wealth, as suggested by Key. Extending his argument, we would expect states with more competition in their legislature to work for an equal distribution of wealth. The data suggest that this is the case.

Key's early finding still holds. Competition between the political parties seemingly results in better distribution of wealth. States that have more competition in their legislature have a lower Gini index or more equal distribution between the richer and the poorer segments of society. The figure also shows that the southern states tend to be uncompetitive and to have poorly distributed wealth. However, the relationship vanishes when the southern states are removed.[13] Although Key studied only the southern states, he did not conceive that only they were affected by the competition among political parties. Competition among political parties is unrelated to distribution of wealth outside the South.[14]

This result seems to be an example of a *spurious relationship*, where a third variable, in this case the south as a region, causes both of the variables initially to seem related, in this case lack of party competition and poorly distributed wealth.[15] A clearer example is the strong relationship in all communities between the number of fire engines responding to a fire and the amount of damage done by the fire. The spuriousness of this relationship is obvious—the severity of the fire is responsible for both the number of engines responding and the amount of damage. If the situation were not so obvious, a council might respond to citizen demands to help cut their home fire insurance costs by passing a city ordinance (law) to the effect that no more than one fire engine can respond to any fire. The intent would be to reduce fire damage but the result would be the opposite, since a single engine responding to a serious fire would be unable to contain it, resulting in additional damage. Only more difficult laws and efforts, such as building codes that emphasize more fire-resistant construction, additional training for fire workers, education programs for homeowners, and so forth are likely to influence damage caused by fires.

A similar situation seems to be the case with efforts seeking to induce party competition in the hope of giving the "have-nots" more say. Since the relationship between the two seems to vanish with the removal of the South, a change in party competition cannot have the intended result. We have not said what it is about the South that causes a lack of competition between

---

13   The equation becomes $y = 0.36 + 0.00021x$, and the correlation drops to 0.09.

14   The relationship still holds within the South, however: $y = 0.39 + 0.0038x$, $R = 0.30$.

15   For the clearest discussion of this problem see Hans Zeisel, *Say It with Figures*, 5th ed. (New York: Harper & Row, 1968), pp. 132–146.

Republicans and Democrats as well as poorly distributed wealth. Certainly, the fact that this region is part of Elazar's traditional political culture, in which government is not expected to redistribute wealth, may explain why the governments of southern states do not do so. The Civil War, or the War Between the States as southerners refer to it, may account for the unwillingness to cast votes for Republicans, the political party of Lincoln. Many other hypotheses could be generated to account for this evidently spurious relationship.

The basic problem with public policy-making is finding effective public policies on which at least a majority of voters can agree. Even if a relationship between a policy and a desired outcome can be found, many of these relationships may be spurious, often without being obvious. The uniqueness of the South is particularly troublesome in comparing the U.S. states.

CONCLUSIONS ABOUT DIFFERENCES

The discussions in this chapter and the preceding ones are so numerous as to be tedious. However, much of what has been introduced will be dealt with more extensively later. First, we have considered differences across the states ranging from economics, political culture, politics and government, and social problems faced that probably greatly influence what a state does. Clearly, there are meaningful differences between states on most, if not all, of such measures. Second, economic and other resources available to states play a very important role in accounting for differences in circumstances or experiences of the states, as well as the policies that they enact to cope with problems. A poor state has few resources with which to solve its problems; however, it should not be implied that economics is the only consideration.[16]

Third, political variations are often institutional changes that can be fairly easily enacted by a legislature. Politics may press the legislature to change political institutions. Just bowing to such pressure, however, need not mean that the institutional change will have any impact on what government does, including the problem the change was supposed to cure. Fourth, the South

---

16   At one point political science was divided into those who said economics was so overwhelming in its influence that political variables were trivial. See Thomas R. Dye, *Politics, Economics, and the Public: Policy Outcomes in the American States* (Chicago: Rand McNally, 1966). The other camp persisted that much variation remained once economics was considered and that political variables were important in accounting for the remaining differences. See Ira Sharkansky and Richard I. Hofferbert, "Dimensions of State Policy," in *Politics in the American States: A Comparative Analysis*, 2nd ed., Herbert Jacob and Kenneth N. Vines (eds.) (Boston: Little, Brown, 1971), pp. 315–353.

typically stands apart in terms of both political and economic variables. Since the problems that policies seek to address also tend to show the South to be different, it often means that if one excludes the South from consideration, relationships vanish. Finally, all of these differences persist although each state is a partner in our federal system of government and subject to the limitations that the federal government (Congress, the presidency, and the federal courts) can impose. They are also nonequal rivals for the resources that the federal government has to distribute, but that also fails to explain the differences between them.

Where you live affects many things in your lives that are of concern to government. Only some of these differences can be manipulated by policymakers in government. These differences, as we will see, permit a comparative analysis of the states, as discussed in this chapter, and among American local governments, such as cities, counties, and school boards. It is apparent from our consideration of political culture and of liberal/conservative differences that even ideas differ between states and influence what the states do. The next chapter deals with many of the ideas that shape what we expect of government.

SUMMARY

1. Differences in politics among the states are expected to influence how they cope with problems in society. Mainly, government is expected to give the poorer segments of society an equal say.
2. Since one political party advocates greater use of government, it is expected that which party controls government affects the policies that are enacted. Also competition among political parties is expected to change the policies enacted by government.
3. Public and decision-maker attitudes concerning what government should do, called political culture, also influences how government seeks to cope with social problems.
4. A state with ample financial resources for coping with problems may have politics or a political culture that encourages or discourages using those resources.

SUGGESTED READINGS

Council of State Governments. *Book of the States, 1988–89* (Lexington, KY: Council of State Governments, 1989). This typically yearly publication includes much data, especially institution differences data, on the states.

Elazar, Daniel (ed.). *American Federalism: A View from the States*, 2nd ed. (New York: Harper & Row, 1972). This book gives a thorough discussion of one person's view of the U.S. political cultures.

Gray, Virginia. "The Socioeconomic and Political Context of States," in *Politics in the American States*, Virginia Gray, Herbert Jacob, and Robert B. Albritton (eds.) (Glenview, IL: Scott, Foresman, 1990). This material covers many of the differences we have discussed in this chapter.

U.S. Bureau of the Census. *Statistical Abstract of the United States: 1990* (Washington, DC: U.S. Government Printing Office). Although this extensive collection of data on the states offers no interpretations, it is the basis of most comparisons of the states. Section 8, dealing with elections, includes many political variables.

Appendix

Table A   Voting Turnout in the Presidential Election of 1984

Rank	State	Percent
1	Minnesota	68.2
2	Montana	65.0
3	Maine	64.7
4	Wisconsin	63.5
5	North Dakota	62.7
6	South Dakota	62.6
7	Iowa	62.2
8	Oregon	61.9
9	Utah	61.6
10	Connecticut	61.1
11	Vermont	59.9
12	Idaho	59.9
13	Alaska	59.3
14	Washington	58.4
15	Ohio	58.0
16	Michigan	57.9
17	Massachusetts	57.6
18	Missouri	57.3
19	Illinois	57.1
20	Kansas	56.8
21	New Jersey	56.6
22	Indiana	55.9
23	Rhode Island	55.7
24	Nebraska	55.6
25	Delaware	55.5
26	Colorado	55.0
27	Louisiana	54.5
28	Pennsylvania	54.0
29	Wyoming	53.3
30	New Hampshire	53.0
31	Oklahoma	52.2
32	Mississippi	52.2
33	West Virginia	51.8
34	Arkansas	51.8
35	Maryland	51.4
36	New Mexico	51.3
37	New York	51.2
38	Kentucky	50.8
39	Virginia	50.7
40	Alabama	49.9
41	California	49.6
42	Tennessee	49.1
43	Florida	48.2
44	North Carolina	47.4
45	Texas	47.2
46	Arizona	45.2
47	Hawaii	44.3
48	Georgia	42.0
49	Nevada	41.6
50	South Carolina	40.7

Source: U.S. Bureau of the Census, *Statistical Abstract of the United States, 1988* (Washington, DC: U.S. Government Printing Office), p. 71.

Table B   Voters Calling Themselves Liberals, 1976–1982

Rank	State	Percent
1	Nevada	30.8
2	New Jersey	26.2
3	New York	25.9
4	Massachusetts	25.5
5	California	24.9
6	Montana	24.8
7	Connecticut	24.5
8	Vermont	24.4
9	Maryland	24.0
10	Rhode Island	23.9
11	Oregon	22.9
12	Wyoming	22.3
13	West Virginia	22.2
14	Colorado	22.1
15	Pennsylvania	21.9
16	Michigan	21.8
17	Ohio	21.7
18	Washington	21.1
19	Illinois	20.9
20	Wisconsin	20.6
21	Minnesota	20.5
22	Iowa	20.0
23	Florida	19.4
24	New Mexico	19.4
25	Delaware	19.3
26	Kansas	19.3
27	Nebraska	19.3
28	Maine	19.0
29	Tennessee	18.9
30	New Hampshire	18.7
31	Kentucky	18.5
32	Arkansas	18.2
33	Georgia	18.0
34	Virginia	17.8
35	Arizona	17.8
36	Indiana	17.8
37	Missouri	17.2
38	Texas	16.7
39	North Carolina	16.4
40	Louisiana	16.3
41	Alabama	16.1
42	South Carolina	15.7
43	Mississippi	15.3
44	Oklahoma	14.3
45	Idaho	13.4
46	Utah	13.2
47	South Dakota	12.4
48	North Dakota	10.5
49	Alaska	NA
50	Hawaii	NA

Source: Gerald C. Wright, Robert S. Erikson, and John D. McIver, "Measuring State Party Identification and Ideology Using Survey Data," *Journal of Politics* 47 (May 1985), p. 445.

Table C   Lower House of State Legislatures, Percentage Democratic

Rank	State	Percent
1	Mississippi	94.30
2	Arkansas	91.00
3	Maryland	87.90
4	Georgia	85.00
5	Alabama	84.80
6	Rhode Island	80.00
7	Hawaii	80.00
8	Massachusetts	79.40
9	Louisiana	78.60
10	West Virginia	78.00
11	South Carolina	74.20
12	Kentucky	73.70
13	North Carolina	70.00
14	Oklahoma	69.30
15	Nevada	69.00
16	Missouri	68.10
17	New Mexico	67.10
18	Virginia	66.30
19	Texas	62.70
20	Florida	62.50
21	Washington	62.20
22	New York	62.20
23	Minnesota	61.90
24	Tennessee	61.60
25	Connecticut	60.90
26	Ohio	60.60
27	Alaska	60.00
28	Michigan	58.20
29	Iowa	58.00
30	Maine	57.00
31	Illinois	56.80
32	California	55.00
33	Wisconsin	54.50
34	Oregon	51.70
35	Pennsylvania	50.70
36	Vermont	49.70
37	Montana	49.00
38	Indiana	48.00
39	Delaware	46.30
40	North Dakota	42.50
41	Kansas	40.80
42	Arizona	40.00
43	Colorado	38.50
44	New Jersey	38.00
45	Utah	36.00
46	New Hampshire	33.00
47	South Dakota	31.40
48	Wyoming	31.20
49	Idaho	23.80
50	Nebraska	NA

Source: Book of the States, 1988–89 (Lexington, KY: Council of State Governments, 1989), p. 89.

Chapter
4

The Origins of Concern with Government

*W*hen government is quite active and makes decisions that greatly affect your life, you are much more likely to be concerned with how its decisions are made. As we shall see later, however, you may not necessarily be concerned enough to invest your time in running for public office, or even in voting. At any rate, the many governments in the United States—national, state, and local—do affect our lives on a daily basis. As noted in Chapter 1, students in Texas are reading this text because their legislature passed a law requiring them to take a course concerning state constitutions and politics. But government has already affected each of you, even if it is early in the morning. You have watched television that the national government regulates; have traveled on roads provided by the state, local, or even federal government; have been subject to rules of driving that are enforced by city governments; and probably have broken no state criminal laws that prohibit murder, burglary, and so forth. In earlier times, government was nearly invisible to the typical American, who was then living on a subsistence farm.

We shall consider several periods of government. Our purpose is to consider the "mind sets" of those who have advocated policy changes during different time periods. Certain ideas arose to shape policy efforts during these periods. Consideration of those ideas will allow us to understand why these

often unsubstantiated policy changes were tried—and why policies introduced to deal with earlier problems that often no longer exist still affect us.
We shall also see the role of politics in many of these policies. Most important,
we shall see how events drive our political system and all political systems
to change in (sometimes successful) efforts to deal with society's troubles.

PERIODS OF GOVERNMENT IN AMERICA

No-Government Period: 1776–1850.   There are many who would probably
take exception both to the characterization of this period as the "no-government period" and with the dates for the beginning and end of this period and
others. There is no question that each period blends gradually into the next
and that some states—notably Massachusetts, New York, New Jersey, and
probably Illinois—left this particular period for the next at an earlier date.
Similarly, some states moved into the later period much after 1850. These
periods suggest events that shaped the dominant tone of thought that in turn
affected our governing institutions.

At the end of the successful fight for independence, as a nation of many
states evolved into a new federal system of government, there were many
details that needed to be resolved. There were external threats in which the
national government played an important role, such as the American Indian
and European threats. There were questions of interplay between the states
and of smoothing commerce by dealing with interstate trade and creating a
stable economy. State and county governments that existed sometimes undertook substantial projects such as the canals in New York and Pennsylvania. Nevertheless, the average American living on a subsistence farm could
fully expect to live a life with nearly no contact with government.

For those who longingly wish for a simpler life free of government inter-
ference, this period is the ideal one to which they wish to return. If you needed
a service, you had to provide it yourself; if you wanted to burn your leaves in
the fall, you did so; and you never, or at least very seldom, had to complete any
forms. The only exceptions were the county clerk's paperwork involved in
reporting a birth or in buying or selling a farm. On occasion, you might also see
the county sheriff, who dealt with theft of property and loss of life.

Everyone was subject to a county government for these record keeping
and law enforcement services. So this might be called the period of county
government. Because contact even with that government was rare for the
average American, "no government" is the most apt label. There were very
few towns of any size. In the first, 1790 census, no U.S. city, not even New
York, Philadelphia, or Boston, had a population of more than 50,000. Only

five cities were larger than 8000 people. Not until 1820 were there any larger than 100,000, and there was no American city with a million people until 1880.[1] Overall in 1820, only 5 percent of Americans lived in areas with 2500 population or more, defined by the Census Bureau as "urban."

Ideas concerning the accountability of government to those being governed had little meaning in such a society. Who cared whether the mayor of New York was corrupt, since few people lived there? Since most did not live in cities, most had no mayor to be concerned about. Even the ideas of corruption or inefficiency meant little, since governments provided little service. Those making decisions to provide these services could do little harm or good. Even issues of states' rights versus those of the central government in Washington, D.C. had no relevance to the average American, at least until the South attempted to secede from the Union in 1860.

To use the language of political culture from Chapter 3, government in this period was "traditional." It defined ownership of property, kept records, and protected property. These services were provided, but no others were needed until people began to concentrate in urban areas.

Municipal Government Period: 1850–1895.   Even during the Civil War, urbanization increased in the United States, driven largely by the industrialization of our economy and the arrival in urban areas of European immigrants needing to earn a living. To industrialize in the 1800s required concentrating industries at points where access to the sea or to other water transportation allowed raw materials to be shipped in and manufacturing goods to be transported to markets. In 1870, seven of the 15 largest cities were seaports and six more were lake or river ports.[2] Furthermore, since the only realistic means to get from home to work was to walk, urbanism—with its concentration of workers in tenements—was the second requirement. A substantial influx of European immigrants provided the unskilled work force necessary for industrialization. These immigrants landed at the seaports and found ready employment there.

In an urban area with many more people concentrated in a square mile than was the case in rural areas, even normal everyday services could no longer be provided by each family. Water was not readily available and often became contaminated because of the lack of understanding of how water waste materials can contaminate drinking water. Thus waste materials could not be merely discarded onto the land or into the water nearby. Families be-

---

1   Noel P. Gist and L. A. Halbert, *Urban Society*, 4th ed. (New York: Crowell, 1956), p. 41.

2   Ernest S. Griffith, *A History of American City Government: The Conspicuous Failure, 1870–1900* (New York: Praeger, 1972), p. 6.

came dependent on someone else to provide services that they previously provided themselves, and they needed new services as well.

With urban concentration, crime increased and more police were needed for each thousand persons. Health and building codes were often demanded. Education became urgent so as to provide the public with a means for adapting to industrialization and the demands of living in an urban area. For example, the public needed to be literate in order to read instruction manuals as well as directions in the streets. Even planning street locations became more effective than using old cow paths. In urban areas, old and new services had to be provided to an increasingly dependent population.

One of the first acts when large numbers of people concentrated in an area was the establishment of a city or municipal government. That government then could pass laws to provide required services, to require people to obey laws and to pay taxes to provide the services, and to establish that certain acts, such as murder or swearing, were considered offenses against society and would be punished. Although state and national governments already existed, asking them to provide these urban services seemed senseless and unnecessarily complicated and indirect. Chicagoans needed services, so why go to the state of Illinois or to Washington D.C. for the services?

At any rate, persons living in these urban areas experienced municipal government through the services and laws that it provided. Thus the first government that had much effect on people was municipal government and, not surprisingly, much of how we think about government was shaped by this first experience. First among these ideas was that government could provide new services and the related idea, noted above, that local services are best provided by local government. Second, the tie between voter support for promised services and for the elected officials providing those services was established. Voters who were dissatisfied with services would merely vote against the incumbent, the present officeholder. Third, the twin ideas of efficiency and corruption took on clear significance. The new urban services provided by government were costly, and taxes were increased. More efficient services meant lower taxes, and corruption of course meant higher taxes.

It was probably inevitable that certain large city politicians, elected from ethnically distinct, perhaps predominantly Italian, Polish, or Irish, districts or wards would recognize the benefits of developing "solid neighborhood loyalty." By being a friend of that neighborhood in providing of city services, the politician assured his party's reelection success.[3] These politicians were

---

3 Kenneth Fox, *Better City Government: Innovation in American Urban Politics, 1850–1937* (Philadelphia: Temple University Press, 1977), p. 6.

called "ward heelers." There is little question that the ideas of the representative seeking to give services to constituents, and those constituents in
turn supporting him for reelection, are basic to our concept of democracy.
Many, however, saw the ward heelers as corrupt, taking bribes or keeping tax
funds for themselves, and demanded change. Certainly some politicians took
advantage of appeals that could be made to urban workers for their support
in winning public office, and others found it easier merely to pay voters to
"vote early and often."[4]

Municipal government did not spring forth in the United States as our
invention. Many of the names and ideas for the shape of this government, as
well as the experience with corruption, came from England. Names such as
sheriff, alderman, borough, township, and bailiff can be traced back to ninth-
century English names. During that century kings structured territorial local
governments and urban concentrations that are the precursors of our county
and municipal governments.[5] These governments too distinguished between
legislative, or at least somewhat representative, bodies and executives, accountable to the Church of England or the crown. Both forms of local government evolved but were initially imposed on local areas by the central
government, the king of England.

Several new ideas, however, did derive from U.S. experiences during the
period we have called the municipal government period. Probably the
foremost idea was that election outcomes could change policies. For many
immigrants, the idea that their day-to-day experience could be changed
merely by voting into office those who promised to improve local life was
probably amazing. Certainly it inspired the highest rates of voting in our history.[6] Related to this situation was the idea that organization was important
to winning, because only by getting immigrants to vote together was victory
assured. Similarly, government services did make a difference; thus the idea
developed that government was a device to provide services. Finally, we had
the idea that the public trust meant that public decision makers had to behave
more responsibly than private decision makers. One scholar of this period
sees those living outside the tenements in urban areas as a community whose

---

4   For a succinct history of urban America during this period, see Kenneth Fox, *Better City
Government*. Other frequently cited works include Robert H. Wiebe, *The Search for Order
1877–1929* (New York: Hill and Wang, 1967) and Sean D. Cashman, *America in the Gilded Age:
From the Death of Lincoln to the Rise of Theodore Roosevelt* (New York: New York University Press,
1984).

5   P. W. Jackson, *Local Government* (London: Butterworth, 1970), pp. 3–7.

6   This phenomenon may, however, have been merely the result of some people fraudulently
voting multiple times. See Jerrold D. Rusk, "The Effect of the Australian Ballot Reform on Split
Ticket Voting: 1876–1908," *American Political Science Review* 64 (Dec. 1970), pp. 1220–1238.

ideas of decency were offended, not only by the excesses of the "robber barons" of private industry, but even more so by the alien elements controlling and abusing city government.[7] Things would be right only if "responsible men" were put back in charge of government.

State Intercity Government Period: 1895–1932. Certainly some of the aspirants for offices such as mayor or city council member, that were defeated by ward heelers were from the community described by Wiebe. They were from families and older waves of immigrants that had been accustomed to holding these offices and to dealing with municipal policy-making before industrialization. For them, government did not have to provide much in the way of services, since the urban concentration and even the numbers of people living in the city were smaller. Many of these individuals also were wealthy or at least more wealthy than the new immigrant, industrial, tenement workers. Given this wealth, they were not disposed to approve of the increased taxes necessary to provide the new services offered by the ward heelers. Thus these older families not only lost elections, but also saw government services changed dramatically from what they considered morally correct. Furthermore, they had to pay higher taxes to pay for these new services. Along with those living in rural areas, these people came to see the new urban centers as hostile, foreign, and contrary to their self-interest.[8]

Those pressuring states to assume a more active role in urban areas seem to have been concerned mainly with political corruption in the cities. The unwillingness of older groups to lose their influence in shaping municipal policy was also a factor. There was also some new thinking, about how to cope with a much more complex society, including the problems posed by the excesses of "robber barons" in the oil, railroads, and steel industries. Prejudices formed against the new immigrants and against their potential support for the socialist ideas then being supported by industrial workers in Europe.

Corruption was certainly rampant. In 1870, of the nation's ten largest cities, New York, Philadelphia, Cincinnati, Chicago, and San Francisco were judged corrupt. Moreover, Boston, Brooklyn, and New Orleans either had corrupt mayors or city councils. Only Baltimore and St. Louis were essentially honest. Generally, the mayor played a lesser role than the ward heelers on the city council. City councils made most political appointments and were divided into subject matter committees that made day-to-day administrative

---

7   Wiebe, *The Search for Order, 1877–1929*, chap. 3 (New York: Hill and Wang, 1967).

8   Wiebe sees this conflict between the values of an older rural society and those of the new urban, worker society; see Robert H. Wiebe, *The Search for Order*.

decisions.[9] There were, however, some instances of citywide political machines in which a mayor played the central role, including the Tammany machine in New York City in 1868, but they were short-lived and perhaps exaggerated in importance.[10]

The economic crash of 1873 caused many cities to default on their debt and even to surrender their charters or to relinquish their status as cities.[11] This event and the fact that cities were competing with each other and over-extending themselves to attract railroads, gave the impetus to seek another solution to the problem in the cities. "State legislative supervision," supposedly motivated by concern for the "moral order of the cities," had been attempted since the 1850s. Those attempts were typically on a state-by-state basis, but the impetus in the 1870s was national in scope. The lawyers, political scientists, and reform-oriented persons responsible for the concerted effort to reform the cities probably never consciously perceived that they were making an end run around the politicians in control of the cities, but this was the case. Reforms included implementation of a civil service system, in which municipal employees are chosen by merit, rather than political loyalty; functional organization of municipal agencies to allow greater efficiency in providing municipal services (the origins of public administration in political science); removal of corruption in municipal elections; and measures to strengthen the hand of the mayor. All of these actions weakened the hand of city councils and all represent reform. But they also weakened the values of the immigrant and working classes that those politicians served.[12]

This is an excellent example of what might be called "changing the arena of conflict" to improve the chances that one group's political interests will prevail over those of another group. The other groups who had lost out in the politics of industrialized municipalities remained in control of state and national governments. If they could pass laws at these levels of government and force them on the municipalities, they could win at the state levels what they had lost at the municipal levels. To do so, they had to establish the right of states to tell municipalities that they had to enact civil service procedures for employment, have voter registration, and keep functional budgets subject to inspection, among other things.

An argument by an academic and the willingness of the state courts to rule actively as to what the cities must and must not do allowed this changing of arenas. In 1878 a lawyer, Thomas Cooley, used common law to argue that

---

9   Griffith, p. 11.
10   Fox, p. 16.
11   Griffith, p. 17.
12   Griffith, p. 91.

local government should deal with services that can be easily, cheaply, and intelligently offered, while state government should have more general powers. He argued that any violations of this rule were unconstitutional.[13] John Dillon extended these ideas and thus shaped how the courts reacted to efforts within the cities and within the legislatures to reform municipal government.[14] He argues,

> It is a general and undisputed proposition of law that a municipal corporation possesses and can exercise the following powers, and no others: First, those granted in express words; second, those necessary or fairly implied in or incident to the powers expressly granted; third, those essential to the declared objects and purposes of the corporation, not simply convenient, but indispensable. Any fair, reasonable doubt concerning the existence of power is resolved by the courts against the corporation, and the power is denied . . . . All acts beyond the scope of the powers granted are void.[15]

As applied by state courts, this became known as "Dillon's rule." It denied cities a solution to their own problems and ultimately provided reformers a constitutional basis for forcing municipal compliance to state statutes.

State governments, especially those of states with large industrialized cities, became active producers of statutes designed to remove corruption and introduce efficiency in municipal services. But this was not the limit of their activity. Some cities decided to franchise privately provided services to provide order to a chaotic situation in which competing utility companies kept the streets dug up endlessly and made the air above the streets a hopeless tangle of wires. Franchising may have helped to provide order, but it also gave the companies a reason to become involved in municipal politics.[16] Similarly, some cities decided to protect residents from hazardous buildings, unsanitary sewage disposal, and unhealthy practices in dealing with contagious diseases, whereas others did not. People who were displeased with their city's efforts in these areas could often find sympathetic state legislators who would seek to enact state statutes. These statutes forced all cities to comply by way of the Dillon rule.

Increasingly, even the common law that we had adopted from Great Britain often proved inadequate to cope with the new problems of an industrialized and urbanized state. Common law is a series of case-by-case principles for resolving disputes, such as what happens when a cow dies

---

13 Thomas M. Cooley, *A Treatis on the Constitutional Limitations Which Rest Upon the Legislative Power of the States of the American Union* (Boston: Little, Brown, 1878), p. 27.

14 John F. Dillon, *Treatis on the Law of Municipal Corporations* (Chicago: J. Cockroft, 1872).

15 John F. Dillon, *Commentaries on the Law of Municipal Corporations* (Boston: Little, Brown, 1881).

16 Fox, pp. 184–185.

shortly after being purchased or when people are denied access across property after having long been allowed to do so. In the first case the common law is to "let the buyer beware," meaning that he or she has no recourse to government. Similarly, if the public has not been allowed access for a year and a day, under common law the property owner can have violators arrested by the police for trespassing. Undertaking a job under common law means that one accepts the possibility of being maimed while doing it. All of these common laws and many others no longer seemed fair in the urban industrialized economies. State legislatures needed to be active. They stepped in and passed statutes that overruled or took precedence over the common laws.

Finally intrastate commerce, most often involving goods moving between the farm and the city, was a concern of state government as well as multiple local governments. Railroads, waterways, and land routes had to be regulated or provided, and only state government appeared to be the appropriate level for such governmental activity.

Again, many ideas derive from thinking during this time. Probably most apparent among these ideas is that local government is a creation of the state government. This afforded the possibility for various interests who lost in a policy-making decision at the local level to "change the arena" to the state level and win there. State government in this period joined municipal government in being active in coping with problems within the state. State government was especially active when those problems crossed the boundaries of several local governments or when there was corruption in a major city in the state. State statutes became the means for overriding common law, which might otherwise have been revered since it represented wisdom derived over hundreds of years. Probably the most important thought or idea that came from this period was that of reform, or the idea that institutions can be manipulated to achieve intended results.

The motivation for reform was to achieve greater efficiency or to weed out corruption and fraud. To cope with inefficiency and fraud, one merely needed to pass election laws, require auditing to ensure proper use of public funds, and select quality public employees based on merit rather than political spoils. To have quality local government, one needed to require checks and balances between the legislative (city council) and the executive (the strong mayor) branches or to combine the two branches into a commission form of government, in which each person served both a legislative and an administrative function. Although many would accuse the reformers of reflecting their class interests in their reforms, it should be noted that they were confident that those reforms would work. Perhaps the primary idea derived from this period is the reform movement and the confidence that there are clear standards by which government can be judged. Furthermore, they thought, government could be reformed to bring it into correspondence with these standards.

Federal Government Era: 1932 to the Present. Two events drove the United States into the next era of government. One of these events, the Great Depression in the late 1920s and the victory of Franklin Roosevelt in the presidential election of 1932, is noted by the beginning date above. The second event was the declaration of war by the United States against Germany and Japan as a result of the bombing of Pearl Harbor on December 7, 1941. Both of these events greatly increased the scope of federal government responsibilities over the few there had been before. The federal government now was responsible for the economy and for *actively* providing for national defense. The Constitution of 1789 gave the federal government responsibility for national defense but until 1941, with few exceptions, only a small part of the national budget was devoted to national defense. In 1940, for example, national defense received only 1.5 billion dollars, or about 16 percent of the $9.5–billion federal government budget. This went to $6 billion, or 43 percent, in 1941 and $24 billion, or 69 percent, in 1942. Since then, it has never been less than 30 percent of the budget.

Figure 4.1, showing the expenditures by federal as well as state and local governments beginning in 1929, demonstrates this sharp increase in federal expenditures in 1941 and the stabilization at high levels of expenditures. The reader should also note that apart from a shallow decline during the wartime years of the 1940s, state and local government expenditures have risen at an almost constant rate of 2.4 billion constant 1958 dollars per year.[17] (It should be noted that a 1958 dollar is worth more than five dollars today.) Apart from the substantial peak in federal expenditures during World War II, its expenditures also have increased at a constant rate, in this case 2.9 billion constant 1958 dollars per year.[18]

The first source of federal involvement came with the "New Deal" programs that were passed by the Roosevelt administration beginning in 1932 and were sharply increased in 1933 and 1934. Figure 4.2 shows public aid expenditures to employ and aid people during this period, again in constant 1958 dollars to control for the inflation this country has experienced since the 1930s. After making a substantial effort at public aid during the late 1930s, state and local governments remained largely unchanged in their ef-

---

17   The slope is 2.4 and the Pearson R is 0.96, meaning that we can very accurately predict total state and local expenditures.

18   The slope is 2.9 and the Pearson R is 0.84, suggesting that events and decisions more substantially shape federal expenditures.

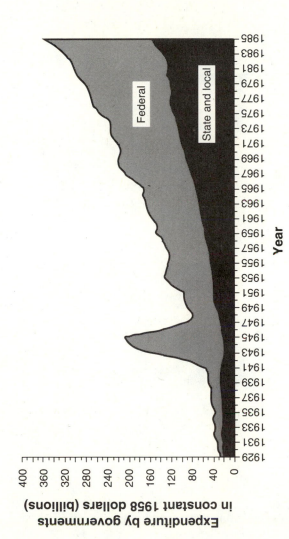

Figure 4.1   Trends in federal and state and local government expenditures over the period 1929–1985.

Sources: Data for 1929–1970: U.S. Bureau of the Census, *Historical Statistics of the United States: Colonial Times to 1970*, Washington DC: U.S. Government Printing Office, pp. 230, 1104, 1126; data for 1970–1985: U.S. Bureau of the Census, *Statistical Abstract of the United States, 1986*, Washington DC: U.S. Government Printing Office, p. 262; *Statistical Abstract of the United States, 1988*, pp. 264, 265, 294.

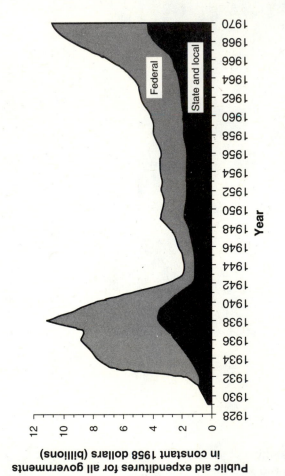

Figure 4.2 Public aid expenditures by all governments: 1929–1970.

Source: U.S. Bureau of the Census, *Historical Statistics of the United States: Colonial Times to 1970,* Washington, DC: U.S. Government Printing Office, pp. 230, 341.

forts at public aid until late in the 1960s. The federal government also showed less enthusiasm for public aid during and after World War II until the late 1960s.

Several ideas derive from this era also. Probably foremost is that of the federal government's income tax. Adopted in 1913, it proved to be bountiful in terms of the revenue it generated, and along with the federal government's right to print money, allowed that government to assume a preeminent position after the depression and World War II. This position was both preeminent and responsible. Washington was responsible for the economy as well as for the suffering of all Americans during an economic downturn or because of old age.

Washington's dominance should not cause us to ignore the fact that state and local governments also greatly expanded their expenditures over this period, as shown in Figures 4.1 and 4.2. Obviously they too had revenue sources that generated many dollars, as we shall discuss later. Some of the growth in state and local expenditures, however, came from transfers from the federal government to the lower governments. Did the generosity of the federal government with its revenue-producing income tax allow the expenditure growth of state and local governments?

Certainly the transfer of funds from higher governments to more local governments did occur, as shown in Figure 4.3. Before the depression, states received less than 10 percent of their revenues from federal government transfer payments. At the peak in the 1960s and 1970s, they received approximately 23 percent of their revenues this way. Similarly, local government first saw federal contributions to their budgets in the late 1930s, rising to a peak of 9 percent in the early 1980s. The biggest increases in transfers, however, were those from state governments to local governments, starting at about 10 percent and reaching 33 percent in the late 1970s. It would be safe to say that local governments, so heavily funded by property taxes, have become increasingly dependent on state and federal revenues to continue to provide local services.

Another idea that came with this process of gathering of revenues centrally and transferring them to lower levels of government is that of attaching "strings" or conditions to the funds. If local governments want state funds or if local and state governments want federal funds, they have to adhere to the limitations and conditions imposed. For example, they may be required to integrate their schools, not discriminate on the basis of race or gender, or impose a 55-mph speed limit and a 21-year-old drinking age. Behind these conditions attached to such funds are more inclusive moral and ethical standards. Since state standards of corruption in public office are imposed on local governments, and national standards for safety or for equal

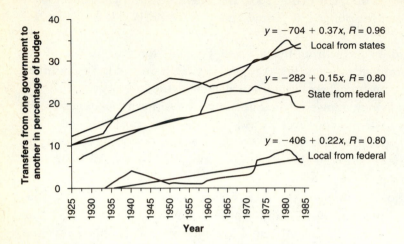

Figure 4.3   Transfer payments over the period 1929–1985.

Sources: John J. Harrigan, *Politics and Policy in States and Communities*, 2nd ed., Boston: Little, Brown, 1984, p. 46; and U.S. Bureau of the Census, *Statistical Abstract of the United States, 1988*, Washington, DC: U.S. Government Printing Office, pp. 264, 265, 294.

opportunity employment are applied to both state and local governments, local standards must give way.

Certainly this period showed that the federal government's ability to tax income and to "deficit spend" put it in a superior revenue position. This idea of superior revenue sources goes with that of invincibility, in that the federal government not only got us out of the Depression but also won the Second World War. Similarly, the federal government was of the right scale to deal with problems that extended beyond not only the borders of local or state government, but also often beyond national boundaries.

Finally, since Franklin Roosevelt's victory in 1932 rested not only on the support he received from the rural poor but also from the major cities with their substantial immigrant populations, we have yet another change of arenas. Those in the cities now could tell their opponents in the state governments that they had to obey federal law because it was the supreme law of the land. Ultimately, the Supreme Court told the state legislatures that they had to be reapportioned to take representation from rural areas and give it to urban areas. We should discuss this in more detail later.

Some observers think that we are entering a new "return to the states" or "New Federalism" era. Nathan argues that there is a cycle in the interplay between state governments and the federal government, with each temporarily leading the way in terms of innovative policy. Beginning in 1980, ". . . the states again are on the move."[19] He sees five factors contributing to this new trend. First is the New Federalism of the Reagan administration that sought to cut federal underwriting to domestic programs, thereby making it encumbent upon the states to undertake these programs at their own expense if they thought it desirable.

He sees additional factors, including the modernization of state governments over the past 20 years with improved managerial and technical capacity. A third factor is the reapportionment of state legislatures, giving more power to those in cities and especially suburbs. Fourth is the fact that the South has caught up with the rest of the states in resources available to government. Finally, Nathan believes that the states overreacted to the sharp recession of the U.S. economy in 1980–1981 by passing new taxes and sharply curtailing expenses. When the economy recovered, the states had ample reserves to innovate with new programs.[20]

Figures 4.1 and 4.3 suggest some truth to these arguments, but not much. Looking at overall expenditures in Figure 4.1, there is no evidence that either federal government or the state and local governments decreased their expenditures. But Figure 4.2 does reveal a modest downturn in federal transfer payments to the states (from 22 percent to 19 percent) and to local governments (from 9 percent to 6 percent). Both of these declines are minor in comparison with the overall trend shown in the figure. Transfers from the states to local governments also declined (from 35 percent to 33 percent). Only the future expenditure levels of the three levels of government will demonstrate whether we are in a new era, but there is room for doubt.

It should be noted that even the minor declines evident in Figure 4.2 does mean billions of dollars that were transferred from the federal government down to those who were poor or ill were not available.[21] After some initial success by the Reagan administration in getting such cutbacks, the states and communities successfully fought additional cuts.[22] As the figure shows, the advance of federal government transfers to the states and communities has not been smooth. New Federalism seems relatively insignificant in this context, no matter how serious it was in human terms.

---

19   Richard P. Nathan, "The Role of the States in American Federalism," in *The State of the States*, Carl E. Van Horn (ed.), (Washington, DC: CQ Press, 1989), p. 18.

20   Also see Carl E. Van Horn, "The Quiet Revolution," in *The State of the States*, Carl E. Van Horn (ed.) (Washington, DC: CQ Press, 1989).

21   Ann O'M. Bowman and Richard C. Kearney, *The Resurgence of the States* (Englewood Cliffs, NJ: Prentice-Hall, 1986).

22   Demetrios Caraley and Yvette R. Schlussel, "Congress and Reagan's New Federalism," *Publius* 16 (Winter 1986), pp. 49–79.

The downturn in federal contributions to both state and local govern-ments and the uncertain economy between 1980 and the present has left many states without the revenue resources they need given the demands for government services. One report notes three major expenditure areas that have left 11 states with revenues below estimates of greater than 5 percent.[23] *Medicaid*, a 56 percent federally underwritten health care program for the poor and disabled, is the fastest growing area of state expenditures. In 1970 it took only 3 percent of state expenditures, but in 1990 it took 12 percent and continues its sharp increase as medical costs soar, as our society increasingly ages, and as the federal government makes more groups eligible. *Education* continues to be the greatest state expenditure, but the federal share has dropped. Finally, *prisons* and their operation and maintenance have grown from taking 21 cents for every state expenditure dollar in 1979 to taking 37 cents in 1989. Although it probably is not new for some states to have budgetary shortfalls, the expectations of the public, economic downturn, and less federal government willingness to transfer funds to the states have made political life in state government uncomfortable as new and greater resources are alway needed.

Again, if there is a new era with many prerogatives for legislation and funding returned to the states, some interests would be benefited. In ef-fect, we would again have a change of arenas. The efforts of the "pro-lifers" to overturn the *Roe* v. *Wade* decision, which allows states to restrict abortions only in the last trimester of pregnancy are largely motivated by a desire to return policy-making on this issue to the state level. At that level, they anticipate that their pressure would be more influential. The history of government in the United States is one of various losing inter-ests who seek to change arenas in the hope that at another level they may be victorious.

CENTRALIZATION OF GOVERNMENT

Apart from the possibility of the states reassuming a substantial share of responsibility for dealing with domestic problems, the pattern we have seen is one of local governments dealing with problems, then states bringing to bear their more central authority under the Dillon Rule. This trend was fol-

---

23 "80's Leave States and Cities in Need," *New York Times* (Sunday, December 30, 1990), p. 1. These states are Maine, New Hampshire, Vermont, Connecticut, Rhode Island, New Jersey, Maryland, Virginia, Georgia, Florida, and Michigan. With the exception of Michigan, all of these are East Coast states. Indeed, the problem seems overwhelmingly one affecting the East.

lowed in turn by the economic muscle of the federal government in dealing with depression and world war, followed by more extensive involvement in domestic programs. The federal government represents the ultimate centralization of problem solving in our system of government. Certainly there are problems apart from national defense that are more global than the authority of our national government. The world economy and the threats of a world depression are but one example. There is also a full range of environmental concerns, such as the depletion of ozone caused by Freon gas, the greenhouse effect caused in part by carbon dioxide gas from burning fuels, and acid rain also caused by such burning. All of these problems extend beyond our national borders. Whether international agreements will prove sufficient to cope with these problems or whether centralization will result in the ultimate centralization, a world government, again remains to be seen.

Presently, however, the state and communities rest in an unstable political environment in which they retain some authority to make decisions that affect us. Given this authority, some state and communities will pass innovative legislation and others will not. Such legislation potentially will make living in some communities more desirable than others. Furthermore, this legislation will reflect the different perspectives of those living in core cities, on farms, or in the suburbs, and the different economic, racial, age, and other circumstances of each group. In this chapter we have seen that events and traditions shape the development of government in the United States; presumably, so will this circumstance.

CONFEDERACY AND FEDERALISM

We have been discussing the history of U.S. government, which rests firmly on the Constitution of the United States and the federal form of government that it entails. We need to consider briefly three forms of national government: unitary, confederacy, and federal, the last two of which are basically American inventions. *Unitary* government is quite simple; there is a national government that oversees the entire nation with the aid, at least in modern times, of regional and local administrative agencies or governments. Laws are proposed to that unitary government to cope with problems in society and, if passed, are administered by the regional and local governments. Under the Dillon rule, in effect, the interrelationship between state and local governments, such as municipalities, school districts, or counties, is one of a unitary government. The state passes the

laws and the local governments administer them. Figure 4.4a shows stylisti-
cally a unitary government.

Except for the fact that they probably would not have succeeded in their
revolt from Great Britain, the 13 original colonies could have become 13 independent unitary governments. Certainly the idea of being "Americans"
rather than "South Carolinians" or "New Yorkers" did not predate the
Declaration of Independence by very long and was strongly opposed by
many. You probably had a similar reaction to the above comments about
the potential for world government. Similarly, Canadians strongly resist
being absorbed by the United States. However, there was a need for the
colonies to give up some of their authority or sovereignty to fight the
revolution. What evolved was a *confederacy*. Ultimately after many years
of fighting the war, the *Articles of Confederation*, 1781–1789, formalized this
organization. Confederacy represents the absolute minimum concession
of authority. A government of governments is set up to deal specifically
with certain actions desired by all constituent governments. In the case of
our confederacy, the central government was set up to fight the war, but
was not authorized even to gather taxes to pay for it or to draft troops to
fight it. Typically, each government in a confederacy retains the right to
stop actions by the central government with a single negative vote. Additionally, the members can withdraw or secede by their individual choice,
often with some prior notification. Confederacy includes these elements,
because they were true of ours. Figure 4.4b shows a confederacy. If we had
still been a confederacy when the depression of the 1930s hit, the "New
Deal" of Roosevelt could have been undertaken only if all 48 states had
agreed to it—a very unlikely prospect.

Ultimately, this confederate form of government proved unsatisfac-
tory to many. As you all know, the states' representatives who met in
Philadelphia to amend the Articles of Confederation exceeded their
authority and drafted a new Constitution. It established a *federal* form of
government, the first ever known to mankind.[24] This form of government
is very complex since it establishes at least two governments for each individual. You can turn to either of these governments to solve problems,
and you must obey the laws of both governments. The purpose of this
complexity is to allow the central government to cope with national
problems without the unanimous consent of the states as was necessary
under confederacy. Figure 4.4c shows a federation.

---

24   There are some who claim that the Iroquois Indians had federalism before we did.

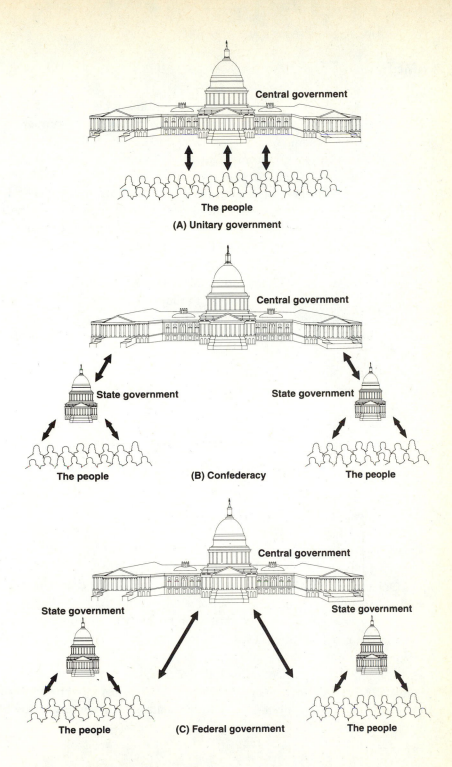

Figure 4.4 Forms of government.

AMERICAN FEDERALISM

Obviously there is the potential for the laws of different levels of government to contradict each other. Someone or some governmental body must resolve conflicts between them. Another alternative is merely to state that the laws of the central or federal government are the "supreme law" of the land. When there is conflict, the regional or state government's laws must give way. If this were the case with our complex system of modern economies and societies, one might well expect that the central government would force the state governments into the status of being administrative governments for the central government's legislation, making it a unitary government by evolution.

The United States Constitution does have the "supremacy clause." "Laws of the United States . . . shall be the supreme Law of the Land: and the Judges in every State shall be bound thereby, any thing in the Constitution or Laws of any State to the Contrary notwithstanding."[25] If this statement were all that the Constitution said on the subject, it seems likely that we would now be a unitary government. State governments, like local governments presently, would be allowed to make laws only until the higher level of government acted.

There are, however, several other statements or clauses in the U.S. Constitution that shape federal and state government interactions. The Constitution enumerates 16 powers that Congress has, plus a seventeenth that entitles it "To make all Laws which shall be necessary and proper for carrying into Execution the foregoing Powers. . . ."[26] To some scholars known as strict constructionists, the 16 *enumerated powers* are all that is given to the federal government. This view is advocated by those controlling the states. Others known as loose constructionists, see the *necessary and proper clause* as implying many more potential actions for the federal government.

One of the enumerated powers, the *commerce clause*, gives Congress the right "To regulate Commerce . . . among the several States. . . ." This clause was, of course, the primary motivation for the new Constitution and has been the basis of much of the federal government's involvement in the national economy.

The Tenth Amendment of the Bill of Rights, the *reserve powers amendment* states, "The powers not delegated to the United States (government) by the Constitution, nor prohibited by it to the states, are reserved to the States

---

25   Article VI.

26   Article I, section 8.

respectively, or to the people." Like the supremacy clause, which seems to give blanket powers to the federal government, this clause seems, apart from the enumerated powers, to give blanket powers to the states *and the people.* The Fourteenth Amendment also has been essential to greater federal government activity in contemporary times. It states, " . . . nor shall any State deprive any person of life, liberty, or property, without due process of law; nor deny to any person within its jurisdiction the equal protection of the laws." This is the *due process and equal protection clause* so often used to force the states not to discriminate.

The Constitution also includes several statements that shape somewhat how the states deal with each other. States must recognize the official acts of other states, such as marriages, divorces, and abortions, because "Full Faith and Credit shall be given in each State to the public Acts, Records, and judicial Proceeding of every other State," which is known as the *full faith and credit clause.*[27] Additionally, "The Citizens of each State shall be entitled to all Privileges and Immunities of Citizens in the several States."[28] This *privileges and immunities clause* means that states have to grant to nonresidents the same privileges and immunities that they accord to their residents. New residents have argued that universities continuing to charge them out-of-state tuition after they have established residency is a violation of the privileges and immunities clause. In Florida, Georgia, and Alabama federal courts, they have been successful.

Finally, "A person charged in any State with . . . Felony or other Crime, who shall flee from Justice, and be found in another State, shall on Demand of the executive Authority of the State from which he fled, be delivered up to be removed to the State having Jurisdiction of the Crime."[29] Under this *rendition or extradition clause*, if a state requests extradition or that a person charged with a crime be made available to be brought back to the state where the alleged crime took place, the requested governor is supposed to make that person available. If the person charged "waives extradition," it merely means no paperwork needs to be filed and that he or she will go voluntarily.

Judicial Interpretation by the U.S. Supreme Court. In the terse language of the U.S. Constitution, many of these clauses seem quite absolute and mutually contradictory. The Constitution makes no provision for limiting the absolute or contradictory nature of these clauses. But very early into our history under the Constitution, one agency of the federal government asserted

27   Article IV, Section 1.
28   Article IV, Section 2.
29   Article IV, Section 3.

its right to judge contradictions—the Supreme Court of the United States. *Marbury* v. *Madison* (1803) was the first case to assert the right of the U.S. Supreme Court to judge the compatibility of actions by government with statements in the U.S. Constitution, or the constitutionality of such acts. Shortly afterwards the Court first interpreted federal actions that restricted the powers of the states. In *McCulloch* v. *Maryland* (1819) the Court broadly interpreted the necessary and proper clause and ruled that a state cannot tax the federal government because that was unconstitutional.

Inasmuch as the U.S. Supreme Court lacks enforcement capability and thus could be ignored, such has seldom been the case. Many of the Court's decisions have shaped policies of state governments, sometimes limiting actions and sometimes demanding actions. There is very little evidence that the U.S. Supreme Court has ever taken a strict constructionist view that limits the powers of the federal government. Although there are now other federal systems of government in the world, including the Soviet Union, none allows one branch of the central or federal government to resolve conflicts between the regional or state governments and the central government.[30] The Court can also be overruled by amendment to the U.S. Constitution. This has been done several times but never to allow that states have powers denied to them by the Court.

A recent case decided by a narrow vote, *Garcia* v. *San Antonio Metropolitan Transit Authority* (1985), denies that there are "traditional" areas of state governing that are beyond the powers of Congress.[31] The Court's majority refused to define such "traditional" areas and instead said that the process of federalism should preserve the states. Since the states have representatives both in the House of Representatives and the Senate, they can have Congress respect the traditional powers of the states. Until Congress enacts a law, they said, the states may take action.

When Congress acts, however, the states must comply. The minority charges that in effect, after many years of trying to resolve conflicts between the various clauses of the U.S. Constitution, the U.S. Supreme Court has opted to give an absolute interpretation of the powers of the central government. Centralization can continue without the Supreme Court restricting it as a result of its interpretation of the U.S. Constitution.

---

30   For a lucid discussion of these matters, see William T. Gormley, Jr., "Custody Battles in State Administration," in *The State of the States*, Carl E. Van Horn (ed.). (Washington, DC: CQ Press, 1989), pp. 131–151.

31   The earlier case was *National League of Cities* v. *Usery* (1976).

CONSTITUTIONS AND THE STATES

No respectable group, city, state, or nation lacks a written constitution. But when the Congress of the United States decided to write down the operating understanding among the states that had allowed them to win the Revolutionary War, the Articles of Confederation that they drafted joined the quickly altered state constitutions as the only written constitutions then existent in the world. Even the state constitutions were quick rewrites of colonial charters, under the tumultuous circumstance of war, to weaken sharply the office of the governor, who up to that time had been the king's governor. Perhaps, had the charters not existed, the Congress would have felt no need for a written constitution and the states and nation today would not have them; however, such was not the case.

A further factor in understanding the concern with state constitutions is the brevity of the second and current constitution of the United States adopted in 1789, which we call the Constitution. This 8700-word document is noticeably lacking in detail. As a result, through the process of tradition as well as through constitutional review or interpretation by the U.S. Supreme Court, detail has been added and often later deleted to allow that now 200-year-old document to adapt to contemporary times. Although two state constitutions (those of Massachusetts and New Hampshire) predate the U.S. Constitution, and share its brevity, it is the national Constitution that most reformers would like to see emulated by state constitutions.

Periods of State Constitution Writing

In terms of their length, we can see in Figure 4.5 that there has been a clear pattern evident over time. Initially, state constitutions typically were about 10,000 words long, leaving little room for detailed procedures and prohibitions. Length began to increase in the middle 1800s and accelerated in the late 1800s and early 1900s, only to decline sharply when many states began to draft new constitutions after World War II. Length and other attributes are the basis for defining several periods of constitution writing.

Until 1780. With the exception of New York, states operated with legislatively dominant governments, largely as a reaction against the excesses of the king's governor before independence. As shown in the figure, these constitutions were short (about 10,000 words). The basic idea was that newly won powers for the legislative branch were the basis of responsive government, in contrast to the unresponsive king's governor. Governors were viewed as dangerous even to the point of being abolished.

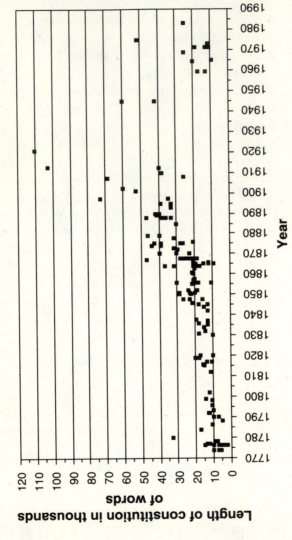

Figure 4.5   State constitutional lengths and time of adoption.

Source: Alfred de Grazia, "State Constitutions—Are They Growing?" State Government, March 1954, pp. 82–83; Constitutions after 1950 are from: *The Book of the States, 1988–89,* Lexington, KY: Council of State Governments, 1989, p. 14.

1780 or 1789 Through 1870. Although these dates are artificially precise, the constitution of the state of Massachusetts in 1780 and the national Constitution of 1789 began the new idea of "balanced" government. A strengthened executive, meaning the governor, was given formal or constitutional powers, such as a veto and power to appoint officials, to offset those of the legislative branch. Since power was vested in at least two branches of government, it was to be controlled by dividing it. This idea was adopted in the U.S. Constitution, as was the idea of two branches of the legislature, each checking and balancing the other.

1870 Through 1920. The Civil War saw the need for much constitutional activity in the South. With the exception of Tennessee, all other Confederate states repeatedly held constitutional conventions. The first was in 1861, in Texas and probably elsewhere, to substitute "Confederate" for "United" States of America. They met again in 1864 or 1865 to reverse this action.[32] Then in 1867 or 1868 they met to enact the new constitution required by Congress under Reconstruction.[33] Finally, during the period 1874–1902, they met to enact post-Reconstruction constitutions that returned power to the wealthy whites who had controlled state governments before the Civil War.[34] It was these post-Reconstruction southern constitutions that contained the antiblack "Jim Crow" laws that disenfranchised most blacks and encouraged racial separation.

Only the last of these southern constitutions was written during the period defined above. During this period no constitution of fewer than 20,000 words was written, and some of the very long constitutions were more than 50,000 words in length. What was included in such lengthy documents? It was obvious to southern whites that there was no protection in "balanced" government. The Reconstruction constitutions balanced the governor against the legislature, but that did not keep the government from, as they saw it, excessive actions against whites. When they regained control, a better protection was sought against government by giving power to the people, or at least to those who could vote.

---

32   J. William Davis and Ruth Cowart Wright, *Texas Political Practice and Public Policy*, 3rd ed. (Dubuque, IA: Kendall/Hunt, 1978), pp. 36–37.

33   This resulted from the Congress's requirement that former Confederate electorates take the "ironclad oath" requirement that voters swear to not having voluntarily served or aided the confederate cause, which disqualified most white voters; see Davis and Wright, p. 37.

34   These dates but not the interpretation are from Albert L. Sturm, *Thirty Years of State Constitution-Making: 1938–1968.* (New York: National Municipal League, 1970), pp. 10–11.

The basic idea is to restrict sharply state government, including both the legislature and the executive, with constitutional restrictions. Only when the voting public approved a constitutional amendment to allow an act could the legislature enact it. These constitutions are lengthy in order to incorporate the many restrictions on government. They are also the most heavily amended, which was perfectly acceptable to those who drafted them. As we will see, the legislatures and executives of these states are the weakest among the U.S. states, as was intended. We can observe in Figure 4.5 that even states unaffected by the Civil War and Reconstruction passed long constitutions during this period. Apparently, activist thinking was responsive to the arguments for giving the public a substantial role in state government.

There are various interests in each state that are advantaged by the restrictions written into every state constitution, but especially these detailed and restrictive constitutions. Of course, since these restrictions predate the growth in complexity and organization of these interests, it is coincidental that the restrictions favor some over others. We shall discuss this organization of interests or interest groups in a later chapter. Some scholars believe that states with long, detailed constitutions retain them because the interests that are advantaged fight to retain them.[35] Others see no such relationship but do note that the lack of competition between political parties may encourage interests to attempt to safeguard their interests in constitutional provisions that are more difficult to change.[36] At this point we will only note that both interest groups with a reputation for being strong as well as uncompetitive political parties are most evident in the South, as are long state constitutions. It may be only coincidental that strong interests and weak political parties are found in long-constitution states.

1945 Until the Present.   No state constitutions were written between 1920 and 1945. As shown in Figure 4.5, those written since 1945 are reduced in size, with many below 20,000 words. Additionally, many states, such as Georgia and Louisiana, have revised their constitutions rather than entirely redrafting them. They have been redrafted to exclude archaic laws and constitutional provisions that seem more appropriate as laws or city charters or constitutions. These new constitutions allow states

35 Lewis A. Froman, Jr., "Some Effects of Interest Group Strength in State Politics," *American Political Science Review* 60 (December 1966), pp. 950–967.

36 David C. Nice, "Interest Groups and State Constitutions: Another Look," *State and Local Government Review* 20 (Winter 1988), pp. 21–27.

to deal more efficiently with state problems by strengthening both the governor and the legislature.[37]

Reforming State Constitutions

Members of the National Municipal League have drafted a "model state constitution" to deal with the problems they see in existent constitutions, chief of which is their excessive detail.[38] Among the benefits to be gained by shortening constitutions is the removal of clauses concerning the state courts, earmarking or dedicating certain sources of taxes to related areas of expenditure, such as gasoline taxes going to maintain roads and highways, and restrictions on local governments. Apart from New York, the states with long constitutions tend to be southern, for the reasons discussed earlier; and most of these states have revised or changed their constitutions as the need to do so became evident. Constitutions reflect the constitutional ideas prevalent at the time of their drafting, but they seldom keep a state from coping or seeking to cope with contemporary problems. When they do prove an obstacle, they are changed.

Amending State Constitutions

With the exception of Delaware, electorates in the states enjoy a power denied to the national electorate concerning amendments to the U.S. Constitution, because they get to vote for or against constitutional amendments. Every state constitution has been amended, and some of the longer ones have been amended many hundreds of times. The process of amending state constitutions, except in Delaware, consists of two stages—*proposal* and *ratification*. Although some states require multiple passage by the state legislature in successive sessions, a simple majority vote for proposal and a single two-thirds vote by the legislature are the most common ways to propose an amendment.

Ratification in all but three states requires a simple majority vote by the electorate voting on the amendment. Wyoming, Tennessee, and Minnesota require that a majority voting in the election must favor the amendment for it to be adopted. Since amendments are at the end of the ballot and many

---

37   For research on concerns in the writing of seven of these constitutions see Elmer E. Cornwell, Jr., Jay S. Goodman, and Wayne R. Swanson, *State Constitutional Conventions: The Politics of the Revision Process in Seven States* (New York: Praeger, 1975).

38   *Model State Constitution*, 6th ed. (New York: National Municipal League, 1963). It should be noted that 23 present state constitutions are shorter than this "model" constitution.

voters do not bother voting for offices or amendments this far down the ballot, it becomes more difficult for amendments to pass in those states. Overall, voters ratify 61 percent of all amendments. However, the fact that in the three more restrictive states the rate is 56 percent suggests little difference.[39] The major point here is merely that the public is asked and generally approves of state constitutional amendments. Long-constitution states use this procedure often.

CONCLUSION

We are the victim of our ideas, and certainly those of us living in the United States are no exception. As we have seen in this chapter, ideas on governance have arisen to deal with immediate concerns faced by society. Some groups support new ideas that are more in line with their interests and preference, whereas others oppose them, and each level of the U.S. government provides a fairly simple mechanism for resolving disagreements about preferred policies. If a majority of elected officials prefer a policy, it is enacted. Seldom if ever, however, is the minority converted to the majority's view. Rather, battles are continually refought; and, more important, a different battleground (a different level of government or arena) can be sought that might result in the other side's winning. That is politics, and state legislatures, governors' offices, and Congress are the halls in which politics happens.

We noted in the first chapter that contemporary legislators seldom attend to research and are even less often persuaded by it to change their votes. Clearly our discussion in this chapter would suggest that government decision makers in the past were no better in this regard. It is also evident that if a serious problem is not resolved by an enacted program, other actions will be attempted until some sufficiently satisfactory solution is found. Higher and higher levels of government historically take these actions, what we have called greater centralization. But despite the *Garcia* case, each state still has latitude to deal uniquely with its problems; and despite the "Dillon rule," city councils and school boards still have a broad range of decisions that can be made without conflict with higher levels of government.

---

39   All data are from *The Book of the States, 1988–89*, (Lexington, KY: Council of State Governments, 1989), pp. 14–17. There have been 8554 amendments proposed, of which 5250 were ratified.

SUMMARY

1. Changes in society have resulted in different expectations of how government is to help us and to shape what we do.
2. Chief among these changes in our society is the movement from farms to the cities; problems in such areas that require government actions; and, more recently, the political and economic influences of events beyond our shores. All of these changes have contributed to the centralization of government.
3. Events, such as those above, have led to problems and proposed governmental solutions. Many were more popular than they were effective, as we have noted is often the case.
4. Often too, some parts of our society are hurt by the majority's policies, such as immigrants who are disenfranchised by the reform of our cities and individuals who have lost government services as, under Reaganomics, federal dollars were withdrawn.

SUGGESTED READINGS

Cashman, Sean D. *America in the Gilded Age: From the Death of Lincoln to the Rise of Theodore Roosevelt* (New York: New York University Press, 1984). A frequently cited interpretation of the history of this period.

Cornwell, Elmer E., Jr., Jay S. Goodman, and Wayne R. Swanson. *State Constitutional Conventions: The Politics of the Revision Process in Seven States* (New York: Praeger, 1975). As the title indicates, this work describes the writing and politics of seven recent constitutional conventions.

Fox, Kenneth. *Better City Government: Innovation in American Urban Politics, 1850–1937* (Philadelphia: Temple University Press, 1977). A succinct history of urban America during this period.

Nathan, Richard P. "The Role of the States in American Federalism," in *The State of the States*, Carl E. Van Horn (ed.) (Washington, DC: CQ Press, 1989).

Chapter
5

Government Revenues and Expenditures

*P*rior to the presidential election of 1984, people interviewed as part of the National Election Studies were asked to respond to the following:

> Some people think the government should provide fewer services, even in areas such as health and education, to reduce spending. Suppose these people are at one end of the scale (they are shown a scale with 1 at the left and 7 at the right) at point 1. Other people feel it is important for government to provide many more services even if it means an increase in spending. Suppose these people are at the other end, at point 7. Where would you place yourself on this scale?[1]

They answered as follows:

Fewer services, reduced spending (scale points 1, 2, 3)	28%
In between (scale point 4)	26%
More services, increased spending (scale points 5, 6, 7)	30%
Don't know, haven't thought much about it	16%

---

1 National Election Studies 1984 survey. Notably, which government is left unspecified, and few, if any, asked, whether the question refers to state, local, or national government.

This question is somewhat unusual in that it successfully confronts the public with the trade-off between services and taxes. The public is obviously divided, with only 58 percent willing to recommend moving in any direction—either for more spending and taxes or for less. Everyone would prefer more services and lower taxes, but that is not possible.

Those who make governmental decisions, such as governors, state legislators, and city council and school board members, must somehow reconcile this contradiction in public opinion. Those in office must either vote for taxes to cover services or decrease services. Either of those actions may draw public disfavor, but public actions to vote the rascals out are rare. We now turn to solutions that have been found by decision makers to cover the expense of government services.

REDISTRIBUTING INCOME

Consider two hypothetical families as described below. They symbolize two sharply distinct components in our society and the government services they receive. In family A, both the husband and the wife work, making them a "two-career" family. They have a combined yearly income of $60,000, substantially above the median family income across the country. They have a single child, who attends public schools. His education, and that of other students in this school system, costs about $3000 per year.

Family B has a single wage earner with a yearly income of $20,000. This family has three school-age children in public schools, meaning that it costs the school system $9000 each year to educate this family's children. Note that it would be quite unusual for two such different families to be living side by side; however, it is not uncommon for both types of families to be in the same school system.

	Family A	Family B
Annual income	$60,000	$20,000
School-age children	1	3
Yearly costs to educate, at $3000/year	$3000	$9000
Cost: User- or client-pay basis	$3000	$9000
Cost: Ability-to-pay basis	$9000	$3000

The question to which we now turn is how to have these families pay for the governmental services they receive—public school education for their children. In a capitalist society, the normal basis of paying for services is that the *user or client pays* for services or goods received. When you bought this book you were paying for the service or good received. On this basis, family

B would have to devote nearly one-half of its before-tax income to educating its children in the public schools, an expense the family probably could not withstand. This would mean that all or some of the three children would remain uneducated. Family A, however, could easily withstand the $3000–per-year cost to educate one child.

Many would argue that government services, as well as private services, should be paid on this basis, but that policy would have several clear implications. In our example it would probably result in three uneducated children. Would there be a cost to society, or to family A, of not educating these children? Most people would say yes. In the short run, family A may well be concerned about whether it is wrong to live in a society where the poor get little or no education. Or family A might be concerned about its property, since family B's children will be at home with nothing to do while family A is away at work or school. Home security might cost family A more than the cost of taxes to support public education. Generalizing to the community level, this argument suggests that those with property may get a better return on taxes paid for public education than for police protection.

There is a more traditional basis for paying for public education, in which taxes are gathered on the basis of *ability to pay* and the services are provided to all who are eligible, regardless of their wealth. Since early times in England, property has been the basis of taxes. If you had $1000 in property, you paid ten times as much in taxes as someone who had only $100 in property. If you were wealthier, you had more ability to pay and did so. In that early time government did not provide public education; but if government is now to pay for education, taxes based on the ability to pay could be used to pay the cost of this government service.

Referring again to our example, if ability to pay is the proper basis for providing public education, family A has three times the ability of family B to pay the costs of public education. On this basis, family A would pay $9000 in taxes to cover the cost of educating four children, those of both families.

Although this arrangement hardly seems to be a bargain for family A, other services, such as welfare or unemployment payments to the family B children, or increased police protection to keep the less affluent from stealing property, might be even more expensive. Also, if family B's children get no education, family A's child might someday be the only taxpayer among these four children. In short, there may be many self-interested reasons for family A to be willing to have funding for public education based on the ability to pay.

The use of taxes based on the ability to pay redistributes the wealth of the rich to the poor. Questions concerning taxes and tax rates are therefore called redistribution policy. The tax rate based on the "ability to pay" shown in the example is a straight proportional rate, with family A having three times the wealth and paying three times the taxes of family B. Many other rates could be conceived and are used, as we shall see shortly. Needless to say, if there must be taxes based on the ability to pay, the wealthy would prefer rates that vary little with the ability to pay, whereas the poor would like the wealthy to pay more. Self-interest is heavily involved here, and much of the controversy in politics centers on redistribution policy.

How Broad Is Social Concern?   In our example, most students support ability to pay as the basis for covering the costs of public education. There seem to be two possible reasons. First, students may be representative of overall society. Ability to pay has always been the basis for paying the costs of public education because of social concern about the consequences of failing to educate the poor, so this answer is the conventional one. Perhaps since students are themselves the beneficiaries of having others substantially underwrite the expense of a collegiate education, they may be persuaded by self-interest. If we move to succeedingly more inclusive geographic areas, however, support for redistribution drops sharply.

Let us consider, not just two families, but rather an entire school district. If a school district has one section that is wealthy and others that are poor, should the wealthy contribute disproportionately to the costs of education in the district? Should many family A's pay substantially more than their share for the services received and family B's pay less? Again, most people probably support ability to pay as the basis for paying districtwide educational expenses. Indeed, this is the norm across the country.

How about statewide? Few states have their wealthy citizens evenly distributed from border to border. Most have poor school districts as well as wealthy school districts. Should the wealth of the rich districts be redistributed to those that are poor? This is not traditional, and the social benefits are less evident, and thus support largely vanishes. States, as we will see, are in competition with one another. A state that fails to educate its students in poor school districts may be uncompetitive in seeking to attract new industry when faced by a competitor state that underwrites poorer school districts with state funds. Supreme courts in several states have ruled that inequitable resources for education are unconstitutional, forcing states to underwrite public education more fully.

Support wanes even more when the idea of redistributing wealth from wealthy states to poorer states is introduced. Uneducated Mississippi children are less troublesome to people in California or Alaska than are poorly educated children within their own states. Also, the federal government would have to be the tax gatherer for redistribution between one state and another, meaning a further expansion of that government. Finally, we could explore support for the position that wealthy nations, such as the United

States, should underwrite the costs of educating children in poorer nations. Apart from the United Nations, no organization is available to redistribute wealth on this scale, and such an idea gains little support from Americans.

PRIVATE GOODS AND PUBLIC GOODS

Economists argue that government should provide public goods and services and that private goods and services should be retained in the private sector. This distinction between private and public depends on several considerations. First, is the good or service beneficial to society, a *merit good* that no one should be denied just because they cannot afford it? Examples of merit goods include health care, clean air and water, and public education.

The second consideration is whether it is *excludable,* meaning that we can meter the service to note when someone uses it and exclude those who do not pay. We can see when a child is in class, so there could be a "user-pay" charge. However, many services are difficult to meter. Water, gas, and electricity meters are now technologically available and have allowed shifting these services to a user-pay basis. Technologically, few services or goods cannot be metered, assuming agreement on what is to be measured. It may, however, be difficult to exclude nonpayers, such as for clean air and water. Basically, since many government services are metered, this criterion does not seem the basis for distinguishing between public and private goods and services.

Finally, if a service in use by one person cannot be used by a second, economists claim it should be a private good. This is most often called a *zero-sum game*. A pie is an example of such a game. If four people were to eat it before you arrived, you would get none of it. When everyone can use it without denying it to others, it is *nonrivaling* and should be a public good. Air and water are normally examples of nonrivaling goods. More examples of nonrivaling goods are difficult to conceive of, so this concept is also not very helpful in making the distinction between private and public goods.

The distinction between public and private goods then hinges on whether those who cannot afford it should be denied the service. Without presenting results from polls, we can say that there is substantial disagreement on which, if any, services are deserved by all regardless of their ability to pay for services received. Few goods or services are clearly either public or private goods; thus this distinction tells us little about what should or should not be provided by government. The basis for payment of services, however, does partially provide such a distinction.

Clearly Governmental Services.   Only the government can gather taxes or money without providing corresponding services. Government can also provide user-paid services, such as charging on the basis of the amount of water, electricity, or highway mileage used. Thus, even if there were agreement that some services should be handled by government, there is no necessary reason why those services should not be paid on a user-pay basis. In fact, many municipal services over the years have been pressed to "pay their own way" or to pay for services without subsidization by general tax revenues. Water, sewage, electricity, and sanitation are all in this group. In order for these services to "pay their own way," user charges would have to equal the costs of the services, even for the poor who cannot pay for them. Thus, "pay-their-own-way" arguments are just the "user-pay" arguments in new clothing.

No clear present instance in which private goods and services are provided based on "ability to pay" comes to mind. An example of this approach might be for General Motors to provide individuals with new cars at a price that was based on how much income they had. The very wealthy would pay perhaps $100,000 and the very poor would pay nothing—a highly unlikely prospect.

Very few, if any, governmental services could not be "privatized" or given to the private sector to provide. Arizona has many normally local government provided services, such as fire protection, provided by private industry. Private police shelter wealthy residential enclaves in many communities. Depending on where you live, water, electricity, fire protection, garbage pickup, schools, street lighting, security, bridges and ferry crossing are provided by private sources on the user-pay basis. Despite these exceptions, the local governments where most of us live still provide all of these services. Probably tradition, rather than some logical distinction, best accounts for whether government or the private sector offers the service. Even if government provides a service, "ability to pay" will not necessarily be the basis of paying for its costs. Meanwhile we now turn to taxes, revenues, and expenditure among the states and communities, much of which depends on how a government covers the costs of its services.

TAXES

Are U.S. Taxes High?   As we can see in Table 5.1, the United States, with 29.2 percent of its gross national product devoted to state, local, and national taxes, ranks eighteenth among the 20 developed democracies included. This figure falls far short of the high percentage of gross national product devoted

Table 5.1   Tax Revenues as a Percentage of Gross National Products in 20 Developed Democracies, 1985

Rank	Country	Percent of GNP
1	Sweden	50.5
2	Denmark	49.2
3	Norway	47.8
4	Belgium	46.9
5	France	45.6
6	Netherlands	45.0
7	Austria	42.5
8	United Kingdom	38.1
9	West Germany	37.8
10	Finland	37.3
11	Greece	35.1
12	Italy	34.7
13	New Zealand	34.3
14	Canada	33.1
15	Switzerland	32.1
16	Portugal	31.1
17	Australia	30.3
18	**United States**	**29.2**
19	Spain	28.8
20	Japan	28.0

Source: U.S. Bureau of the Census, *Statistical Abstract of the United States, 1988* (Washington, DC: U.S. Government Printing Office), p. 810.

to government services in Sweden and other northern European countries. State and local governments in the United States gather only about one-third of our taxes, at least since 1970. Some countries provide more services on the basis of ability to pay than the United States, which provides about 70 percent of its services on a user-pay basis.

Types of Taxes.   In the United States we have basically three types of taxes—property taxes, sales taxes, and income taxes. As we shall see, state, local and national governments depend on different taxes. The reason for this variation goes back to when the different governments became active, as discussed in Chapter 4. There is no reason we could not have one tax gathered once a year and distributed to the various governments. As we shall see, however, persons of differing wealth are not equally advantaged or disadvantaged by different taxes. Thus some would like to see the income tax dropped, and others dislike the property tax. Some taxes are judged to be fairer or more equitable than others, at least by some people. Certainly politics is always a factor concerning taxes, and any change in the tax structure mobilizes enormous concern and hot political interest. Thus the likelihood of having a single tax is close to zero. Rather, as mentioned above, the diversity of taxes probably reflects the history of their invention. The type of tax used reflects which government has imposed it as well as the influences of the multiple centers of political power inherent in a federal system of government. If one interest controls the city council and another the state government, two different taxes are likely to be collected.

Property Tax. Property taxes are collected in proportion to the amount of property that you own. In all cases it is a flat rate, or the same rate regardless of how much or how little property you own. Thus if the millage or *mill rate* (how many mills or thousandths of a dollar of value are to be collected in this year) is 130, or 13 cents for each dollar of assessed property, and you own $50,000 worth, your tax is $6500. If you own only $25,000 worth of property, it is $3250. Since property can be seen and its worth *appraised*, or have a value placed on it, it was a tax that could be imposed hundreds of years ago. At that time the average person subsisted on a farm, bought few goods with money on which sales tax might be gathered, and had no income that could be taxed. Thus the property tax is much older than sales or income taxes.

The mechanics of collecting property tax are complex, and in a modern economy often it becomes an unfair tax. The key to collecting property tax is in identifying and appraising property. The government must pay to have the property appraised and must retain records of who owns what property. At one time, the king's agents could break in, note all property, appraise it, and collect the appropriate taxes on the spot. Appraisers today seek to avoid the need to enter property. They resort instead to external appraisals, in which the size of the home, the quality of its construction, the size of the garage and other structures, as well as the size of the lot are all measured and noted. Even the use of the property, such as residential or agricultural, is a factor. This information then is used to set a value on the property, typically by comparing it with recently sold, similar, and nearby property for which the market value is clear.

There are two problems even apart from the difficulty of the act of appraisal. The first is that personal property, such as your stereo set, furniture, clothing, and animals, is excluded because it is too difficult to assess. Furthermore, savings in the bank, travel expenses, and even stocks and bonds are not included as property. Second, the value of real estate property, which is typically all that is assessed property taxes, changes over time. Frequent appraisals, although expensive, can deal with this problem. Few governments, however, reappraise more than once every 5 years, with 20 percent of all property being reappraised each year. Some governments have not reappraised all property since the early 1800s, when an appraised value of $300 was placed on the property that now sells for $125,000! Meanwhile, new homes nearby are being appraised for their selling price; hence this tax is clearly unfair.

The first problem, in which some property is excluded from being taxed, results in the tax being unfair for the poor because it is *regressive*. When it was imposed on all property, it had *equity* because the wealthy, who had more property, paid proportionately more than the poor, who had little.[2] But the convenience of assessing only homes, where the poor must invest a larger percentage of their income, means that the property tax is collected on a greater proportion of their wealth than in the case of the rich. In effect, as wealth goes up, the percentage of one's wealth on which the property tax is collected decreases. This example is one of a *regressive tax*. Although, as mentioned earlier, property tax rates are flat, since the tax is not collected over all property, it becomes regressive. There have been efforts to make the property tax more equitable, such as exempting the first $5000 or $10,000 of appraised value in a home from taxes, called the *homestead exemption*. Another method is to set a maximum percentage of a person's income that will be collected as property taxes, called the *circuit breaker*. However, the property tax still is challenged as unfair.

Despite its inequities, the property tax continues because it is the primary source of local tax revenues. People are accustomed to paying it. And because the appraised value of all property in the city is known, setting a tax rate yields very predictable amounts of revenue. Although dependence by city, schools, and county governments on property taxes has declined since World War II, there is little question that it will be with us in the future. The states, initially dependent on property taxes, have since learned to gather more of their revenues from the other two basic taxes. The federal government has never used a property tax. It is difficult to imagine how it might be collected.

Income Tax. Both federal and state governments had imposed income taxes before 1900. The federal government had used it to finance the fighting of the Civil War and then dropped it. The states had tried unsuccessfully to use it. In 1911 Wisconsin introduced the first successful state income tax, only to be followed by nine other states by 1920.[3] Forty states now have an income tax.[4] Administration of the income tax is easier than that of the property tax; people and corporations fill out forms, and send them in to the state along

---

2 Economists speak of many types of equity; see J. Richard Aronson and John L. Hilley, *Financing State and Local Governments*, 4th ed. (Washington, DC: Brookings, 1986), pp. 97–100.

3 Aronson and Hilley, p. 86.

4 *The Book of the States, 1988–89* (Lexington, KY: Council of State Governments, 1989), p. 257.

with their due taxes. The state checks the forms and makes some effort to ensure proper completion and the payment of due taxes.

The mechanics of this tax typically include a personal exemption for each dependent, varying between very little to $6000 in Mississippi.[5] Also, these taxes are mildly *progressive;* that is, those with more income pay at a somewhat higher rate. Two criticisms are raised concerning the progressivity of state income taxes. First, the highest and lowest rates differ little, averaging 2.47 percent for the lowest income and 7.23 for the highest. Second, the highest rate is applied to such low incomes that nearly everyone is paying the highest rate, making it in effect a flat-rate tax. The highest bracket for the state income tax, for example, is $10,000 or less in 12 states.

It should be noted that progressive and regressive taxes are not mere opposites. Progressive tax rates increase with wealth or ability to pay. Regressive taxes, however, are flat-rate taxes that, effectively, gather a higher percentage from the poor because they are not applied to all wealth. Although most people concede that the federal income tax is progressive and the state income taxes mildly so, there is no reason that the rate could not be constant as income increases. The result would be a flat rate, which is used in the income taxes of six states. No government uses a truly regressive tax rate or a tax rate that decreases with income. A regressive income tax is certainly conceivable, such as a 15 percent rate on yearly incomes below $10,000 decreasing to zero above $100,000. Income taxes, in short, need not be progressive, and in many states are not.

Sales Tax.   The sales tax is the most recently introduced tax. A general sales tax on a broad range of items purchased in retail establishments within the state was first introduced in Mississippi in 1932. This tax followed more selective sales taxes, such as the tax imposed on gasoline, which Oregon introduced in 1919 and which spread rapidly to all states by 1929.[6] The general sales tax also spread rapidly, as 13 more states introduced it in 1933; now 45 states have it. Typically you pay more than 5 percent but less than 10 percent of the value of what you are purchasing in sales taxes, most of which goes to state government. Twenty-six states also collect and remit sales taxes for local governments.[7]

---

5   *The Book of the States,* p. 257.

6   Aronson and Hilley, p. 90.

7   Aronson and Hilley, p. 147.

In all cases the sales tax is a flat-rate tax, since everyone pays the same percentage regardless of the price of the item being purchased. Moreover, since the wealthy purchase items that are not taxed, such as services, bonds, stocks, and travel, this tax is criticized also as regressive in application. Partially to offset the fact that a higher percentage of the poor's money goes toward buying food, 28 states exempt at least nonluxury foods from sales taxes. This results in some comic distinctions, such as ice cream purchased by the scoop in a cup being nonluxury, whereas in a cone it is a luxury and is subject to sales tax. Florida briefly enacted a sales tax on services as well as goods, which of course would have shifted more taxes to the wealthy. Its application to national advertisers drew much protest, threats to stop advertising in Florida, and some canceling of conventions. The Florida legislature hurriedly repealed the measure.[8] Massachusetts actually lends an element of progressiveness to its sales tax since individual pieces of clothing are not subject to a sales tax unless they cost more than $175. If the clothing costs more than $175, the sales tax applies to the entire value of the item.

The federal government has never used the sales tax, although its excise taxes on tires and liquor are a limited sales tax. Increasingly, the declining revenues produced by property taxes for local governments are being offset by rebated sales taxes from the states. Now the sales tax provides about 5 percent of the revenue of local governments. Thus the sales tax, or gross receipts tax as it is sometimes called, remains the best source of funds for the states. However, state income taxes now generate revenues nearly equal to those produced by state sales taxes.

PATTERNS OF STATE DEPENDENCY ON DIFFERENT TAXES

The South introduced the state sales tax and the Upper Midwest the income tax. Present dependency on one or the other of these taxes is still somewhat evident in Figure 5.1. There is a substantial range in the percentage of tax receipts coming from either of these taxes. Oregon, without a state sales tax, gets 62 percent of its tax revenue from its state income tax, whereas Tennessee gets only 2 percent. Those states with no income tax, of course, have zero

8   Marilyn Marks, "Florida's New Tax: The Budget 'Cure' That May Be Contagious," *Governing* (October 1987), pp. 48–55.

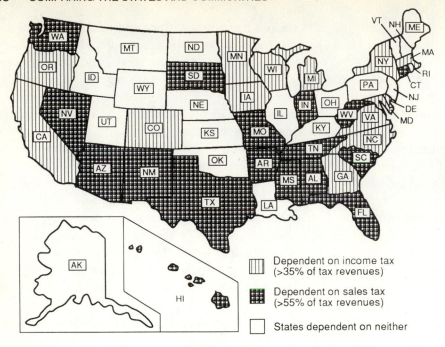

Figure 5.1   State dependency on either the income tax or sales tax, 1986.

Source: U.S. Bureau of the Census, *Statistical Abstract of the United States, 1988,* Washington, D.C.:
U.S. Government Printing Office, p. 270.

dependence on that tax. Similarly, Nevada, which is one of seven states
without a state income tax, draws 86 percent of its tax revenues from its sales
tax. South Dakota, Florida, Washington, and Texas, all lacking an income tax,
derive at least 69 percent of their tax revenues from sales taxes. As shown in
Figure 5.2, dependence on the sales tax tends to be inversely related to dependence on the income tax.

Since Figure 5.1 shows that many southern states depend on the sales tax
for a substantial part of their revenue, one might expect that states in
which the Democrats dominate the state legislatures would tend to depend
on the sales tax. Given the Democratic party's attempt to appeal to the poor,
we might expect just the opposite finding. Or is this a spurious relationship, inasmuch as the South both tends to use that tax and tends, as we
have seen, to be Democratic? Even among nonsouthern states, the tendency is for more Democratic states to rely more on the sales tax.[9]

9   The equation for the nonsouthern states becomes $y = 24 + 19x$, $R = 0.21$.

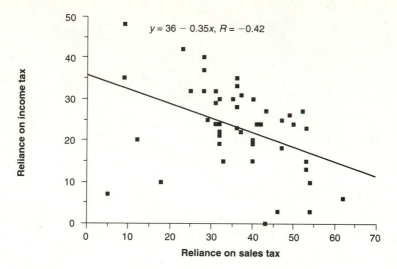

Figure 5.2   Relationship between reliance on income taxes and sales taxes.

PROGRESSIVITY OF STATE AND LOCAL TAXES

There are many ways to assess how progressive or regressive a government's taxes are.[10] In Figure 5.3 we have one such assessment. The percentage of income paid in taxes to both state and local government by individuals with incomes below $20,000 per year is divided by the percentage paid by those with incomes over $100,000. Shown in the figure are states that fall into four different categories in terms of this ratio. The most progressive states are shown in white. In those states, the poor pay less than 85 percent of the taxes in percentage of their incomes as do the wealthy. If the wealthy pay 10 percent of their income in taxes, the poor pay 8.5 percent or less.

In the states shown with darkest shading, the poor pay more in terms of percentage of their income than do the wealthy, which is the definition of regressive. If the wealthy pay 10 percent of their income in taxes, the poor pay at least 10.1 percent. Again, no geographic pattern or pattern of in-

---

10   Susan B. Hanson, "Extraction: The Politics of State Taxation," in *Politics in the American States*, 4th ed., Virginia Gray, Herbert Jacob, and Kenneth N. Vines (eds.) (Boston: Little, Brown, 1983), pp. 415–453.

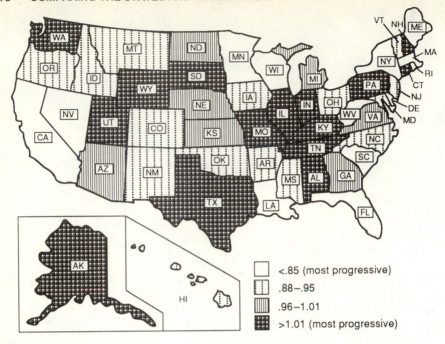

Figure 5.3 Progressivity of state and local taxes: The ratio of taxes paid as a percentage of income of those earning less than $20,000 divided by percentage paid by those earning more than $100,000.

Source: State Policy Databook, 1988, Alexandria, VA: State Policy Research, Inc., 1988, Table D-35.

dustrialized versus nonindustrialized states is evident.[11] This result may imply that there is no deliberate planning to make the mix of taxes at the state and local level more progressive or regressive. It may be that coping with needs, and the limits of public patience with the level of a particular tax, such as a sales tax in excess of 10 percent, shapes the states' tax structures. In effect, it may be argued that progressive tax policy is an incidental consideration in decision makers' efforts to find funds to cover expenditures.

Some confirmation for this conclusion can be found in the relationship between the percentage of a state calling themselves liberals and how regressive that state's taxes are. We might expect that citizens of more liberal states would support moving toward the less regressive income tax and that our measure of regressiveness would find these states less regressive. However,

---

11   We might expect that out of self-interest, the states with high per capita personal income would not use the income tax. However, there is a modest opposite relationship, $y = 10 + 0.0009x$, $R = 0.22$.

no positive relationship is found. In fact, there is a very slight negative relationship.[12]

SEVERAL OTHER TAXES AND SOURCES OF REVENUE

Severance Tax. The severance tax is a tax paid by the producers or extractors of certain minerals taken from the earth, such as oil, coal, natural gas, and sulfur. Obviously, if a state has resources that are in demand within their state as well as in others, a severance tax can produce substantial revenue with much, if not nearly all, being paid by customers in other states. Substantial revenues are available to the Texas legislature from oil bought by non-Texans to heat their homes. Although 33 states have some severance tax revenue, only 11 received more than $100 million in 1986 from this tax.[13] Texas, Alaska, Louisiana, and Oklahoma lead the list with over 500 million dollars in revenue.

Lotteries. Although the vast majority of Americans approve of state-run lotteries, and the 1989 failure of a revenue plan in Louisiana is attributed to the fact that it included no lottery, it has been found that lotteries contribute insignificantly to the revenues of the states.[14] Of the 32 states with lotteries, none gains more than 5 percent of its budget from lottery returns, although the returns sometimes seem significant, such as California's $2.5 billion. However, this is only 4.3 percent of that state's total revenues. Thus far, with the exception of Florida, the South has not adopted lotteries—largely perhaps because of lobbying by religious groups. Some oppose this source of revenue as regressive, but studies suggest that wealthier people are more likely to play than the poor. Some even suggest that they are poor bets with only 50 percent going to prizes, and that bookies pay better. Nevertheless, the public, as judged by the Louisiana experience, presently insists on a lottery before other taxes can be raised further.

Borrowing. Apart from transfers from the federal government, which contributes about 18 percent of state budgets, states borrow about 8 percent

---

12 The relationship with Democratic control does, however, show modest support for the anticipated decrease in regressiveness of taxes with Democratic control.

13 U.S. Bureau of the Census, *Statistical Abstract of the United States, 1988* (Washington, DC: U.S. Government Printing Office), p. 272.

14 "Lotteries Shaping Up as the New Political Reality," *Houston Chronicle* (June 18, 1989), p. 1.

of their budgets.[15] All states have some debt outstanding, led by New York, California, New Jersey, and Massachusetts.[16] Since only Vermont and Wisconsin are not bound by a balanced budget, the bulk of this debt is capital investment in buildings for which bonds have been sold and interest has to be paid.

VARIATIONS IN THE TAX EFFORTS THE STATES MAKE

We noted in Chapter 2 that some states are judged wealthy on the basis of the high per capita income of their residents. Not surprisingly, the states with high per capita wealth derive more taxes. Ultimately, a state's potential tax revenues are dependent on the wealth of its residents. A poor state cannot impose taxes above a certain level that would deny the public an ability to provide for shelter and food. Overall, as shown in Figure 5.4, the states increase their tax revenues in proportion to the wealth of their residents. As shown, Connecticut has a per capita personal income of just over $21,000 and gets just an average of under $2000 per year in taxes from every woman, man, and child residing there.

New Hampshire is also shown as quite some distance from the regression line, which would predict that given that state's per capita income it would have more than $400 additional tax revenues per capita. New York and Wyoming are a different case; they have higher revenues than expected. This consideration of whether a state is taxing at a level that would be expected given the wealth of its residents is called its *tax effort* or *tax burden*. New Hampshire makes little effort and Wyoming a great effort.

In Figure 5.5 we merely computed how much in the way of tax revenues per capita each state should gather given its per capita income and subtract this from actual tax revenues. We can see that most of the low-tax-effort states are in the South and in the lower Midwest. A wealthy individual could expect to have less of his or her income taken in state and local taxes in a low-tax-effort state. A poor individual would also pay low taxes in such a state but would receive low government services unless the federal government largely paid for them.

---

15   *Statistical Abstract of the United States*, p. 266.
16   *The Book of the States*, p. 246.

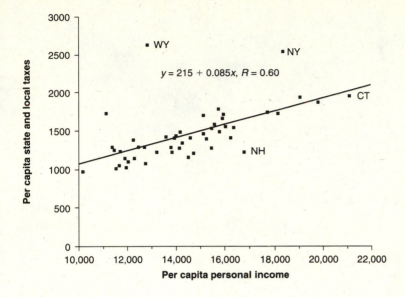

Figure 5.4   Per capita state and local tax revenues vs. per capita personal income in 1986.

THE LOCAL TAX SITUATION

Local governments still draw most, 75 percent, of their tax revenues from property taxes, down from 87 percent in 1967.[17] Of course, transfer payments from the state and the federal governments have increasingly supplemented local tax revenues, as we saw in Chapter 4. Even with these transfers, the cities still depend on a regressive tax on the appraised value of houses and other real estate. In many cities, especially older central cities, this appraised value is sharply declining. Income taxes imposed on those working within cities have been tried, primarily in Ohio and Pennsylvania, but as employment opportunities also move to the suburbs, these taxes too will prove to be an inadequate source of revenue. Sales taxes rebated by states now constitute about 13 percent of local government tax revenues. This source might seem promising, but there is resistance among legislatures to exceed the 10 percent

---

17   Aronson and Hilley, p. 16.

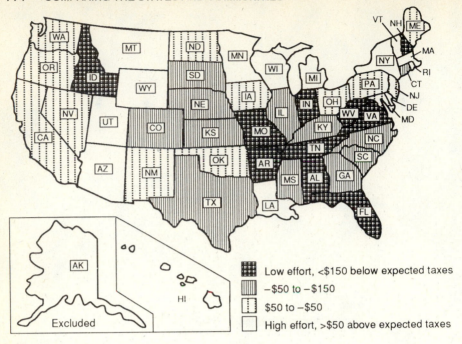

Figure 5.5   State tax effort: State expected taxes per capita from Figure 5.4 subtracted from actual per capita tax revenues.

sales tax barrier, and many states are close to meeting it. Local governments then can expect sales taxes revenues remitted to them to grow little.

STATE AND LOCAL GOVERNMENT SOURCES OF REVENUE AND EXPENSES

Revenues. State governments typically derive their revenue from four major sources, as shown in Figure 5.6. About one-fourth comes from sales taxes, which here includes motor fuel and tobacco taxes. Federal transfer payments contribute nearly as much. The income tax, both individual and corporate, is growing in importance and now contributes about 18 percent of state government revenues. The fourth major source is different since it is payments into two trust funds—state employee retirement funds and unemployment compensation. The legislature may not use these funds for other programs.

Local government revenues come primarily from two sources. More than one-third of local government funds comes from transfer payments from

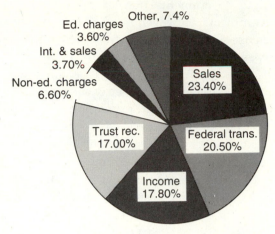

(a) State sources of revenue

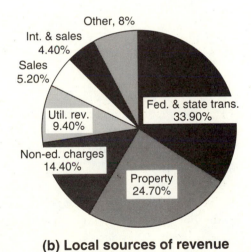

(b) Local sources of revenue

Figure 5.6 State and local government sources of revenue, 1986.

Source: U.S. Bureau of the Census, *Statistical Abstract of the United States, 1989*, Washington, DC: U.S. Government Printing Office, p. 265

other than state and federal governments. Property taxes have declined in significance for local governments, but they are still the primary tax source.

Expenditures. State governments transfer nearly one-third of their resources to local governments. However, much of this money comes from the federal government (see Figure 5.7). Apart from these transfers, education is the biggest state expenditure. Furthermore, nearly all of state transfers are to local school boards for educational expenses. Ignoring whether the local school board or the state makes the expenditure of such transfer funds, it has been found that about one-third of all state expenditures go to public education. Welfare payments to supplement federal payments constitute 13 percent of state expenditures. Notably, corrections expenditures for prisons and jails represent only about 2 percent of state expenditures.

Local governments invest overwhelmingly in public education, with much of this funding coming from transfer payments. Combined expenditures for police, fire, health, hospitals, sewers, and sanitation come next. Parks and recreation are a substantial part of this category, but other expenditures included in this category range greatly. The cost of running utilities, including street lighting, claims 13 percent of local funds. Police, fire, and corrections cost less than 10 percent of local expenditures.

BUDGETING BY THE STATES

We shall later consider differences among the states in how they spend their revenues. As noted in Chapter 2, they do vary greatly in both their per capita revenues and per capita expenditures as well as in the personal wealth of their citizens. In Chapter 13 we shall consider educational, welfare, and crime expenditure differences more completely.

Each year in 29 states or every other year (biennially) in 21 states the legislative and executive branches must pass a state budget. Most often a state's budget is a line-by-line listing of how the state's revenues will be spent by the many agencies providing services to the public. If an agency is awarded $5 million for the next year to provide the pay to state employees that provide its services, that is the agency's budget. The agency can spend less than that amount, but cannot spend more. It would be bad management for an agency to run out of money before the end of the year and to have to cut services. No doubt those responsible would be rebuked or even fired, and the clients for those services would no doubt complain to the agency as well as to their legislators. To spend only part of the budgeted money would get no such complaints, but the administrators of the agency would minimally

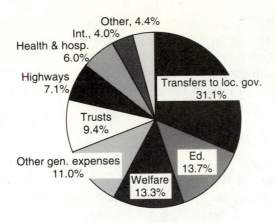

(a) State expenditures

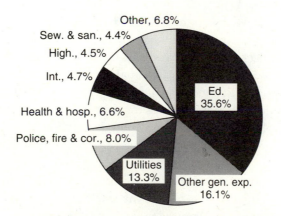

(b) Local government expenditures

Figure 5.7   State and local government expenditures, 1986.

Source: U.S. Bureau of the Census, *Statistical Abstract of the United States, 1989,* Washington, DC: U.S. Government Printing Office, p. 265.

be noted as politically naive and probably should expect to have their budget cut in the next budget. In short, an agency's budget is fundamental to its accomplishing its task to provide services, and certainly spending it is also important.

A state's budget must be passed identically in both houses of the state legislature and must be endorsed, not vetoed or partially vetoed (the appropriations item veto) by the governor to become official. As noted earlier, most states require that the budget be balanced, meaning that revenues equal expenditures. Since there is never an abundance of state revenues, the passage of this budget is a troublesome time for all those involved. The least-needed services and the most-inefficient agencies vie with the most-needed and most-efficient for appropriations to allow them to continue. The age-old task of legislators and the governor is to identify correctly the needed and the efficient, but this is easier said than done. Some legislators will be supporters of some agencies and will see them doing no wrong. For example, a legislator from an agricultural area will see the department of agriculture as providing essential services and seek to increase its budget. Those from urban areas may covet agriculture funding for human services agencies providing services to their constituents. The agencies will soon learn who their friends are in the legislature as well as noting the pressure groups that will come to their aid in pressing the legislature to pass their desired budget. Much of what we characterize as politics centers on the drafting and passing of the state's budget.

The public may welcome the services provided in the budget, but most often will disfavor any increase in taxes. The best of all possible happenings would be for services to be improved and taxes unchanged. A growth in the state's economy might generate additional revenues to allow tax rates to be unchanged while services increase. Or state agencies could be forced to be more efficient, allowing more services for the same tax revenues. The public, however, will seldom be involved, although wave after wave of hopeful politicians seeking public office will promise to make government more efficient.

Certainly some successful politicians ignore public concerns about improving the efficiency of state government. Others, however, have sought to honor their campaign pledges; there are a multitude of budgetary efforts to improve government efficiency. The 1960s and 1970s saw many new forms of budgeting introduced that were intended to improve efficiency. These reforms compared the cost of government against the goal or goals of the agency in providing these services. *Planned program budgeting*, for example, charged agencies to compute the costs of each of their services, thus making it quite evident which services were most costly, which then could either be stricken from the budget or pressed to become more efficient. *Zero-based budgeting* forced each agency to defend not only the increase in their budgets but also all funds. Without adequate defense of even the last year's budget, the agency might get a zero budget or no funds for the next year. Essential to such innovations in the allocation of state funds is the legislative and executive branches' paying closer attention to an agency's total program rather than to the increases it seeks. While these innovations and others have been broadly adopted among the states, there is little evidence that they improve efficiency. Perhaps the most damaging evidence of the failures of any such efforts to improve government efficiency by having the legislature and the governor's office thoroughly consider each agency's budget is the incremental way that state budgets grow.

One disturbing fact in budgets of governments and private industry is that they are quite linear, with each year's budget highly predictable from those that precede it. This is the pattern in Figure 5.8, where five successive budgets for education in three select states—Alabama, California, and Texas—shows a very slight wobble about a straight-line prediction. The very high correlations suggest how tightly the budgets stick to the predicted values. This pattern, in which each year's budget is that of the preceding year

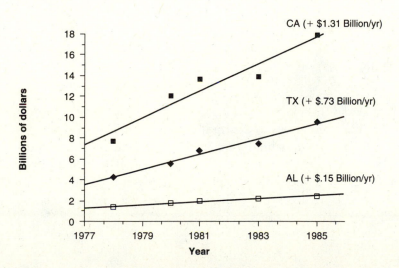

Figure 5.8   Actual and predicted budgets for education in three states, 1978–1985.

Source: Book of the States, Lexington, KY: Council of State Governments; 1981, pp. 288–289; 1983, pp. 382–383; 1986, pp. 324–325; 1987–88, pp. 256–257; 1988–89, pp. 242–243.

plus a certain increment of several percent is called *incrementalism*.[18] Clearly, anyone with simple mathematical capabilities could seemingly replace the great efforts on the part of all those involved in the budgeting process. Great time and money could be saved.

Similar data for welfare and highway expenditures show nearly identical results, but with changed increments. No single state consistently has the highest percentage increase. Figures 5.9 and 5.10 show the results for these programs.

Corrections expenditures, however, show a different pattern, as shown in Figure 5.11. The increment is quite substantial, suggesting that some consideration is contributing to the growth other than a simplistic adding of the increment. Texas might be explained by Justice Justice's court order to improve conditions in Texas prisons, but Alabama also is under court scrutiny and shows no unusual increment. Furthermore, although California is not under pressure from the courts, it shows a substantial increment.

It is possible that incrementalism reflects the staggering cost to government of modern services and the continual search for additional sources of funds. For the two biggest programs, education and welfare, expansion of the programs can come only with the growth of the economy or with new sources of revenues. Since the latter seems uncommon, the major programs, regardless of the demand, are bound to incremental growth unless other major programs are cut. Corrections expenditures, however, are not a major program, and so substantial growth in percentage terms can be undertaken without hundreds of millions of dollars needing to be found.

CONCLUSION

What we have seen in this chapter is a certain inventiveness on the part of legislators in finding alternatives to the traditional property tax. This inventiveness has been quickly emulated by others with local, state, and national government vying for each new basis for taxing. There will probably never be sufficient funds in a modern, complex economy for paying for all demanded services. Thus this rapid imitation of the first innovative states seems rational on the part of the legislators.

---

18   Thomas J. Anton, "Roles and Symbols in the Determination of State Expenditures," *Midwest Journal of Political Science* 11 (February, 1967), pp. 27–43. Also see Gerald E. Sullivan, "Incremental Budget-Making in the American States: A Test of the Anton Model," *Journal of Politics* 34 (May 1972), pp. 639–647.

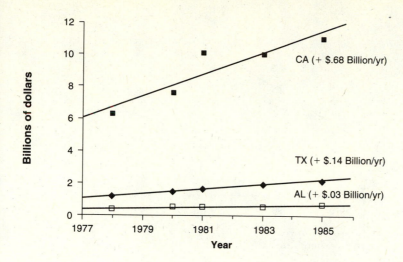

Figure 5.9   Welfare expenditures for three different states.

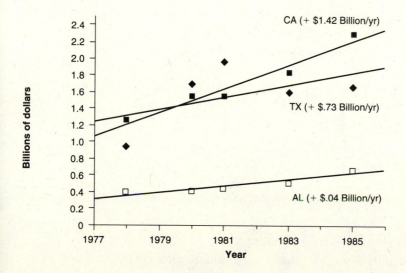

Figure 5.10   Highway expenditures for three different states.

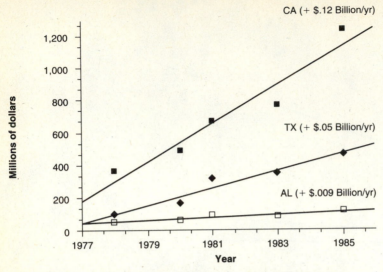

Figure 5.11   Corrections expenditures for three different states.

We have also seen variations among the states, in terms of both their dependencies on sales and income taxes and the regressiveness of state and local taxes. Certainly, taxes vary in their regressiveness or equity, as well as how economic turndowns affect them. If you are unemployed, you pay no income tax, although you must still purchase some things that may require you to pay sales tax. You also may strive to hold onto your home, but you will have to pay property taxes. Although these variations between different taxes seem fairly substantial, we have little to suggest they are large enough to make much difference. People who move from New York to Texas may save many thousands of dollars in taxes. In return, however, they also get fewer services, necessitating the reinvestment of some savings into providing privately for lost services.

SUMMARY

1. Taxes, like other ideas for how to allow government to operate, have changed with changes in our society.
2. Generally speaking, states have added each newly conceived tax, such as the income tax, to previous tax sources to gather the funds needed to run their services.

3. The different sources of tax revenues have implications as to whether the wealthy or the poor pay a higher percentage of their income in taxes.

4. If you are poor, there are some states where, comparatively speaking, you would be better off, such as wealthy states where there are ample dollars to underwrite government services. Similarly, it is better to be wealthy in some states than in others. Again, the wealthy would be better off in a wealthy low-tax-effort state.

5. Curiously, the strength of one or the other of the major political parties seems little related to the type or the extent of taxes in a state.

SUGGESTED READINGS

Hansen, Susan B. "The Politics of State Taxing and Spending," in *Politics in the American States*, Virginia Gray, Herbert Jacob, and Robert B. Albritton (eds.) (Glenview, IL: Scott, Foresman, 1990).

Nathan, Richard P. "The Role of the States in American Federalism," in *The State of the States*, Carl E. Van Horn (ed.) (Washington, DC: CQ Press, 1989). Changes in the financial circumstances of the states and communities in modern federalism and also the politics of taxes are considered.

Sears, David O., and Jack Citrin. *Tax Revolt: Something for Nothing in California* (Cambridge, MA: Harvard University Press, 1982). With its initiative process, California awakened politicians everywhere to the possibility of a "tax revolt" coming to their state. These anxieties failed to materialize.

Chapter
6

The Individual in Democratic Government

*T*he general public has never governed itself for very long. At one time communication and transportation made such direct government all but impossible. In the days before amplification no one could be heard in a gathering of many hundreds of people. Even taking a vote would be difficult. Counting hundreds of raised hands or having everyone cast only one vote would be most difficult with any large number of people. Even assembling everyone in one location would be difficult. Before public transportation, the automobile, and modern highways, a trip of 50 or more miles would have been a day's travel. Modern communication and transportation may make such direct governing more practical, but our procedures remain.

Most people think of the New England town meetings as an example of such direct public governance. The normal circumstance, however, is for some few, typically called the elite, to govern for the many. In a democracy the many elect these few and can hold them accountable for their actions in governing if they seek reelection. In the next several chapters we shall focus on the activist elite, such as political party leaders, pressure groups, legislators, governors, and judges. In this chapter, however, we consider the general public's role in governing.

POSSIBLE FORMS OF PARTICIPATION

Seeking Public Office

The federal system has many elective offices at all levels of government. Overall in the United States there are probably more than 300,000 elected offices to be filled. Only one of these has a national constituency, the office of the president, with a vice president sharing the ticket. Although there are other elected officials who serve in the national government, 100 senators and 435 representatives to Congress, they are all elected by either state or local districts. There are 7394 state legislators, most elected for two-year terms and all from local districts. Finally there are by conservative estimate more than 275,000 city council, school board, county commission, and town or township board members to be elected.[1] In short many hundreds of thousands could directly participate in government by holding one of these offices.

Even if we include the many who run for office and fail and those who have served in the past, plus those serving on special appointed local boards, it is an extremely small minority that directly participates in governing. Certainly far less than 1 percent of the public is so active. This small number makes it appear "abnormal" to run for public office. Some have suggested that only abnormal personalities must be so attracted. To endure the constant criticism, the loss of privacy, and the need to gather substantial dollars for campaigning, means that one must be gaining something from public office other than salary and gratification for being civically active. This may just be vanity, but it may be more serious. Lasswell suggests a "psychopathology of politics" to capture this idea.[2] Certainly, lesser offices, such as city council or school board member (where the impact of public office-holding on one's life is less than that involved in being a governor, senator, or president), might attract more "average" persons and thus result in more normal personalities in those offices. Political science has yet to provide research on such questions.

Democratic elections provide a safety valve to relieve the displeasure of people whose positions on issues are ignored by government. If you feel strongly about an issue, you can seek to influence the decision directly by

---

1 There are 3042 counties, 19,205 municipalities, 16,691 towns and townships, and 14,741 school districts in the United States. Each varies in size but most have at least five elected representatives, thus my estimate of 268,395 local elected legislative officials. Additionally there are 29,487 special districts usually with no independently elected officials. But some may be elected. Furthermore, there are elected school superintendents, mayors, local judges, and many others that could well swell my number greatly.

2 Harold D.Lasswell, *Psychopathology and Politics* (New York: Viking, 1960).

seeking and winning public office. This option is seen as dampening the threat that people will resort to violent means to get their preferences in public policy.[3] Nevertheless, another direct form of participation is protest, rebellion, revolution, and assassination. None of these activities is at all common in the United States, and only the first is even condoned.

Even at the height of Vietnam protest, fewer than 1 percent were ever involved.[4] We have no information on the minuscule percentages involved in other direct acts. Nevertheless, beginning with "Shay's rebellion" in 1786 and with the excesses by the general public in the French revolution, many have been alarmed by the potential of public excess in democracy. This subject too will be discussed later.

Attending Public Meetings

As we move from more direct forms of participation to those forms that affect policy less directly, the number of people involved increases. We next come to attending various public meetings. The audiences at public meetings can let elected officials know how they feel. Attendance at meetings encompasses a broad range of such contacts. There are official public hearings by standing committees within the state legislature concerning possible new laws, such as permitting a state lottery, or reforming worker's compensation provisions. The average citizen is unlikely to be heard in such hearings. There are actual business meetings of the city councils and school boards in which the audience may speak; and there are less formal public meetings to interact with the candidates preceding elections. Elected officials schedule these latter types of meetings to assure their reelection by impressing the public that they "care" about constituents.

The extent of public participation in such activities is not clearly known, but we can make estimates. Across five democracies 28 percent of the public claims to have ever attempted to influence the outcome of a government decision in their local community and about 16 percent at the national level.[5] Nineteen percent claim to have attended at least one "political" meeting or rally in the last three years; 30 percent to have worked with others in trying

3 Robert A. Dahl, *Who Governs?* (New Haven: Yale University Press, 1961). Dahl speaks of the "penetrability of the elite," meaning that we all can become members of the elite, as important to society's stability (p. 92).

4 Sidney Verba and Richard Brody, "Participation, Policy Preferences, and the War in Vietnam," *Public Opinion Quarterly* 34 (Fall 1970), p. 330.

5 Reported in Sidney Verba and Norman H. Nie, *Participation in America: Political Democracy and Social Equality.* (New York: Harper & Row, 1972), p. 27.

to solve some community problem.[6] The National Election Studies of how people vote in presidential and congressional elections typically find about 8 percent claim to have attended a political meeting, and this figure has varied little over time.[7] Only about one in ten attended a school board meeting within the past year.[8] In short, at most about one American in four is visible at public hearings. Moreover, many of them say nothing at these meetings.

Communicating with Representatives

A next less direct, but more common, act is to write to an elected official. Writing to your congressional representative is probably the most common of these, even if Congress has nothing to do with the problem written about, such as garbage pickup schedules. About three in ten claim to having written to an elected official.[9] Certainly members of Congress devote much of their staff's time to answering and tabulating these letters by issue area as part of their efforts to serve their constituency and thereby to be reelected. We know that such writers are both well educated (probably because they feel comfortable in writing) and ideological (in that they appear to be sufficiently motivated to write).[10]

The Public Initiating Laws

The next most direct of public involvement is found in only a few states and communities—that is, allowing the public to vote public policy directly. Sometimes this voting is on actual policies, such as the initiative and referendum in California, and sometimes it is on budgets, such as the practice in New York and several other states of having the public endorse (or reject) the school district's budget.

Under the direct *initiative and referendum* procedures, a draft of a proposed law is distributed for sufficient voters' signatures. Typically, if 3 to 10 percent of the number voting for governor in the last election sign (Califor-

6 Verba and Nie, p. 31.

7 David B. Hill and Norman R. Luttbeg, *Trends in American Electoral Behavior*, 2nd ed. (Itasca, IL: Peacock, 1983), p. 99.

8 Norman R. Luttbeg, *Florida Educational Needs: Public Satisfactions and Dissatisfaction with Their Schools.* (Tallahassee, FL: Survey Data Center, Florida State University, 1970), p.7.

9 Hill and Luttbeg, p. 99.

10 Robert S. Erikson, Norman R. Luttbeg, and Kent L. Tedin, *American Public Opinion: Its Origins, Content, and Impact,* 2nd ed. (New York: Wiley, 1980), pp. 256–259.

nia requires only 5 percent), it is placed on the ballot as a referendum. A majority vote can pass it into law.[11]

A handful of mainly western states encourage this act of direct public participation. They include Alaska, Arizona, Arkansas, California, Colorado, Idaho, Missouri, Montana, Nebraska, North Dakota, Oklahoma, Oregon, and Wyoming.[12] These issues are placed at the end of the election ballot, which is almost certainly headed by the contest for either the governor or the president. Thus turnout is determined largely by these contests. Many who bother to vote in contests at the top of the ballot fail to do so toward the bottom of the ballot. Fewer than 90 percent of voters bother to vote for referendums.

As noted in Chapter 4, nearly all states have public referendums on state constitutional amendments, the ratification stage. Constitutional referendums are also placed at the end of the normal state election ballot, meaning they again are chiefly affected by turnout for higher offices, such as the governor or the president. Most states permit local governments on some issues to hold public referendums on local legislation.[13] The city council, rather than the public, decides whether it wants to test public opinion in such cases. Some states also use this technique, often calling these public votes "straw votes."

Like the laws considered by legislatures, often the initiative process brings up "bad" laws that could seriously injure the state and its future or that would be just dumb policy. Several years ago Californians were asked to vote on an initiative that would have limited the governor's salary to $80,000 and to set a maximum compensation of other state and local officials at 80 percent of this, or $64,000 including fringe benefits and retirement. Had this measure passed (it did not), several thousand school superintendents, police chiefs, and other officials would have had to take pay cuts or to have sought jobs in other states. Although the debate over the advisability of direct initiative will no doubt continue, the evidence suggests that the resulting legislation is not easily classified as conservative or as liberal.[14] Furthermore, critics can point to a few dumb referendums that have passed. Certainly, the same cannot be said of laws passed by state legislatures!

---

11 Eugene C. Lee, "California," in Referendums: A Comparative Study of Practice and Theory, David Butler and Austin Ranney (eds.) (Washington, DC: American Enterprise Institute, 1978), pp. 87–122.

12 The Book of the States, 1988–89, (Lexington, KY: Council of State Governments), p. 217.

13 Austin Ranney, "The United States of America," in Referendums: A Comparative Study of Practice and Theory, David Butler and Austin Ranney (eds.) (Washington, DC: American Enterprise Institute, 1978), pp. 67–86.

14 Ranney, pp. 82–85.

Voting

Voting for public officeholder is the sole act that finds a majority of Americans at least occasionally participating. These elections can be viewed as indirect voting. Voters can only affect policy indirectly by finding candidates who stand for preferred policies and getting these officials elected. Once in office, presumably they will cast votes for these policies.

The necessary information and consideration that precede a choice among several candidates is enormous. With two candidates, A and B, and with a single issue, where candidate A favors enacting the policy and B opposes it, the voter need only decide whether he or she favors or disfavors the policy. With that decision the vote preference follows easily. The complexity of this process grows enormously with additional candidates and issues, with lack of clarity of the candidates' positions, and with the voter's need to decide which issues are most important. The typical election is more likely to be more complex than the single issue with clear alternative candidate positions first suggested above.

If we consider the example below, we can see how the task becomes unmanageable. On each of the six issues, one has to become informed and to form one's personal opinion. Then one has to gather information from the candidates, and they may not want to take clear positions for fear of losing votes to an opponent. Finally one must choose between the two. Probably in most cases, as in that shown here, one must decide additionally which issues are more important. Thus in this example if issue 1 is more important than any others, a vote for candidate A is rational in that A pledges, if elected, to vote consistently with the voter's personal position. *Active involvement* in gathering information and participating, *being informed*, and *rationally supporting* the candidate who best reflects one's personal positions are the desirable, if difficult, goals to achieve. They are the standards for voters in a democracy.

Issue	You	Candidate A	Candidate B
1	pro	pro	con
2	pro	pro	con
3	pro	uncertain	con
4	pro	con	pro
5	pro	con	pro
6	pro	con	uncertain

Finally, there is one additional requirement for voting that makes the voter's task all but impossible. One has to select the candidate that takes your position on *unanticipated issues.* If at the time of the election, no one anticipates a shortfall in the budget or the need to ratify a national constitutional amendment, the voter nevertheless must select the candidate that will vote consistently with the voter's personal positions. But, you ask, how can anyone do that? If something about the candidate allows predictions as to how that candidate will vote on unanticipated issues and the voter knows it, the choice can be made. The fact that the candidate is "conservative" or a "Democrat" perhaps will allow such a selection. But this approach violates the careful calculus, noted above, that is ideally expected of voters.

Turnout in Various Elections.   In the 1988 presidential election George Bush, the Republican candidate, won the support of 47,946,000 voters. He got 53.9 percent of the vote and, of course, was the winner. Just under 90 million Americans voted. These millions of voters are only just over half of those who seem eligible to vote. In the presidential primaries that most influenced the candidates selected by the parties, typically only about 10 percent of those eligible bothered to vote. We shall shortly consider why Americans turn out to vote for national offices in such small numbers. What should be noted, however, is that the presidency is the office for which there is the highest turnout. All other national, state, and local offices have lower turnouts, often much lower.

In 1986 just under 60 million voted for members of Congress—only about one-third of those eligible to vote. In the elections for governor held in 1986 or the election closest to that year, just over 43 percent of those eligible voted. Statewide elections for members of Congress or for governor tend to show a turnout that is 7 to 10 percentage points lower than the turnout for president.

Few study the turnout of voters for local elections. One nationwide survey reports that municipalities claim a 33 percent turnout.[15] Research in the San Francisco Bay area shows a 31 percent turnout.[16] There is reason to doubt whether city clerks in calculating local turnouts divide by the number of those eligible (which they seldom know), or by those registered (which they do know). Since few of those who move bother to register to vote for local elections, we cannot even be certain of the percentage of those eligible who are registered. Typically only about two-thirds of those eligible are registered. Thus, true turnouts in local elections probably barely exceed 20 percent. No city council member or mayor can claim much of a mandate for a

---

15 Albert K. Karnig and B. Oliver Walter, "Municipal Elections: Registration, Incumbent Success and Voter Participation," in *The Municipal Yearbook 1977* (Washington DC: International City Management Association: 1977), pp. 65–72.

16 Heinz Eulau and Kenneth Prewitt, *Labyrinths of Democracy* (Indianapolis: Bobbs-Merrill, 1973).

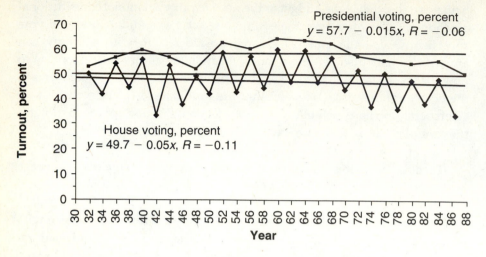

Figure 6.1   Patterns of voter turnout since 1932.

Source: U.S. Bureau of the Census, *Statistical Abstract of the United States, 1986,* Washington, DC: U.S. Government Printing Office, p. 255.

governmental action, inasmuch as probably no more than one in ten voting-eligible adults voted for him or her.

Declining Turnout.   Figure 6.1 shows the percentage of eligible adults voting in presidential and off-year elections (those when the president does not run) both scheduled in November of even-number years. With only a few exceptions, states elect their state legislatures, both upper and lower houses, and their statewide elected executives, such as the governor, during one of these elections. Since 1960, in thirteen states the gubernatorial election date was changed to correspond to the off-year election timing.[17] Thus, although these election data are for presidents and congressional election turnouts, most elections for state officeholders fall at one of these times. Since they are further down on the ballot, turnout for them is slightly lower.[18] We can see that voting for president only briefly exceeds 60 percent only between 1952

---

17 Norman R. Luttbeg, "Differential Voting Turnout in the American States, 1960–82," *Social Science Quarterly* 65 (March 1984), pp. 60–73.

18 Luttbeg finds over the period that he studies that turnout for governor is approximately 5 percent higher than that for Congress in off-years (p. 62).

and 1968 and that off-year election turnout never exceeds 50 percent. Whatever is causing these variations from election to election is similarly affecting both off-year and presidential election turnouts and shows a very glacial-like decline over this long period.[19] Voting may be the most common form of public participation; but apart from voting for president, typically fewer than half of those eligible bother.

Why Do Americans Vote Less?   We can see in Table 6.1 that only one developed democracy had a lower turnout than we did in the 1980s. Three factors largely account for our voting less, but only two of them can be altered by passing laws. First and most important is our lack of a sharp correspondence between one party and a major segment of society, such as blue-collar workers, whereas the other political party gains overwhelming support from nonworkers or the middle class.[20] This is called *party-group linkage*. The Democrats represent the working-class voters and the Republicans the middle-class voters much less distinctly than do political parties in other countries. This situation makes it much more difficult to recognize and mobilize supporters, and the result is lower turnout. Obviously, legislation could only with great difficulty affect any change in this pattern. Perhaps district boundaries could be made to correspond to areas with predominantly blue-collar or white-collar residents. Politically, if one political party chooses to abandon one group to improve its appeal to another, we might expect sharper divisions. In today's political campaigns this situation seems quite improbable.

Second in importance, however, is *registration restrictions*. The states organize and run elections; and largely as a result of the excesses of an earlier era, we have the most restrictive registration procedures of any democracy. To vote we must register to do so before the registration rolls close, typically 30 days before the election. Canada, by contrast, employs registrars who are charged to go door to door just before an election to assure that all who are

19 The primary focus on participation decline is over the period 1960 through 1980 for some reason. Much has been suggested to account for this period's decline. But none of it seems justified. See Michael M. Gant and Norman R. Luttbeg, *American Electoral Behavior: 1952–1988* (Itasca, IL: Peacock, 1991), chap. 3; Luttbeg, "Differential Voting"; Norman R. Luttbeg, "Attitudinal Components of Turnout Decline: Where Have Some States' Voters Gone?" *Social Science Quarterly* 66 (June 1985), pp. 435–443; and Carol A. Cassel and Robert C. Luskin, "Simple Explanations of Turnout Decline," *American Political Science Review* 82 (December 1988), pp. 1321–1330.

20 Actually landholding and religion are also seen as important cleavages, depending on which country is considered. G. Bingham Powell, Jr., "Voting Turnout in Thirty Democracies: Partisan, Legal, and Socio-Economic Influences," in *Controversies in Voting Behavior*, 2nd ed. Richard G. Niemi and Herbert F. Weisberg (eds.) (Washington, DC: CQ Press, 1984), pp. 34–53.

Table 6.1   Voting Turnout in Selected Countries in 1985–1988

Country	Percentage of those eligible voting
Australia	89
Iceland	89
Austria	87
New Zealand	87
Belgium	87
Netherlands	86
Italy	85
Sweden	85
West Germany	84
Norway	84
Greece	83
Israel	79
Denmark	75
United Kingdom	75
Canada	75
France	75
Portugal	74
Ireland	73
Finland	72
Japan	70
Spain	69
United States	**50**
Switzerland	49

Source: Thomas T. Mackie, "General Elections in Western Nations During 1988," *European Journal of Political Research* (1989), pp. 747–52; (1988), pp. 573–84; (1987), pp. 717–22; and (1986), pp. 695–97. Only one election is shown (that closest to 1988).

eligible are registered and, of course, to inform them that an election is upcoming. If the states were to change our laws to be more like those in Canada, we might expect more to turn out. One study suggests that with easier registration procedures turnout could be increased by 14 percent. Such an increase in the United States would leave us still low but at about the level of turnout in Spain, the next-lowest-turnout democracy in Table 6.1.[21]

Finally, many countries apply fines and *penalties for failure to vote.* You would, for example, receive in the mail a citation for failure to vote. Again, were the states to impose such a penalty, our turnout apparently would in-

21 G. Bingham Powell, Jr., "American Voter Turnout in Comparative Perspective," *American Political Science Review* 80 (March 1986), p. 35.

crease. Presumably a severe fine would have a larger effect. Some would question, however, the value of a vote from someone who did so only to avoid a fine. Nevertheless, many democracies do penalize those who fail to vote, with no apparent loss of quality in voters' decisions.

Americans may participate at lower levels because they are exhausted by the number of times they must go to the polls.[22] As noted earlier, we elect nearly 300,000 officials, with most elected to 2- or 4-year terms. Primary elections proceed nearly all of these elections. In primary elections, rival candidates within the two major political parties vie for the designation of their party's candidate for that particular office. Inasmuch as most of us live under many governmental jurisdictions—a city council, a school board, a county, a state, and a nation, we can expect every 4 years to be asked to vote for as many as a hundred officials in probably four elections and four more primaries. Citizens of many other democracies have three officials representing them—a member of parliament, a city council member, and a mayor. Is exhaustion, impatience, or possibly uncertainty as to who is in charge of a problem at the root of lower U.S. participation?

Using Mail Balloting to Encourage Turnout. Since World War II, most states have allowed some voters to cast their ballots by mail (or absentee vote, as it is called). Those who are hospitalized or expect to be out of the state on election day can apply for such a ballot, which is completed and returned by mail, where the signature is checked against that on the voter registration. Since the 1970s these procedures have been followed for all voters in many elections. Consistently, turnouts of more than 50 percent have been recorded when all vote by mail.[23] In San Diego 61 percent of those registered voted in a by-mail election concerning a convention center. In prior referendums fewer than 20 percent voted.[24] Such elections have proved to be about one-third less expensive and show little fraud.[25] Although no other nation has used such procedures for elections, these experiences would suggest that U.S. turnout could be greatly increased with such procedures.

---

22 Ivor Crewe, "Electoral Participation," in *Democracy at the Polls*, David Butler et al. (eds.) (Washington, DC: American Enterprise Institute, 1981), p. 232; Richard W. Boyd, "Decline of U.S. Voter Turnout: Structural Explanations," *American Politics Quarterly* 9 (April 1981), pp. 133–159.

23 General Accounting Office, *Voting: Some Procedural Changes and Informational Activities Could Increase Turnout* (Gaithersburg, MD: GAO, 1990), pp. 35–41.

24 Charles G. Abdelnour, "The City of San Diego Mail Ballot Election Experience" (San Diego: Office of the City Clerk, 1981).

25 *Voting*, p. 41.

REQUIREMENTS TO VOTE IN THE AMERICAN STATES

As noted above, the states set voting requirements, except for age (the Twenty-sixth Amendment to the U.S. Constitution sets the voting age at *18 years old*). All additionally require that you be a *citizen* of the United States and a resident of the state to vote, and 49 states require that you be *registered* to vote, at least in most urban areas. The exception is North Dakota.[26]

Registration is an outgrowth of our reforms enacted to stop corruption in our cities beginning just before the turn of the century. Most states now allow voting registration through the mail. You merely complete a form and send it into the registrar. If you are notified through the mail without it being returned, you can expect to find your name on the voter rolls on election day. If you vote typically at least once every four years and do not move, your registration remains active. Unfortunately, many move between elections (the 1980 census reported that 47 percent had moved in the previous 5 years) and thus must remember to reregister at least 30 days before an election if they expect to vote.

Several states encourage registration and voting turnout. Oregon, for example, mails a packet of information to registered voters before the elections. California also sends information on referendums including pro and con statements. Several states pay deputy registrars to enroll voters, paying between 20 and 50 cents per person registered.[27] There also has been some experimentation among the states in using what is called "election day" registration where one merely needs to go to the polls with proof of residency, such as a driver's license with the correct address, to vote. There is an advantage in terms of greater turnout with such procedures, between 5 and 13 percent; and no additional fraud, such as persons voting who are not eligible, is evident.[28]

There are two other constitutionally allowed restrictions on who is allowed to vote. Most states deny the vote to those convicted of a felony even after they have served their sentence, and this restriction has not been found unconstitutional.[29] Finally most states disallow the vote of the mentally ill and those protected by guardians. The Supreme Court has not acted on such restrictions.

---

26 The *Book of the States, 1988–89* (Lexington, KY: Council of State Governments), p. 211.

27 William J. Crotty, *Political Reform and the American Experiment* (New York: Crowell, 1977), p. 89.

28 Richard G. Smolka, *Election Day Registration* (Washington, DC: American Enterprise Institute, 1977); David P. Glass, Peverill Squire, and Raymond E. Wolfinger, "Voter Turnout: An International Comparison," *Public Opinion* (December/January 1984), pp. 49–55.

29 *Richardson* v. *Ramirez* (1974).

Other Laws Affecting the Vote.   There is a certain legal presence when one enters a voting place. In most states the building is a public building, and certain laws affect it. For example, campaigning is forbidden in the building and usually for 100 feet or so in every direction. Access to the voting booth or machine is limited to registered voters and their smaller children. Talking is discouraged, and your vote is to be private with no one looking over your shoulder. The ballot that you cast is provided by the state and, although sample ballots can be brought with you, only the official ballot can be cast. Even how you mark the ballot may be restricted; some states require an "X" rather than a "✓" to be a proper vote.

Moreover, ballots differ from state to state; some use *office ballots*, in which the candidates for each office are grouped together, whereas others use the *party column ballot* with a column of Democrats running for each office side by side with one for Republicans. The office ballot was thought to restrict partisanship by requiring the ardent Republican to scan through each office to find Republicans rather than simply going down the column on the party column ballot and voting for all Republicans. Many states provide a single box that, if marked, casts one's vote for all Democrats or for all Republicans. As with all institutional efforts to restrict partisanship, ballot form efforts work best for the least partisan. The partisan will cast a *straight ticket*, voting for all candidates in one political party, regardless of inconveniences.[30]

Finally, the selection of polling places has an effect. The preference for using public schools means that polling places are away from arterial highways where people would notice that there was an election while en route to work. Some states and communities place large flags or signs indicating polling place so that people will notice. Others place small signs in windows, where they are unlikely to be noticed. There is little research that would support the idea that high visibility of polling places raises turnout, but it is certainly plausible.

It should be noted that most local elections and many elections of judges are *nonpartisan* elections, in which case the ballot does not list the candidates' political parties. Many times the law forbids the candidates to advertise their party affiliations. It is usually argued that without partisan labels on the ballot, voters will be less inclined to vote blindly for all Democrats or all Republicans. This practice was another part of the reform effort to overcome machine politics in U.S. cities in the late 1800s. The hope was that issues

---

30 Angus Campbell, Philip E. Converse, Warren E. Miller, and Donald E. Stokes, *The American Voter* (New York: Wiley, 1960), pp. 266–289.

would replace such blind partisanship. Many other democracies use no party labels on their ballots, without any apparent loss of partisan voting.

Voting Requirements in the Past. Although registration has been added, the overall pattern in the United States has been one of reduced requirements over time. At one time, age requirements were higher, one needed to be white and a free citizen, property was required, and females were excluded. The South also used a poll tax[31] (many states until the 1960s), literacy tests (more than 20 states in 1960), understanding of the state constitution, and white primaries to restrict black participation. The Voting Rights Act of 1965 and extensions thereof disallowed literacy and constitutional understanding as qualifications for voting in many southern states. The last of these additional requirements (holding property to vote in bond elections) ended in the 1960s.

STUDIES OF VOTING BEGINNING IN 1940

Nearly all that we know about how Americans vote when they vote derives from studies of national samples focusing, first, on presidential elections and, second, on off-year elections of representatives to Congress. Furthermore, the results are dependent on the use of survey research. Although we probably know more about how people vote by asking them, we are also subject to natural desires on the part of people not to appear ignorant in front of the interviewer. Sometimes the answers we receive are thus fiction and at other times true representations about whom they voted for and why. The most difficult problem is knowing which is which.

Survey Research and Polling. Picking a *sample* of people whose answers are to be taken as representing all other people is the least of researchers' worries. We know with high certainty that about 1500 people *randomly* chosen, in 95 samples out of 100, will give answers that are within 3 percent of those we would receive were everyone interviewed. To pick a random sample there must be no bias in how they are chosen, such as having their names picked out of a hat. Often a computer randomly picks telephone numbers, and the interview is conducted over the telephone.

If 57 percent of a randomly drawn sample were to say they would vote for the Democratic gubernatorial candidate, we can probably assume that on

---

31 This tax was stricken down in *Harper* v. *Virginia State Board of Elections* (1966).

election day somewhere between 54 and 60 percent (3 percent) will support that candidate. If we deviate from a random sample, such as using telephone interviewing when not everyone has a telephone, our results become less certain by an unknown amount.

Not all of those interviewed will actually vote. Typically, fewer than half will. Asking people whether they will vote always results in substantial more than half saying they will—one example of the *unreliability of people's answers*.[32] An equally troublesome example is shown in Figure 6.2. Four "quality organization" national polls asked people if they called themselves Democrats, Republicans, or independents. All were conducted in June 1982. How can it be that the percentage saying "Democrat" varies between 34 and 52? Were independents a small minority, 19 percent, or a near majority of 48 percent? Which poll is accurate? What is suggested here is that people's answers are greatly dependent on how the question is asked, but some people would probably not change their answers regardless of the question's wording. Despite such difficulties, or perhaps more accurately with an awareness of them, we can learn much from the voting studies.

The American Voter. The earliest voting studies discovered the willingness of Americans to express which political party's candidates they would support and presumably did support on election day. Most of those who, in June before the November election, said they would vote either for the Democrat or the Republican presidential candidate actually claimed to have done so after the election.[33] Furthermore, these studies found people insufficiently interested in the presidential campaign to be affected by it. Politics, even presidential politics in the election of 1940 with a war going on in Europe, was not of abiding concern to Americans. The effects of using the mass media, newspapers and radio at the time were minimal—what they called the *"minimal effects model"* of mass media influence.

The American Voter focused on the presidential elections of 1952 and 1956, adding confidence to the earlier findings by studying a national sample rather than a single community as was true in the earlier study.[34] They also conceived of the party identification question, "Generally speaking, do you usually consider yourself as a Republican, a Democrat, an Independent, or

---

32 For a discussion of such difficulties see Robert S. Erikson, Norman R. Luttbeg, and Kent L. Tedin, *American Public Opinion*, 3rd ed. (New York: Macmillan, 1988), chap. 2 and 3.

33 Paul F. Lazarsfeld, Bernard R. Berelson, and Hazel Gaudet, *The People's Choice* (New York: Duell, Sloan & Pearce, 1944); Bernard R. Berelson and William N. McPhee, *Voting: A Study of Opinion Formation in a Presidential Campaign* (Chicago: University of Chicago Press, 1954).

34 Campbell et al., *The American Voter*.

Question: Are you a Democrat, Republican, or what? (From *Time* / Yankelovich, Skelly, and White)

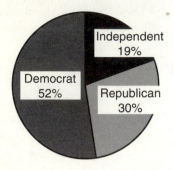

Source: Survey, June 8–10, 1982.

Question: Regardless of how you have voted in the past, do you consider yourself a Democrat, a Republican, an Independent, or what? (From *Los Angeles Times*)

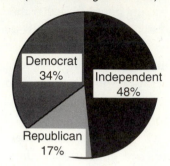

Source: Survey, June 27–July 1, 1982

Question: In politics today, do you usually think of yourself as a Republican, a Democrat, an Independent, or what? (From *NBC News* / *Associated Press*)

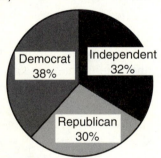

Source: Survey, June 14–15, 1982.

Question: In politics, as of today, do you consider yourself a Republican, a Democrat, or an Independent? (From a Gallup poll)

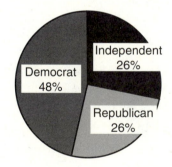

Source: Survey, June 25–28, 1982.

Figure 6.2 Democrats, Republicans, and independents and question wording.

Table 6.2   Political Party Identification in the American National Electorate 1952–1988

Party Identification	1952	1956	1960	1964	1968	1972	1976	1980	1984	1988
Strong Democrat	22%	21%	21%	26%	20%	15%	15%	16%	18%	17%
Democrat	25	23	25	25	25	25	25	23	22	18
Leaning Democrat	10	7	8	9	10	11	12	11	10	12
Independent	5	8	8	8	11	13	14	12	6	11
Leaning Republican	7	8	7	6	9	11	10	12	13	13
Republican	14	14	13	13	14	13	14	14	15	14
Strong Republican	13	15	14	11	10	10	9	10	14	14
Other	4	3	4	2	1	2	1	2	2	2

Source: National Election Studies.

what?" which allowed the prediction of how most would vote. Along with follow-up questions, this technique allowed people to be placed for their party identification, as shown in Table 6.2. In the 1952 and 1956 elections, 78 percent and 83 percent, respectively, voted consistently with their party identification, Republicans voting for the Republican presidential candidate and Democrats for the Democrat. In Table 6.3 we see that in 1984 and 1988, 86 percent and 85 percent, respectively did so. Especially in the normal two-man presidential race, party identification has lost none of its predictive capacity.

Table 6.3   Party Identification and Claimed Voting Support in 1984 and 1988 Presidential Elections

Party Identification	In the 1984 Election Voted For			In the 1988 Election Voted For		
	Reagan	Mondale	Other	Bush	Dukakis	Other
Strong Democrat	11	87	1	6	93	1
Democrat	32	67	1	27	70	3
Leaning Democrat	21	79	—	12	88	—
Independent	71	27	2	61	33	6
Leaning Republican	92	6	1	84	15	1
Republican	92	6	1	83	17	—
Strong Republican	96	3	—	98	2	—

Source: National Election Studies, 1984 and 1988.

In *The American Voter* party identification plays a central role. It originates early in childhood, as parents pass their party identification on to their children; it seldom changes as one ages; it colors perceptions of the political world; and its intensity strongly motivates attention to the campaign and likelihood of actively participating in it. Strong partisans both of the Republican and Democratic parties are more likely to participate, most likely to be informed, and least likely to vote for the opposition political party. This conclusion is true regardless of what positions are taken by the candidates or which candidates are chosen by their political party.

Independent voters, by contrast, are not partisan, but they lack the "good citizen" characteristics of being interested, concerned, and participant. In the 1984 presidential election, for example, only 60 percent of independents claimed to have voted versus 86 percent of the strong partisans of both political parties.

In all the elections discussed (1952, 1956, 1984, and 1988), those calling themselves Democrats greatly outnumbered those calling themselves Republicans (see Table 6.2). Nevertheless, the Republican presidential candidates won. The answer to this paradox is that, although most voted their political party identification, those who claimed none, the independents, and some of the partisans did not. The concern then shifts to the quality of the votes cast by independents as well as by those who defect from "their" political party. Concerns apart from the issues in the elections have always been found chiefly important for such votes. Among these voters, those who defect and independents show little or no concern with issues.[35]

Party Identification Across the United States.   The identification with a political party is not evenly distributed across the country, as is shown in Figure 6.3. Therefore to the degree that partisans cast loyal votes for the party's candidates in races other than the presidency, we might well expect Democrats to win in Democratic states. The most Democratic states are Louisiana (57 percent) and Georgia (51 percent), whereas Nebraska (40 percent) and Utah (38 percent) are the most Republican. With the exceptions of Wyoming and Minnesota, the states with more than 35 percent identifying as Democrats are in a broad belt across the bottom half of the country. States with 30 percent or more identifying as Republicans center in the interior central mountain and plains states. Again Wyoming is an exception, although, as we saw in Chapter 3, that state has few Democrats in its lower state house.

---

35 Hill and Luttbeg, p. 50, plus a later update by Luttbeg.

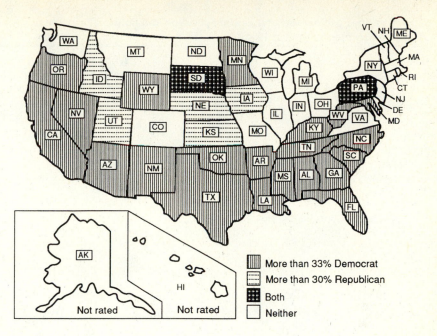

Figure 6.3   Party identification in the states (percentage of the public saying they are Democrats, Republicans, or independents).

The reader will no doubt remember that the traditional political culture tends to be concentrated in the South. Certainly, Figure 6.3, shows a strong southern commitment to the Democratic party. The traditional political culture's unwillingness to use government for any purposes other than the traditional protection of property would seem to be at odds with the program of the Democratic political party, or at least the national program of that party. We shall make only two comments on this subject. One, this seeming contradiction may suggest how adaptable and enduring party identification can be in the face of changed national programs. People can stick with the party of their parents despite the movement away from earlier position by that political party. Second, political culture suggests that historical experiences endure in present-day perspectives of what politics should be like. Party identification as well as orientation on how much government should be used is not the same in different parts of our country.[36]

36 Robert S. Erikson, John P. McIver, and Gerald C. Wright, Jr., "State Political Culture and Public Opinion," *American Political Science Review,* 81 (September 1987), pp. 797–813.

Table 6.4   Issue Positions on Services and Spending and Political Party Identification in Affecting Presidential Vote in 1984

Issue position	Strong Democrats	Weak and leaning Democrats	Independents	Weak and leaning Republicans	Strong Republicans
Both fewer services and reduced spending	12%[a] (8)	56% (9)	68% (9)	97% (35)	100% (44)
In between	15% (75)	27% (114)	87% (39)	93% (138)	98% (54)
Both more services and more spending	10% (30)	7% (28)	50% (4)	71% (7)	100% (4)

Source: National Election Studies, 1984.

[a]Cells show percent voting for Reagan in 1984, in this case 12 percent with 88 percent voting for Mondale.

Voting Issues. Probably the high point of discouragement with the capability of the U.S. electorate came when most of a panel of respondents interviewed in 1956 and reinterviewed in 1958 and 1960 proved to change their opinions on issues in a largely random manner.[37] If you were to predict people's opinions in 1960 and some were changing, you seemingly could better predict using their opinions in 1958 rather than the older opinions of 1956. In this research, however, predictions were equally poor using 1958 as they were using 1956 opinions. This result could best be explained if most who randomly answer opinion questions were perhaps being liberal in 1956, conservative in 1958, and liberal once again in 1960. No doubt some, approximately 20 percent, of the opinions are consistent, but the opinions of most seem irrelevant.

Some additional insight into the role of issues in U.S. voting patterns can be gained by looking at Table 6–4. The table shows the percentage in each cell voting for Reagan in 1984. Each cell in the table is determined by two questions with the first being their party identification. The second question is how they feel about whether services should be cut to achieve cuts in taxes or whether taxes should be increased to allow more services. In that election, Reagan's position was to cut both services and taxes. Strong Democrats (column 2) believe in the position advocated by Reagan; thus they are in the wrong political party. They are Democrats but should defect and vote Republican or for Reagan.

---

37 Philip E. Converse, "The Nature of Belief Systems in Mass Publics," in *Ideology and Discontent*, David E. Apter (ed.) (New York: Free Press, 1964), pp. 206–261.

The percentage shown in that group, 12 percent, is the percentage voting for Reagan. Most, 88 percent, voted their party rather than their position on the issues. Looking at the lower right cell in the table, that for strong Republicans who favored more services and taxes, we again have people in the wrong political party. They should be Democrats and should have voted for Mondale, but none did! Looking from left to right in the table, we note a very strong impact of party identification regardless of the respondent's personal position. Looking from top to bottom, we see little impact of personal positions on this issue, especially among strong partisans. Results are quite similar for other issues.

Finally we should note that the number of people falling in the upper left and lower right cells, shown in parentheses, is quite small in comparison to those where party identification and issue position are compatible. *The American Voter* strongly suggests that this outcome is the result of most people choosing a candidate and then learning what that candidate's positions are and personally supporting them. Certainly there has been an enormous outpouring of research on the matter of the importance or lack of importance of issues in how people vote.[38] Then, too, this subject is a very important matter for democracy. Is it democracy if people do not vote issue positions? It is equally certain that political science cannot definitively state whether people vote issues sufficiently to be contributing to the preservation of democracy in the United States.

Voting in Congressional Elections.   The most extensive study of an election other than that for president came in 1978. The focus of the 1978 study was the election of the U.S. House of Representatives. As noted earlier, this office is locally elected and thus gives better insight into how people vote in most elections in the United States. Presidential elections are hardly like any other of our elections, since both candidates are known to nearly all voters, contests are publicly funded, and the media pay much attention to the candidates' daily actions.[39] The major outcome of the 1978 congressional election studies was that few incumbents, those presently in office, faced serious challengers. This finding was the result of concern as to why so many incumbents won reelection. In 1978, of 382 incumbents (88 percent) seeking

---

38 See the summary in Erikson, Luttbeg, and Tedin, 1988, chap. 9.

39 Hardly like in the sense that a very lengthy and expensive mass media campaign certainly makes the major candidates known to all, that this campaign and close media coverage as "news" certainly makes the vast majority aware that the election is upcoming, and that clear claims and disclaimers are offered to associate the candidates as defenders or opponents to policies and trends in society, the economy, and the world. No other election matches this hoopla.

reelection, 94 percent won. Although in 1986 and 1988, approximately 99 percent of running incumbents won, this figure dropped to 96 percent in 1990. This high success rate, called *incumbency advantage,* seems to be increasing, at least in the U.S. House of Representatives.[40]

From our perspective, what is most important here is how people who call themselves Democrats vote if they have a Republican incumbent, and the same for a Republican with a Democratic incumbent. The research suggests that they often defect and support the incumbent.[41] The apparent decision rule is to vote for the incumbent regardless of one's party identification. But if one has heard something unfavorable concerning the incumbent, which is uncommon, then one votes one's political party identification.[42] Note that for most people the incumbent is the candidate of their political party, which means that most representatives are from the dominant party of their district. If there were substantial incumbency advantage for state legislators (there is![43]) and for city council and school board members (there is![44]), we might fully expect similar behavior on the part of the electorate for those offices.

CONCLUSION ON HOW PEOPLE VOTE

The overall impact of the voting studies is that the electorate is minimally involved and concerned with the selection of elected officials. This is not to say that they do not want to be asked. In view of the fact that so many vote in presidential elections despite no interest, as well as the fact that many claim to have voted even when they have not, it is clearly suggested that few would willingly give up their vote and its potential impact. Various shortcut devices could be used by people in voting. One could merely randomly select

---

40 Barbara Hinckley, *Congressional Elections* (Washington, DC: CQ Press, 1981), p. 41. This work is the best account of the 1978 study from the perspective of how people vote. Also see Gary C. Jacobson, *The Politics of Congressional Elections* (Boston: Little, Brown, 1983) for a focus on the candidates.

41 Hinckley, p. 67.

42 Hinckley, pp. 83–86.

43 Craig H. Grau, "The Neglected World of State Legislative Elections," a paper presented at the annual meeting of the Midwest Political Science Association, 1981; Malcolm E. Jewell and David Breaux, "The Effect of Incumbency on State Legislative Elections: A Preliminary Report," a paper presented at the annual meeting of the American Political Science Association, 1988.

44 Norman R. Luttbeg, "Multiple Indicators of the Electoral Context of Democratic Responsiveness in Local Governments," a paper presented at the annual meeting of the Midwest Political Science Association, 1986. A now somewhat dated project found that about 78 percent of city council incumbents win reelection; see Albert K. Karnig and B. Oliver Walter, "Municipal Elections: Registration, Incumbent Success and Voter Participation," in *The Municipal Yearbook 1977* (Washington, DC: International City Management Association, 1977), pp. 65–72.

among the candidates or vote for the first person listed on the ballot, but that would be irresponsible. Political party identification and incumbency offer shortcuts that are not irresponsible. What is wrong with voting the party you and your parents have so long found favors programs you can endorse? What is wrong with rewarding the incumbent for a job well done? It remains to be demonstrated, however, that such thinking about issues underlies either voting for one's party or for the incumbent.

Americans seem even less involved in state and local elections, at least as judged by their lack of voting in such elections. Turnout for city council and school board elections varies greatly from community to community but averages about 25 percent.[45] This percent is of course far below that for even state elections. It should be noted that many city and school elections are held in the spring. Without a presidential or gubernatorial campaign or even the attraction of state legislative elections to spur some interest in the mass media, which in turn might spur public interest and participation, these elections have very low turnouts.[46]

Figure 6.4 shows turnout for gubernatorial, congressional, and presidential elections since 1960. No data are presented for state legislative election turnout or for turnout for other statewide elected executives, such as treasurer or attorney general, because these elections are scheduled at the same time as gubernatorial elections. With the governor or with the president at the top of the ballot, nearly all who bother to vote in the election make their preferences known for these offices. Further down the ballot, however, many will not bother to make a choice. Thus we can expect turnout for these lesser offices to be lower yet.

As can be seen in Figure 6.4, all three elections show substantially the same pattern of declining turnout since 1960.[47] Thus we can speak about what turnout was like in 1960 or in 1980, but it drops between the two dates in most states. Whatever factors are affecting turnouts for presidential elections are equally affecting off-year national congressional elections as well as gubernatorial elections regardless of their timing. This result would suggest that an explanation for the decline in voting for president must also explain

---

45 Karnig and Walter, p. 69. A study of local elections in larger Texas communities in 1985 finds turnout varying between 1 and 32 percent; see Luttbeg, 1986, Table 1.

46 Norman R. Luttbeg, "The Role of Newspapers in Local Election Coverage and in Political Advertising," *Journalism Quarterly* 66 (Winter 1988).

47 Norman R. Luttbeg, "Differential Voting Turnout in the American States, 1960–82," *Social Science Quarterly* 65 (March 1984), pp. 60–73. Data since 1980 were added by the author. The regression coefficients are 0.47 percent for president per year, 0.54 percent for off-year congressional, 0.43 percent for governor in presidential years, 0.59 percent for governor off-year, and 0.21 percent for governor in odd years.

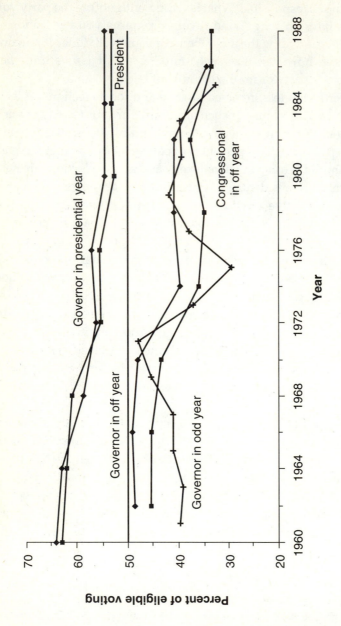

Figure 6.4 Turnout decline compared for presidential, off-year congressional and gubernatorial elections.

declining turnout in gubernatorial elections. Therefore to say that Americans are voting less because they find the presidential candidates selected by the political parties unexciting would fail to account for why both congressional and gubernatorial election turnouts are also down. We do know that some western democracies have seen an even greater decline, whereas others show some increase in turnout. These results are shown in Figure 6.5. Note that during this period U.S. participation declined at a rate of 0.19 percent per year less than in the countries shown.

TURNOUT VARIATIONS AMONG THE STATES

Apart from the overall decline in gubernatorial turnout, there are also substantial variations among the states. Whereas turnouts for gubernatorial and congressional elections are strongly related, as shown in Figure 6.6, those states with gubernatorial turnouts substantially above 1986 congressional turnouts all had gubernatorial elections in the presidential election year of 1984 rather than in 1986.

In 1986 it was found that 58 percent of eligible voters cast ballots for governor in South Dakota, and 56 percent did so in Idaho; however, only 27 percent in Georgia and 29 percent in Texas bothered to vote. In 1962 the variation was greater, with 66 percent voting for governor in Idaho and 64 percent in North Dakota, but only 12 percent in Georgia and 17 percent in Alabama. The states that had the highest turnouts in the 1960s have dropped quite sharply, nearly 1 percent each year.[48] No simple explanations can account for the sharply declining turnouts shown in Figure 6.7.[49]

VOTER TURNOUT AMONG THE STATES— DOES IT MATTER?

Because citizen participation is seen as essential to a true democracy, turnout in elections plays a vital theoretical role. It is expected to be encouraged by many factors, and high participation is expected to have many, mainly salutary results. We turn first to an additional factor that is fully expected to encourage public participation—electoral *competition* among political parties for public offices. In focusing on both the lack of turnout and party competition in the South, V. O. Key sees more effort on the part of political parties to

---

48 Luttbeg, 1984.
49 Luttbeg, 1984; Luttbeg, 1985.

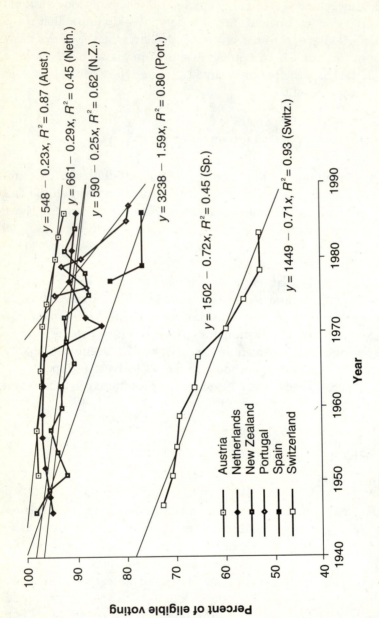

$y = 548 - 0.23x$, $R^2 = 0.87$ (Aust.)

$y = 661 - 0.29x$, $R^2 = 0.45$ (Neth.)

$y = 590 - 0.25x$, $R^2 = 0.62$ (N.Z.)

$y = 3238 - 1.59x$, $R^2 = 0.80$ (Port.)

$y = 1502 - 0.72x$, $R^2 = 0.45$ (Sp.)

$y = 1449 - 0.71x$, $R^2 = 0.93$ (Switz.)

Austria
Netherlands
New Zealand
Portugal
Spain
Switzerland

Year

Percent of eligible voting

1940 1950 1960 1970 1980 1990

40 50 60 70 80 90 100

Figure 6.5   Declining turnouts in various nations.

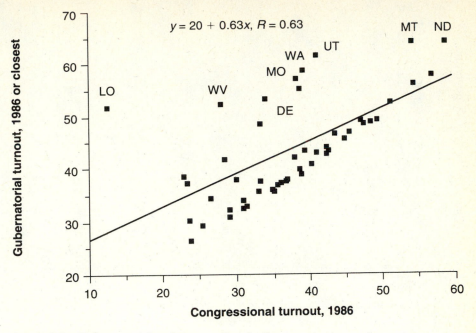

Figure 6.6   Gubernatorial and congressioanl off-year voter turnout.

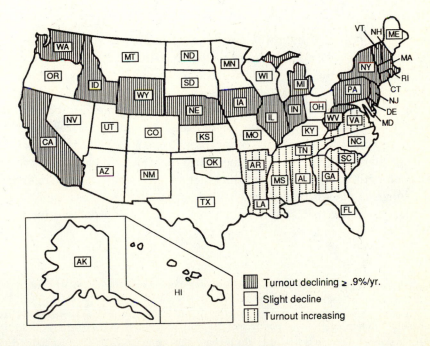

Figure 6.7   Turnout decline in the 50 states, 1960–1980.

Source: Norman R. Luttbeg, "Differential Voting Turnout in the American States, 1960–82," *Social Science Quarterly* 65, March 1984, pp. 60–73.

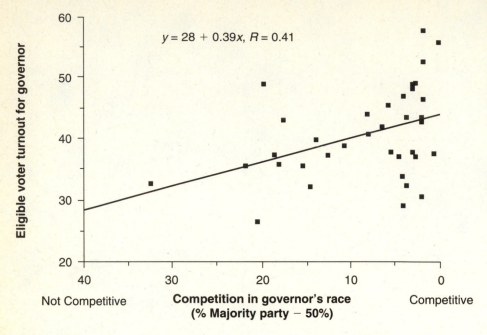

Figure 6.8   Turnout and competition in gubernatorial races, 1986.

turn out supporters if the contest is likely to be close—that is, where each additional supporter may represent victory.[50]

In Figure 6.8, the often-demonstrated relationship is again noted.[51] The figure shows each of the 50 states on two variables, turnout of eligible voters in the gubernatorial elections of 1986 and whether the Democratic and Republican candidates got close to the same percentage of the vote. We would expect the states with the more competitive gubernatorial elections to show greater turnouts. We see in the figure that this is indeed the case. The most competitive states have turnouts that are typically greater than 40 percent, whereas the less competitive states have turnouts of less than 40 percent. It does appear that if a state were to become more competitive, increased turnout could be anticipated.[52]

---

50 V.O. Key, Jr., *Southern Politics in State and Nation* (New York: Random House, 1949), p. 307.

51 I chose to present only those states with off-year gubernatorial contests as those in 1984 have artificially high turnout given the presence of the president on the ballot.

52 An important question is how it might become more competitive. Higher expenditures in competitive contests seem most important in affecting turnout. See Samuel C. Patterson and Gregory A. Caldeira, "Getting Out the Vote: Participation in Gubernatorial Elections," *American Political Science Review* 77 (September 1983), pp. 675–689. But how do you encourage greater

There is evidence, however, that this relationship is not as strong within individual states. Some states in fact over time show little or no relationship between the competition in a particular race and turnout.[53] Comparing U.S. turnout with that in other nations suggests that our national, and presumably, state turnout would increase by 13 percent were we to have the party competition so common in other developed democracies.[54] Of course, the question still remains how party competition might be increased, especially since it would not be in the interest of state legislators, who would be required to vote for such an effort to increase competition.

The Impact of Participation. There is some concern over whether voters brought to the polls by efforts to improve participation would be "quality" voters. Although we shall say much more about this subject in a later chapter, certainly the voting studies would cause us to suspect, at least initially, that they would not be informed or concerned about the issue positions of the candidates. However, few would take exception to the idea that more participation by the public in a democracy is better than less. Several factors are usually mentioned.

First is improved *legitimacy* for governmental decisions. Legitimacy is a psychological attitude, meaning that one feels that since proper officials made the decision, one must voluntarily obey it. Officials are proper if they are elected in fair contests in which all who want can express their opinions in their votes. It is very difficult to measure this concept with any confidence that one is getting real opinions that matter in terms of how people behave. Some research suggests that turmoil and violence are reduced as nations become more participatory.[55] On the other hand, no research suggests that those states with low participation have more turmoil and violence. Although it is beyond the scope of this book, there is consideration of whether high personal crime reflects a loss of legitimacy. If data were available for personal crimes against laws that were made by authorities whose legitimacy was questioned, we might be able to assess this concept. We shall leave this concern with turnout with only the guarded statement that it does not appear

---

expenditures? Even if expenditures are held constant, more competitive districts have higher participation, suggesting that expenditures are not the sole way in which competitiveness affects turnout. See Gary W. Cox and Michael C. Munger, "Closeness, Expenditures, and Turnout in the 1982 U.S. House Elections," *American Political Science Review* 83 (March 1989), pp. 217–231.

53 Virginia Gray, "A Note on Competition and Turnout in the American States," *Journal of Politics* 38 (February 1976), p.156.

54 G. Bingham Powell, Jr., "American Voter Turnout in Comparative Perspective," *American Political Science Review* 80 (March 1986), p. 34.

55 Powell, p. 37.

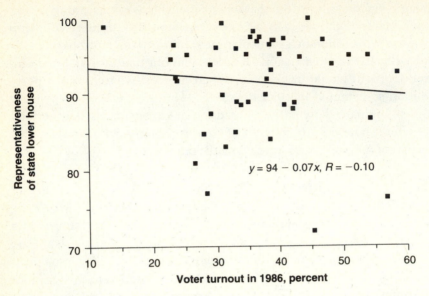

Figure 6.9   Relationship between representativeness of state lower house and voter turnout in 1986.

that the differences in turnout among the states affect the legitimacy accorded governors and legislators.

A second concern about turnout centers on the potential *lack of correspondence between public policy and public opinion* when many, and often most, fail to vote. This linkage between what the public wants and what it gets in terms of policy is expected in a democracy. How is it to be achieved if those who are elected are selected by a minority? Do the opinions of those bothering to vote reflect those who do not? There is research to suggest little difference between voters and nonvoters.[56] Again data are limited, but Figure 6.9 considers the question.

Representativeness here is measured by the proportion of Democrats in the lower house of the state legislature relative to the proportion of the state's electorate having a Democratic party identification. Taking Alabama as an example, we find that, of those with partisan identifications, 75 percent of its electorate consider themselves Democrats, and 85 percent of the Alabama lower house is Democratic, meaning a difference of only 10 percent, or fairly close representation. Low values would mean Democrats in the legislature

---

[56] Key again first assessed this question; see V.O. Key, Jr., *Public Opinion and American Democracy* (New York: Knopf, 1961), p. 182.

and in the public are nearly equal, meaning they are quite representative. Thus low values would mean greater representation. This concept might be difficult to grasp, and therefore this difference is subtracted from 100 percent in the figure. It can be seen that there is a discouraging drop in representativeness when measured with increased participation. The correlation is quite weak, however, and thus we probably should conclude that there is no relationship.[57]

We might suspect that another instance in which nonvoters' opinions might differ from those who are driven to vote is in the self-interest they reflect. The better-off vote more and would favor taxes that do not increase with how much you earn. Therefore, do taxes prove more regressive in low-participation states where presumably only the better-educated vote? Again, we get the wrong direction in the relationship between turnout and regressive taxes. Higher-turnout states have more regressive state and local taxes. Again, however, because of the weakness of the relationship, we should probably just conclude that none exists.

CONCLUSION

Although there may be little to suggest that variations in public turnout in elections have much impact, many still believe that a true democracy must have avid public participation. Competition among candidates seeking public offices seems to be the primary source of public interest in voting; and, as questioned earlier, the concern thus shifts to how to generate more competition. Although the political parties, interest groups, and candidates themselves may be our only hope for increasing competition, there is no incentive for any of them to seek greater competition. We turn finally to the potential of the electorate itself to contribute to greater competition.

Certainly were the electorate to take a greater interest in elections and to hold officials accountable to campaign promises as well as getting those promises to center on important issues, we might expect incumbents to be defeated occasionally. Prospective challengers then might see the potential for winning if they were to run. Unfortunately, there is little to suggest such public capability at present or much potential for such an improvement in the future.

---

57 Turnout in 1986 for the U.S. House of Representatives is used rather than governor turnout because the latter is so dependent on when the election is scheduled relative to the presidential election.

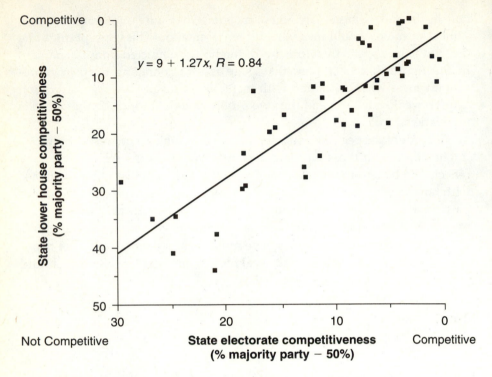

Figure 6.10   Relationship between competitiveness of state lower house and state electorate.

As it now stands, the electorate can contribute to greater competition only where Democrats and Republicans are mixed in nearly equal numbers in districts. Currently districts that are close to being either homogeneously Democratic or Republican tend to be drawn. Figure 6.10 shows the correspondence between competitiveness in the public and in the lower house of the state legislature. Where state electorates are close mixes of Democrats and Republicans, state legislatures are competitive. Obviously there will be states and certainly local congressional and state legislative districts that cannot have or do not have sufficient numbers of partisans of one political party to offset those of the dominant political party.

When the partisan mix is close, candidates do compete and voters do turn out. But when districts are safe with one political party's supporters dominant, the dynamics of when Americans vote and which candidate they support may make it seem that voters are not capable of playing a role in democracy. As V. O. Key states, " . . . voters are not fools . . . the electorate behaves about as rationally and responsibly as we should expect, given the clarity of the alternatives presented to it and the character of the information available to it."[58]

SUMMARY

1. Americans have numerous opportunities to participate in their governments, but few do anything more than vote. Very few are politically involved.
2. Only in presidential elections do most Americans even bother to vote. And in such elections parentally transmitted loyalty to one of the major political parties seems to afford the best prediction of how most people vote. People, however, do *not* vote for candidates for other offices the same way as they do for president.
3. Even comparing turnout for our presidential elections with turnouts in other countries finds us to be poor participants. Several differences account for this low turnout, one of which is our requirement that prospective voters must register to vote at least 30 days before elections.
4. Typically, more than 85 percent of incumbent representatives, those presently in public office, win reelection. Voters seem to support the incumbent if they have heard nothing unfavorable about his or her actions. This outcome is true for state legislators as well as for the U.S. House of Representatives.
5. Local participation is the lowest, and there is little hope that Americans at this level show greater concern with taking stands on major issues.

SUGGESTED READINGS

Erikson, Robert S., Norman R. Luttbeg, and Kent L. Tedin. *American Public Opinion,* 3rd ed. (New York: Macmillan, 1988). Although this text focuses primarily on congressional and presidential representation, it does consider the role of public opinion in policy-making.

Gant, Michael M., and Norman R. Luttbeg, *American Electoral Behavior: 1952–1988* (Itasca, IL: Peacock, 1991). This book considers differences in how

---

58 V.O. Key, Jr., *The Responsible Electorate* (Cambridge: Harvard University Press, 1966), p. 7.

Americans now vote for president and members of Congress in contrast to how they did in the past.

General Accounting Office, *Voting: Some Procedural Changes and Informational Activities Could Increase Turnout* (Gaithersburg, MD: GAO, 1990). This report considers the research on state and local differences in encouraging turnout, and includes many recommendations.

Jewell, Malcolm E., and David M. Olson, *American State Political Parties and Elections* (Homewood, IL: Dorsey Press, 1982). Although some of the material is now somewhat dated, the focus here is exclusively on state elections.

Salmore, Barbara G., and Stephen A. Salmore, "The Transformation of State Electoral Politics," in *The State of the States*, Carl E. Van Horn (ed.) (Washington, DC: CQ Press, 1989). This study focuses on the "congressionalization" of state legislatures, pointing out that running for a state legislative seat has become much like running for Congress.

Chapter
7

Political Parties, Pressure Groups, and the Idea of Competition

*P*olitical parties and interest or pressure groups are a natural outgrowth in a democracy. Although the founding fathers who wrote the Constitution of the United States may have wanted to resist "factions" or political parties and interest groups, their efforts were unsuccessful. In fact they formed the first interest group or political party to seek the ratification of the new constitution they had drafted. No democracy today lacks either political parties or pressure groups.

Fundamentally, political parties and pressure groups differ little from each other. They both are organizations of like-minded individuals seeking certain government actions. The drafters of the new national Constitution in 1787 obviously shared an interest in getting it ratified. They organized to do so and succeeded, probably because those opposed to its ratification were poorly organized. There are many thousands of interests in a complex society. Pressure or interest groups organize such interests to exert their influence on legislating bodies to get their interests reflected in public policy. Those opposed to handguns organize to seek laws requiring registration, restricting who can buy handguns, or even banning them. The National Rifle Association organized long ago, using its magazine to convince like-thinking readers to pressure their legislators to resist such restrictions. Evidently, the NRA has been better organized.

The pro-life, antiabortion segment of opinion has been well organized for several years and has had success in disrupting abortion clinics and drawing public support for their arguments. Now that the Supreme Court has stepped back from its position on *Roe* v. *Wade*, state legislatures may vote for more restrictions on abortion. Pro-choice supporters have been much less organized, but with the renewed potential for state legislative restrictions, they can be expected to become organized.

Clear patterns are evident in these few examples. Organization is obviously more successful than the lack of organization, and one side's organization forces other sides to organize to counter their opponents. Second, little is gained by organizing those who are unconcerned or in the vast majority. Few would organize to resist a banning of apple pie as too fattening because there is no need to do so. Nor is there need to organize the vast majority, whose votes can easily be used to affect the election outcome. Third, small segments of society with no resources other than their votes achieve nothing by organizing. Generally, small poor groups are useless. Wealthy small groups, however, have had great success, largely because they are able to contribute campaign funds to "deserving" candidates. As campaigning for public office has gotten very expensive, candidates have increasingly turned to small but wealthy interests for campaign contributions. Costly campaigns have greatly increased the influence of interest groups.

Size is probably the fundamental difference between interest groups and political parties. Inasmuch as political party organizes to pass policies in the legislature or to select candidates, large numbers of legislators or voting supporters are necessary. This size consideration, of course, means that political parties must have interests that are a good deal broader to attract more voters and must "patch over" many differences among prospective supporters. But although compromise is a necessary word in political parties' lexicon, interest groups, especially wealthy interest groups, have more reason to be uncompromising. Even if small, their generous contributions to campaigns can give them great say.

POLITICAL PARTIES

As mentioned earlier, the first political party in the United States, the Federalists, organized to ratify the Constitution. One of the reasons for a political party to organize is to gather the necessary votes to win in the legislature. Normally, what is required is a simple majority, 50 percent of those voting plus one. Working together to achieve such a majority can be called *legislative organization*. It is always easier for a legislative body to do nothing, allowing a new bill to fail rather than enacting it. Thus proponents seem most likely to organize. When one side organizes, especially if it has any success as a result, the other side also swiftly organizes.

When, as often is the case, certain legislators think similarly about a broad range of issues, the organization becomes more enduring. They seek to retain their numbers within the legislature or to increase them to be successful in the future on other issues. This second function, organizing for purposes of appealing to the electorate for votes, can be called *electoral organization*. The purpose of the Jeffersonian Republicans was to resist the centralization of government advocated by the Federalists following the anti-Federalists' unsuccessful effort to stop the ratification of the Constitution.[1] They further organized to seek like-minded voters who would return them and like-minded candidates to public office.

The Jeffersonian Republicans, the second U.S. political party, served as an example for later political parties. Ultimately this electoral organization by the Jeffersonian Republicans, and the inability of the aristocratic Federalists to stoop to appealing for voter support, resulted in the Federalists becoming irrelevant to national politics.

A BRIEF HISTORY OF AMERICAN POLITICAL PARTIES

As already mentioned, the new Constitution served as the origin of the Federalists. That constitution provided a strong central government that was less sensitive to the general public's demands. Areas of commerce, primarily in seaports such as Boston, New York, Philadelphia, and Baltimore, sought to ratify the Constitution. A stronger central government would be able to smooth commerce between the states, and many living in these areas earned their livings in commerce.

The inland areas, where farming was the main occupation, saw in a stronger central government the renewed threat of the king's government that had only recently been overthrown. Those of this belief, as noted, were disorganized and were generally labeled "anti-Federalists." In 1787–1789

---

1 For a more extended discussion see V. O. Key, Jr., *Politics, Parties, and Pressure Groups*, 4th ed. (New York: Crowell, 1958), pp. 221–225.

only a fool would have run as an anti-Federalist for a state legislative seat or one in the U.S. House of Representatives from a Boston district, given the popular support in that area for the new Constitution. The district would have been *uncompetitive* since only Federalists were likely to be successful in seeking election. Rural districts were also uncompetitive. In these districts, however, only anti-Federalists were likely to be successful.

Competition in a statewide district, such as for governor or U.S. senator, differed from that in a local district. If a state had a close mix of mercantile and rural areas, such as Massachusetts, it might be balanced politically. The anti-Federalists in the rural areas of the state would offset the Federalists of the more urban areas. Statewide districts might have been competitive just by the chance of urban and rural areas being nearly equal in size. Other states, such a Georgia, were all rural and therefore uncompetitive.

For a time, however, the Civil War and its aftermath ended party competition altogether. The deaths and emotion associated with the Civil War divided the country into a Republican North and a Democratic South. In the North, the Democratic party was associated with the Confederacy and the deaths of many thousands of northern troops. No candidate running as a Democrat could have been elected. Similarly no Republican could run in the South after Reconstruction because of what Sherman had done to the South. So neither statewide districts nor local districts were competitive politically. Everyone lived in a one party state and locality. Since the North had a greater population than the South, even after southerners were allowed to vote, Republicans were also able to dominate the presidency.

Before and after the Civil War, northern cities continued to grow. The heavy immigration after 1850 and the pressing need in urban areas for municipal services returned party competition to many northern states. Because the Civil War held little meaning for immigrants, a ward heeler who appealed for their vote for Democratic candidates with the promise to provide municipal services found them quite willing to do so. Soon no nonurban machine candidates could win in such cities. At the city or local level, politics had changed from uncompetitive for the Republican party into uncompetitive for the machine's party.

Machine supporters focused on local issues and seldom considered competing for state and national offices. However, if a state had a large city to offset Republicanism in rural areas, state politics and statewide districts often proved competitive. Each political party has a good chance to win an office, such as governor or U.S. senator. Of course, with little industrialization or urbanization, the South remained uncompetitive at both the state and local levels.

Franklin D. Roosevelt put together a coalition of urban northern city residents and southerners, most of whom already called themselves Democrats.

The purpose of the coalition was to relieve the unemployment in the depression of the 1930s, as discussed in Chapter 4. However, it did little to change the competitiveness of any office other than the presidency. The end of the Second World War, however, did represent a change in competitiveness in U.S. politics.

The mobility of Americans was at the root of this change. We moved from South to North, and later vice versa. We moved from urban to suburban areas and from rural to urban areas. Most of this mobility was to seek better jobs or a better life-style. Middle-class Republicans moved to the suburbs, making the older core cities, such as St. Louis and Chicago, overwhelmingly Democratic. Urban party organizations, endorsing the "New Deal" programs of Roosevelt, proved appealing to southern Republican blacks and converted them to the Democratic party. This Democratic party was different from the one they had known in the South.

Many Republicans moved to the South. The South's cheap, nonunion labor attracted northern industry, and many Republican managers moved along with their companies. Most often these people moved into urban areas and persisted in voting for the Republican presidential candidate and whatever other local Republicans that were running. Gradually some Republican candidates found enough votes to win seats in state legislatures and the U.S. House of Representatives. Lately many Republican candidates for governor have been successful. The overall pattern in the South is one of growing Republican strength in urban areas.

In the North and West, mobility has furthered the competitiveness at the state level but without affecting the lack of competition always evident in local districts. There has been a continued duality in U.S. politics. We were first divided on the Constitution, then on slavery and states' rights, then on federal efforts to safeguard us against economic cycles, and then on civil rights. Urban and rural and North or South differences correspond to these opinion differences. If issues divided those living in urban and rural areas and if a state had nearly equal urban and rural populations, its statewide politics became competitive. Local areas, however, have seldom been competitive. Wherever you live there is little likelihood that your neighbors will be of a different political party. It is equally unlikely that your locally elected representative for Congress, state legislature, or local government will face competition from the other political party.

WHY ALWAYS TWO MAJOR POLITICAL PARTIES?

In the United States there have always been only two political parties. The Jeffersonian Republicans evolved into the Democratic political party, and faced only a single opposition party. This opposition party was initially the Federalists and later the Republicans. Although political scientists may decry the dominance of one political party, especially in the South, competition between more than two political parties is also viewed as undesirable. Countries, such as Italy and France, with more than two political parties endure many struggles to put together a coalition to govern. Members of several political parties are needed in these countries to achieve the majority in their parliaments necessary to establish a government. These precarious governing majorities and the uncertainty of government no doubt caused this concern about multiple political parties. Competition between more than two political parties might be destabilizing.

Several factors explain our being blessed with only two major political parties. First is that we had the *good fortune* to face only one divisive issue at a time. The agricultural versus mercantile division on the Constitution gave way to the North versus South division and the Civil War. Similarly, the civil rights movement of the 1960s replaced the controversy between the wealthy and poor reactions to Roosevelt's New Deal programs. In each of these disputes, the Democratic party took one stance and its opposition took the other. V. O. Key calls this *dualism*.[2]

Institutional factors, such as the "winner-take-all, single-member districts" are also seen as central to our two-party system. If there is only a single victor in a district, the chance of a third political party candidate winning is slight. If there were multiple representatives to be selected from such a district, however, a third party capable of getting a third of the popular vote might win one of the seats. All U.S. House districts are single-member districts, so third parties have little chance for victory in those races. Most state legislative districts and local government districts are also single-member districts.

Primary elections are another factor. All candidates for state and national offices are assured a place on the ballot only if they win either the Democratic or the Republican primary. The sole exceptions are candidates for president who get on the ballot in nominating conventions. Third parties have no primaries! Their candidates can get on the ballot only by exceptional means. Typically, they need a petition signed by many registered voters (several percent of the vote last cast for this office). Although primaries weaken the major political parties by taking candidate selection out of their hands, there is little question that they are fatal to third parties.

---

2 Key, p. 228.

Party identification and the slowness with which it changes also contribute to our two-party system. Fewer than 18 percent of Americans refuse to identify themselves with either the Democrats or the Republicans. Since parents transmit their party identification with great success to their children, a third political party would have to convert people as adults. Research has shown that only events such as the Civil War or the Great Depression of the 1930s have such a potential for converting people. Since the Vietnam War and World War II proved to be incapable of converting people's partisanship, however, third parties seem to have little or no chance.

Finally, nearly all two-party democracies are *Anglo*, or English by heritage. In addition to the United States, Canada, Australia, New Zealand, and the United Kingdom are all Anglo, two-party democracies. What is it about English heritage that results in two-party government? The reduced influence of the Roman Catholic Church in these countries may underlie their having only two parties. Other countries may have a pro-Catholic working-class party as well as an anticlerical (against the Catholic Church) working-class party. In non-Anglo democracies, even if the middle class is not divided into pro- and anti-Catholic political parties, there are usually at least three political parties. Often the communists provide a fourth, at least somewhat successful, party. More recently, environmental parties, such as the German Green party, have also attracted many votes.

Two of the explanations of our having a two-party system, the historical reasons, are accidental and could not be copied by other political systems. The explanations of structural barriers to third political parties would suggest that we could encourage third political parties if we wanted to do so. The party identification explanation, while not accidental, would be difficult to change to encourage third political parties.

Regulating Political Parties

Although political parties are not a branch of any government, but rather are informal organizations, all states regulate political parties. This feature is apparently unusual among democracies and probably can be traced to the efforts to undo urban politics in the late 1800s, as discussed in Chapter 4. State laws regulating political parties are of five types: (1) defining membership, typically as being registered as a Democrat or as a Republican; (2) defining a formal party organization and its selection, including a state party chairman and central committee with some limited responsibilities; (3) allowing access to the state election ballot or denying it if the party lacks popular support; (4)

providing procedures for nominating candidates and holding primaries; and (5) restricting campaign financing or providing public funds.[3]

Despite the overall decline in party control represented by increased state regulation, some state political parties persist in influencing politics. In some states they more actively recruit candidates, contribute more campaign funds, and train candidates in necessary modern campaign skills, such as soliciting campaign funds and using election polls.[4] All of these efforts, no doubt, endear their political party to successful candidates; but as compared to earlier eras when a tightly organized political party could bring large numbers of loyal supporters to the polls and assure its candidates success in winning elections, modern political parties are weak imitations of those in the past. By contrast, wealthy interests have gotten the attention of candidates by way of their ability to contribute the campaign funds that are needed in modern, television-centered campaigns.

Primaries. Many states have weakened political parties by requiring primary elections.[5] Earlier political parties could select their candidates however they wished and then notify voters of these selections. Frequently elected state legislators of the party would meet and select their candidates for all legislative seats including those then held by the opposition party. No one from those districts could be sure they would have any say on nominees. Criticism of such *legislative caucuses* centered on constituents having little say. *Party conventions* replaced these caucuses to give average party members more say in candidate selection. Conventions also have been criticized as being conspiratorial, with decisions made in smoke-filled rooms, which was not what the public wanted. *Primary elections* allow the public a say, but at the expense of not allowing the party to say who is truly a Republican or who is a Democrat. All states use primaries to select candidates for state offices.

There are several types of primary elections used among the states. The most common type is the *closed primary* used by 38 states. To vote in the Republican primary in one of those states, for example, you must affirm that you are a Republican. This usually is done when you register to vote as a Republican, a Democrat, or an independent. Independents may not vote in either the Republican or the Democratic primaries. An *open primary* requires

3 John F. Bibby, Cornelius P. Cotter, James L. Gibson, Robert J. Huckshorn, "Parties in State Politics," in *Politics in the American States: A Comparative Analysis*, 4th ed., Virginia Gray, Herbert Jacob, and Kenneth N. Vines (eds.) (Boston: Little, Brown, 1983), pp. 69–75.

4 James L. Gibson, Cornelius P. Cotter, John F. Bibby, and Robert J. Huckshorn, "Assessing Party Organizational Strength," *American Journal of Political Science* 27 (May 1983), pp. 193–222.

5 V.O. Key, Jr., *American State Politics: An Introduction* (New York: Knopf, 1956), pp. 85–194.

no such affirmation of partisanship. You merely ask to vote in either the Republican or Democratic primary, not both. Texans, for each voter registration period, may choose to vote in either primary but cannot change thereafter. Alaska and Washington use a *blanket primary* in which you can vote in the Democratic primary for one office and in the Republican primary for others.

The open and blanket primaries are thought to encourage partisans of one party to vote in the opposition party's primary. They might do so to select weak candidates that can more easily be defeated in the later general election. There is, however, little evidence that this kind of voting takes place to any significant degree. The 12 states lacking closed primaries are in a belt running from Michigan to Washington, plus Vermont and Alaska. Louisiana has yet another type of primary, the *nonpartisan primary*, where all candidates of each office run in a combined primary. If one candidate receives 50 percent of the vote, he or she is the victor. If not, the top two candidates, regardless of party, face a runoff election.

Political parties have sought to counter the effects of primaries by selecting and endorsing desirable candidates before the primary. Although this approach has been partially successful, the primaries have nevertheless greatly weakened the importance of political parties for prospective candidates.[6] With sufficient money and in a race with no incumbent, anyone can run in a primary for whichever party is dominant in the area, win it, and ultimately win the general election. This result can be achieved without the political party involved having any say. In this situation a Democratic candidate need not necessarily have the policy positions expected of that political party.

The Importance of Political Parties and Competition Among Them

Responsible Political Parties.   Although we share the system of two dominant political parties with Great Britain, ours are often seen as not offering the clear choice that the Labour and Conservative parties offer there. When political parties take clear stands, select candidates upholding those stands or party positions, educate the public on these positions, remove officeholders who do not uphold those positions, and organize themselves within the halls of government to enact these positions into law, many see this party system as a very desirable one. It is called a *responsible party system*.[7] Many believe that Britain has such

---

6 Malcolm E. Jewell and David M. Olson, *American State Political Parties and Elections*, rev. ed. (Homewood, IL: Dorsey, 1982), pp.112–120.

7 E. E. Schattschneider, *Party Government* (New York: Rinehart, 1942), and "Toward a More Responsible Two-Party System," *American Political Science Review* 64 (September, 1950), supplement.

a party system and that we would be better off if we were to have more responsiblepoliticalparties.

It is unlikely that the United States ever really had the potential for developing such a system; moreover, many factors now all but preclude our doing so. As we have seen, most Americans are loyal supporters of their parents' political party. Many candidates can ignore political parties at election time by relying on campaign contributions they gather themselves. And as we shall see, primary elections for selection of candidates weaken the political parties' ability to exclude candidates not sharing their positions.

Is the Party Over?[8] There has been much concern that American political parties are in decline. Certainly Americans in survey after survey seem more than willing to see parties vanish. They feel "the man rather than the party" should be the basis of the voting choice. Parties are seen as confusing the issues, creating conflict where none really exists; and not keeping their promises.[9] Nevertheless, most people call themselves Democrats or Republicans. *Antipathy toward political parties* is often cited as one reason parties today are not as vital as they were before World War II, but there are other reasons.

Primary elections, as we have noted, have weakened the parties by denying them the ability to reward loyal and hard-working individuals of known political beliefs with a nomination as a candidate. They also cannot develop the *"balanced slate"* of candidates that they once could, combining a Jewish candidate and an Irish candidate, to bring such groups together to assure victory. Now, if the Irish outnumber all other groups, all Irish candidates win the primary. In the general election, however, the other groups may no longer endorse the party's candidates. Also, with the primary a candidate can win the nomination without the party's support or even in spite of the party's opposition.

There is a *new-style politics* of campaigning that drops the person-to-person contact between party workers and voters and the appeals for party unity. Instead, candidates make every effort to seem trustworthy and statesmanlike, without taking positions on the issues.[10] What is being

---

8 This play on words is taken from David S. Broder, *The Party's Over: The Failure of Politics in America* (New York: Harper & Row, 1971). Also see Larry J. Sabato, *The Party's Just Begun* (Glenview, IL: Scott, Foresman, 1988).

9 Jack Dennis, "Support for the Party System by the Mass Public," *American Political Science Review*, 60 (September, 1966), p. 605.

10 Edwin Diamond and Stephen Bates, *The Spot* (Cambridge: MIT Press, 1984).

emulated in this new style of politics is the same advertising campaigns that are used to sell cola and cars. When John Kennedy won with such a campaign and Nixon turned around a loss in 1960 with a win in 1968 by campaigning in this style, candidates embraced the technique as effective.[11] Now candidates, even for lesser offices, must match an opponent's media-based, new-style campaign with one of his or her own. This technique has enriched consultants and public relations firms, weakened political parties, and contributed little to the quality of democracy.

In Chapter 6 we found very little decline in political party identification. If you look only at the number of people who first say they are independent and then admit to leaning toward one of the political parties, you will find that their number has increased over the years. Despite what they say however, they vote overwhelmingly for the political party toward which they lean. They are, in effect, "closet partisans." Still, one can see a *decline in partisanship in the electorate*, which some see as further evidence of the decline of U.S. political parties. As we noted earlier, incumbency seems to have replaced party identification as the first reason to support a candidate for a congressional or state legislative seat.

For whatever reasons, Americans are less "strongly" committed to their political party than in the past. Furthermore, primaries have taken out of the political parties' hands the choice of which candidates will be called "Democrats" or "Republicans." Certainly the advantage of the incumbent in seeking reelection has increased in Congress through the use of "candidate centered" campaign techniques focusing primarily on the use of television. The parties nevertheless persist, perhaps because they are organized. [12]

Party Organization   There are many ways in which we might assess the strengths of political parties in the states. In most developed democracies, the political parties get loyal votes from their party's elected members of parliament on important bills. If they fail to get this support, the parties can refuse to list (or slate) offenders on the ballot in the next election. Moreover, they can assure the reelection of those who are loyal, even if they are strongly opposed by offended interest groups. The parties have loyal supporters in the electorate and many volunteer workers to go from door to door to find supporters and perhaps to convince some to vote for the party's candidates. Getting out the party's supporters on election day can help win the election. Again volunteers are needed.

---

11   George McGinnis, *The Selling of the President 1969* (New York: Pocket Books, 1969).

12   Samuel C. Patterson, "The Persistence of State Parties," in *The State of the States,* Carl E. Van Horn (ed.) (Washington, DC: CQ Press, 1989).

By this standard, we might say that the political parties in a state are strong if nearly all Democrats vote one way with nearly all Republicans in opposition. The concept of party strength is best captured by the ability to defeat those who are disloyal and to reelect those who are loyal. Unfortunately we have no such measures. We do, however, have a single study of many factors of party organizational strength. Both state and county-level party leaders were surveyed.[13] If the political parties are well organized, we can expect that at least a good effort is made to optimize the support that party gets. We cannot be assured that the effort is sufficient to reelect those legislators that have worked loyally for the party's programs. Certainly, however, weak organization does not suggest a strong political party.

In terms of distributing campaign literature, raising money, conducting local registration drives, and other campaign efforts, parties were stronger, not weaker, in 1979 than they were in 1964.[14] Similarly at the state level such efforts have certainly not declined over the period 1960–1980.[15] These criteria are measures of the activity of political parties, not necessarily of their success. Although this type of measure is not exactly what we might want for assessing the political parties' strength in each state, it probably is the best we can do. Despite our misgivings, however, at least the local party organization measure largely explains the differences among the states in competition between the political parties.[16] It seems to assess differences in organizational strength.

Whatever it is that encourages or allows a local political party to be strong also strengthens the other political party. One political party's strength encourages or drives the other to become stronger.[17] New Jersey, Pennsylvania, New York, Delaware, Indiana, Ohio, and Connecticut rate high for both political parties, whereas many southern states, plus Nebraska and Kansas, rate low in organization for both political parties. This organization is related to competition between the parties, or at least their relative balance in the lower state house, as is shown in Figure 7.1.

---

13 Cornelius P. Cotter, James L. Gibson, John F. Bibby, and Robert J. Huckshorn, *Party Organizations in American Politics* (New York: Praeger, 1984); James L. Gibson, Cornelius P. Cotter, John F. Bibby, and Robert J. Huckshorn, "Whither the Local Parties?: A Cross-Sectional and Longitudinal Analysis of the Strength of Party Organization," *American Journal of Political Science* 29 (February, 1985), pp. 139–160.

14 Gibson, p. 143.

15 Cotter, p. 31.

16 Samuel C. Patterson and Gregory A. Caldeira, "The Etiology of Partisan Competition," *American Political Science Review* 78 (September, 1984), pp. 691–707.

17 The organizational strengths of the parties correlate at a 0.78 level at the county level but only 0.34 at the state level.

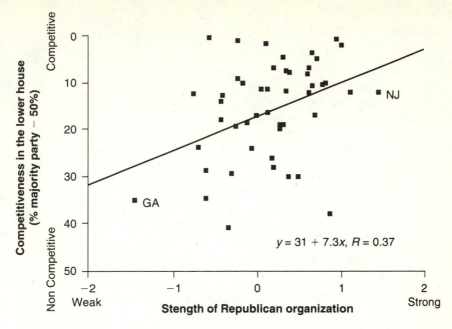

Figure 7.1   The relationship between competitiveness in the lower house and Republican party organizational strength within state legislatures.

Georgia and New Jersey are identified in the figure. Georgia has the lowest degree of organization in its Republican Party and is the third least competitive state. By contrast, New Jersey's Republican Party is the best organized and, while its lower house is no where near the most competitive, it is quite competitive. The Democratic party shows the same pattern.[18] If one party organizes to achieve more victories in elections so does the other party. Furthermore organization and competition go hand in hand. This is true looking at state level organization also, as is shown in Figure 7.2. The direction of the causality is unclear, however. It may be that organization encourages competition or that when the political parties are competitive they organize to optimize their chances. Figure 6.10 showed us that when the electorate was competitively balanced between Democrats and Republicans, the state legislature was competitive. This finding would suggest then that organization follows competitiveness rather than preceding it.

18 The correlation for the Democratic party's organization is 0.42.

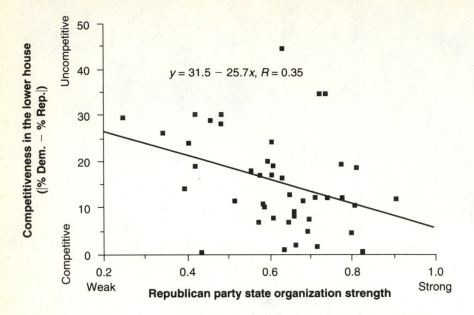

Figure 7.2   The relationship between competitiveness and organization at the state level.

We need to be cautious in assessing the strength of U.S. political parties. Compared with political parties in most democracies, ours can little influence the reelection success of those legislators who vote as the party would prefer in passing laws and making policies. There seems little question that our parties were stronger in the past and that today even the best organized would be judged quite weak when compared either with U.S. parties in the past or present day parties in other democracies.

But political parties' inability to influence elections does not necessarily mean that liberal Democrats and conservative Republicans are equally likely to be elected from all districts across the United States. As we have discussed, some areas are overwhelmingly likely to elect Republicans and others Democrats. And most conservatives will run as Republicans and liberals as Democrats. Weak political parties also do not mean that Democrats and Republicans will be nearly equally in number in state legislatures. Some states have one dominant political party. We now turn to the question of whether Republican legislatures enact different legislation than do Democratic legislatures, and whether a close mix of Democrats and Republican in the legislature differs from what happens when one political party dominates.

The Impact of the Party in Control

Political party leaders, such as members of Congress, state party leaders, and delegates to presidential conventions have been found to differ sharply between the political parties in terms of issues and ideology. Therefore, we would expect that a Democratically controlled legislature would enact more liberal programs, such as civil rights legislation. Some research has supported this theory,[19] but others have not.[20] We would also expect to find the liberalism reflected in progressive taxation and higher AFDC payments, but there are mixed results on those measures.

Figure 7.3 shows that states with more Democrats in the lower house are those with less regressive taxes. In the figure, if the poor paid the same percentage of their income in taxes as did the wealthy, the measure would be 0.00. Democratic control of the lower house of the state legislature results in less regressive state and local taxes. This is not a strong relationship and is not strengthened with the South deleted.

Unexpectedly, these same Democratic state legislatures authorize lower average Aid for Families with Dependent Children payments. However, this too is a quite modest relationship. Moreover, the relationship reverses when the South, with its low payments and Democratic dominance, is excluded. It then becomes a quite weak relationship with Democratic control now resulting in higher AFDC average payments.[21] The regressiveness of the tax structure seems somewhat affected by which political party is in control, but AFDC average payments are unaffected. Our only conclusion is that further research is necessary.

Interparty Competition.   Competition between the political parties has long been thought to be important in our democracy.[22] The basic idea is that to compete, political parties will select their candidates more carefully and better orchestrate the passage of needed legislation. They will be more responsive to public demands and more effective in passing policies preferred by the public. As a result, there has been a long tradition of measuring such competition.[23]

---

19 Robert S. Erikson, "The Relationship Between Party Control and Civil Rights Legislation in the American States," *Western Political Quarterly* 24 (March 1971), pp. 178–182.

20 Thomas R. Dye, "Party and Policy in the States," *Journal of Politics* 46 (November 1984), pp. 1097–1116.

21 The equation is $\$296 + 0.74 \times$ percentage Democratic, $R=0.13$.

22 V.O. Key, Jr., *Southern Politics in State and Nation* (New York: Random House, 1949), p. 307.

23 For a summary, see Austin Ranney, "Parties in State Politics," in *Politics in the American States: A Comparative Analysis,* Herbert Jacob and Kenneth N. Vines (eds.) (Boston: Little, Brown, 1965), footnote 10.

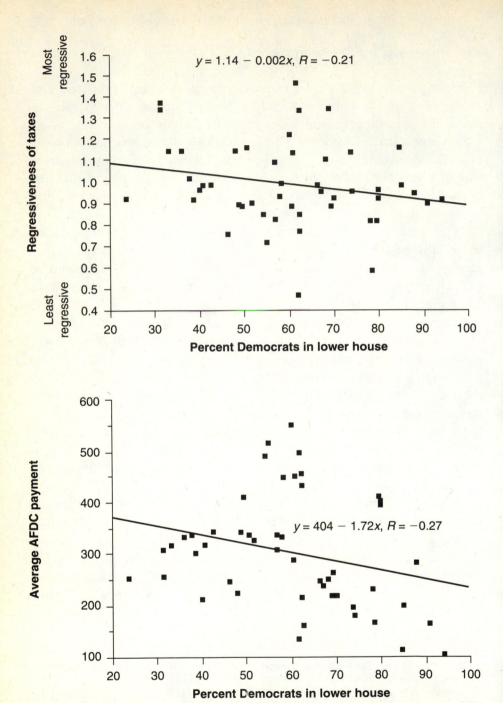

Figure 7.3 Regressiveness of taxes and average AFDC payment vs. percent Democratic control in lower house.

The most common measures of competition include the percentage of Democrats in both the upper and lower houses; the percentage of the vote won by the Democratic gubernatorial candidates; the division of which party controls the legislature houses and the governorship; and the duration of one party's control. All of these measures have been weighed equally into a single measure.[24] Competition at the state level, which is assessed, fails to find corresponding competition in individual districts.[25] States that are competitive statewide may have few districts in which incumbents are much challenged. Generally, the concept of competition is based on the incorrect assumption that a competitive state will be competitive regardless of how competition is measured.[26] Furthermore, since it increasingly has been the case that the governor is of one political party and a majority of at least one house of the other, a combined measure confuses the issue, as shown in Figure 7.4.

We shall therefore stick with statewide competition within the lower house of the state legislature, which relates closely with competition within the states' upper houses, as shown in Figure 7.5.

This measure simply subtracts 50 percent from the percentage in the lower house of the larger political party. A more competitive state therefore would be quite close to 0, meaning that both political parties held half of the seats. The five most competitive states and their percent deviations from being perfectly competitive are Vermont, 0.3; Pennsylvania, 0.7; Montana, 1.0; Oregon, 1.7; and Indiana, 2.0. The least competitive states are Mississippi, 44.3; Arkansas, 41.0; Maryland, 37.9; Georgia, 35.0; and Alabama, 34.8. Figure 7.6 shows the competitiveness of the states.

As we can see on the map, the South includes most of the uncompetitive lower houses where one party's percentage is greater than 70 percent.[27] Idaho, Massachusetts, Rhode Island and others, however, are also uncompetitive by our measure. No southern state is truly competitive, but Florida, Tennessee, and Texas are moderately so. Several states are surprisingly competitive, such as Montana, North Dakota, Kansas, Vermont, and Maine. Because many of the same states have less per capita personal income and fewer services, uncompetitive states seem less responsive to public demands for

---

24 Ranney, pp. 63–65.

25 Harvey J. Tucker, "Interparty Competition in the American States," *American Politics Quarterly* 10 (January 1982), pp. 93–116.

26 Norman R. Luttbeg, "Multiple Indicators of the Electoral Contest of Democratic Responsiveness in Local Governments," a paper presented at the annual meeting of the Midwest Political Science Association, 1986.

27 This percentage is an absolute value, with the percentage Democrat subtracted from 50 percent. Thus North Carolina's lower house has 70 percent Democrats. Subtracting 50 percent and taking the absolute difference yields 20 percent, which falls in the uncompetitive category. Nebraska elects state legislators on a nonpartisan ballot.

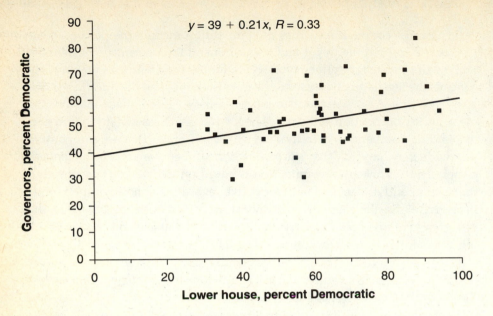

Figure 7.4 Percent of governors who are Democrats vs. percent Democrats in lower house of state legislatures.

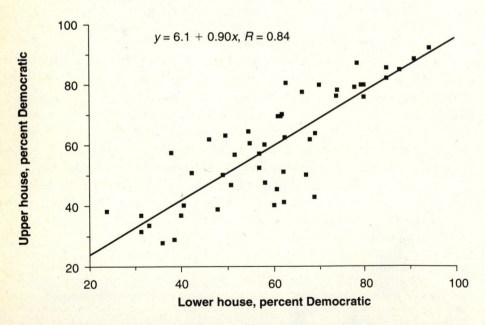

Figure 7.5 Percent Democrats in upper house vs. percent Democrats in lower house of state legislatures.

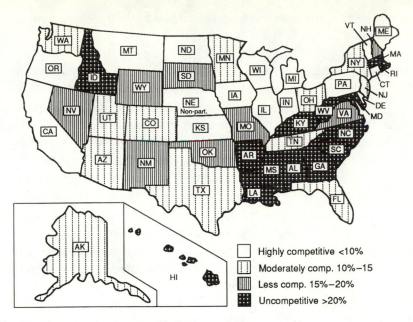

Figure 7.6   Political party competition in state legislature lower houses.

Source: U.S. Bureau of the Census, *Statistical Abstract of the United States, 1988,* Washington, DC: U.S. Government Printing Office, p. 246.

services. Nevertheless the presence of so many southern uncompetitive states can trouble our analysis.

Sources of Statewide Party Competition.   When the electorate of a state is nearly equally divided between Democrats and Republicans, the parties in the legislature are also more equally divided. We saw this situation earlier in Figure 6.10. An equal division between Democrats and Republicans within the legislature is the definition of statewide party competition. The figure therefore suggests that one source of party competition is a more nearly equal division of voters supporting each of the parties. Of course, this situation still leaves open the question of why some states have nearly equal numbers of Democrats and Republicans.

We also have seen in Figure 7.1 that party organization strength and competition are related. In interpreting that figure, however, we hesitated to say that organization results in competition, rather than the other way around. If greater competition between the parties is sought, however, party organization improvements or encouragements to do so by state government would seem likely to succeed.[28]

The Impact of Competition.   The highest correlations between competition and policies have been found in expenditure data centering on welfare payments.[29] When the political parties of a state closely compete, welfare payments are larger. Figure 7.7a shows that more-competitive states are those with higher Aid for Families with Dependent Children average monthly payments. We might expect this. A dominant political party facing no competition need not appeal to those on welfare for support. Raising AFDC or other welfare payments are an unnecessary expense to attract supporters. Southern states, being both uncompetitive and poor, may inflate this relationship. Figure 7.7b, which excludes southern states, shows the expected, much weaker pattern.

However, when we look at measures less sensitive to the wealth of the states, we find that party competition is of little importance. One example appears in Figure 7.8. The regressiveness of state and local taxes differs little with increased party competition. This area is one in which we might most expect political parties to be responsive. No pattern is shown on expenditures either. Taking state and local expenditures for each $1000 of personal income in the states removes the impact of wealth. When this is done for welfare expenditures, the correlation with competitiveness is only 0.16, again showing little or no relationship. The same is found for educational expenditures, with a correlation of 0.11; however, state and local health and hospital expenditures per $1000 personal income sharply decline with competition, with a correlation of 0.44. With the exclusion of southern states this relationship drops to 0.09.

It is plausible that party competition might force political parties and politicians to be more responsive to the wants of the electorate. There is evidence, however, to suggest that the declining importance of parties might weaken such responsiveness. The growth of primaries and the growing importance of direct mass media appeals to voters paid by individual campaign funds rather than the parties have greatly weakened political parties. Party leadership now perhaps can do little to respond to competition. Individual candidates, as a result, might well be expected to avoid appearing responsive to any one segment of constituents rather than being responsive to all. Perhaps at one time party competition or the lack of it in the South resulted in different public policies, but the evidence shows it makes little difference now.

---

28 Patterson and Caldeira, p. 702 (see note 16).

29 Tucker, p. 109 (see note 25).

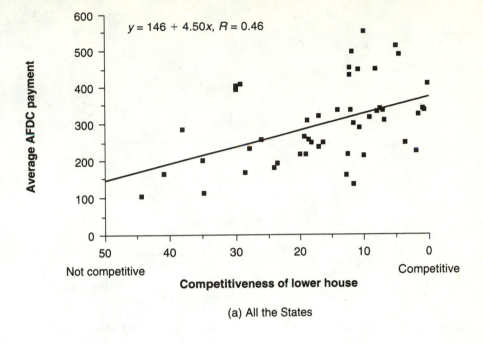

(a) All the States

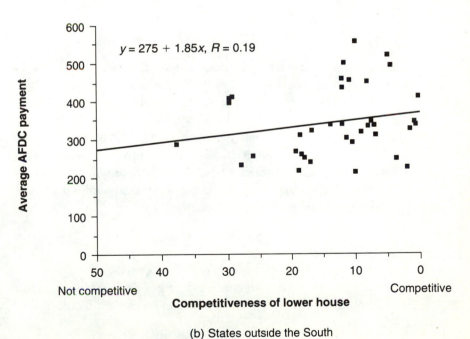

(b) States outside the South

Figure 7.7 Average AFDC payments vs. competitiveness of lower house in (a) all of the states and (b) states outside of the South.

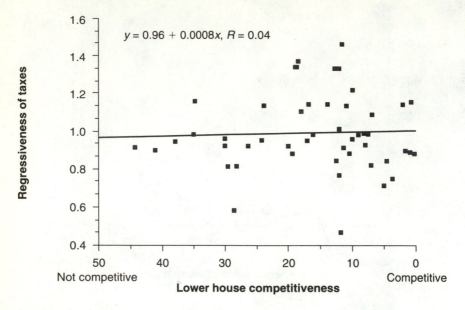

Figure 7.8   Regressiveness of state and local taxes vs. competitiveness in lower house.

Although overall state party competition would seem most likely to shape public policy, there is evidence that local competition is decreasing.[30] Statewide political party competition may be merely the coincidence of having nearly equal local areas dominated by either the Democrats or the Republicans. Since World War II, there has been little public resistance to the further weakening of the political parties. Not surprisingly, then, there is little difference between competitive states and states where only a single party dominates politics. Furthermore, the weakening of political parties may have encouraged the strengthening of interest groups.

INTEREST GROUPS

It has been hard to come to an understanding of political parties and their importance to politics in the United States. It is even more difficult to deal

---

30 Harvey J. Tucker and Ronald E. Weber, "Electoral Change in U.S. States: System Versus Constituency Competition," a paper presented at the annual meeting of the American Political Science Association, 1985.

with interest or pressure groups. It is certain that they too represent organizations of persons of similar interests and opinions to seek to influence public policy. Despite Americans' ambivalence toward political parties, few would argue that they are undemocratic, that somehow their existence compromises democracy. Perhaps they have resulted in biased public policy, inefficiency, and corruption, but since people voted freely for them, they are part of democracy. Such is not the case for pressure groups. Many people may be members of these groups, but no one votes for them. Furthermore, in reality they organize to offset popular votes since they act between elections as well.

Although it is useful to have large numbers in a pressure group, this approach has a cost because some members will not be similarly affected by policies. They might therefore obstruct group efforts on particular bills and laws. What is most useful for a pressure group is money. Ample money allows interest groups to win appreciation from candidates for substantial campaign contributions to underwrite very expensive television campaigns. Ample money allows interest groups to have full-time lobbyists present in state capitals to attend and speak at public hearings. These lobbyists can advise legislators of the group's interests and gather information concerning how other sympathetic state legislatures had coped with a problem. Or they can seek to bribe or offer free meals and entertainment to legislators to encourage their sympathetic response to the group's interests.

Some would encourage the more neutral term "interest group" rather than "pressure group." These pluralists, whom we will soon discuss, focus on the desirable aspects of interest groups. They argue that millions are either members or rely on them as reference groups, a guide to how legislation is likely to affect them. These thousands of groups work to the benefit of democracy. Such activity is seen as another form of participation, in which some people's opinions are brought to bear in making public policy. The pluralists see many channels by which the public can speak to their representatives, only one of which is through interest groups.

These interest groups also contribute information to the political process. They are likely to have more technical competence than do legislators. Although they may present only their perspective in offering this technical information to legislators at public hearings, at least that information is made available. Other groups may present other relevant technical information. Across the 50 states legislators accept the notion that such groups provide valuable technical information and thus contribute to better public policy.[31]

---

31 Clive S. Thomas and Ronald J. Hrebenar, "Interest Groups in the States," in *Politics in the American States*, 5th ed., Virginia Gray, Herbert Jacob, and Robert B. Albritton (eds.) (Glenview, IL: Scott, Foresman, 1990), p. 126.

Case studies of many states suggest that the interaction between lobbyists and legislators is more constructive in some states than in others. Some research shows Oregon to lead this ranking.[32]

The Strength of Interest Groups

Because interest groups do not stand for election, their number and relative strength in various states are uncertain. Most states register at least some groups, most often if they wish to appear in public hearings, and most states require budget information on at least the largest groups. This information, however, leaves uncertain the relative strengths of interest groups. Although groups may be asked to indicate the number of their members and even their budgets in such reports, neither of these pieces of information may determine which are most effective in getting their way. Not all states require such reports.

Informants (i.e., informed persons living in each state) also can identify which groups they think are most influential as well as whether they think groups in general have great influence in their states. In short, we have no certain knowledge about how important or strong interest or pressure groups are within any state, much less which states have the stronger groups.

Despite arguments that interest groups contribute to better public policy and to affording the public alternative avenues to affect public policy, the suspicion remains that more fundamentally they pull public policy away from what we would expect were interest groups totally absent. Basically, no one has ever found that all segments of society are equally prevalent among interest groups. Those who are wealthy, better educated, white and male, and involved in the business world are better represented by numerous interest groups.[33] Although the most effective groups in some states are public school teachers' organizations, such as those affiliated with the National Educational Association, business groups dominate the most effective ranks in most states.[34] General business organizations, such as the Chamber of Commerce, bankers' association, and manufacturers' groups, are second, third, and

---

32   L. Harmon Zeigler, "The Effects of Lobbying: A Comparative Assessment," in *Public Opinion and Public Policy*, Norman R. Luttbeg (ed.), 3rd ed. (Itasca, IL: Peacock, 1981).

33   E.E. Schattschneider, *The Semisovereign People: A Realist's View of Democracy in America* (New York: Holt, Rinehart, and Winston, 1960) and L. Harmon Zeigler, "Interest Groups in the States," in *Politics in the American States*, 4th ed. Virginia Gray, Herbert Jacob, and Kenneth N. Vines (eds.) (Boston: Little, Brown, 1983).

34   Thomas and Hrebenar, pp. 144–145.

fourth, respectively, in most states. If interest groups are effective, there seems to be little question that they do more harm than good.

Efforts to Control Pressure Groups

Not everyone would like to see pressure groups and their impact on government removed. Some see these groups as one of the many channels through which people can influence government policy. Similarly, legislators who get the bulk of their campaign funds from such groups may be hesitant to limit their effectiveness, much less to outlaw them. It should be noted also that the activities of pressure groups would probably be seen as constitutionally protected free speech.

Not surprisingly, efforts to control pressure groups have been halfhearted and largely ineffective. A pressure group, as with all individuals, cannot *bribe* an elected official to vote as the group wants. Groups can, however, offer a free meal or make contributions to campaigns with the expectation of a supportive vote being understood. Many states also require *registration* by pressure groups especially if they wish to speak before legislative committees. The public can then learn about the activity of pressure groups from those registrations, if they bother to check. Some states continue to experiment with *publicly financed campaigns* to relieve legislators from the temptation of pressure group campaign funds.[35] If candidates get funds from the state, they need not obligate themselves to pressure groups to get funds for running their campaigns. Public campaign funds, however, are sufficient to underwrite only a portion of a campaign's expense, so candidates still must seek some pressure group funds.

Perhaps pressure groups' effectiveness could be undercut by restricting their involvement in the election process. Probably this could be accomplished by restricting how much money candidates could spend in election campaigns. With the costs of new style campaigns, stressing expensive television advertisements, few candidates can resist the temptation to accept a $250,000 campaign contribution from an interest group. Even if the group makes no direct demands on the candidate accepting such funds, he or she

35 Jack L. Noragon, "Political Finance and Political Reform: The Experience with State Income Tax Checkoffs," *American Political Science Review* 75 (September 1981), pp. 667–687, and Ruth S. Jone, "State Campaign Finance: Implications for Partisan Politics," *American Journal of Political Science* 25 (May 1981), pp. 342–361.

is compromised by accepting this money. Election success will have to some degree have been paid for by this group, and it is even possible that without this group's "help," the election would have been lost. When the group next asks for a certain vote, few can resist complying.

If candidates were able to spend only $100,000 in their campaigns rather than the millions of dollars that are now spent, the limited funds needed could come with fewer strings attached. Political party and individual contributions could provide all the funds a candidate was allowed to spend. Interest groups could then not "buy" votes.

The U.S. Supreme Court has ruled that restrictions on campaign expenditures by candidates are unconstitutional, a violation of the First Amendment's freedom-of-speech clause, despite the fact all other developed democracies do restrict campaign expenditures.[36] Thus with the exception of a constitutional amendment to the effect that campaign expenditure restrictions are *not* a violation of the First Amendment, restrictions on contributions or public financing would seem the only recourse.

Congress has made some attempt to organize and limit the role of money and interest groups in election establishing a Federal Elections Commission and requiring candidates for Congress to file reports on the sources of their campaign funds and where they spent those funds. Political Action Committees (PACs) were also established. Although PACs were required to register, to provide information on their membership, and limited in how much money they could contribute to the campaign of each federal candidate, they could contribute supportive campaign activities. PACs have grown enormously and are rivals to political parties. Often they provide the majority of campaign funds to candidates, especially incumbents.[37] The purpose of these regulations may have been to limit the influence of interest groups; however, the effect has been just the opposite.

Following the lead of Congress, many states have sought to regulate contributions by requiring the formation of state PACs. Like the national efforts, these reforms have merely increased the money channeled by pressure groups to candidates. PAC spending in state elections rose from $95 million in 1972 to $400 million in 1984. PACs financed 60 percent of the campaign costs for the California Assembly in 1984 and 40 percent of the funds collected by Illinois

---

36 *Buckley* v. *Valeo* (1976).

37 Frank J. Sorauf, *Money in American Politics* (Glenview, IL: Scott, Foresman, 1988), p. 265; John F. Bibby, Cornelius P. Cotter, James L. Gibson, and Robert J. Huckshorn, "Parties in State Politics," in *Politics in the American States: A Comparative Analysis*, 5th ed., Virginia Gray, Herbert Jacob, and Robert B. Albritton (eds.) (Glenview, IL: Scott, Foresman, 1990), p. 113.

legislators in 1984–1985.[38] Such increases are commonplace throughout the states.[39]

The present restrictions on contributions from individuals and PACs for candidates seeking national offices or legislative and executive offices in most states are totally ineffective. There is no restriction on how many groups can contribute. An individual can therefore contribute unlimited funds merely by forming unlimited groups.

Several states have experimented in partial public financing. Until this financing is sufficient to require that taking public funds precludes using any additional funds, such as is true for presidential candidates, the effectiveness of such public financing remains unknown.

Political Parties Versus Pressure Groups. It has long been suggested that political parties can be an effective, perhaps the *only* effective, limitation on pressure groups.[40] If a political party had substantial influence in determining which people become its candidates and proved effective in reelecting those incumbents who followed party programs in voting, a candidate would have little to fear from pressure groups. A pressure group's threats to fail to contribute to a candidate's campaign fund or to get group members to vote against the candidate would be meaningless. The candidate could in effect show pressure groups to the door.

In evaluating this situation we have two problems. First, we have no objective measure of pressure group strength or influence. We do have a measure based on informants' assessments in states they know well.[41] It is the outgrowth of the combined research of many political scientists in a combined 50-state project.[42] A second problem is that we do not have a valid measure of political parties' ability to reelect or to be selective in its choice of candidates. We do have the measure of local party organization used earlier that would seem close to what we want.

With these measures, we can see in Table 7.1 that the pattern is the opposite of what we might expect.[43] When parties are strong, so are pressure

---

38 Thad L. Beyle, "Introduction to Politics: Parties, Interest Groups, and PACs," in *State Government: CQ's Guide to Current Issues and Activities, 1989–90,* Thad L. Beyle (ed.) (Washington, DC: CQ Press, 1989), p. 40.

39 Larry Sabato, *PAC Power* (New York: Norton, 1985).

40 E. E. Schattschneider, *Party Government* (New York: Rinehart, 1942), pp. 197–198.

41 Sarah McCally Morehouse, "Pressure Group Influence," *State Politics, Parties and Policy* (New York: Holt, Rinehart and Winston, 1981).

42 Clive S. Thomas and Ronald J. Hrebenar, "Interest Groups in the States," in *Politics in the American States,* 5th ed. Virginia Gray, Herbert Jacob, and Robert B. Albritton (eds.) (Glenview, IL: Scott, Foresman, 1990).

43 These data range from negative numbers indicating party organizational weakness to positive numbers indicating strength. For the table, those of 0.30 or greater were labeled "strong," those—0.30 or less, "weak," and "medium" in between.

Table 7.1   Republican Party Organizational Strength and Pressure Group Strength

Republican Party Strength	Dominant	Dominant/ complementary	Complementary	Complementary/ subordinant
		Pressure Group Strength		
Strong	44% (4)	33% (6)	11% (2)	20% (1)
Medium	44% (4)	33% (6)	33% (6)	0% (0)
Weak	11% (1)	33% (3)	56% (10)	80% (4)

Source: Clive S. Thomas and Ronald J. Hrebenar, "Interest Groups in the States," in *Politics in the American States*, 5th ed., Virginia Gray, Herbert Jacob, and Robert B. Albritton (eds.) (Glenview, IL: Scott, Foresman, 1990).

groups. The table shows the results for the Republican party, but Democratic party organizational strength shows the identical pattern. Party strength has no effect on limiting pressure groups. Probably the positive relationship is spurious, caused by metropolitan states with complex economies that have strong pressure groups as well as strongly organized political parties.

The Impact of Pressure Groups on Policy

The general expectation is that the existence of pressure groups throughout the United States means that business interests predominate. Nearly 60 percent of registered lobbyists represent business,[44] and they are recognized as the most influential lobbyists.[45] Among the states with weak pressure groups, however, labor assumes a more active role.[46] Our overall impression, however, is that pressure groups generally shape public policy in a direction preferred by business.[47] Other literature suggests that neither business groups nor any interest group has much success in shaping public policy as compared with others who influence public policy, such as political party and institutional leaders.[48] There is substantial variation from state to state in

---

44 L. Harmon Zeigler, "Interest Groups in the States," in *Politics in the American States: A Comparative Analysis*, 4th ed., Virginia Gray, Herbert Jacob, and Kenneth N. Vines (eds.) (Boston: Little, Brown, 1983), p. 99.

45 Wayne L. Francis, *Legislative Issues in the Fifty States: A Comparative Analysis* (Chicago: Rand McNally, 1967), pp. 44–45.

46 Zeigler, p. 103.

47 Thomas and Hrebenar, pp. 140–145.

48 Charles W. Wiggins, Keith E. Hamm, and Charles G. Bell, "Interest Group and Party Influence Agents in the Legislative Process: A Comparative State Analysis," a paper presented at the annual meetings of the American Political Science Association, 1984; and Charles W. Wiggins, "Interest Group Involvement and Success Within a State Legislative System," in *Public Opinion and Public Policy*, 3rd ed., Norman R. Luttbeg (ed.) (Itasca, IL: Peacock, 1981), pp. 226–239.

Table 7.2   Pressure Group Influence and Regressive Taxes

Regressive-ness of taxes	Pressure Group Strength			
	Dominant	Dominant/complemen-tary	Complemen-tary	Complementary/subordinant
Progressive (<0.85)	33% (3)	6% (1)	22% (4)	40% (2)
0.88–0.95	33% (3)	39% (7)	22% (4)	20% (1)
0.96–1.01	0% (0)	22% (4)	17% (3)	20% (1)
Regressive (>1.01)	33% (3)	33% (6)	39% (7)	20% (1)

Source: Clive S. Thomas and Ronald J. Hrebenar, "Interest Groups in the States,," in *Politics in the American States,*, 5th ed., Virginia Gray, Herbert Jacob, and Robert B. Albritton (eds.) (Glenview, IL: Scott, Foresman, 1990).

Table 7.3   Political Party Competitiveness and Pressure Group Influence

AFDC Average Monthly Payment	Pressure Group Impact or Strength			
	Dominant	Dominant/complemen-tary	Complemen-tary	Complementary/subordinant
Low (<$200)	0 (0)	7 (1)	0 (0)	0 (0)
$200–$300	67 (2)	36 (5)	24 (4)	20 (1)
$300–$400	0 (0)	36 (5)	53 (9)	20 (1)
High (>$400)	33 (1)	21 (3)	24 (4)	60 (3)

Source: Clive S. Thomas and Ronald J. Hrebenar, "Interest Groups in the States,," in *Politics in the American States,*, 5th ed., Virginia Gray, Herbert Jacob, and Robert B. Albritton (eds.) (Glenview, IL: Scott, Foresman, 1990).

which groups are most influential although, as stated earlier, business groups predominate.[49]

In Tables 7.2 and 7.3, we attempt our own analysis. We might well expect the middle class and business bias of pressure groups to result in regressive tax policies. Such regressive taxes would result in the middle class paying a smaller proportion of taxes. The table does show that 40 percent of the states with the weakest pressure groups have the progressive state and local taxes that we would expect pressure groups to oppose. It is the two middle

---

49 Thomas and Hrebenar, pp. 144–145.

categories of interest group impact, however, that have the most regressive state and local taxation. Knowing that southern states have at least the reputation for having strong pressure groups and have regressive taxes, we checked for the possibility that this is a spurious relationship. It is not.

Tabble 7.3 shows the relationship between average monthly AFDC payment levels and the reputed strength of pressure groups. Southern states are excluded, however, since eight of the southern states have strong pressure groups and low AFDC payments. Given the bias of interest groups to press the point of view of business, we might expect states with more dominant interest groups to succeed in holding welfare payments at a low level to keep taxes low. Even with the South excluded, this does indeed seem to be the case. The less influence interest groups have in the political process, the higher the average monthly AFDC payments. While it is beyond the scope of this text, however, a regression model including pressure group strength, competition between the political parties, and per capita income as explanations of AFDC average payments finds that all three have substantial independent impacts on the payments, with pressure group strength being the weakest relationship.

Conclusions on Pressure Groups

As noted in the introduction to interest or pressure groups, there is an absence of research concerning the importance of interest groups to policymaking. There is also uncertainty about whether they are democratic. We have not been able to justify many conclusions on these groups. Certainly they exist for a purpose. Hundreds of millions of dollars are spent each year to support these groups. It is possible that if an interest organizes and pays for a lobbyist, a rival group might feel the need to countervail by organizing itself. This situation might occur even if the first group gets no clear return on its investment in terms of favorable public policy.

There are clear examples at the national level of interest groups that seem to shape public policy effectively. They include the National Rifle Association, which has deterred restrictions on guns, and the American Medical Association, which has successfully fought a national health insurance. Certainly there has always been concern that groups, sympathetic legislators, and related state agencies work together to further the interests of the groups. Agriculture might be a good example, but there are others. With growing incumbency advantage, a group might get a high return on its investment in a young legislator. After repeated reelections, that legislator could assume a very responsible committee position dealing with matters of great concern to the group. The more systematic studies noted above, however, show much less success and even involvement with issues than what might have been expected. Interest groups' impact on our political system may be largely limited to underwriting the high cost of the modern election campaign.

The Potential for Competitive Politics

Both political parties and pressure groups are organizations that achieve the political purpose of passing desired public policies. The idea is that they reflect the politics of society, not that society is shaped by them. There is little that can be done to limit or encourage either political parties or pressure groups. The sole exception is the debilitating effects of primaries on political parties. But if we were to reverse this action, to allow parties to select their candidates by whatever means they please, would they strengthen politically? And if they did, would people whose views are underrepresented by pressure groups, such as the poor, be appealed to by at least one of the strengthened parties? Although many believe or hope so, studying the variation in the strength of political parties in the states and the variation in regulations of those parties offers little confidence in this result.

True, we have found modest support for many of the hypothesized relationships between political parties, pressure groups, and policy. The party of the poor, the Democratic party, in some analyses appears to be the advocate of that class, but often that is not the case. Competition between the political parties also fails to have clear implications of public policy. Sometimes competition appears to have an effect, but often it does not. Competitive political parties do not seem to be found in states with weaker pressure groups. Such may not have always been the case, however, since the parties may have once controlled pressure groups. It is more probable, however, that time has just changed the role of political parties.

At one time, political parties may have been perfectly adequate for representing divisions between what people in urban, mercantile areas wanted versus what people in rural, agricultural areas preferred. With economic complexity, however, subtle economic differences may be lost when there are only two or perhaps even several parties. Automotive workers, the elderly, students, or residents in states with poor health facilities may be too small in number for a political party to be concerned with either their plight or their votes. Interest groups may allow such groups to express their views, supplementing the role of political parties.

Political parties in states with competitive parties and weak pressure groups may be able to reflect political divisions within the state that do not entail the more subtle reflection of interests available through pressure groups. Again, the party and pressure group system may just reflect the politics of the state. Confidence that parties truly limit or make pressure groups less important would be helped if a state with weak political parties and strong pressure groups were to see a strengthening of political parties. If this strengthening was followed by a decline in pressure group influence and by policies better reflecting the desires of society, rather than just those of the middle class and business, we might advocate such changes for other states. We have no such example, however.

Pressure groups also may reflect, rather than shape, society. Their great activity today thus may reflect the need society has for them. Can we envision a political system with numerous pressure groups and no political parties vying in elections? It probably would look very much like a multiparty system, including the need for compromise among the multiple groups to pass policies. We might suspect that candidates would then find middle ground to appeal to more groups, win elections, seek out like-minded fellow representatives, and organize to pass policy. Those policies would be used to appeal for further voter support, by arguing that it is better to get something that they want rather than nothing. In effect, this scenario would suggest that political parties would still reappear.

SUMMARY

1. Those of like mind on the issues of the day can often overwhelm their opponents by organizing to get their supporters elected and to pass the desired policies into law. Political parties were the first such organizations, but interest groups too represent organizations formed to help enact policies.

2. At one time political parties were stronger than they are today in the United States. Political primaries and a new style of campaign using expensive television commercials paid for by interest groups have weakened political parties. There is evidence that political parties have sought to offset this by organizing the services they can provide candidates.

3. States and probably districts with nearly equal numbers of Democrats and Republicans have more competitive political parties, and improved organization results from the parties seeking to optimize their chances.

4. Interest groups also are organizations hopeful of influencing public policy to be consistent with their interests. Their interest is overwhelmingly that of business.

5. Money is one of the major sources of influence for interest groups and is mainly applied by way of contributing to the campaign funds of incumbent legislators in the hopes of getting them to feel obligated to vote as the groups want.

6. With campaign expenditure limitations being judged by the Supreme Court as unconstitutional, the main technique for controlling interest groups is lost. No other restriction is effective.

SELECTED READINGS

Beyle, Thad L., "Introduction to Politics: Parties, Interest Groups, and PACs," in *State Government: CQ's Guide to Current Issues and Activities, 1989–90,* Thad L. Beyle (ed.) (Washington, DC: CQ Press, 1989). A brief but quite current statement on parties and interest groups in the states.

Bibby, John F., Cornelius P. Cotter, James L. Gibson, and Robert J. Huckshorn, "Parties in State Politics," in *Politics in the American States: A Comparative Analysis*, 5th ed., Virginia Gray, Herbert Jacob, and Robert B. Albritton (eds.) (Glenview, IL: Scott, Foresman, 1990). A thorough study of local party organization.

Sorauf, Frank J., *Money in American Politics* (Glenview, IL: Scott, Foresman, 1988).

Thomas, Clive S., and Ronald J. Hrebenar, "Interest Groups in the States," in *Politics in the American States*, 5th ed. Virginia Gray, Herbert Jacob, and Robert B. Albritton (eds.) (Glenview, IL: Scott, Foresman, 1990). A first report on a coordinated study of interest groups in the 50 states using academics as informants in each state.

Chapter
8

The First Active Government: That at the Local Level

Today you receive substantial services from both state and national governments in addition to that from municipal government. Municipal government was the first active government. Even today, with a substantial amount of public services underwritten by the federal and state governments, it is local government that provides most of our services. Since all local governments have been found subject to state rules and actions, some might argue that they are merely administering state laws and programs. This conclusion, however, would ignore the fact that much of the cost of local government services is borne by local taxes, usually property taxes.

SERVICES OF LOCAL GOVERNMENTS

Probably the first services we think of as coming from local government are those for which it first became active. Police, fire protection, street construction and maintenance, sewage, and often drinkable water and garbage disposal are the most obvious municipal services. As Figure 8.1 shows, police, sewers, and streets constitute nearly 43 percent of city government expendi-

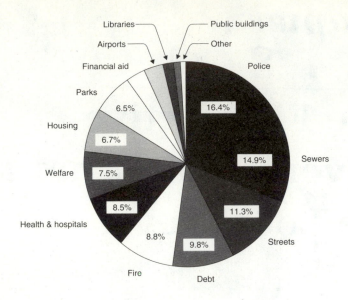

Figure 8.1   City government expenditures.

tures on the services shown. Some cities, however, provide many other services. The poor are aided with food and health care and are often provided with public housing at very low rents. Additionally, hospitals, parks and recreation, and airports are among some cities' services. Most cities also provide streetlights, sidewalks, and libraries. Public schools are normally a service provided by a separate school system. It is still the case that the government most evident in our daily lives is local government.

LOCAL GOVERNMENTS

Local government is no doubt the most complex of our government levels. You are subject to multiple local governments even if you live in the most remote rural areas. If you live in a large metropolitan area with one or more older core or central cities surrounded by multiple incorporated municipalities, you may have as many as 10 or 12 local governments, each providing you with some services. Overall, there are nearly 82,000 local governments.[1]

---

1   U.S. Bureau of the Census, *Statistical Abstract of the United States, 1988* (Washington, DC: U.S. Government Printing Office), p. 274.

The first government we will discuss is the oldest local government, *county government*. Apart from Connecticut and Rhode Island, all states have county governments, mainly to provide governmental services, such as maintaining property records, providing public health care, and maintaining roads, even in the most rural areas. There are a number of titles for the commission that governs in counties. In the Northeast, those governing the county are called the board of supervisors. Elsewhere, the title is most commonly the county commission.

Apart from a handful of quite urban counties, this commission combines the functions of both legislative and executive branches. Commissioners both pass county policies and see to their administration. Many county executives are elected, however, such as the sheriff, clerk, and tax assessor, but there is no chief executive to check and balance the commission acting as a legislative body. In some urban counties, such as Suffolk in New York, county government provides services that are more like those provided by municipalities. Many of these governments have an elected or appointed chief executive also.

There were 3042 counties in 1987, and there has been little change in this number over time. The size of the county commission varies greatly between states, with many having 50 supervisors and others having five commissioners—typically a part-time and low paying job. Since in most counties there is little for county government to do, this low pay does not discourage those interested in the satisfaction of being a commissioner.

Municipal government, or government in incorporated cities, is what we normally think of as local government. It too is a relatively old form of government adopted from England. As the oldest form of municipal government, the *mayor/council* form of government has the division between legislative and executive branches that Americans expect of government. The mayor is the executive branch and the city council the legislative branch. Some mayors have substantial formal powers, such as budget making and veto power; they are labeled *"strong" mayors*. "Weak" mayors lack these powers; often they have only a tie-breaking vote in the council.

Frequently weak mayors have other elected executives to vie with in addition to the city council. Additionally, they lack powers to influence the city's budget. These formal powers, or the lack of them, can be offset by other powers of the individuals involved. Mayor Daley's strong influence on Chicago politics during the 1950s and 1960s was achieved despite his being formally a weak mayor. Personality, political influence through organized political parties, and other informal powers can be more important than formal powers.

The mayor/council form of municipal government rests on the *checks-and-balances* ideas of how to form public policy. Cities, however, have now abandoned the bicameral or two-house form of legislature that is normally associated with the idea of checks and balances. Now the check of the second house on excesses of the first is not present in our cities, even those with mayor/council governments. What remains is the rivalry between the legislative and executive branches, checking and balancing each other in making public policy. Only those policies that both think are desirable become law. The best policy is the one that meets the approval of both the executive and the legislative branches—*policy-making by competition*. Better than half of all cities still use this form of local government, especially cities larger than 250,000 in population as well as those smaller than 10,000.[2]

The *commission* form of municipal government derives from a hurricane that hit Galveston in 1900 and the incompetence or unwillingness of the mayor and city council to clean up the damage swiftly and to restore order. A key element in this form of government is the combination of both legislative and executive roles within one institution, the city commission.

This commission, of course, is identical to the county commission. Moreover, during the peak of the reform movement, states frequently established state commissions to deal with corruption in the police department or other corrupt local services. In the municipal form, a commissioner is the representative of a district within the city, fulfilling the normal expectations of a legislator. In addition, the commissioner also serves as a department head within the executive, such as being the mayor, police chief, head of streets and sanitation, or personnel director. Since the executive and legislative are the same individuals, there is little conflict between them. The best policy now is the result of *cooperation*, not the competition of checks and balances.

For a brief period, 1900–1950, the commission form swept through many cities as a better or "reform" means of government. It proved largely unworkable, however. No one had the long-term planning responsibilities traditionally undertaken by the mayor in the mayor/council form. As a result, there was no coordination of effort, with each department head operating independently. Budget making often found commissioners supporting each other's budget requests rather than questioning the need for items on the budgets. Thus commissions were often inefficient. Only about 3 percent of all cities retain the commission form of municipal government. Overall, the commission form of municipal government can claim few successes.

The *council/manager* form of municipal government copies the form of government used in most U.S. *school district governance*. Both are based on the

---

2 *The Municipal Yearbook, 1986* (Washington, DC: International City Management Association), p. xv.

basic idea that there should be no partisan way to provide services. This notion is true whether the service is educating children or paving streets. The basic administration of both should be *professional* rather than partisan. There not only is no Democratic or Republican way to teach Johnny to read, but also no Democratic or Republican way to pave streets. The best policy is the professional one, which need not be either competitive or cooperative.

Under this form there is a publicly elected city council that appoints a professional city manager to administer municipal government during the term of his or her contract. In school governance there is a professional school superintendent who is appointed by an elected school board. Both the city manager and the school superintendent are products of university professional schools with degrees in government or education. There are national professional associations in both specialties. Since city managers and school superintendents follow careers that take them from city to city, many local residents see them as outsiders.

This form of government is used in nearly all independent school districts, in nearly half of all cities with populations between 10,000 and 250,000, and several urban counties. It is most common outside the Northeast and Midwest, where the unreformed mayor/council form predominates.[3]

No state has ever attempted to have a professional, appointed executive (akin to a city manager) and elected legislature, and most of the few large cities that tried it have returned to the mayor/council form. The professional manager is in a difficult circumstance politically because supportive council members may lose to those who are less supportive of the manager's programs. The manager is often tempted therefore to become involved in seeking the reelection of supporters. Often the manager's professional judgments as to where sewers are needed results in the loss of support in the areas that are denied such services. In short, especially in larger cities, two political parties form; one supportive of the manager and one opposed.

School superintendents run into an additional charge, that they lead the school board, with their information and claims on professional judgment, into areas that the public opposes. Because there is no rival form of government for our independent school districts, usually this opposition merely results in firing the superintendent rather than abandoning the form of government. The school superintendent and the city manager, of course, do not win elections to get their offices; they are appointed. Since such is the case, they can make no claims that the public has endorsed their programs

---

3 Paul G. Farnhorn and Stephen N. Bryant, "Forms of Local Government," *Social Science Quarterly* 66 (June 1985), pp. 386–400.

by electing them. They can make the claim of professionalism, but the elected boards can merely say the public does not support that program. Both the manager and the superintendent thus welcome supportive elected officials, but they must be most careful in encouraging their election. The professional administrator must play a balancing act between being professional and political.

City councils with city managers also have mayors, although they are not the counterparts of strong mayors under the mayor/council form. Often the major will run citywide, whereas other members of the council run in smaller districts. The mayor, however, is just a member of the city council with many symbolic functions, such as signing proclamations and greeting visitors. By way of presiding at council meetings and because of the label, mayor, the local mass media often turn to him or her to find out what is happening. This situation gives mayors unusual access to the media and enhances their influence. Table 8.1 shows the various forms of municipal government.

Nationwide a different local government typically provides for public schools. Many New England municipalities, however, do provide schools. Until recent years there were many examples of municipalities controlling schools, but the movement to independent schools is all but complete. After World War II there were more than 100,000 school districts in the United States. With the steady increase in urbanization after the war, many rural districts lost school attendance and consolidated with surrounding rural districts. Thus by 1962 we had only about 35,000 school districts. This decline bottomed out by 1977 with about 15,000 districts.

Special districts, by contrast, are becoming more numerous. These districts deal with limited services, such as mosquito abatement, soil conservation, public transit, water supply, and recreation. Typically the governance of these districts is a *confederacy,* with multiple municipalities joining together to form a central government to provide the special service only. Each municipality has a single vote in the governance of these districts, with the right to secede

Table 8.1   Attributes of Different Forms of Municipal Government

Mayor/council	Commission	Manager/council
Checks and balances between legislative and executive	Executive and legislative the same	Appointed executive and elected legislative
Mayor with formal powers	Symbolic mayor only	Symbolic mayor only
Also used by state and federal governments	Also used by county government	Originated in school government
Competition to make public policy	Cooperation to make public policy	Professional public policy

with advance notice. The public has no say in most special district governance, except through the city council member who serves on the special district board of governance. As we shall see when we discuss metropolitan problems, special districts provide one solution to the fragmentation of most of our metropolitan area governments. At any rate, the 12,340 special districts in 1952 grew to more than 29,000 in 1987.[4]

THE MACHINE AND REFORM

As we saw earlier, U.S. cities experienced tremendous growth and troubles under the twin forces of industrialization and immigration. New industries needed a work force. Given the lack of transportation available in the late 1800s and early 1900s, sufficient workers could be found only in growing urban areas. Immigration brought a willing and substantial work force to our cities.

When the political machine—or, perhaps more accurately, the "ward heelers"—organized immigrants so as to gain control of municipal governments and to provide urban services, the counterorganization of reformers won support from state courts for the idea that cities were the creations of the states—Dillon's rule. Through this interpretation, charters were forced on municipalities, sharply restricting their powers. Various imposed reforms were intended mainly to disable the machines and to return power to proper persons.

There are many elements to these reforms. We have already discussed some of these. Probably foremost was the state-provided Australian ballot, or *secret ballot,* as the only lawful way to cast one's vote. Until that time any way of indicating one's voting preferences had been accepted as a legal ballot, including precast ballots by political machines. Poll watchers for the machines could watch patronage workers cast these precast ballots to ensure that they voted correctly. With the secret ballot and secrecy in the casting of one's vote, no one could now know how a person voted. This practice disabled the machine's ability to be certain that its supporters did indeed support the candidates of the machine.

The *primary elections* also hurt the machine. Voters in the primary, rather than party leaders, chose the candidates. The careful balancing of the slate of candidates to attract support from all ethnic elements in the machine's coali-

---

4   All statistics on the number of governments are taken from the *Statistical Abstract of the United States, 1988*, p. 256.

tion was lost with this reform. Of course it also disabled the political party from excluding candidates whose issue positions were at odds with those generally accepted by that party. The primary election thus muddied the meaningful distinction between who is a Democrat and who is a Republican. Overall, the primary takes candidate selection out of the hands of political parties and thereby weakens them.

Nonpartisan elections, with candidates not identifiable by a party label, were intended to make it difficult for less-literate and less-involved machine supporters to know how to vote and perhaps even to discourage their voting at all.[5] The illiterate could no longer vote for the donkey or the elephant candidates. The requirement of *literacy* to vote furthered this effort. Presently more than 70 percent of all American cities elect their councils and commissions on nonpartisan ballots; only the Middle Atlantic states holdout for partisan elections.[6]

The *merit system* of selecting public employees was intended to disable the machine's awarding public jobs to those supporting the machine. In a merit system, public jobs have job descriptions and associated competency tests. Candidates judged competent receive jobs with no consideration of their party affiliation. Workers under the machine were expected to give up to 10 percent of their earnings back to the party organization that helped underwrite the expense of running that effort. Obviously, civil service employees owe nothing to the political parties for their jobs and, not unexpectedly, contribute little to the political parties. In fact, many states discourage political involvement by civil service employees.

The *strong-mayor* form of municipal government, with the mayor having many appointed positions, was also a part of the reform movement. This practice clarified who was responsible for government actions. It also better protected important agency heads, such as the police chief, from politics by making them appointed. With fewer officials to elect, the ballot would be shorter, so this reform is often referred to as the *short-ballot* reform. Later both the commission form of government, with less competition between the legislative and executive branches, and the professionalism of the city manager in the *manager/council* form of government were advocated by reformers.

---

5 Carol A. Cassel, "Social Background Characteristics of Nonpartisan City Council Members: A Research Note," *Western Political Quarterly* 38 (September 1985), pp. 493–501. Also see Eugene C. Lee, *Nonpartisan Politics* (Berkeley: University of California Press, 1960); and Susan Welch and Timothy Bledsoe, "The Partisan Consequences of Nonpartisan Elections," *American Journal of Political Science* 30 (February 1986), pp. 128–139.

6 Heywood T. Sanders, "The Government of American Cities: Continuity and Change in Structure," *The Municipal Yearbook, 1982* (Washington, DC: International City Management Association), pp. 178–186.

Finally, *at-large elections*, in which all members of the city council or commission are elected citywide, were intended to weaken the ability of ward heelers to provide local services in order to ensure local election. Political leaders in the South used at-large elections even more effectively to assure that blacks won no elections. Blacks, who were a concentrated minority, might have been able to win in a district in which they were the majority, but they could not win citywide contests. Even today, at-large elections to a substantial degree deny blacks, and probably other minorities, the representation on city councils that would be expected given their percentage in the community.[7] Federal courts have forced district elections both on city councils and, more recently, on school boards.

Obviously the political machine died in U.S. cities. There is a question, however, as to whether the reforms were responsible. The machines may have not been viable to begin with, as immigrants swiftly acculturated into U.S. society and moved past the need for the organization provided by the machine. It is also unclear whether reformers won back control of the cities. Since the cities had changed much over this period, city leaders after the machines were unlike those that the machines had overthrown. The machine, however, was clearly not all bad.[8] The reformers' efforts may, indeed, have taken municipal government away from the public and made it less democratic.[9]

CITY HOME RULE

There is little question that the notion of cities as the creations of their state government, captured in Dillon's rule, displeased city governments. They have continued to seek greater independence from state laws. *Home rule* has been the sought-after goal. Basically home rule is a state legislative act saying that Dillon's rule does not apply to this particular city. The city is authorized to shape its government form and to provide municipal services as it sees fit, without getting approval of the legislature.

---

7 Albert K. Karnig, "Black Representation on City Councils," *Urban Affairs Quarterly* 12 (December 1976), pp. 223–243; and Thomas R. Dye and Theodore P. Robinson, "Reformism and Black Representation on City Councils," *Social Science Quarterly* 59 (June 1978), pp. 801–829.

8 Robert K. Merton, *Social Theory and Social Structures* (Glencoe, IL: Free Press, 1957); and Edward C. Banfield, *Political Influence* (Glencoe, IL: Free Press, 1962).

9 Although there certainly have been no definitive assessments, see Susan Blackall Hansen, "Participation, Political Structure and Concurrence," *American Political Science Review* 69 (December 1975), pp. 181–199; and Robert Presthus, *Men at the Top* (New York: Oxford University Press, 1964).

Although many cities have won home rule, the description above is more of an idealized or totally free home rule than the reality of how it exists in most cities. Most cities with the good fortune to have home rule charters are only somewhat more free to act as they want than they were when still subject to general charter provisions and Dillon's rule.

The politics of home rule are not unlike those surrounding city machine politics earlier. Rural areas and the more well-to-do segments within cities oppose freeing cities to provide services and to raise taxes. There are few studies to assess the impact of home rule; and because of its many varieties, such research would be most difficult. Because most cities' success in winning home rule are at best only partial, the victory is largely symbolic. In practice, home rule does not matter in terms of the services provided, tax levels, or quality of life in U.S. cities.

METROPOLITAN DIFFICULTIES

Following World War II, there was an explosion of movement by American families. Some moved from the rural South to the urban North seeking jobs. Probably the most significant movement, however, was from the older and decaying neighborhoods of central cities to newly developed residential areas surrounding those cities—what became known as the *suburbs*. The availability of the *automobile* and the *long-term graduated repayment mortgage*— with the federal government guaranteeing repayment for veterans—made it possible to move to the suburbs. It was the middle class that could afford such a move, and move they did in great numbers.

The areas to which they moved with increasing population concentrations were swiftly pressed to provide municipal services, such as schools, better streets, sewers, and water supplies. Most states provided for easy organization of such areas as new municipalities (a process called incorporation). Most states also discourage annexation by municipalities of urban concentration around them. So, with the exception of Texas, where incorporation is difficult and annexation easy, older cities were surrounded by substantial numbers (often many hundreds) of small, newly incorporated suburban municipalities.

Because of their substantial number and diversity, one could shop for a suburb that most closely corresponded to one's personal characteristics. One could seek a well-to-do Jewish community, a less well-to-do Jewish community, a middle-class Polish community, or an Italian community. Nearly all of these communities, however, lacked the size or wealth to deal with many of the problems that they soon faced. Where was an adequate water supply to be found? Where was the money to build a new high school? How was sewage to be disposed of? Who would pay for new arterial highways to speed workers into the city where they worked? We refer to these numerous but insufficiently large governments in suburban areas as *fragmented governments*. They typically result in inadequate municipal services provided at high expense. Most avoid redistributive services. The poor are in another municipality that is too poor to provide any services. In such a case, unless the state undertakes redistributive services, there are none between the wealthy and poor municipalities, even if they are adjacent.

Texas allows municipalities to annex surrounding areas by a simple majority vote of the city council doing the annexation. This annexation can be up to 15 percent of their present geographic areas each year. Furthermore, each city can announce its intent to move into an area extending out 5 miles in any direction, and no incorporation is allowed within that area. One solution to the fragmentation in metropolitan areas evident in most states is to do what Texas does. Unfortunately, the time to have done so has long passed.

A second recommended, but little followed, solution was city/county consolidation. Many U.S. cities and counties held votes to do so, but most lost.[10] The idea was simple. Since most of these fragmented municipal governments and the central city that they surrounded were in a single county, that county government could be made more like one big municipality. Of course a metropolitan area, such as Atlanta, that is in multiple counties could not be so helped, nor could metropolitan areas overlapping into several states or even into another country. City/county consolidations no longer have devotees.

Certainly the racial integration questions involved in joining white suburban areas with black core city areas, the unwillingness of suburban whites to see their tax money paying for central city facilities, and just simple hostility toward the central city and its politics that fueled the reform movement all contributed to the failure of this solution.[11] It should be noted that such a consolidation would have made municipal government larger and more remote, and this situation too may have motivated opponents. Also with fragmented government, one can easily get fed up with one municipal government or school system and move to where one prefers the policies. As mentioned in an earlier chapter, this practice is called voting with your feet.

10 John C. Bollens, Henry J. Schmandt, et al. *Exploring the Metropolitan Community* (Berkeley: University of California Press, 1961); and Philip B. Coulter (ed.), *Politics of Metropolitan Areas* (New York: Crowell, 1967).

11 For a discussion and analysis see Scott Greer, *Metropolitics* (New York: Wiley, 1963); and Vincent L. Marando and Carl Whitley, "City-County Consolidation: An Overview of Voter Response," *Urban Affairs Quarterly* 8 (December 1972), pp. 181–203.

The primary solution apart from just living with fragmentation has been to join in *special districts*. When multiple suburban municipalities join together in a water, sewer, recreation, or transit district, they have the scale to deal with the problem financially. The geographic area that they cover also may be sufficient to deal with many problems, such as finding a waste disposal site or a way to dispose of effluent from sewage. As we saw earlier, special districts have proliferated since the 1950s.

Special districts and more ad hoc solutions, such as metropolitan planning agencies and councils of government, have partially coped with our fragmented cities. Nevertheless, it still is the case that most metropolitan areas barely cope with day-to-day problems. Most metropolitan residents complain about congestion, poor or nonexistent services, such as a lack of sidewalks or streetlights, and high government expense. Nothing is organizationally on the horizon that would alleviate this situation.

DEMOCRACY IN LOCAL GOVERNMENT

In Chapter 6, which deals with how people vote, we noted that there has been no systematic study of how people vote in local elections for the city council, school board, or county commission. We do know from aggregate information, such as the number of votes cast and simple mass media accounts, that participation and involvement are low in such elections. We are most informed by studies of activists as to the state of democracy in local elections. Our information here comes from four sources: (1) several surveys by the Council of City Managers; (2) a study of city council members in 87 San Francisco Bay area councils; (3) a study of 35 Texas cities' city councils and school boards; and (4) the community power structure literature.

Local Elections. The International City Management Association has several times solicited questionnaire responses from cities concerning their city council and mayoral elections as well as on turnout in such local elections. Incumbent advantage is evident in U.S. cities, since 72 percent of incumbents seek reelection and 78 percent of them win; mayors have slightly less success.[12] Later data show that 63 percent of incumbent mayors seek reelection and 85 percent win.[13]

---

12   Albert K. Karnig and B. Oliver Walter, "Municipal Elections: Registration, Incumbent Success, and Voter Participation," *The Municipal Yearbook, 1977* (Washington, DC: International City Management Association, 1977), p. 66.

13   Edward C. Page and Harold Wolman, "Mayoral Profiles," *The Municipal Yearbook, 1987* (Washington, DC: International City Management Association, 1987).

Nearly all (83 percent) of local elections are held at a time other than that for state and national elections. As a result, turnout is low (21 percent for council seats only and 33 percent for the election of the mayor).[14] Overall there would appear to be little potential for electoral accountability in our cities. Few vote and incumbents overwhelmingly win.

Most city council members serve with little or no pay. Only in the largest cities can one make a living as a city council member. Council members devote several evenings a week, for a two- or four-year term, to their duties. Certainly there is prestige associated with being called "his honor" or "her honor" or just "councilwoman" or "councilman." Everywhere you go, however, people take exception to council actions or lobby you for future actions. Many citizens feel it is their right to call you throughout the night to complain about garbage pick-up or annoying neighbors. Additionally, many smaller cities cannot afford to buy insurance protection for you in case you are sued for actions of the council, and thus you are held personally responsible for any awards granted by courts. Perhaps so few run because it is thankless. Were it not the case that state legislators and members of Congress also have weak opponents and seldom lose, we might suggest that the thanklessness of the job accounts for election results in our cities.

Volunteers. The San Francisco Bay area study is the most inclusive yet undertaken. It has two shortcomings, however. First, it centers on the overall characteristics of the 87 communities involved, ignoring variations. Second, California is probably unrepresentative of the United States. In New England, municipalities have responsibilities across a very broad range of services including public education. As one goes west and south, municipal governments shed services to special districts—beginning with education, as independent school districts are established.[15] California, with its sprawling suburbanization, represents the culmination of this trend; few services remain for municipal government, making serving on a city council largely symbolic. Thus perhaps the most striking finding from this study, the eagerness of city council members to leave office, is explained by the irrelevancy of those offices.

Among the Bay area council members, most initially were involved in voluntary civic roles where we do not expect public accountability. Rather it is civic duty that drives people's involvement in activities, such as serving on the United Fund, or the zoning board.[16] About 12 percent run for office to repay the

---

14 Karnig, p. 69.

15 Roland J. Liebert, "Municipal Functions, Structures and Expenditures: A Reanalysis of Recent Research," *Social Science Quarterly* 54 (December 1974), pp. 765–783.

16 Kenneth Prewitt, *The Recruitment of Political Leaders: A Study of Citizen-Politicians* (Indianapolis: Bobbs-Merrill, 1970), p. 89.

community for their successful businesses. About one-fourth are initially appointed, 80 percent win reelection, and given low turnouts so few votes are necessary to win that an extended circle of friends can win the election for a candidate.[17] Finally, only about half say they will again seek office and most who do will seek only one additional term to complete a project.[18] These council members seem mainly "volunteers," who seldom face electoral challenge and who are unlikely to feel any obligation to constituents. They are only in office out of civic duty. Lacking ambition both for reelection and for higher office, they seem beyond public accountability.

Were all of these characteristics to apply to other elected officials, we might question whether democracy can function. It seems unlikely, however, that there is so little ambition for continuing in public office or moving up to higher offices in state legislatures or in the halls of Congress. It may well be that these cities are unrepresentative of others across the country. Local officials thus might be the least-responsive elected officials—certainly not what we might expect from the government that is closest to the people.

Competition at the Local Level. Certainly a study of Texas local elections in 1985 found that members of city councils and school boards were not all volunteers.[19] Perhaps what was most surprising in this study is the variation shown in Table 8.2. Using multiple assessments of the degree of competition experiences in these communities, we can certainly see that some experience competition. Council members in one city won narrowly with only 52 percent of the vote, while one school board's candidates won 99 percent of the vote, hardly competitive. Although not all council and board members are up for election at the same time, some communities had new people in those seats up for reelection and others had all incumbents returning. These results, of course, represent maximum and minimum change in the council or board.

The number of contesting candidates on average per seat who were up for election also varied greatly. All incumbents ran in one school district and faced no opponents. Another had an average of 5.5 candidates per seat. Finally, turnout varied from 1 percent of eligible adults voting to nearly 32 percent. On average in these city council elections, only 13 percent voted, which is

---

17   Prewitt, pp. 131, 137, 147.

18   Prewitt, pp. 180–181.

19   Norman R. Luttbeg, "Multiple Indicators of the Electoral Context of Democratic Responsiveness in Local Government," a paper presented at the annual meeting of the Midwest Political Science Association, 1987.

Table 8.2   Measures of Electoral Competition in 37 Cities

	City council			School board		
	Min.	Max.	Mean	Min.	Max.	Mean
Average winning percent of vote	52%	95%	70%	34%	99%	68%
Change as a percent of possible change	0%	100%	34%	0%	100%	51%
Percent of incumbents seeking reelection	0%	100%	74%	0%	100%	68%
Percent of incumbents winning	0%	100%	84%	0%	100%	79%
Candidates per seat	1.2	5.5	2.4	1.0	5.0	2.1
Eligible adults voting	3.3%	31.7%	12.6%	1.0%	22.6%	8.7%
Average number of years of present council or board	0.8	8.6	2.8	0	7.1	4.1
Percent turnover in last 9 years	10%	34%	20%	5%	37%	15%

substantially below the 31 percent reported in the Bay area study and 33 percent in the national study.[20] As we have seen, Texans are low participators in state and national elections. Thus it would be no surprise to find them low participators in local elections.

Since overall 74 percent of incumbent council members and 68 percent of school board members seek reelection and 84 percent and 79 percent respectively won reelection, there is little electoral challenge or competition evident on the whole. It might be expected that some communities would show competition across these measures while others lacked competition. Such was not the case, for several reasons. First, many of the measures proved only poorly correlated, resulting in some communities having few incumbents seeking reelection and thus much change in who was on the council, and many candidates seeking the open seats. Second, other communities had many incumbents seeking reelection and losing with high turnout. Finally, others had long-tenured councils. School boards show equal but somewhat different patterns. Surprisingly, those cities with competition for city councils lacked it for school boards.

The variation evident in this study is encouraging because it might allow us to assess how competition might be increased and to determine the impact of competitive political systems. Although overall competition may not be evident, there are some communities that do enjoy it. Moreover, the com-

---

20 Heinz Eulau and Kenneth Prewitt, *Labyrinths of Democracy* (Indianapolis: Bobbs-Merrill, 1973); and Karnig and Walter.

plexity of competition suggests that political science conceptually lacks a full understanding of what is important. Do we want to encourage incumbents to seek reelection with the resulting dearth of challengers and low turnout but with occasional losses? Or do we want to discourage reelection efforts, thereby promoting many open seats and higher turnout? Furthermore, what can account for the negative relationships between city council competition and school board competition? Weak evidence from this study suggests that better-educated communities and those with substantial Hispanic minorities have competitive school district elections but pay little attention to city council elections. Why?

COMMUNITY POWER STUDIES

We have already come across several concerns over the role of the public in a democracy. Some are concerned about the general public's being too participant—particularly with regard to the more violent forms of participation, such as revolution and assassination. We have seen also the anxieties created by immigrants organizing into urban machines at the turn of the century. There are many who would not want a democracy in which the public plays a more active role than it now plays.

The voting studies, for example, found an unwillingness on the part of most voters to spend much time in the process of choosing candidates. Only the strong partisans proved interested in political campaigns and informed, and they could not be persuaded to vote other than for their political party. This disinterest and less than avid monitoring of elected officials may afford those officials the latitude that they need to compromise in making public policy. Frequently the less favorable term, "masses," is substituted for the public in such discussions about the public's role in democracy.

People who make decisions that government imposes on us also have their detractors, who see these decisions shaped by personal self-interest rather than by the public's interest. They pejoratively refer to these decision makers as the "elite." We have seen the public playing a very limited role in governing. Legislators, political parties, and pressure groups cope with problems of their state, with only occasional public interest and input. Some would like the public to be more active in protecting its interest while reducing the elite's role. Others want no change that would excite the masses into potential excesses.

Much, but certainly not all, of the controversy evident in these contrary perspectives derives from case studies of certain U.S. communities. What is studied is not just what the city council or mayor did. Rather the overall process is studied, including all who are involved. Such studies include those who are not elected to public office but nevertheless are influential in the decisions that are made. These decisions include not only those made by the city council and school board. Additionally, banks' willingness to lend money to local government and local industries' benefiting from governmental decisions and seeking to influence elected officials are all part of the scenario. Undertaking so inclusive a study at the state or national level would be unmanageable, although it has been tried.[21]

What is being attempted in these studies is a characterization of the cities studied, as open or closed. Those that are *open* give the public ample opportunity to shape decisions, but in *closed* communities only a select few make decisions that influence all. Athough it would seem obvious that there must be gradations between open- and closed-community decision making, most of the studies seem to view cities only as a dichotomy, either open or closed. It is also assumed that the *power* or *influence* to make a decision may not rest with elected officials. This assumption is an awkward, but obvious, one. We would certainly expect those who lend money to politicians seeking election to expect a say on important issues if those candidates are elected. This expectation would be characteristic of pressure groups, party leaders, and even those whose advice is sought or at least willingly received. Public policy is made by those elected to public office, but certainly others have a great amount of influence. This assumption is awkward, although while it is easy to identify who holds public office, it is not easy to identify those with influence or power outside the halls of government. The methodology for doing so itself is controversial.

Stratificationists. This is a clumsy word, but others that have been used, such as elite theorists, elitists, critics of democracy, are even less satisfactory. Researchers had earlier studied cities and frequently found persons of substantial wealth dominated in both small and large cities. Floyd Hunter's studies of Atlanta, Georgia, in his book *Community Power Structure*, however, provided the spark for a brief flurry of what are called community power studies.[22] Hunter's method for identifying those who influenced decisions, even if not in public office, was to ask informants who had influence as they saw it. This became known as the *reputational method*. In Atlanta using this method, he identified the president of Coca-Cola as the most

---

21 C. Wright Mills, *The Power Elite* (New York: Oxford University Press, 1956); and G. William Domhoff, *Who Really Rules?* (Santa Monica: Goodyear, 1978).

22 Floyd Hunter, *Community Power Structure* (Chapel Hill: University of North Carolina Press, 1953).

influential person, with several others, all leaders of local businesses, nearly as influential.[23] He argued that there was a *hierarchy of power,* with a few in the top stratum having great influence and wealth, the *elite,* and many at the bottom having little of either, the *masses.*

Only well down in this influence hierarchy did he find public officeholders, such as the mayor. Those with influence groomed the elected officials.[24] Those at the top stratum of power were all businessmen, chiefly concerned with their own interests. In effect democracy, or its institutions and the public's use of those institutions, was a sham; government was influenced by an elite that was neither publicly responsible nor *accountable.* How could the public get to the president of Coca-Cola for a bad decision; buy Pepsi? What was necessary to improve Atlanta was change. Democracy would have to come to Atlanta.[25]

Most typically, researchers of this perspective are called elite theorists or elitists. Although they certainly see an elite dominating government, they certainly do not approve. Calling them elitists therefore is inappropriate because this term might be taken to mean that they approve of elitism. Most important, they see social strata in society based fundamentally on wealth, see political decisions as dominated by the upper strata, and see decisions as serving those interests. This concept of social strata therefore results in our label.

Pluralists.   The charge that democracy anywhere was a sham motivated political scientists to consider whether their studies of democratic institutions were sufficient to understand U.S. democracy. They questioned the validity of the reputation method, however, as forcing informants to say that someone had influence and dealing with the reputation rather than the reality of influence. Of course, they too could not study the reality of influence. Instead in a study of New Haven, Connecticut, Robert Dahl investigated, in newspaper accounts and with interviews, how decisions in three areas were made.[26] This method is referred to as the *decisional technique.* On each of the three decisions there was a hierarchy of influence, with an influential few at the top.

---

23   Hunter, p. 64.

24   Hunter, p. 200.

25   Two additional studies of Atlanta suggest that at least that community has changed for the better: M. Kent Jennings, *Community Influentials: Elites of Atlanta* (New York: Free Press, 1964); and Clarence N. Stone, *Regime Politics: Governing Atlanta 1944–1988* (Lawrence: University Press of Kansas, 1989).

26   Robert A. Dahl, *Who Governs?* (New Haven: Yale University Press, 1961).

Dahl thought it was significant that there were three distinct hierarchies. If one hierarchy should become undemocratic, the others could appeal to the public as alternatives. With multiple hierarchies or elites, there is *competition among elites*. Community conflict and the *loss of stability,* Dahl felt, would hurt a community more than the lack of competition among activist elites.[27] Certainly no change was necessary in New Haven in his view. Those living in New Haven could always "take up the slack" in the system by becoming more active if they were dissatisfied with one or more of the governing elites. Dahl thought he had dispelled the unfavorable criticism leveled by Hunter. In his review of Dahl's *Who Governs?*, Hunter suggests that New Haven is just like Atlanta. Businessmen and their personal interests govern in both.[28] Stratifications were little persuaded by the research of the pluralists, nor vice versa.

The study of decisions rather than the reputation for influence has been criticized as ignoring *nondecisions*.[29] If an influential person can keep an issue from even arising, keeping the issue as a nondecision, that person must have substantial influence. The decisional technique ignores such influence. Presumably informants in the reputational technique would be aware of such influence.

The idea that power and influence in society rest in a large number of centers gives the pluralists their name. Each center of power might compete with another and thereby spur public interest. When power to make decisions is so distributed, pluralists are less likely to see decisions as made by upper strata in their own self-interest. Also the stability of American democracy is preserved. Table 8.3 enumerates several distinctions between the pluralist and stratificationist perspectives.

Other Sources of Pluralistic Thinking.   In the last chapter of *Voting*, Berelson comes to the conclusion that the U.S. voter fails to satisfy the criteria for democratic voters. Ideally they are to be active or participant, informed, and rational in choosing between candidates for public office.[30] But Americans are not. To use his words, the democratic practice falls short of the expectations of democratic theory. Somewhat surprisingly, he would suggest

27   James S. Coleman, *Community Conflict* (Glencoe, IL: Free Press, 1957).

28   Floyd Hunter, "A review of *Who Governs?*" *Administrative Science Quarterly* (March 1962).

29   Peter Bachrach and Morton C. Baratz, "Decisions and Nondecisions," *American Political Science Review* 57 (September 1963), pp. 632–642.

30   Bernard R. Berelson, Paul F. Lazarsfeld, and William N. McPhee, *Voting* (Chicago: University of Chicago Press, 1954), pp. 305–323.

Table 8.3 Pluralist and stratificationist perspectives

Pluralists	Stratificationists
Study decisions	Study influence
Competition among elites important	Strata of decision makers important
Stability of democracy important	Accountability in democracy important
Maintain status quo	Change is necessary
The public is not democratic	An elite is undemocratic
Public can become more participant	Public plays no role

that what is wrong is the theory not the practice. What is needed is balance, he argues.

He sees voters as heterogeneous, with some more intemperate, some more involved, and some indifferent. The distribution of actual U.S. voters shown in Figure 8.2 is superior to a society of what he calls "ideological man." Such voters would have the desirable attributes of being participant and informed along with the undesirable attributes of being rigid and prone to violence in the event of losing a public decision.[31] They would vote as democratic theory expects but would ultimately destroy democracy. The rejection of democratic theory and preference for the practice puts this statement in the pluralist camp. It adds the idea of a balance between those ideologically involved and those indifferent to the pluralist perspective.

Another concern arose from the rise of Nazism in Germany. Was the public there responsible for it happening and could it happen in other democracies, especially in the United States? An *authoritarian personality* was conceived as responsible for Nazi growth. Such a personality was subservient to authority when subject to it and demanding of being obeyed when superordinate. To assess this, researchers developed a fascism or "F" scale.[32] *Example "agree" or "disagree" questions are:*

1. Obedience and respect for authority are the most important virtues children should learn.
2. If people would talk less and work more, everybody would be better off.
3. What this country needs most, more than laws and political programs, is a few courageous, tireless, devoted leaders in whom the people can put their faith.

---

31 Berelson, p. 323.

32 T.W. Adorno, Else Frenkel-Brunswik, Daniel J. Levinson, and R. Nevitt Sanford, *The Authoritarian Personality* (New York: Harper and Brothers, 1950).

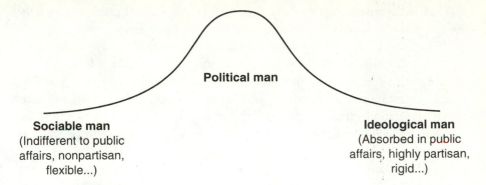

Political man

Sociable man
(Indifferent to public
affairs, nonpartisan,
flexible...)

Ideological man
(Absorbed in public
affairs, highly partisan,
rigid...)

Figure 8.2   Distribution of U.S. voters.

Persons who agreed with these statements were labeled "authoritarians." They tend to be less educated and from lower social strata. Since decision makers come from upper strata, these findings further raise the concern about changing the practice of democracy or the public's role in the United States or in any democracy.

Later studies, which reversed the questions, now requiring a "disagree" response to be giving the authoritarian response, found the upper social strata to be the authoritarians. Merely reversing the meaning of the question by substituting a "no" reversed the conclusion as to who was authoritarian! The only explanation for this is that those interviewed paid little or no attention to the content of the questions. Rather the better educated had a "response style" of disagreeing to any statement. The less educated too had a "response style" of agreeing to all statements. In effect, the study is meaningless.[33] Regardless, however, it set the tone for viewing the general public with suspicion.

Other studies have also suggested that the less educated public is more dangerous than the better educated elite and cautioned against changing our democracy to be more responsive to the public.[34] This authoritarian study

---

33   If a different set of individuals is identified by a question merely by changing whether an agree or disagree response is needed, it suggests strongly that there is a response style with some agreeing with questions regardless of the content of the question and others disagreeing. See Angus Campbell, Philip E. Converse, Warren E. Miller, and Donald E. Stokes, *The American Voter* (New York: Wiley, 1960), p. 512.

34   Seymour Martin Lipset, *Political Man: The Social Bases of Politics,* expanded ed. (Baltimore: Johns Hopkins University Press, 1981), pp. 87–126; Samuel A. Stouffer, *Communism, Conformity, and Civil Liberties* (New York: Wiley, 1966).

and follow-ups that suggest there is danger in the general public, especially the less educated, contributed to the credibility of pluralism.

Stratificationists have greater confidence in the public. They may concede that now the public may rashly support undemocratic ideas, such as denying certain minorities' freedom of speech.[35] If the public were asked to vote on more meaningful matters, such as offering clear choices among candidates or even to make public policy directly, the public's tendency to be undemocratic might lessen—that is, its "civic health" might improve.[36] If they participate more and have contact with persons of opposing views, they may learn tolerance of those views. They may realize that opponents are not evil, as well as learning that sometimes they may lose but at other times win.

An ultimate question separating the pluralists and the stratificationists then seems to be what would happen were the public to become more participant. The pluralists see no good coming from greater participation and the stratificationists see an improved electorate. There is evidence that more participant portions of the electorate are more tolerant and informed. Unfortunately, there are no research findings to suggest that persons who are somehow spurred to greater participation will change as a result of that participation. Also, these concerns are clearly not limited to our local governments.

A study of how decisions are made and who has influence at the state level would, however, be a major undertaking. Since there has been no demonstration either that the decision-making or reputational method is valid, it would seem desirable to use both. Following state decisions in newspaper accounts, however, would seem insufficient, and thus informants would seem necessary even if specific decisions are studied. In Chapter 7, we discussed a study of the reputation of interest group impact in the 50 states using political scientists knowledgeable in their individual states. The same methodology could be used in a study of who has influence in the states. Of course, the same concern about whether the informant is truly informed would still hold.

The results of such a study would, as was the case in the interest group impact study, be a classification of states. Some might well be expected to have elected officials, such as the governor and legislative officers, exercising their authority in confronting the state's problems. Other states, however, might see nonelected individuals shaping the state's actions. From the

---

35 James W. Prothro and Charles W. Grigg, "Fundamental Principles of Democracy," *Journal of Politics* 22 (June 1960), pp. 276–294.

36 Jack L.Walker, "A Critique of the Elitist Theory of Democracy," *American Political Science Review*, 60 (June 1966), pp. 285–295.

perspective of what we expect of a democracy, the latter states would be called "undemocratic" or at least "less democratic." The former states would be labeled "democratic" or perhaps "more democratic."

In many respects such a study would duplicate the study of the impact of interest groups. Probably the majority of influence on state legislators and executives is by way of interest groups. But there is the additional question of more direct influence, exercised privately over the telephone or at private meetings. At any rate, there are no such studies.

COMPARING LOCAL GOVERNMENTS

As we have seen and will further consider, there are major problems with comparing state governments. For one thing the South is different, but for unclear reasons. It is poor, traditionalistic, and, until recently, uncompetitively Democratic. This situation leaves many relationships uncertain. We cannot, for example, be sure that a tie between party competition and higher levels of services means that party competition results or causes higher service levels. Since the South is uniquely low in both, perhaps only the Civil War and the South's poverty explain what only appears to be a relationship. Perhaps it is spurious.

Also comparing the states limits us to the small differences that are evident between the states. Cities, or more correctly municipalities, vary more than states. Just to use the service levels and competition discussed above, we can find cities that provide very few services and those providing very extensive services. Just considering what the 50 largest cities spend for housing, health, welfare, police, and fire, we find great differences. Washington spends the most per capita at $2018, followed by New York at $1405. El Paso, by contrast, spends only $114 per capita on these services and San Antonio only $138. Furthermore, some city councils have all incumbents reelected with no opposition, and others find all incumbents losing reelection efforts. The range of what we are interested in would be greater were cities compared.

We could also find cities in traditional political culture areas with substantial wealth and with substantial competition. Comparing cities would give us examples that are not to be found among the 50 states. Most important, we could have many more examples to study. There are nearly 20,000 municipalities in the United States, although many are quite small. The same argument applies to the study of local school district governance. There are nearly 15,000 school districts; and in terms of the money they spend, they are more important than municipalities.

Unfortunately, there are two major problems with comparing local governments—the data are fleeting and no one is interested. Our comparisons of the states are made possible by compilations by the Bureau of the Census and by the Council of State Governments. Although the Bureau of the Census does a survey of governments that gathers some data on municipalities, for the most part data on local elections, laws passed, actual expenditures by areas, the character of local politics is often discarded, sometimes never gathered, and at best buried in the archives of state secretaries of state.

Political science does have a subfield of urban politics, but comparative analyses are rarely attempted. The data difficulties enumerated above partially explain this problem; however, since the analysis is in depth, it tends to emphasize the uniqueness of the city studied. Even the cities studied are unrepresentative of U.S. cities because they are nearly exclusively the largest ones, such as New York, Chicago, and Los Angeles. Scholars seldom study cities such as Eugene, Carbondale, North Wales, Tallahassee, Stony Brook, and Bryan. Perhaps someday at least a random sample of cities will be compared for the same purpose that we have compared the states in this text.

DEMOCRACY IN PUBLIC SERVICE DELIVERY

As we have seen, municipal governments were first to become active in the United States. The stimulus for this increased activity was the need for government services that individuals could no longer provide. Ten thousand people concentrated into a single square mile in an urban area need government to provide planning, water, sewers, crime protection, and transportation among many other needs. When distributed over many hundreds of square miles, they can provide most of these for themselves at their own expense.

In providing such services, municipalities would be expected to be unbiased in their response to the needs of individuals and neighborhoods. A government that provides more services to some individuals or neighborhoods is likely to draw first public criticism, then challenge, and ultimately removal from office. The assumption, of course, is that it has meaningful democratic elections and that those disadvantaged by the delivery of the services are in a majority. Even in a democracy, a government that discriminates against a minority is unlikely to face a serious challenge at the polls unless the unfairness of the situation finds many in the majority to vote with the minority.

Despite the complexity of dealing with questions of government discrimination in providing services and public protest, this problem has been an active area of research in U.S. cities. From the stratificationist viewpoint, we might well expect that those without influence in a community might not enjoy the same attention from government in providing for their needs. Adding the assumption that those without influence are the poor, we get what has been labeled the "underclass hypothesis."[37] The poor do not get equal services.

Many case studies of larger U.S. cities have found that some services reach the middle and upper classes more, others reach the lower classes, and yet others show no pattern. The underclass hypothesis thus has little support in this unsystematic research.[38] This finding, however, has not ended concern with such services and any bias in their delivery. The focus has shifted to citizen demands or complaints about municipal services. Again this question is asked within the context of thinking about democracy. One possible act of a democratic public is making such demands, and a democratic government should be responsive to those demands. Government responsiveness to such demands may exceed in importance the role of elections in a democracy.

When the public votes for elected officials in our normal elections, we have noted the apathy of the public, the indirectness of allowing the public a say in what government does, and the complexity of the information needed in making a choice. This topic was covered in Chapter 6. By contrast, citizen complaints are likely to be quite important to those complaining, quite direct, quite unambiguous, and based on clear information.[39] We believe that services have been inadequate, and those complaining have noticed and exercised their democratic right to be heard by those responsible for the service delivery. Garbage has not been picked up; there is a pothole in the street; the police have been ineffective in controlling noise, crime, or drugs; or Johnny cannot read.

The underclass hypothesis also exists in the study of contacts. It is assumed that contact initiated by citizens are based on deficient services and that if these complaints come from the lower classes then their services must be poorer. There has been no assessment of whether services are poor for those complaining. Nevertheless, contacts have been often studied, although

37 Robert L. Lineberry, *Equality and Urban Policy: The Distribution of Municipal Public Services* (Beverly Hills, CA: Sage, 1977).

38 Bryan D. Jones, *Governing Urban America: A Policy Focus* (Boston: Little, Brown, 1983), pp. 360–362.

39 Philip B. Coulter, *Political Voice: Citizen Demand for Urban Public Services* (Tuscaloosa: University of Alabama Press, 1988), p. 7.

they have never been compared between cities.[40] Again the results have been mixed, largely depending on the study. There are findings supportive of the underclass hypothesis as applied to contacts. Additionally, there are also studies showing that the underclass gets superior service (meaning they complain less), studies showing that the middle class is advantaged or disadvantaged in contrast to the upper and lower classes, and studies showing no pattern.

Although no doubt there are method differences between these studies that can partially account for these different findings, some differences are probably real.[41] It seems entirely plausible that cities vary in providing services to their publics. In Floyd Hunter's Atlanta study one might well expect that poor neighborhoods would receive fewer and lower-quality services, with an elite in control knowing that complaints would be unlikely to have implications in elections. It is equally plausible that an urban machinelike political party might intercede on the behalf of its supporters to meet their complaints quickly.[42] And it is conceivable that a middle-class university town would be most responsive to the middle class.[43]

Government responsiveness to its citizens is provocative and important. Unfortunately, this research literature on municipal services is insufficiently far along to answer many questions. This literature leaves us only with the interest in having comparative research. With such research we might see whether government serves those who participate or whether there is sufficient public accountability forced on those providing the service, as the pluralists would argue, to assure unbiased services. Many studies have failed to find unbiased services. We cannot be sure, however, whether the methods used in such studies, incompetence on the part of some city workers, crushing needs in some parts of especially older cities, a different appetite for municipal services or failed democracy accounts for who receives services.

State services are less obvious and probably the average person is more likely to complain to a member of Congress than to a state legislator or civil servant. Thus, although we can be comparative at the state level, the question is better considered at the municipal level. Probably, we should say at the local level, inasmuch as citizen complaints about their schools may exceed those concerning their municipal government. No one has analyzed this sub-

---

40   Coulter exhaustively reviews all of this research.

41   Coulter deals with many possible explanations for these different findings.

42   Bryan D. Jones, "Party and Bureaucracy: The Influence of Intermediary Groups on Urban Public Service Delivery," *American Political Science Review* 75 (September 1981), pp. 688–700.

43   Luttbeg, "Multiple Indicators" (see note 19).

ject, but it appears that, within a community, democracy in the city government and in school government may differ.[44]

CONCLUSION

Because of their substantial number and differences in size, cities range enormously. In addition, there is a great range of formal structures imposed on them by the states. Certainly the states do place limits on local governments. No matter how strong a city's home rule might be, it still is substantially limited by its state's laws and constitution. Moreover, local governments are not immune to taxing and charging to provide governmental services. There are local governments that are so poor that they can barely provide fundamental services such as police. Recently some California counties have had to close bridges because of a lack of funds to pay for their repair. Despite all of their problems, local governments seem to offer prospective residents nearly everything that they might want in terms of taxes, services, employment opportunities, climate, and so forth.

This range might also attract the interests of those concerned with how democracy operates. Much about local government differ from that at higher levels. Perhaps most discouraging, few data are readily available concerning most local governments. Election records, for example, are most often decentralized to the cities themselves. Nonpartisan elections are the rule, meaning that political party competition is meaningless. Despite the potential for comparison, there are few; thus studies of local governments have little informed us of what is important to their governments acting as they do.

The debate between the pluralists and the stratificationists has not been productive. It seems obvious that some communities and some states must be more open and accessible to the public, and public policy decisions should be directed less toward the upper stratum's self-interest. No comparative literature, however, is available to help us. Where are open states and communities to be found, and what difference does it make in terms of the policies they enjoy?[45] We just do not know. In large part since the decisional

---

44   Luttbeg.

45   Actually, there were several limited comparative works with exciting findings. See Robert E. Agger, Daniel Goldrich, and Bert E. Swanson, *The Rulers and the Ruled* (New York: Wiley, 1964); and Robert Presthus, *Men at the Top* (New York: Oxford University Press, 1964). Also see Claire W. Gilbert, "Community Power and Decision-Making: A Quantitative Examination of Previous Research," in *Community Structure and Decision-Making: Comparative Analyses*, Terry N. Clark (ed.) (San Francisco: Chandler, 1968).

technique used by the pluralists determined that they would find multiple elites, the method for doing the research was judged to determine the results.[46] At any rate, research died on this subject early in the 1970s without any definitive findings.

The implication of these perspectives, however, is far broader than just the study of community politics. It is very difficult for either of these schools to convince the other with research findings. The two schools differ on the dangers of influence being centered in the public or the elite. They also place different value on stability and freedom from civil strife and on account-ability or having democracy respond to public wants and interests. Both schools of thought will no doubt continue to have research findings that con-vince only like-minded believers.

No one, however, has shown that pluralistic democracy, which the perspective of the pluralist is called when full blown, is more stable than other democracies. Stratificationists also have never shown that democracy can overcome the upper-status bias that is characteristic of all democratic governments.

SUMMARY

1. Although the institutional formats of our national and state governments differ little and are seldom changed, government at the local level is often altered and varies greatly.

2. Local governments include city or municipal governments, county governments, school district governments, and other special district governments.

3. Much of the change in local governments is directed toward improving efficiency and effectiveness and reducing corruption in government. There are many reforms that have been in favor at different times.

4. The public's role, or at least some part of that public's role, in government is often an element in reforming local governments.

5. Pluralists and stratificationists sharply differ in how democratic they find all levels of government to be. There is little probability that either side will ever convince the other.

---

46 John Walton, "Substance and Artifact: The Current Status of Research on Community Power Structure," *American Journal of Sociology* 71 (January 1966), pp. 430–438.

6. We know little about how local governments differ or what effect these differences have on public policies.

SELECTED READINGS

Dahl, Robert A. *Who Governs?* (New Haven: Yale University Press, 1961). The classic alternate view of the operation of community politics.

Hunter, Floyd. *Community Power Structure* (Chapel Hill: University of North Carolina Press, 1953). Although it is not the first study on the subject, this volume captures the conspiracy of community politics.

Lipset, Seymour Martin. *Political Man: The Social Bases of Politics,* expanded ed. (Baltimore: The Johns Hopkins University Press, 1981). Chapters 3 through 5 express many of the views of pluralists.

Prewitt, Kenneth. *The Recruitment of Political Leaders: A Study of Citizen-Politicians* (Indianapolis: Bobbs-Merrill, 1970). One of the major publications coming out of the study of city councils in the San Francisco Bay area.

Stone, Clarence N. *Regime Politics: Governing Atlanta, 1944–1988* (Lawrence: University Press of Kansas, 1989). A recent book that expands on the considerations of both Dahl and Hunter.

Stone, Clarence N., and Heywood T. Sanders (eds.). *The Politics of Urban Development* (Lawrence: University Press of Kansas, 1987). This reader deals with contemporary problems in large cities.

Chapter
9

Legislating Policy and Representing the People

*T*he legislative branch of state governments, like its national counterpart, Congress, is the lawmaking branch. Thus we can call the holders of its elected positions legislators and lawmakers, in addition to terms such as members of the assembly, of the House, or senators. All of these officeholders can also be called representatives, since representing constituents is one of their primary actions.

PROVIDING REPRESENTATION

When very small numbers of people, perhaps as many as several thousand, form a government, they can all participate in the acts of making government policy. They can all be given their say, with the vote of each counting equally. If they lose, moreover, they should feel some obligation to comply with the policy they personally opposed because a majority favored it. There is little question as to how each should decide when voting on the policy. It should be on the basis of *informed* personal opinion. Those participating are supposed to know facts concerning the issue and to have formed their own opinions thoughtfully and logically.

When the size of a government exceeds this number, however, some individuals must make governmental decisions for the others. These specialists in governmental decision making are called *representatives*. This representative government brings with it many troublesome concerns. Should the representatives vote on the basis of their informed personal opinions or of those of their constituents? What is the constituent's obligation to comply if his or her representative did not vote as the constituent preferred? Does a majority decision by the representatives equal a majority decision among the constituents? In other words, is the decision representative? And how do we ever know whether a decision is representative or not?

Geographic Selection of Representatives. All representatives to all governments in the United States are selected on the basis of geographic districts. Some times these geographic districts are the nation itself. Only the president is elected in such a district, along with his vice presidential ticket mate. Sometimes the districts are the states, such as for U.S. senators, governors, and other statewide executives. Most often the districts are local, or small portions of states, typically with populations of well below 500,000. Although there are some very minor exceptions, the vast majority of representatives in all democracies are selected by similar geographically based districts. Let us consider this mechanism.

Given a state of 2 million people and a decision to have 50 representatives, one merely needs to divide the population by the number of representatives to get the target number of people to be in each geographic district—in this case, 40,000. With this figure and a map showing populations based on some very small geographic areas, such as counties or census districts of 10 to 15 city blocks, and standards, such as compactness and contiguity, one can divide the state into districts, a process called *apportionment*.

Briefly, *compactness* means that the district should closely match a square, which is the most compact way to divide area. *Contiguity* means that all portions of the district must be in contact with each other. Districts are not contiguous if they have a little portion here and another several miles away. Given these considerations, we would expect to see a district map with various-size squares. The smaller ones would be in populous urban areas where only several city blocks might have a population of 40,000. Few actual districts are actually square, however.

The above example assumed a *single-member district* with a single representative being selected from each district so drawn. There is no reason, however, that two, three, or more representatives cannot be selected in each district. These would be *multiple-member districts*. Multimember districts are becoming less common, however, perhaps because they have been criticized for making it difficult for minorities to win seats.[1] Once apportionment is completed, the state announces elections from these districts, candidates stand for election, some win, and the winners decide public policy.

This procedure dates to a time when it was the only workable solution for selecting representatives. At one time communication was difficult. Candidates seeking to appeal to voters for their support could speak face-to-face with them. Only if the representative represented a geographic district that was small enough for constituents to gather to hear the appeals of the candidate could they communicate. We should remember that most constituents were *illiterate*, so only face-to-face communication could be used. Similarly, voting could be accomplished only by physically gathering people in polling places to cast their ballots. With illiteracy and expensive mail, the best solution to casting ballots was to have the voters come to polling places. In short, geographic representation was necessary at one time in our history.

The costs or liabilities of geographic representation were not great at one time. When government did not do much, there was little need to cast an informed vote and little cost to gathering necessary information. Even the costs of being misinformed were minor. In a state were nearly all were subsistence farmers growing their own food, those in a given district were equally likely to be affected by the weather, such as the lack of rain, or by other natural events, such as poor soil or threatening insects. Thus their representative could clearly see the desired policy, given the improbability of government doing anything. In modern society, however, there are high costs to be paid for geographic selection of representatives.

Chief among these costs is the difficulty of representing a heterogeneous district. With a complex economy, most geographic districts now include constituents who share few views, if any. They are not equally affected by either natural events or by government policies directed at such events. A district may include poor farmers eager to sell their products at high costs and poor workers eager to buy farm products at low costs. It may contain many unemployed workers hoping to have extended unemployment insurance and owners of small businesses barely able to make a living because of present state taxes. If, as is so often true, one type of constituent predominates, such as farmers or industrial workers, the representative may be forced to ignore the others. But what if his or her personal opinions favor the others? As in so many other areas, the growing complexity of society has

---

1 Samuel C. Patterson, "State Legislators and the Legislatures," in *Politics in the American States*, 5th ed., Virginia Gray, Herbert Jacob, and Robert B. Albritton (eds.) (Glenview, IL: Scott, Foresman, 1990), p. 166.

greatly complicated the procedures for selecting representatives as well as the actions of those representatives.

Alternatives for Selecting Representatives. Literacy and inexpensive communication could emancipate us from the dependency on geographic representation. We certainly no longer need to gather prospective voters to hear candidate appeals. Although it is expensive, television is the preferred technique to advertise oneself before an election. A candidate who can look like a "statesman" and appear "wise and honest," as compared to the opponent who is "tricky" and just a "politician," is most likely to win an election. If interest groups are willing to supply the money for such campaigns, all is well for legislators desiring to continue their employment. They can be reelected time after time. Are they representatives, however? Reelection may have nothing to do with how representatively a legislator acts.

Although it is not used, technology now allows for vote gathering other than by having people visit polling places. Since World War II the states have allowed absentee voting by mail if you are to be out-of-town on election day.[2] San Diego and other local governments have experimented with allowing all voters to cast their votes through the mail. These experiments have greatly increased turnout. Much of our daily banking is accomplished over the telephone or by way of cash cards. Establishing similar procedures for vote gathering seemingly could make voting as easy as a telephone call or a visit to the counterpart of a cash card machine. Voters would no longer need to gather at polls. Through technology, then, it is no longer necessary to rely on geographically based districts that increasingly are hard to represent.

Apportionment now could assign representatives to segments of society defined by their likelihood of sharing opinions on governmental policies. If one-quarter of the state is agricultural, one-quarter of the representatives could be selected by farmers. Moreover, if most of these farmers are poor, one could apportion 80 percent of these representatives to poor farmers. Similarly, if wealthy businessmen were to constitute only 2 percent of the state, they might get only a single representative in such an apportionment based on occupation and income. Race, gender, and age are other bases on which such a system might be constructed.

There is no question that there would be technical difficulties in implementing such a system, but they are not insurmountable. Certainly some segments of society that are overrepresented presently would oppose any

---

2   Texas allows people to vote by machine at selective locations in the two weeks preceding elections. Perhaps other states too have such provisions.

Table 9.1   Occupations of State Legislators in Percentages (1986)

Occupation	New England	Middle Atlantic	East North Central	West North Central	South Atlantic	East South Central	West South Central	Mountain	Pacific	Nation
Attorney	10	21	18	10	24	21	26	11	13	16
Business owner	12	4	10	13	13	19	19	11	18	14
Educator	7	4	6	8	7	12	4	6	7	8
Full-time legislator	12	52	25	7	3	0	2	3	12	11
Homemaker	4	0	0	3	2	1	1	1	1	2
Business	6	4	6	5	5	6	6	6	6	6
Real estate										4[a]

[a]Data not provided by regions.

Source: State Legislators' Occupations: A Decade of Change, State Legislative Report (Denver: National Conference of State Legislatures, December 1986), p. 7.

such restructuring of our procedures for selecting representatives. This solution to the problem is only one among several that we shall discuss as we consider the nature of state legislators, as well as executives and judges.

REQUIREMENTS TO BE A STATE LEGISLATOR

To become a state legislator one typically (but not always) has to be a citizen, a resident, and above a certain age. This minimum age is typically 21 years old for the lower house and 25 for the upper house or senate.[3] There are other common characteristics, which are so common among legislators that they might be called "informal requirements." Although it is possible to be elected without meeting these informal requirements, it is improbable.

For example, as Table 9.1 shows, representatives' occupations are predominantly professional or managerial, the upper-middle-class end of occupations. Lawyers and businessmen are particularly overrepresented in state legislatures. Attorneys are most common in the Middle Atlantic and

---

3   In 24 states the minimum age is 21 for the lower house, and in 16 states it is 18. In the senate the minimum age is 25 years in 20 states and 18 years in 15 states.

southern states, ranging from New York south along the coast through Texas. The national percentage of attorneys in state legislatures has dropped from 22 percent nationwide in 1976 to 16 percent in 1986. Additionally, greater percentages of legislators are white, male, Protestant, and over 30 years old than are found for the general adult population.[4]

As shown in Table 9.2, the bias of state legislatures is not limited to their being occupationally atypical. Although no state even approaches being representative in terms of gender, New Hampshire, Colorado, Maine, and Washington stand out as having more than one-quarter female legislators. The South is least representative by gender. The range for the percentage of black legislators varies from 0 percent for Hawaii, Idaho, Maine, Montana, New Hampshire, New Mexico, North and South Dakota, and Utah to a high of 17.1 percent in Alabama. Not surprisingly, given the substantial percentage of their total population that is black, the South leads in this regard. Illinois, Michigan, and Maryland are also included among legislatures with a substantial percentage of black legislators. The non-native-born legislator percentage varies greatly from 83 percent in Nevada to 11.6 percent in Oklahoma. Not surprisingly, growth states, which tend to be in the Sunbelt, tend not to reflect their substantial non-native-born-populations in the composition of their legislature. Perhaps with time they will.

Table 9.3 considers the difference between legislators and their constituents from another perspective. The state legislatures differ greatly in how accurately the percentages of legislators with some attribute, such as being a black or male, mirror that percentage in the populace of their state. In Table 9.3 the .67 figure for Alabama means that the legislature has about two-thirds of the number of black legislators that one might expect given the percentage of that state population that is black. Ratios below 1.00 indicate underrepresentation of an attribute and are most noticeable for women, labor union members, and government employees.[5] The obvious greatest overrepresentation is for attorneys. The typical state has more than 48 times as many attorneys in its legislature as in its population!

Figure 9.1 merely shows the sums of these biases for each state legislature.[6] A state legislature that perfectly represented all seven of these attributes would have a score of 7. No state has anywhere near such perfect repre-

---

4   Malcolm E. Jewell and Samuel C. Patterson, *The Legislative Process in the United States*, 4th ed. (New York: Random House, 1986).

5   It should be noted that these figures represent available data, not data that were sought to best reflect our concern with upper-status bias.

6   Many attributes were inverted to make all range from 0 (total lack of representativeness) to 1.00 (perfect representation).

Table 9.2   Characteristics of State Legislators in Percentages (1986)

State	Characteristic			State	Characteristic		
	Women[a]	Blacks[b]	Non-native[c]		Women[a]	Blacks[b]	Non-native[c]
AL	5.7	17.1	—[d]	MT	15.3	0	36.0
AK	18.3	1.7	73.3	NE	18.4	2.0	12.5
AZ	23.3	3.3	68.8	NV	15.9	4.8	83.0
AR	6.7	3.7	18.0	NH	32.5	0	45.3
CA	13.3	6.7	34.1	NJ	10.0	6.7	—
CO	29.0	4.0	—	NM	9.8	0	—
CT	21.9	5.3	43.5	NY	10.0	9.5	—
DE	16.1	4.8	41.9	NC	14.1	9.4	17.1
FL	20.6	7.5	58.8	ND	12.6	0	—
GA	11.0	11.9	—	OH	10.6	9.8	—
HA	19.7	0	21.0	OK	8.1	3.4	11.6
ID	20.6	0	—	OR	17.8	3.3	56.6
IL	18.1	11.9	23.1	PA	6.3	7.1	—
IN	12.7	5.3	—	RI	16.0	4.0	26.9
IA	14.7	.7	22.6	SC	7.1	11.8	17.3
KS	18.8	2.4	—	SD	17.1	0	15.4
KY	5.1	1.4	—	TN	9.1	9.8	20.6
LA	4.2	13.2	—	TX	9.4	8.3	—
ME	28.5	0	—	UT	7.7	0	14.4
MD	20.7	14.4	—	VT	24.4	.6	48.6
MA	18.5	3.5	19.7	VA	7.1	6.4	38.5
MI	14.9	10.8	15.0	WA	25.2	2.0	51.3
MN	15.4	.5	—	WV	15.7	.7	—
MS	2.3	11.5	—	WI	20.5	3.0	13.6
MO	15.7	7.6	19.6	WY	23.4	1.1	38.2

[a]Percentage of state legislators who are women in 1987. Source is Table A-36 in *State Policy Data Book, 1988.*
[b]Percentage of state legislators who are black in 1987. Source is Table A-40 in *State Policy Data Book, 1988.*
[c]Percentage of state legislators born in state in 1987–88 session.
[d] A dash denotes no report.

Source: State Legislators' Occupations: A Decade of Change, State Legislative Report (Denver: National Conference of State Legislatures, December 1986), p. 7; and Joel Thompson and Gary Moncrief, "Residential Mobility of American State Legislators," a paper presented at the annual meeting of the American Political Science Association, 1988.

sentation. The most-representative states are Washington, Arizona, Illinois, Wisconsin, Ohio, Pennsylvania, New York, New Jersey, Connecticut, Rhode Island, and Massachusetts. The least-representative states prove to be southern, north central, and western states.

Table 9.3   Representation Ratios of State Legislators and State Publics (1986)

	Group						
State	Women[a]	Blacks[b]	Attorneys[c]	Agriculture[d]	Labor Unions[e]	Education[f]	Government[g]
AL	.11	.67	47.29	2.40	.00	10.14	.13
AK	.39	.50	34.48	2.43	.00	1.77	.00
AZ	.46	1.18	13.32	2.09	.00	4.78	.14
AR	.13	.27	102.63	2.68	.00	2.05	.05
CA	.26	.87	55.16	3.29	.00	3.39	.00
CO	.58	1.14	51.43	5.79	.00	6.51	.20
CT	.42	.76	43.78	1.33	.00	3.71	.10
DE	.31	.30	.00	2.38	.00	8.73	.38
FL	.40	.54	89.29	.46	.00	4.43	.04
GA	.21	.44	74.00	5.22	.00	2.47	.00
HA	.40	.00	77.41	.91	.05	6.20	.00
ID	.41	.00	42.00	3.75	.00	2.67	.05
IL	.35	.81	71.91	1.67	.00	1.52	.26
IN	.25	.70	103.35	2.38	.00	6.76	.17
IA	.29	.50	29.76	2.82	.00	3.18	.09
KS	.37	.45	61.30	3.88	.00	1.24	.04
KY	.10	.20	124.74	2.16	.07	4.45	.05
LA	.08	.45	125.00	4.18	.00	3.84	.04
ME	.55	.00	20.41	1.67	.00	2.55	.16
MD	.40	.63	92.47	3.22	.03	6.52	.23
MA	.35	.90	46.37	.00	.05	3.56	.08
MI	.29	.84	57.96	4.76	.02	8.10	.68
MN	.30	.38	39.07	2.45	.04	6.11	.14
MS	.04	.33	156.25	5.64	.00	3.61	.10
MO	.30	.72	43.28	2.78	.02	4.05	.00
MT	.31	.00	36.33	3.13	.00	3.49	.00
NE	.36	.65	37.78	2.76	.00	2.47	.00
NV	.32	.75	38.08	6.30	.00	1.84	.36
NH	.63	.00	9.14	1.82	.00	1.88	.09
NJ	.19	.53	83.32	.67	.09	4.22	.67
NM	.19	.00	83.41	2.30	.00	.69	.12
NY	.19	.69	62.41	1.17	.00	1.98	.03
NC	.27	.42	162.67	2.50	.00	2.85	.00
ND	.25	.00	39.95	2.72	.00	4.41	.03
OH	.21	.98	81.80	2.37	.00	1.54	.06
OK	.16	.50	88.88	2.06	.00	3.26	.19
OR	.35	2.36	44.14	3.56	.04	6.34	.00
PA	.12	.81	63.83	1.40	.00	.72	.07
RI	.31	1.38	98.81	1.00	.07	13.28	.10
SC	.14	.39	213.00	4.15	.00	2.23	.04
SD	.34	.00	50.88	2.22	.00	2.42	.13
TN	.18	.62	103.63	1.80	.00	4.01	.17
TX	.19	.69	145.04	1.92	.00	.68	.00
UT	.15	.00	60.10	3.55	.00	5.41	.00

Table 9.3   Representation Ratios of State Legislators and State Publics (1986)
(*continued*)

State	Women[a]	Blacks[b]	Attorneys[c]	Agriculture[d]	Labor Unions[e]	Education[f]	Government[g]
					Group		
VT	.48	3.00	28.08	3.29	.00	3.50	.00
VA	.14	.34	193.00	1.00	.00	4.50	.00
WA	.50	.77	38.15	2.60	.02	3.44	.23
WV	.30	.21	129.33	1.57	.08	5.55	.08
WI	.40	.77	73.32	2.58	.00	1.49	.00
WY	.48	1.57	45.95	4.84	.00	4.49	.05

[a]Percent women in the legislature divided by percentage of women in the state.
[b]Percent blacks in the legislature divided by percentage of blacks in the state.
[c]Percent of attorneys in legislature divided by the percentage of attorneys in population.
[d]Percent of legislators whose major occupation is agriculture divided by the percentage of the agriculture in the civilian population of the state.
[e]Percent of legislatures whose major occupation is covered by a union divided by the state's union membership as a percentage of nonagricultural employment.
[f]Percent of legislators whose major occupation is education divided by public educational employment per 10,000 population.
[g]Percent of legislators whose major occupation is by government divided by percentage of civil employment in government.

Source: Norman R. Luttbeg and Keith Hamm, "Representation and Policy Making in the American States," in *Representation and the Policy Process in Federal Systems*, David M. Olson and C.E.S. Franks (eds.) Data on legislators from *State Legislators' Occupations: A Decade of Change*, State Legislative Report (Denver: National Conference of State Legislatures, December 1986), p. 7.

Legislatures that underrepresent blacks, agriculture, and labor unions and overrepresent attorneys all tap the status bias of state legislators. To the degree that state legislatures are unrepresentative on these attributes, they reveal a middle-class bias. Figure 9.2a considers whether participation in the form of greater turnout in elections, here using gubernatorial elections, affects the degree to which the legislature reflects the public of the state. As turnout increases, attribute representation declines sharply! Since so many southern states have both low voting turnout and poor attribute representation, they are deleted in Figure 9.2b. This relationship is even stronger! No ready explanation comes to mind for this curious pattern. Other political variables such as whether the Democrats or Republicans dominate the legislature, the competition evident in state legislative politics, and pressure

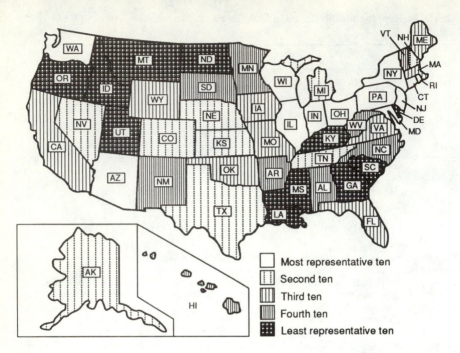

Figure 9.1   Attribute representativeness of the states.

group strength (see Figure 9.3) show negative relationships, mostly quite weak.[7]

Another measure of representation, party representativeness, also proves only weakly related to attribute representation. The measure of what could be called party representativeness was developed in Chapter 7. When the percentage of Democrats in the legislature mirrors that in the general public, it is more party representative. A state with 58 percent Democrats in its electorate and with 58 percent of its lower house being Democrats would be perfectly representative. As can be seen in Figure 9.4, the two measures are very weakly related. At least as judged by these data, states are not consistently representative.

Figure 9.5 shows a relatively strong relationship between per capita income and attribute representativeness. Wealthy states have substantially more attribute representative state legislatures. Intuitively, one might expect legislatures always to be middle-class institutions; and as a state's public be-

---

7   The correlation with Democratic control is -0.10 and that for all states for competition is -0.33 but this figure drops to -0.11 for nonsouthern states.

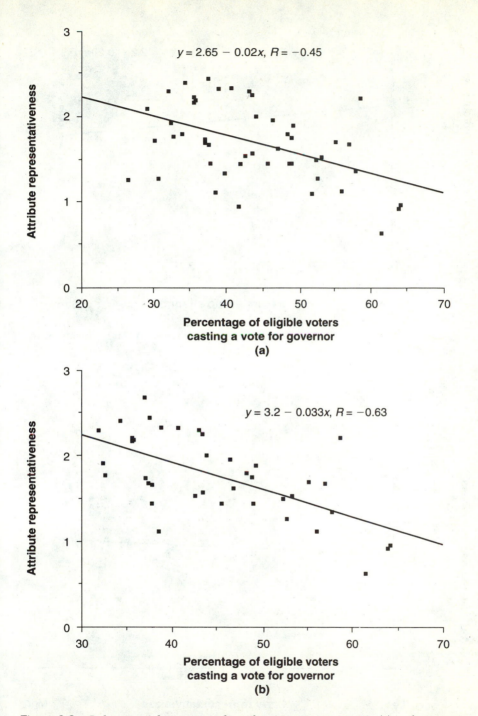

Figure 9.2 Gubernatorial turnout and attribute representativeness (a) in the country as a whole and (b) in the states outside of the South.

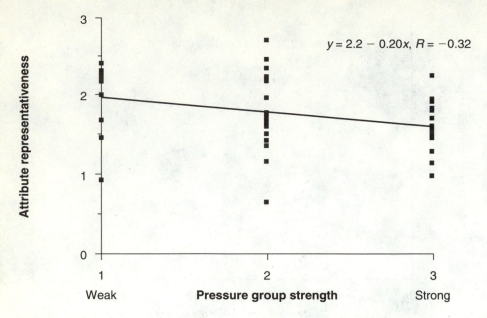

Figure 9.3 Pressure group strength and representativeness in states outside of the South.

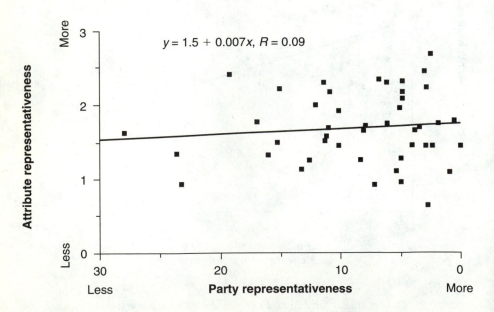

Figure 9.4 Attribute representativeness vs. party representativeness.

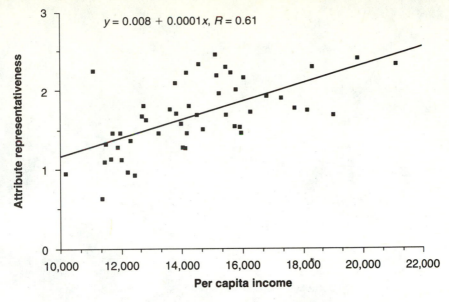

Figure 9.5   Attribute representativeness vs. per capita income.

comes more middle class, the unchanged legislature better reflects these attributes. This finding suggests that no credit can be given to more-
metropolitan, middle-class state legislatures for being more representative;
their publics have merely become as middle class as the legislatures.

   The Impact of Status Bias.   All of the above considerations just assess
what leverage we might have if we desired to make legislatures more attribute representative. Political variables seem to have little import. Our
primary question remains: Do status-biased legislatures enact status-biased
legislation? Again we turn to a straight redistributive issue, that of average
Aid for Families with Dependent Children, and to our measure of the regressiveness of state and local taxes. Status bias in a legislature would suggest
that low payments and regressive taxes would prevail. There is a modest improvement in AFDC payments with improved attribute representation. The
noted southern states, however, all tend to be low both in AFDC payments
and in attribute representativeness, and removing these states further dampens an already weak relationship.[8]

   Figure 9.6 shows that more attribute representative state legislatures tend
to have more regressive state and local taxes. This relationship is largely un-

---

8 The regression coefficient becomes 42 rather than 79 and the correlation is 0.22 rather than 0.34.

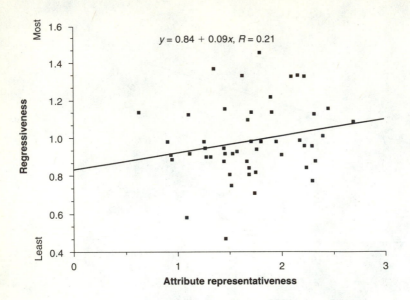

Figure 9.6   Regressiveness of state and local taxes vs. attribute representativeness.

affected by the presence of the southern states. Neither the pluralists nor the stratificationists could find much to be happy about in this relationship, because it is in the direction predicted by the pluralists, though quite weak.

The Impact of Representative Bias in Low-Participation Circumstances.   The essence of the pluralist's argument is that representatives' upper-class bias fails to take precedence because of the institutions of democracy and the competition among elites. At the state level this view can be stated as a hypothesis. Where the public uses the institutions of democracy by turning out in elections, the middle-class bias of legislators will be less evident, especially for policies preferred by the more working-class public.

Figure 9.7 divides the 41 states that held their gubernatorial elections other than in 1984 into the 21 highest-turnout and 21 lowest-turnout states. Those with gubernatorial elections in 1984 would have had turnouts in those elections inflated by a high presidential election turnout. Among the low-turnout states, the more substantially middle-class-biased states (the low end of the representation ratio scale) have only slightly lower AFDC payments. Where turnout is high, representative bias has a substantial impact. This result is, of course, opposite of what we hypothesized.

Although they are not shown, the comparable figures for regressiveness of state and local taxes show no impact of controlling for turnout. As with the overall pattern shown above, the less-representative states reveal a weak

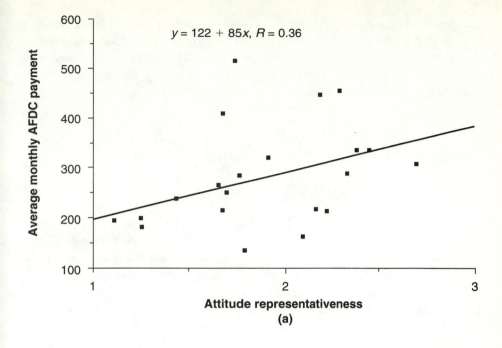

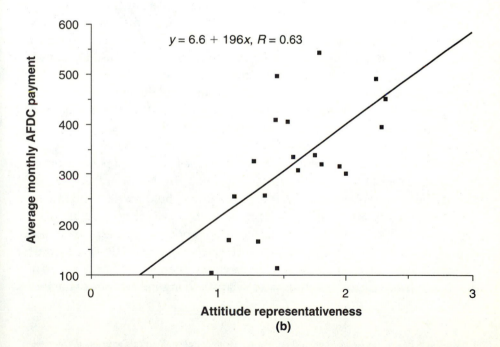

Figure 9.7 AFDC payments vs. attribute representativeness in (a) low-turnout and (b) high-turnout states.

pattern of having more-progressive (or less-regressive) state and local taxes. We are going well beyond the normal pluralist argument and assessing state data rather than data for local government. Nevertheless the public's exercise of democracy does *not* appear important in offsetting the attribute bias evidence in state legislatures.

APPORTIONING POPULATION RATHER THAN GEOGRAPHIC AREA

Failure to Reapportion. We noted in discussing geographic apportionment that in earlier times people were spread more evenly across the land. Then most constituents were farmers. Industrialization and the accompanying concentration of people in cities resulted in equal-sized geographic districts no longer including the same number of people. Because those living in rural areas were in power and had no desire to give up that power, most state legislatures failed in their charge to reapportion districts within their states.

The Supreme Court of the United States repeatedly ducked the issue of whether those living in urban areas were being treated unconstitutionally. With each urban representative expressing the desires of many more people than those in rural areas, policies were not those of the majority. The Court said that this was a political issue to be dealt with by legislatures.[9] Of course, those representatives overrepresenting rural areas had little reason to vote for change. The U.S. Census of 1960 made the inequity all the more evident. For example, in Florida, state senate districts ranged from 10,000 to 935,000; and in California, Los Angeles with 40 percent of the state's population held only 1 of the 40 seats in the senate.[10]

The Supreme Court accepted a Tennessee case involving a poorly apportioned state legislative lower house. Surprisingly, in this case, *Baker* v. *Carr* (1962), the Court ruled that federal district courts could consider this issue. The district court ordered reapportionment on the basis of population. Conceding the inevitable, many state legislatures reapportioned rather than face court challenges. Just two years later in *Reynolds* v. *Simms* (1964) the Court extended the "one man's vote should be equal to another's" or "one man, one vote," principle to the state senates. Many had argued that one of the two

---

9   Gordon E. Baker, *The Reapportionment Revolution: Representation, Political Power and the Supreme Court* (New York: Random House, 1966).

10   Malcolm E. Jewell, "What Hath *Baker v. Carr* Wrought?" in *State Government, 1989–90,* Thad L. Beyle (ed.) (Washington, DC: CQ Press, 1989).

state houses should retain equal representation on a geographic basis to protect rural interests. Chief Justice Earl Warren confronted these arguments with his statement that "legislators represent people, not trees or acres." Actually the phrase, "one man, one vote," is not only sexist but misleading, because the decisions merely insist on districts of nearly equal population not of equal number of voters.

The rule of thumb now is that the largest-population and smallest-population districts must have populations within 1 percent of each other. The federal courts have now extended these equal-population considerations to U.S. House districts and to local governments, including school boards.

The Results of Reapportionment.   It is somewhat difficult to be certain of the impact of these reapportionments. Urbanization and suburbanization continued unabated during the 1960s, 1970s, and 1980s, and state governments increasingly turned to urban problems.[11] However, it is always difficult to say when two trends coincide that one is causing the other. For example, does the fact that family farms have declined swiftly since the reapportionment decisions demonstrate that urban and suburban legislators have ignored these constituents, resulting in the failure of small farms? Certainly there are more legislators from urban and suburban areas now than was the case before the early 1960s. There are more Democrats from the cities in northern legislatures and more urban Republicans in the South. It seems nearly certain that reapportionment based on population has given legislators more desire to attack urban problems and to devote expenditures to those areas.[12]

GERRYMANDERING

Thus far the Supreme Court has not seen its way to becoming involved in the shape and implications of the equally populated representative districts it has assured by its decisions discussed above. It did declare in a 1986 decision, *Davis* v. *Dandemer*, however, that "identifiable political groups" could challenge district mapping. Presumably, political parties are so identifiable, so the

11   Timothy G. O'Rourke, *The Impact of Reapportionment* (New Brunswick, NJ: Transaction Books, 1980).

12   See Yong Hyo Cho and H. George Frederickson, "The Effects of Reapportionment: Subtle, Selected, Limited," *National Civic Review* 63 (July 1974), pp. 357–362; Timothy O'Rourke, *The Impact of Reapportionment* (New Brunswick, NJ: Transaction Books, 1980); Michael A. Maggiotto et al., "The Impact of Reapportionment in Public Policy," *American Politics Quarterly* 13 (January 1985), pp. 101–121.

Census of 1990 and the reapportionment by state legislatures afterward may long preoccupy the courts.

Obviously the population of a state could be apportioned into districts in an entirely impartial manner. Each district could be a close approximation of a square with closely matched populations. We could ignore possible problems, such as the possibility that several incumbent legislators might have to face each other for a single seat. It is also possible that one political party would be advantaged because just enough of its supporters were concentrated in a district to win the seat. It is unrealistic to expect this in the apportionment process. Instead the process has the biases suggested by the term *gerrymandering.*

This term, which implies having political purpose in drawing district boundaries, comes from a political cartoon in the early 1800s. The Jeffersonian Republicans had concentrated Federalist voters into a district where they would overwhelmingly win a single state legislative seat, while the surrounding areas could elect Republicans. The cartoon exaggerated the appearance of this district to look like a dragon or salamander or what the paper called a "gerrymander" because the governor involved was a Governor Gerry.

Concentration of the minority party, such as that used in the above example, is but one technique used in the majority party drawing district lines to the disadvantage of the minority party. *Dilution* is even more artful. In Figure 9.8 we see an example of diluting the minority party so that they win no seats. This particular example was called "bacon stripping." If the majority party's supporter gave it more than one half of the vote in each district, the

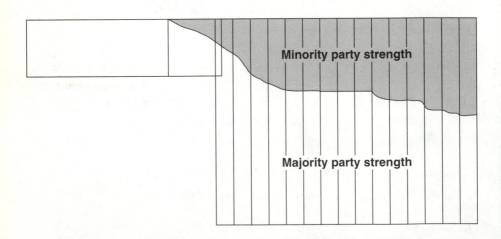

Figure 9.8   Dilution of minority party strength through "bacon stripping."

minority would win no seats. Since the Democrats control most state legislatures, most gerrymandering is pro-Democratic. Both political parties, however, do all they can to assure electoral success in the future by drawing district boundaries to their own advantage.

It should be noted that the courts are increasingly ordering municipal and school-governing bodies to gerrymander single-member districts locally to assure representation to minorities. What is used might be called court-ordered gerrymandering, with a racially based concentration of minorities in certain districts to assure their election. Going to "at large" elections in which all representatives to a city council are elected citywide was common in the South. The motive was the dilution of minorities so that none won election to the council. With "at large" districts all council members are elected by voters across the city. A minority of 25 or 30 percent of the vote would win no seats.

COMPENSATION

Although the mean salary of state legislators in 1987 was just over $18,000, there is substantial variation. The highest yearly salary for state legislators is in New York at $57,500.[13] Pennsylvania legislators have the second highest salaries at $47,000, with California at $40,816, Massachusetts at $40,992, and Michigan at $39,881 closely behind.[14] Additionally, many states provide a per diem to legislators while they are in session. Often this is substantial, such as California's $87 per day. Since these salaries are well over the median family income in the United States, one can see individuals attracted to making a career as a state legislator, at least in these states. Additionally, many of these states have good health insurance and retirement plans and provide legislators with gasoline and telephone credit cards.

Some states pay so poorly that it is inconceivable that one could live on a legislative salary. For example, New Hampshire pays $200 a year, Rhode Island pays $5 per day for a 60–legislative day session, and Alabama pays $10 per day for a 105–day session. North Dakota, Nebraska, West Virginia, and Texas pay $2160, $4800, $6500, and $7200 per year, respectively. They also tend to offer low, if any, benefits, making a legislative career difficult.

---

13   National Conference of State Legislatures, *Summary: Legislators' Compensation and Benefits*, October 31, 1987.

14   *The Book of the States, 1988–89* (Lexington, KY: Council of State Governments), pp. 96–97.

SIZE OF LEGISLATURES

All lower houses in the states are larger than their senate or upper-house counterparts. The average lower house has 112 members and the senate 40 members. This figure does vary greatly, with the smallest lower houses being Alaska (40), Delaware (41), and Nevada (42), and with the largest being New Hampshire (400) and Pennsylvania (203). The smallest senates are in Alaska (20) and Nevada (21) and the largest in Minnesota (67) and New York (61). There are two considerations in setting the size of a legislative house, neither of which probably concerned those who wrote state constitutions.

Even with present technology the upper limit on the size of a legislature is time. With thousands of bills to consider, each legislator's opportunity to speak on a bill would be restricted further if the house were larger. This situation is especially the case in those states that restrict legislative sessions. To be certain, technology in architecture as well as in public address systems allows the housing of quite large groups, such as in domed stadiums, as well as allowing individuals to be heard. Because lower houses are larger than senates, they typically have leaders of greater authority as well as limited debate.

Senators in California represent about 692,000 people, and those in Texas about 560,000 people. By contrast, New Hampshire lower-house legislators represent merely 3000 people. Can they thus give better representation than their senate counterparts in the populous states? Although it has not been demonstrated, it would appear easy to be a representative in New Hampshire. Obviously, if the California senate was increased to 9320 members, those senators would have the ease of representation of New Hampshire legislators! It would be possible to house them and to allow them to be heard, but each might have only a few seconds to speak on each bill.

Choosing 1500 California legislators randomly we know would give quite accurate representation. Thus 9300 representatives is overkill, except for the fact that they are selected by elections with only certain individuals really eligible to run. Nevertheless, representatives selected from low-population districts seem more likely to reflect those districts than would be the case in large districts. Large districts seem more likely to be varied and small districts more homogeneous.

PROFESSIONALISM IN STATE LEGISLATURES

State legislatures have drawn much criticism for their lack of professionalism. Reformers recommend several goals.[15] They generally recom-

---

15   The Citizens Conference on State Legislatures, *The Sometimes Governments: A Critical Study of the 50 American Legislatures* (New York: Bantam Books, 1971).

mend smaller legislatures to increase the prestige of the office, to allow the public to know clearly who is responsible, and to encourage free debate. They also recommend nearly full-year sessions to avoid the repeated special sessions common in limited session states. They would advocate commensurate salary increases, to provide a livelihood for individuals who are exclusively legislators. In less-professional circumstances, legislators can hold primary occupations, such as attorney or real estate agent, since their time in the legislature is limited.

Staff and office facilities to provide additional information are also seen as desirable in a more professional legislature.[16] Finally, many long, detailed constitutions restrict legislative latitude by prohibiting certain actions without constitutional amendments. Additionally, "earmarking" funds from some sources, such as gasoline taxes, for use in related areas, such as for roads, restricts legislative latitude. These funds cannot be used in more pressing policy areas.

Generally speaking, reformers would like the state legislatures to follow the path of Congress as it became an active, professional, and high-paying legislature. Some criticize these reform goals, however. The amateur legislature of old is preferred by many as being less likely to enact unwanted legislation, such as excessive salaries for themselves. With the low salaries of amateur legislatures, the representative would need to have other employment within his or her district and thus could not be out of touch with constituents.

Smaller legislatures too, for reasons discussed above, might be less representative. With larger districts, such as those in the California senate, minorities might be lost in the large numbers of majorities thus gaining few if any representatives. As we can see in Figure 9.9, the size of legislative districts for the lower house substantially improves the representativeness of state legislatures in terms of including more blacks, Hispanics, and women. Reformers seem largely irrelevant in the state legislatures moving toward professionalism. The driving force seems to be the industrialization of a state, which of course brings on associated problems.

Figures 9.10, 9.11, and 9.12 show the impact of a state's metropolitanism and economic complexity and the growing professionalism of its legislature. In Figure 9.10 it can be seen that for each percentage-point increase in its metropolitan population, 90 additional bills are introduced. As shown in Figure 9.11, there is a strong pattern between the number of bills introduced and

---

16   Patterson, p. 186 (see note 1); Brian Weberg, "Changes in Legislative Staff," *Journal of State Government* 61 (1988), pp. 190–197.

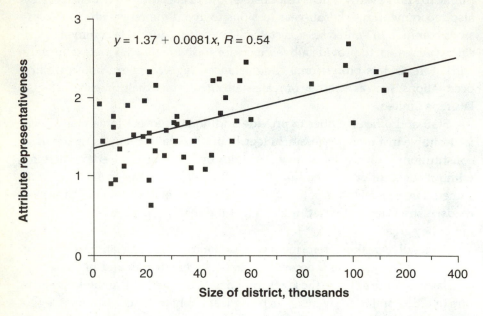

Figure 9.9 Attribute representativeness vs. district size for lower house (California excluded).

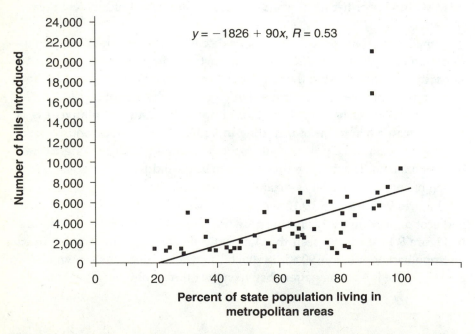

Figure 9.10 Number of bills introduced vs. metropolitanism of states.

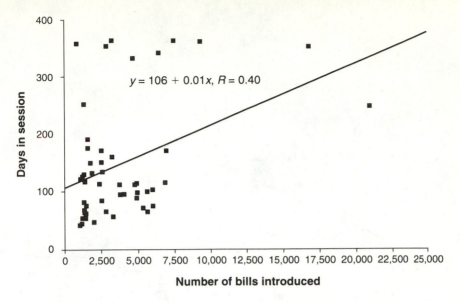

$$y = 106 + 0.01x, R = 0.40$$

Figure 9.11   Length of legislative session vs. number of bills introduced.

the lengths of the legislative session (every ten additional bills leads to one additional day in session). The more days a legislator has to devote to legislative activities the fewer days he or she will have available for earning other income. A legislator who has legislative activities nearly every day of the year cannot earn much outside income. Fortunately, as shown in Figure 9.12a, across the states legislators typically earn about $83 per day in salaries and per diem. The number of bills introduced is also correlated with salary levels, as shown in Figure 9.12b.

Turnover.   Too much turnover of personnel from one legislative session to the next has been of concern to some. The experienced legislator knows how to pass legislation and has expertise on matter of public policy. More turnover means fewer experienced legislators and fewer with the necessary skills. Although turnover between sessions is decreasing, the map in Figure 9.13 shows much variation in the lower houses of the state legislatures.[17] Turnover in the upper and lower houses, however, is closely related, as

---

17   Alan Rosenthal, "Turnover in State Legislatures," *American Journal of Political Science* (August 1974), pp. 609–616; Jerry Calvert, "Revolving Doors: Volunteerism in U.S. State Legislatures," *State Government* (Spring 1979), pp. 174–181; and Malcom E. Jewell, *Representation in State Legislatures* (Lexington: University of Kentucky Press, 1982).

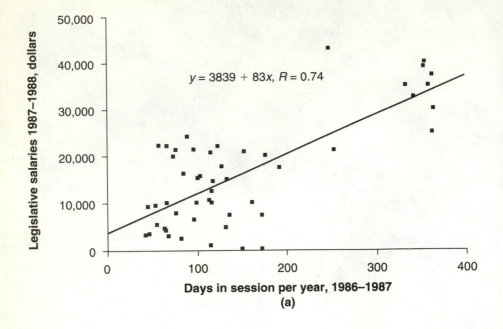

$y = 3839 + 83x$, $R = 0.74$

Days in session per year, 1986–1987

(a)

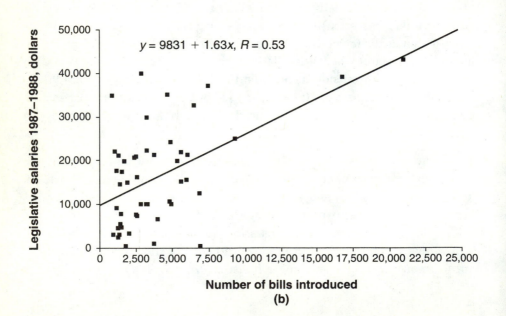

$y = 9831 + 1.63x$, $R = 0.53$

Number of bills introduced

(b)

Figure 9.12   Increase in legislative salaries with (a) length of session and (b) number of bills introduced.

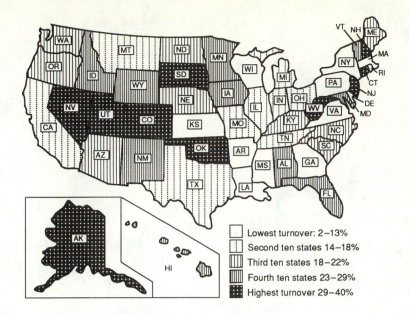

Figure 9.13   Turnover in the lower houses of the states, 1986–1987.

Source: The Book of the States, 1988–89, Lexington, KY: Council of State Governments, p. 90.)

shown in Figure 9.14. There is little that can be said about the geographic distribution of turnover in the state legislatures, although the western mountain states seem to have a high turnover. The lowest-turnover states include industrialized states, such as New York and Pennsylvania, as well as southern states, such as Mississippi, Arkansas, and Louisiana.

Declining turnover also seems part of the dynamics of legislative professionalism, as shown in Figure 9.15. For each $10,000 of increased legislative salaries, turnover declines by 3 percent. The obvious explanation is that such salary increases make the career as state legislator more attractive. Preliminary research suggests that even in states with high salaries, few state legislators stay in office for more than eight terms, or approximately 16 years. This period falls far short of a 40-year career. Of course, many legislators leave to run for other elective offices, such as Congress or a judgeship.[18]

---

18 Norman R. Luttbeg, "The Search for a Career Likely to Be Responsive," a paper presented to the Lexington Conference on State Legislative Elections, March 1–3, 1990.

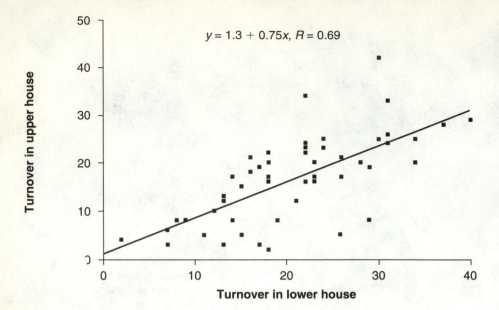

Figure 9.14   Relationship between turnover in upper and lower houses.

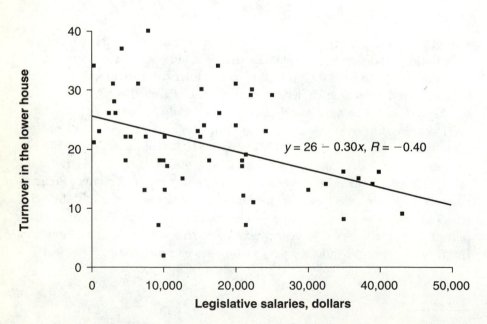

Figure 9.15   Relationship between turnover in the lower house of state legislatures and legislative salaries.

Life in the Legislature.   There is little question that individual legislators must adapt to the procedures of the legislature if they are to exercise any influence.[19] Legislators must learn informal rules under which the legislature has been run, and no doubt they need to learn how to deal with constituents and to win campaign contributions and reelection.[20] Apparently, part of this adaptation involves developing friends within the legislature to whom one can turn to for advice. Legislators consult such friends more so than they do any other actors in the policy-making arena.[21] A legislator's early success in getting on desired committees that deal with policies of interest to their constituents rests with party leaders and the presiding officers in their house. Correct behavior for a beginner can affect the chance of getting on a desired committee. Such assignments seem to weigh the occupational background of legislators, inasmuch as educators are typically put on education committees and farmers on agriculture committees. This practice, no doubt, is desired by the legislators involved, but it plays into the hands of interest groups who would desire such responsive individuals to be put on committees that deal with policies with which they are most concerned. An agriculture group could expect that a farmer assigned to an agriculture committee would push the group's policy preferences.[22] Since the legislature as a whole often proves to be influenced by the committee's recommendations, such a pattern leaves the general nonagriculturally employed public unprotected by a legislature watching out for their interests.

One of the concerns with too rapid change in personnel within a legislature is that newcomers may not learn from old-timers and that the legislature may not function smoothly. The recent popularity of a fixed number of terms in the legislature, such as in Oklahoma and California, may contribute to the inability of those in leadership positions to pass on their understanding of how the legislature works. Since it appears that most legislators across a broad range of states leave before the 10 or 12 years that would be allowed by such limits, it would appear to be these older leaders who would be most affected by term limits.[23]

---

19   E. Lee Bernick and Charles W. Wiggins, "Legislative Norms in Eleven States," *Legislative Studies Quarterly* 8 (May 1983), pp. 191–200.

20   Charles G. Bell and C. M. Price, *The First Term: A Study of Legislative Socialization* (Beverly Hills: Sage, 1975).

21   Eric Uslaner and Ronald Weber, *Patterns of Decision Making in State Legislatures* (New York: Praeger, 1977).

22   Keith E. Hamm and Ronald D. Hedlund, "Occupational Interests and State Legislative Committees," a paper presented at the Midwest Political Science Association meeting, 1989.

23   Luttbeg, p. 20 (see note 18).

Committees Most of the work in any legislature is accomplished by committees. As we shall see, nearly all bills are assigned initially to a group of several legislators who deal with bills on agriculture, business, taxes, and many other substantive areas. All states have such continuing or *standing committees*. Typically, there are 11 to 20 such committees.[24] They greatly shape the content and potential success of the bill as it moves through the procedures to become a law. State committees, however, are not as powerful as are their counterparts in Congress.[25]

HOW LAW IS MADE

Figure 9.16 schematically depicts the many steps that must be taken for an idea for how to cope with a problem in a society becomes a law that affects our lives. All the states use this very complex process. National and local governments use the same procedures. *Drafting* of a bill is a complex task in and of itself, since the language must be clear, and many, if not all, eventualities must be considered. Legal and technical advice is quite important, as is research on other governments' efforts to deal with the problem in a similar manner and their success or failure with it. Although only a legislator in a given house can introduce a bill for consideration in his or her chamber, help in drafting can be gathered from many sources. Political parties, interest groups, fellow legislators, staff, constituents, and in most cases the governor's office are such sources. As we will see, one of the admired attributes of governors is having a program of legislation drafted in the governor's office that is introduced in the legislature by sympathetic and supportive legislators.

The *introduction of a bill* is the simple act of placing it on the desk or in a basket of the presiding officer, typically called the "speaker" in the lower house and the "president," "lieutenant governor," or "president pro tem" in the senate. An unsympathetic presiding officer can assign a bill to a hostile committee, which could see that it is not considered. The act of introduction and assignment to a standing committee is called the *first reading*. When most legislators were illiterate, a clerk would read introduced bills to alert legislators.

Bills are *assigned to standing committees* for the purpose of improving them with information from the expert legislators on these committees as well as information from *public hearings* in which alternative views are heard from

---

24   Patterson, p. 185 (see note 1).

25   Harry H. Basehart, "The Effect of Membership Stability on Continuity and Experience in U.S. State Legislative Committees," *Legislative Studies Quarterly* 5 (1980), pp. 55–68; Keith E. Hamm, "U.S. State Legislative Committee Decisions: Similar Results in Different Settings," *Legislative Studies Quarterly* 5 (1980), pp. 31–54.

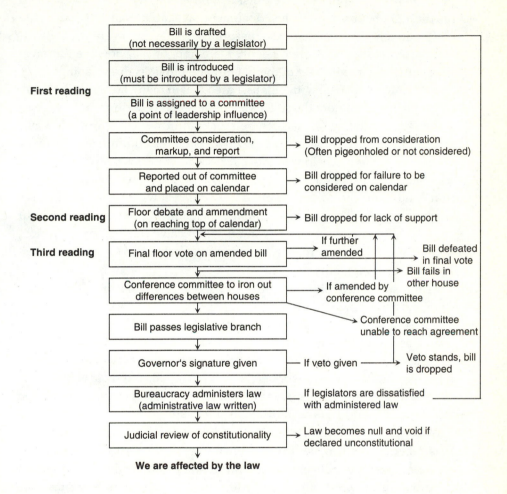

First reading

Bill is drafted
(not necessarily by a legislator)

Bill is introduced
(must be introduced by a legislator)

Bill is assigned to a committee
(a point of leadership influence)

Committee consideration,
markup, and report → Bill dropped from consideration
(Often pigeonholed or not considered)

Reported out of committee
and placed on calendar → Bill dropped for failure to be
considered on calendar

Second reading

Floor debate and ammendment
(on reaching top of calendar) → Bill dropped for lack of support

Third reading

Final floor vote on amended bill

If further
amended

Bill defeated
in final vote

Bill fails in
other house

Conference committee to iron out
differences between houses → If amended by
conference committee

Conference committee
unable to reach agreement

Bill passes legislative branch

Governor's signature given — If veto given → Veto stands, bill
is dropped

Bureaucracy administers law
(administrative law written) → If legislators are dissatisfied
with administered law

Judicial review of constitutionality → Law becomes null and void if
declared unconstitutional

We are affected by the law

Figure 9.16 Procedures for making public policy.

the general public and interest groups. Announcements of such public hearings range from posting a notice outside the hearing room on 3- by 5-inch cards the night before to published documents available to all. Obviously, the use of limited notice is intended to discourage public involvement. Regardless of how inadequately these hearings are announced, however, interest groups are likely to be aware of them. Only the public is disadvantaged.

A committee can deal with bills assigned to it in many fashions. Probably most common is to ignore them. This act of never considering a bill assigned is called "pigeonholing." A bill can be much improved by information and opinions gathered in public hearings. As a result, the committee can "mark up" or rewrite the bill before sending it back to the house, reported out of committee, for further consideration, with a favorable, unfavorable, or no recommendation. The bill then is put on a *calendar*, at which point it will have its second reading. The typical calendar is just a listing of bills reported out of committee and a schedule of when it will receive further consideration. Most states also have emergency and consensus calendars to accelerate considerations of certain bills.[26]

At the scheduled time, the bill receives its *second hearing*. This is the debate and amending process we consider as typical of legislatures. When a bill comes up on the calendar, legislators will have printed versions of the bill, as reported out by the committee, at their desks. They may speak for or against it, often with a time limit imposed in the lower house. Amendments can be introduced and passed or defeated. If amended, and most bills are, the clerk sees that the amendments, as passed, are included in a reprinted version available to legislators at the *third and final reading*.

Although the purpose of the third reading is to take the final vote on the bill as previously amended, further amendments are permitted. If amendments are made, the bill comes back for another final reading. In the third and final reading, most often a recorded vote is taken, with all states now using electronic voting machines. If a majority of those casting votes approve, the bill has been passed in that house.

Using identical procedures the other house too may pass the bill. This, of course, assumes a *bicameral* (two-house) legislative body. With the exception of Nebraska, which has a *unicameral* (one-house) body, all states have bicameral

---

26   The emergency calendar includes bills to deal with emergencies when the legislature wants to act as swiftly as possible; assignment to committee may be bypassed. The consensus calendar typically includes minor bills, such a compensation of individuals for losses incurred by state action, having a cow killed by a state highway truck, and local bills supported by the local delegation of senators and representatives to change local government. Both calendars are typically considered early in each legislative day and passed by voice or unrecorded votes.

legislatures, as does the U.S. Congress. Few if any local governments, however, have bicameral legislative bodies, although bicameral city councils were not uncommon in the past. There is no evidence that there is any difference in policy-making between bicameral and unicameral legislatures.

A bicameral legislature, however, complicates passage of a bill. It must pass in an identical version in both houses to become law.[27] If there are differences between the senate and house versions of a bill, a *conference committee*, composed of members of both houses, must iron out the differences. Sometimes this task is easy, and other times it is all but impossible. Many bills passed by both houses fail to become law because the conference committee cannot agree to a single version of the bill. Once agreement is reached in the conference committee, its representatives from each house take the redrafted version back to their house for another third and final reading or vote. If the bill passes both houses in identical form, it is sent on to the governor for his or her signature, at which time it becomes law.[28]

All but one state's governors can deny their supportive signature on a bill. This is called a *veto*.[29] Without that signature, despite the efforts in both houses, the bill does not become law. As we shall see in the next chapter, some governors can veto portions of a bill, especially bills appropriating money. The legislative branch can *override the governor's veto* if enough votes can be found in both chambers. In most cases two-thirds of both houses must vote for the legislation in order to override the governor's veto. If that override vote is obtained, the legislation is enacted. Although they are often threatened by governors, vetoes are seldom used. Few vetoes, however, are overridden. In 1986–1987 sessions of the state legislatures, just over 1 percent of the enacted bills were vetoed, and only 4.3 percent of these veotes were overridden.[30]

Two other procedures further influence each new law. First, it is assigned to an agency to administer, which entails forms and procedures. These are called *administrative laws*. Either through misunderstandings or opposition by agency personnel or confusion between different sections of the law, the bureaucracy or agency can administer the law in a manner contrary to what the legislature and governor intended. If the problem is serious enough, the entire process can be used again to force the agency to follow legislative intent

---

27 Nebraska, with only a single house, passes bills with the simple majority vote of that house.

28 Some states require a period of up to 90 days after enactment before the law takes effect.

29 The North Carolina governor has no veto power.

30 There were 194,436 enacted bills, 2169 vetoes or item vetoes, and 93 overrides. *The Book of the States, 1988–89* (Lexington, KY: Council of State Governments, 1989), pp. 116–119; Charles W. Wiggins, "Executive Vetoes and Legislative Overrides in the American States," *Journal of Politics* 42 (November 1980), pp. 1110–1117.

more closely. In effect, a new law can be passed to override the bureaucracy's administrative law.

Second, once the law is implemented, someone who is affected by it can appeal a case to the state supreme court, arguing that it is *unconstitutional*. This process is called *judicial review*. In some states the state attorney general can make a judgment on a bill's constitutionality. However, the supreme courts need pay no attention to such judgments. If the courts judge a law unconstitutional, it is declared null and void. This need not be the end. The legislature can propose a constitutional amendment,at least to the state constitution, and if ratified, the state supreme court's ruling no longer applies.

REPRESENTATION IN AMERICAN STATE LEGISLATURES

As we noted at the beginning of this chapter, one of the primary functions of the legislative branch is to represent the public. Unfortunately, no one can give a definitive statement of how representative state legislatures are. Moreover, no one can tell us how to encourage better representation. Although we have previously considered the overall representativeness of the governing elite versus the mass public, we now turn to specific considerations of the state legislatures.

How Legislators See Their Roles.   Several researchers have explored how legislators believe they should behave as representatives. They consider a broad range of roles, but we are only concerned with how legislators see their role vis-à-vis their constituencies (their representational roles). Three are identified, including the *trustee*, a legislator who "sees himself as a free agent that as a premise of his decision-making behavior, he claims to follow what *he* considers to be right or just, *his* convictions and principles, the dictates of *his* conscience."[31] The trustee is fully confident that his or her constituency expects that kind of behavior.

The opposite conclusion from that of the trustee is held by the *delegate*, who feels that the opinions of constituents should be enacted, even if they are contrary to his or her own. Finally, because the researchers found many representatives who claimed they needed to play delegate on some controversial issues while they could be trustees on others, a conditional or mixed role, the *politico*, was defined.

Table 9.4 shows the distribution of the three role types found within several state legislatures and the U.S. House of Representatives. We would expect that

---

31   John C. Wahlke et al., *The Legislative System* (New York: Wiley, 1962), p. 73.

Table 9.4   Distribution of Representational Roles (in Percentages)

Role	N =	CA	NJ	OH	TN	WI	PA	MI	CA	IA	U.S. House
		49	54	114	78	89	106	77	38	175	87
Trustee		55	61	56	81	21	33	35	58	52	28
Politico		25	22	29	13	4	27	31		23	46
Delegate		20	17	15	6	66	39	34	42	25	23
Not classified		—	—	—	—	9	1	—	—	—	3

Sources: John C. Wahlke et al., *The Legislative System* (New York: Wiley, 1962), p. 281 for the first four listed states; Frank J. Sorauf, *Party and Representation* (New York: Atherton Press, 1963), p. 124, for Wisconsin; Malcolm E. Jewell and Samuel C. Patterson, *The Legislative Process in the United States* (New York: Random House, 1966), p. 398, for Pennsylvania; John W. Soule, "Future Political Ambitions and the Behavior of Incumbent State Legislators," *Midwest Journal of Political Science* 13 (August 1969), p. 452, for Michigan; James H. Kuklinski and Donald J. McCrone, "Electoral Accountability as a Source of Policy Representation," in *Public Opinion and Public Policy*, 3rd ed., Norman R. Luttbeg (ed.) (Itasca, IL: Peacock, 1981), p. 334, for California; H. Paul Friesema and Ronald D. Hedlund, "The Reality of Representational Roles," in *Public Opinion and Public Policy*, 3rd ed., Norman R. Luttbeg (ed.) (Itasca, IL: Peacock, 1981), p. 318, for Iowa; and Roger H. Davidson, *The Role of Congressman* (New York: Pegasus, 1969), p. 117, for the U.S. House.

delegates who are inclined to vote their constituents' views would be the most accurate representatives. Many legislators would find it humiliating to admit to being merely the voice of others. Indeed, most of us applaud the "courage" of "statesmanlike" legislators who vote their independent judgments rather than the views of their constituency, however uninformed— especially when we agree with that judgment. Nevertheless, Wisconsin's legislature stands out for its high proportion of delegates, perhaps because of the state's "progressive" political history. The one southern state, Tennessee, has the fewest legislators who feel it is their role to reflect constituents' views.

Since we might expect that the public would not endorse a trustee's indifference to public opinion, we might expect that delegates "learn" their role by facing more competition. Two studies give contradictory results.[32] The

32 Roger Davidson, *The Role of the Congressman* (New York: Pegasus, 1969), pp. 34–71; James H. Kuklinski and Donald J. McCrone, "Electoral Accountability as a Source of Policy Representation," in *Public Opinion and Public Policy*, 3rd ed., Norman R. Luttbeg (ed.) (Itasca, IL: Peacock, 1981), pp. 320–341.

trustees are more reflective of constituency opinions. It may be that the trustee enjoys an easy election from an uncompetitive district and reflects that district. But a second possibility is that with repeated success in reelection, the incumbent grows more confident about how closely constituents are watching and gives a more realistic answer to the role questions. Having been forced by a largely indifferent public into behaving like a trustee, a legislator with longer standing may admit to being a trustee.

An Iowa legislative study found that the roll call voting of delegates in proposing four constitutional amendments corresponded with the majority of their district's later vote on those amendments only 61 percent of the time.[33] The correspondence for politicos was 72 percent and for the seemingly unresponsive trustees was 76 percent.

A study in California perhaps accounts for this unexpected finding. Because California has frequent referendums and initiative votes, it is possible to divide legislative districts into those providing a consistent cue to the legislator by clearly voicing a liberal or a conservative response across these public votes and those that were less consistent in that on occasion they cast liberal votes and at other times conservative votes. Table 9.5 finds that the delegates achieve great consistency *when* they can get consistent cues from their constituents.[34] Lacking such cues, the table shows trustees and politicos to be the better representatives. Speculatively, trustees and politicos may have the advantage over more junior delegates in being around long enough to know their constituents' opinions better. Or legislators show themselves poor estimators of constituency opinions, often seeing them as more conservative than is actually the case. Thus the trustee and politico may avoid the errors of the delegates because they are more indifferent to public opinion.

Few representatives enjoy the information on their constituents provided by the frequent initiative votes in California. One might speculate that the franking privilege of Congress may allow constituent opinion polls, but there is great danger in using survey research to assess public opinion. But non-opinion may obscure true public opinion. The votes on initiatives may thus be a more accurate indication of public opinion. Lacking a source for learning constituent opinion, legislators elsewhere may, if motivated to be a delegate, prove worse at reflecting public opinion than the trustee.

An Overall Attempt to Assess Representation at the State Level.   One study seeks to make such an assessment using "simulated public opinion."

---

33   H. Paul Friesema and Ronald D. Hedlund, "The Reality of Representational Roles," in *Public Opinion and Public Policy*, 3rd ed., Norman R. Luttbeg (ed.) (Itasca, IL: Peacock, 1981), pp. 316–320.

34   Kuklinski and McCrone, 1981, p. 337 (see Table 9.4 footnote).

Table 9.5   Representational Roles of Legislators and Consistency Opinion Cues, and Correspondence Between Constituency Opinions and Roll Call Votes

Representational role	Consistency of constituency cues	
	Consistent	Less consistent
Delegate	0.68[a]	0.20
Nondelegate	0.36	0.39

[a]Unstandardized regression coefficients.

Source: James H. Kuklinski and Donald J. McCrone, "Electoral Accountability as a Source of Policy Representation," in *Public Opinion and Public Policy*, 3rd ed., Norman R. Luttbeg (ed.) (Itasca, IL: Peacock, 1981), p. 337.

Opinions were not available for each state but were available for the nation. Researchers noted how blacks and whites, the rich and the poor, and other demographic groups differed in opinions. Opinions were simulated for each state given these characteristics for that state. A state with 35 percent blacks and 65 percent whites would have black opinions times 35 and white opinions times 65 assigned to it.

Using these "simulated opinions" the researchers assess four possibilities: (1) a "poorly informed elite," where legislators "simply (are) not in a good position to estimate public opinion"; (2) an "isolated elite," in which legislators "may not know what public opinion is even though they can tell you what they think it is"; (3) an "uninformed electorate," where legislators "may be able to tell you what they believe is the prevailing view within their constituencies, but they do not believe that the rank-and-file electorate pays much attention to the issues," giving the legislators little incentive for heeding public opinions; and (4) an "electoral secure elite," where safe seat holders feel little concern with the issue of representation.[35] This last concern, of course, underlies much of the concern about the meaning of incumbency advantage.

There is some support for the "isolated elite," as those who "almost always know" constituency opinions have higher congruence between their personal opinions and their perceptions of constituency opinions. There is "little support" for the "uninformed electorate," because legislators who

---

35   Uslaner and Weber (see note 21).

believe that constituents have positions on an issue have little more congruence between their personal opinions and those they perceive to be held by that public than those who do not share this belief. Finally, "electoral security" is not supported because legislators from safe districts again are no more congruent in their perceptions of constituent opinion and their personal positions than those from competitive districts.

Paraphrasing Key, the researchers conclude, "State legislators are not overwrought by an inclination to seek out the views of constituents on which policy alternative should be selected."[36] They suggest that "the information quest may itself be the most elusive part of the representation puzzle." Without readily available information on public opinion, legislators may not seek it; and without their seeking it, the public "may not raise its collective voice loudly enough to be heard." They conclude, "Perhaps, then, we expect too much policy congruence from those who govern us and for many legislators, the state of ignorance of public opinion may indeed be 'blissful,' if not always intentional."

The Pressure of Approaching Elections.   We might also expect that shorter terms or proximity to elections would encourage responsiveness on the part of the representative. Indeed, another California study finds this to be the case (see Figure 9.17). The figure shows the correspondence between votes on initiatives and referendums and legislator roll call votes. Lower house (assembly) members, with two-year terms, tend to reflect constituency votes and opinions accurately on a continuing basis, but senators, with four-year terms, prove even more accurate representatives when a reelection effort is eminent, but not afterward.

CONCLUSION

Concern with representation among elected officials tends to focus on the legislative branch. Since this branch makes the law, biases here are likely to be reflected into laws. Although there has been much research in areas that relate to the representation, we actually know very little concerning which legislatures are most representative and which not. If most legislatures were quite representative and only several were not, it probably would matter little. Probably, however, none even approximates being representative.

---

36   V.O. Key, Jr. *American State Politics* (New York: Knopf, 1956).

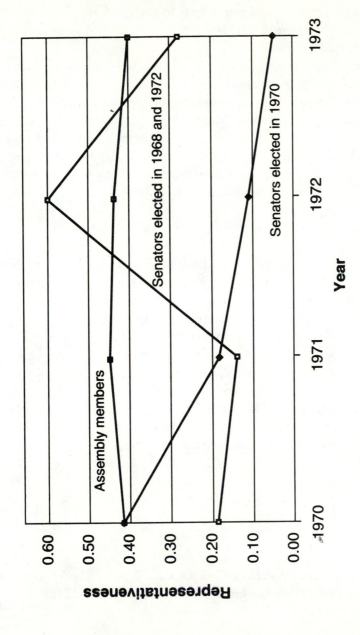

Figure 9.17 Relationship between representativeness of California state legislators and the temporal proximity of elections.

Source: James H. Kuklinski, "Representativeness and Elections: A Policy Analysis," *American Political Science Review* 72 (March 1978), p. 174.

SUMMARY

1. The legislative branch not only is expected to check and balance the executive branch in making public policy but also is expected to represent constituents.

2. Although it was once necessary given communication difficulties and illiteracy, geographically based selection of legislators no longer is necessary and no longer allows representatives to have a consistent constituency that is easy to represent.

3. Judged in terms of the percentage of blacks, women, and various less-middle-class attributes of state legislatures, some are considerably more biased than others. Although the significance of this bias among representatives is hotly debated, it seems to have little impact.

4. State legislatures apportion their states' populations into both state upper (senates) and lower house districts and U.S. congressional districts. The drawing of district lines can greatly disadvantage the minority party that has little say in the matter.

5. Many more metropolitan states with many bills to consider have made their legislatures more professional with higher pay, longer sessions, more staff, and greater office areas.

6. The process of enacting a bill involves the "three-reading" procedure adopted from England. Very few bills pass these hurdles, although there are variations.[37]

7. Although it seems likely that some state legislatures do a better job of representing their public, there is little we can say about which they are or what difference it makes.

SELECTED READINGS

Darcy, Robert E., Susan Welch, and Janet Clark. *Women, Elections, and Representation* (New York: Longmans, 1987). Explores male bias in public office holding.

---

37 Wayne L. Francis, "Costs and Benefits of Legislative Service in the American States," *American Journal of Political Science* (August 1985), pp. 626–642.

Patterson, Samuel C. "State Legislators and the Legislatures," in *Politics in the American States*, 5th ed., Virginia Gray, Herbert Jacob, and Robert B. Albritton (eds.) (Glenview, IL: Scott, Foresman, 1990).

Rosenthal, Alan. "The Legislative Institution: Transformed and at Risk," in *The State of the States*, Carl E. Van Horn (ed.) (Washington, DC: CQ Press, 1989).

Chapter **10**

Executing the Laws and Representing the People

*T*he reader can expect that much information pertaining to the executive branch in our national government applies to the executive branches of the states and communities. Since the bicameral legislature and executive checks and balances in the national Constitution copied the government form of the states and municipal governments at the time, this should not be surprising. This analogy should not be taken too far, however, because the powers of the governors differ from one state to another. Moreover, governors are not just junior versions of the president.

AMBIVALENCE TOWARD THE EXECUTIVE

American ideas toward the executive, the governor in particular, have ranged over our history. Americans initially viewed the governor with *outright hostility,* given their experiences with the king's governor. Ten of the original 13 states had a single-year term for their governors, believing that they could quickly remove those who acted irresponsibly.[1] At present the executive is expected to provide *policy leadership*. Governors have become "vigorous, incisive, and thoroughly trained leaders . . . "[2] This change has been caused by the competition of states in a very complex world economy as well as by the problems, such as crime and urban decay, inherent in the concentration of people in metropolitan areas.

Initially, as noted in Chapter 9 dealing with the legislative branch, representation was primarily expected of only that branch. The governor had been appointed by the king of England prior to the Declaration of Independence. His lack of accountability had led the colonies to demand powers for the representative legislative branch. Similar demands for powers for the legislative branch had long existed in England. When they could throw off the influence of the king's governor, most states simply weakened the office of governor to the point of being irrelevant. Several state constitutions, including Massachusetts's 1780 constitution, however, had used the office to offset what was seen as a too-powerful legislature, representative though it might have been. This concept, of course, is the basis of "checks and balances." The governor also was expected to have governing powers.

Andrew Jackson's idea that the president should also be a *representative* of the public, along with the growing role of the public in selecting the president, influenced thinking among the states about governors.[3] Also part of his perspective on presidential politics was the idea that "to the victor belonged the spoils" of government. What resulted was called the *spoils system*, wherein the winning president or governor would appoint supporters to all available governmental offices as a reward for that support. With a turnover in the executive branch, supporters of the new officeholder would replace all previous government workers.

Although some were entirely satisfied with this situation, the "better elements" of society sought to reform the executive branch to make "merit" the basis of public employment. We have already discussed this concept in Chapter 4. At any rate, powers were taken from the executive branch. The southern states were certainly willing to go along with this trend, given their experience with "carpetbagger" governors. Ideas at this time called for a gover-

---

1 Thad L. Beyle, "Governors," in *Politics in the American States*, 5th ed., Virginia Gray, Herbert Jacob, and Robert B. Albritton (eds.) (Glenview, IL: Scott, Foresman, 1990), p. 219.

2 Larry Sabato, *Goodbye to Good-time Charlie: The American Governor Transformed*, 2nd ed. (Washington, DC: CQ Press, 1983).

3 See Herbert Kaufman, "Emerging Conflicts in the Doctrines of Public Administration," *American Political Science Review* 50 (December 1957). I became aware of these terms in John J. Harrigan, *Politics and Policy in States and Communities*, 3rd ed. (Glenview, IL: Scott, Foresman, 1988), pp. 242–244.

nor who could check the legislative branch, but was otherwise *weak*. Until some states experienced the need to use government to cope with the new problems of industrialization, it mattered little whether the governor was weak or strong.

The situation changed, however, as states faced the need to cope with such problems as crime, regulation of business and industry, the inequitable distribution of wealth in local school districts, and other problems that come with contemporary economies. Legislatures reacted to problems rather than anticipating them. The office of the governor, however, could draft a program of legislation to deal with upcoming problems. *Executive leadership* from the governor thus became urgent in our expectations. "Good-time Charlies" could no longer be tolerated as governors.[4]

THE MODERN GOVERNOR

The institutional powers of governors vary greatly across the states largely because of the different feelings toward the office noted above. Among these powers derived from the state constitutions are length of term, veto powers, fragmentation of the state executive and appointive powers for lesser offices, and budget-making powers.

Term of Office.   At the low point in gubernatorial powers, most governors were elected for two-year terms as are lower-house legislators. These short terms encouraged responsiveness and representativeness. With only two years between elections, representatives must always be aware that the voters may defeat them for failing to act as the voters prefer. Some states, such as Alabama, when George Wallace was governor, would not even allow a governor to succeed himself after this two-year term. Wallace sought unsuccessfully to avoid this by having his wife win the governorship for the next two-year term, presumably to be followed by George Wallace the next term. These short terms of office failed to allow the governor to develop a program of legislation and permitted legislators simply to await the exit of a disliked governor. Longer terms would seem to strengthen the governor's opportunity to influence policy.

After much change since 1960, only three states now retain a two-year gubernatorial term: New Hampshire, Rhode Island, and Vermont. This is

4   Sabato, 1983.

down from 19 states with two-year terms in 1956.[5] None of the three limit the number of such terms. A four-year gubernatorial term has become the norm.

There are differences in how many terms the governor may serve. Three states limit the governor to a single four-year term; 23 to two such terms; and 21 put no limit on the number of such terms. Since limits have been placed on legislative terms only recently, governors with limits on the number of their terms would seem weaker with regard to dealing with the legislature. In states with no limits, a governor theoretically might be continually reelected and make a career as governor of that state. In actuality, however, few governors serve more than eight years.

Veto Powers.   As previously noted, a governor's signature on a bill passed by the legislature is required for it to become law. North Carolina is the exception; there the bill becomes law after it has passed the legislature only. A governor that denies this required signature has *vetoed* the bill. The president has such a power, but many governors have an even more flexible power, the *item veto*. All but seven states give their governor the power to veto portions of a bill while allowing the remainder to become law. Typically, item vetoes are limited to appropriation bills. With this power the governor need not compromise with the legislature to get a budget passed. He or she can item veto those budget items not desired. Sometimes the governor can merely reduce the money given to an agency.[6] As we have seen, legislatures seldom override gubernatorial vetoes. Governors with no veto or no item veto power are less able to influence legislation.

Fragmentation of the State Executive.   The president and vice president of the United States are the only nationally elected executives. The president appoints all other executives, such as the secretaries of state and defense, with the approval of the Senate. They are the president's assistants and may be ask to resign for "personal reasons," if the president asks. The governors of Maine and New Jersey are the only state chief executives who enjoy equal independence and power.[7] Most governors share power in the executive branch with other statewide elected executives.

---

5 Thad L. Beyle, "The Governors, 1986–87," in *The Book of the States, 1988–89* (Lexington, KY: Council of State Governments, 1989), pp. 24–34.

6 R. C. Moe, *Prospects for the Item Veto at the Federal Level: Lessons from the States* (Washington, DC: National Academy of Public Administration, 1988).

7 Additionally, the governor of New Hampshire has to deal only with an elected executive council.

In many of the 42 states with lieutenant governors, they are elected independently of the governor, meaning they can be of the other political party. Similarly, the attorney general (in 43 states) and the secretaries of state (in 38 states) owe nothing in their election success to the governor. These executives must seek their own reelection and owe their election success to their own efforts rather than to anything done by the governor. Governors seeking their cooperation then are backed by neither threats to fire them nor promises to share in the electoral benefits of successful policies. Finally, the federal courts have even undercut the governor's ability to fire appointive officeholders.[8]

On average the governor shares executive power with ten other elected executives—a downward trend from 1956 when the average was 14. North Dakota leads with nine executives plus two statewide elected commissions in addition to the governor. Typically, southern states—not surprisingly, given their constitution writers' desires to weaken all government—have the most executives. On average they have two more executives than do northern states. Clearly, many who wrote state constitutions saw multiple, elected executives as a means for weakening the powers of the governor.

Appointive Powers.   When offices such as those discussed above are not elected, often the governor can appoint them. This arrangement is not unlike the president's appointments of cabinet members. In the case of boards of higher education, though, terms may be staggered, with only a portion of the body to be appointed in a single term, thus delaying gubernatorial control. On average, governors can appoint approximately 18 top state executives, but the range is from 5 to 32.[9] Using data from 1960 on, researchers have appraised the appointive powers of the governors, with strong governors competing with few elective executives and having direct appointive powers with no legislative approval. There has been no change over this period.

Budget-Making Powers.   The budget can be enormously influential in terms of what the state does. The person who controls the budget or purse strings controls policy. A policy with no funding for enforcement is worthless, and governors differ in their influence on budgets. Those in Texas and South Carolina, for example, cannot independently develop their own executive budgets to submit to their state legislatures. Rather the legislature itself is involved in drafting a proposed budget. In other states, governors in effect have access to information not available to the legislatures, and obviously this advantage strengthens the governor's hand. Furthermore, they have the

---

8   Thad L. Beyle, "From Governor to Governors," in *The State of the States*, Carl E. Van Horn (ed.) (Washington, DC: CQ Press, 1988), pp. 39–40.

9   Beyle, p. 40.

opportunity to take an initial position on the budget, to which the legislature can only introduce amendments to reduce or raise an agency's budget.

Other Powers of the Governors. The above powers are institutional powers written into state constitutions and statutes, but there are other sources of influence available to governors, as there are for presidents. Probably chief among them is the *power of personality*. Many governors are effective administrators but lack the personality that could make them memorable as a "great" governor. Former president and governor Jimmy Carter comes to mind. Others lack even this virtue. Obviously a governor with few institutional powers and having a "dry" personality can expect to make little or no impact on the state.

Few governors are not members of one of the major political parties, which gives them the *power of party organization*. Recalcitrant legislators can be pressured to support the governor for the good of the party. The expectation is that voters will reward that party in subsequent elections. This approach works only if governors have the good fortune of having their party in the majority of both state legislative houses, a circumstance becoming increasingly uncommon, as shown in Figure 10.1. Most governors face at least one house that is controlled by the opposition party, and thus the governor's position is weakened rather than strengthened.[10] Contemporary governors would seem to gain little influence from their being the top statewide elected official of their political party.

Another power of the governor is provided by the *patronage system* or spoils system, which was probably more important in the past than currently. When the party faithful could be given jobs with the state, their loyalty could be rewarded as well as their continuing actions in support of the party's position expected. Patronage workers failing to comply with the governor's program could be fired and replaced with those more supportive of the program.

The *merit system* changes this situation. Reformers sought this system as a way of weakening the support political machines might gain with offering people public jobs. Employment in such a system uses a civil service testing procedure. For each government job there are associated tasks for which people take competency examinations. Those passing such examinations are placed at the bottom of a listing of eligibles. When the name of each, along with two others, reaches the top of this list, the three names are sent to an agency needing someone with those skills. The agency must hire one of the top three, for a probationary period. Once that probationary period has passed, the government employee can be fired only for a specific reason.

---

10 P. Sherman, "Power-Split: When Legislatures and Governors Are of Opposing Parties," *State Legislatures* 10 (May-June 1984), pp. 9–12.

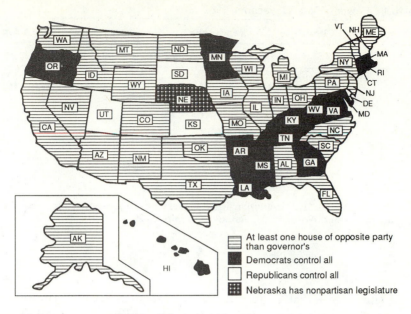

Figure 10.1   Party control of both houses of legislature and the governorship.

Obviously such employees owe no allegiance to a political party or to the governor. A governor facing resistance in the bureaucracy for his or her program initiatives can do little against such civil servants. Thus the merit system weakens the governor and other elected executives.

Presidents can easily gain prime-time access on the television networks to the U.S. public. With this access, he can "go over the head of Congress," appealing directly to the public for their support and put pressure on Congress to respond as the president wants. This advantage might be called *media power*. Governors have no such media access to the state's public. The print and broadcast media in the United States are organized on the national level as well as on the community level. Like the president, a mayor can seek access to the community through local television or radio stations or newspapers. There are no state-level media, however. The governor can tailor press releases, can visit localities and appear on their local stations, and can even make video messages available for use on television stations, but all can easily be ignored by local outlets.[11] They are aware that other news stories sell newspapers or gain bigger television or radio audiences.

---

11   Thad L. Beyle, "Governors," in *Politics in the American States*, 5th ed., Virginia Gray, Herbert Jacob, and Robert B. Albritton (eds.) (Glenview, IL: Scott, Foresman, 1990), p. 238; William T. Gormley, Jr., "Coverage of State Government in the Mass Media," *State Government* 52 (1979), pp. 76–81.

Table 10.1   Power of State Governors, 1985

Very weak			Weak			Moderate			Strong			Very strong	
14	15	16	17	18	19	20	21	22	23	24	25	26	27
SC		TX	MS	NV	ME	KY	AZ	AL	AR	CT		NY	MD
		NC	OR	WA	MT	MO	DE	AK	CO	LA		WV	MA
			RI		NH	WI	ID	CA	FL	NE			
			VT		NM		IN	GA	HE	UT			
					VA		KS	IL	MI				
							OK	IA	MN				
							TN	OH	NJ				
							WY	PA	ND				
									SD				

Source: Thad L. Beyle, "The Institutionalized Powers of the Governorship: 1965–1985," *Comparative State Politics Newsletter* 9 (February 1988), pp. 23–29.

The simple idea that Congress, even members of the opposition party, cannot afford to oppose a *popular* president, has resulted in uncertain confirmation of this power of the president.[12] Not surprisingly, the popularity of a governor would seem to be of an advantage in competing with the state legislature by the same mechanism. Rosenthal presents gubernatorial popularity in 12 states.[13] The popularity of governors varies greatly from state to state and over time, but even after unpopular actions such as raising taxes, governors tend to be more popular than the legislature. Rosenthal discusses several circumstances in which governors have been able to translate that popularity into government actions that they prefer.[14] Popularity is one of the powers of the governor.

ASSESSING THE GOVERNOR'S STRENGTH

Using most of the above indicators of gubernatorial strength, it is possible to assess their overall institutional powers as shown in Table 10.1. With the exception of the Dakotas, more rural states tend to have weaker governors. It

---

12 George C. Edwards, *Presidential Performance and Public Approval* (Baltimore: Johns Hopkins Press, 1990); Jon R. Bond and Richard Fleisher, *The President in the Legislative Arena* (Chicago: University of Chicago Press, 1990).

13 Alan Rosenthal, *Governors & Legislatures: Contending Powers* (Washington, DC: CQ Press, 1990), pp. 30–31.

14 Rosenthal, pp. 34–35.

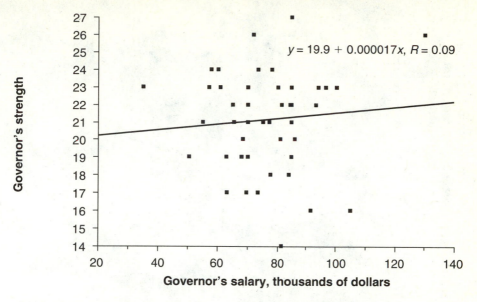

Figure 10.2   The relationship between gubernatorial strength and gubernatorial salary.

is the least metropolitan states that have had the greatest strengthening of their governors over the period from 1965 to 1985. Indeed, it tends to be rural states' lengthening the term of office for their governor that shows the biggest change of this period.[15] It is, of course, cheap to lengthen the term of a state's governor. Thus this measure of the governor's overall strength may not relate to the pressures on the office created by a state's increasingly complex economy. As when we were dealing with the professionalism of the state legislature, salary may be the better measure. Figure 10.2 indicates, however, that gubernatorial institutional strength is poorly related to gubernatorial salary level. Although the subject has not been studied in depth, measures of governors' strength suggest that the placement of a given governor depends on how strength is measured. One study asks informants to rate the influence of the governor on appropriations relative to that of the legislature. As shown in Figure 10.3, this measure only moderately relates to gubernatorial institutional strengths.[16]

---

15   Thad L. Beyle, "The Institutionalized Powers of the Governorship: 1965–1985," *Comparative State Politics Newsletter* 9 (February 1988), pp. 23–29.

16   Glenn Abney and Thomas P. Lauth, "Legislative Influence in the Appropriations Process: A Comparative Analysis," a paper presented at the annual meetings of the American Political Science Association, September 1983. It is cited in Rosenthal, p. 169.

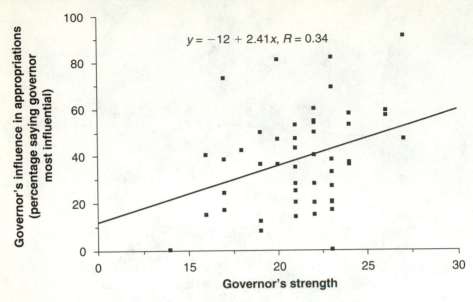

Figure 10.3   Influence of governor on appropriations vs. governor's institutioanl strength.

Rural states are unwilling to pay their governors high salaries, as is evident in Figure 10.4.[17] The salary of the governor rather than his or her institutional strength is most related to the number of bills introduced, as shown in Figures 10.5 and 10.6. It seems evident that salary best captures the fact that the governorship, as in the state legislature, responds to the press of problems coming with modern economies and the concentration of people in metropolitan areas. As Figure 10.7 shows, our two preferred measures of professionalism, that for the legislature and for the governorship, are strongly related. It is possible to speak of a more professional state government, if we are willing, for the moment at least, to ignore the judicial branch.

PROFESSIONAL STATES VERSUS THOSE LESS SO

The idea of professionalism applies both to state legislatures and governors. Both legislatures and governors are affected by the increasing complexity of

17   The correlation between percentage metropolitan and governor's institutional strength is 0.24 and that for salary is 0.61.

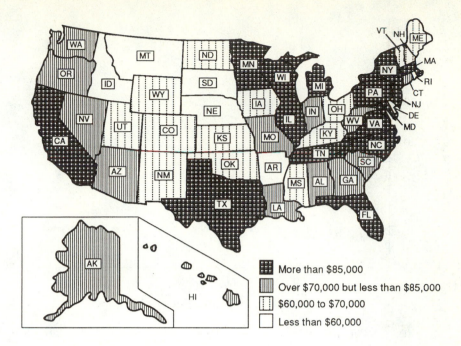

Figure 10.4   Gubernatorial salaries.

Source: The Book of the States, 1988–89, Lexington, KY: Council of State Governments, p. 38.

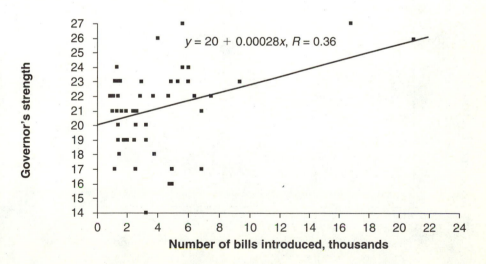

Figure 10.5   Relationship between governor's strength and number of bills introduced.

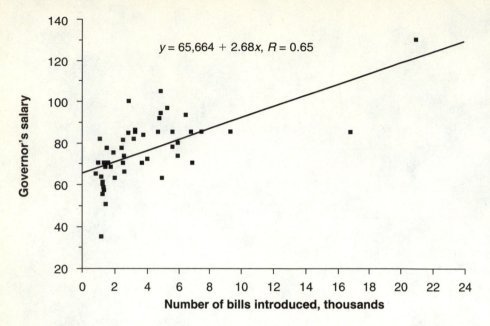

Figure 10.6   Relationship between governor's salary and number of bills introduced.

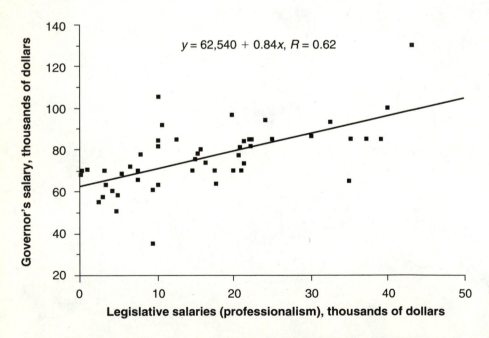

Figure 10.7   Relationship between gubernatorial and legislative salaries.

a state's economy, or the degree to which the state is a microcosm of the United States in general. In such an economy, many work in service industries, many are unemployed, most live in urban or metropolitan areas, and crime and other urban problems beset them. It is thus suggested that professionalism in a state's government comes not as a policy choice by the state and its electorate but rather as a result of the state's entering modern times.

This is not the claim of advocates of professionalizing state government. With professionalism they see more efficient and responsive government better able to cope with problems. In short, they see a state's willingness to become professional as resulting in improved public policy rather than a situation in which the problems are responsible for professionalism, as suggested above. We can partially evaluate this difference on the benefits of professionalism.

The relationships shown in Figure 10.8 are troublesome to explain from the reformers' perspective. There is a very strong relationship between per capita income in the state and the salaries received by the governor and legislators, our state professionalism measures. It is implausible that legislative or gubernatorial salaries result in everyone else receiving more income. Causality may run the other way, however, from higher per capita income to a more-professional state. If so, it suggests that the adoption of state professionalism is the result of the both improved and troublesome modern economy into which the state has moved.

Similarly the relationship between state professionalism and the percentage of the state's public that declares themselves "liberal" may be the result of that professionalism or may be the cause. It is plausible that a public may see the increased government activity that we will see is associated with state professionalism and decide that such activity is what liberals prefer. Since they prefer such policies, they then call themselves liberals. Or it could be that a more liberal state wants more governmental programs and adopts a government form that facilitates the passage of such programs, as measured by state professionalism. It is hard to conceive that more-professional state governments result in more-liberal electorates.

The Results of State Professionalism.   Using our two measures of representativeness, we can note the effects of a state's being professional. These two measures are party representativeness and attribute representativeness. *Party representativeness* is the correspondence between the percentage Democrats in the public and in the lower house of the state legislature, with low values indicating closer correspondence or representativeness. *Attribute representativeness* is the degree to which the lower house of the state legislature reflects seven demographic attributes in the state's public, such as the

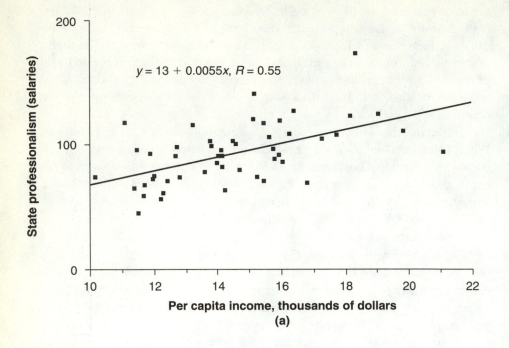

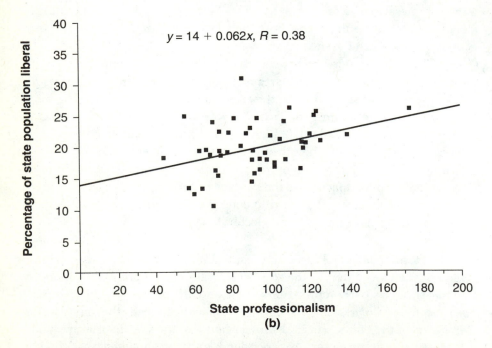

Figure 10.8   (a) State professionalism vs. per capita income and (b) liberalism vs. state professionalism.

percentage women or blacks. A higher value means more representativeness. More professional state government results in better representation, as shown on both measures in Figure 10.9.

Policy differences between professional and not yet professional states are much less clear. In professional states, taxes are less regressive, fewer live in poverty, and fewer lack health insurance, as shown in Figuress 10.10, 10.11, and 10.12, respectively. Those advocating a professional state government might claim these desirable outcomes as the result of reform. Figures 10.13, however, shows that a sharp decline in state expenditures in education as well as a sharp increase in welfare expenditures comes with professionalism in state government. Note that both measures are in dollars per thousand dollars of per capita income, which removes the effect of wealthy states spending more because they can easily afford it.[18] Although the increase in welfare payments might be heralded, the shortsighted failure to invest in educating future generations is not.

Further assessment is beyond the scope of this text; however, it may be concluded that the movement toward both a professional legislature and governorship is driven by the need for processing more bills and programs to deal with problems in a more complex economy. This increasing complexity is the easiest explanation for our findings. The decline in educational expenditures may just reflect the many demands for state spending in such economies, with an apparent lessening of emphasis on education.

GUBERNATORIAL QUALIFICATIONS AND COMPENSATION

Qualifications. Thirty-three states require that a governor be at least 30 years old in addition to being a resident for typically 5 years and a citizen. Again we note several "informal requirements" not written into the constitution but so common as to discourage those not conforming. For example, 38 of the sitting governors in 1988, or 76 percent, were born in the state they serve. Three are women, 6 percent; all but one are white, and their average age is 54. They all have probably a better-than-average education and, before and after serving as governor, will have incomes considerably higher than that of the average family. Like legislators, governors are not representative of their constituents in these regards.

---

18   Thomas R. Dye, "Executive Power and Public Policy in the United States," *Western Political Quarterly* 22 (December 1969), pp. 926–929.

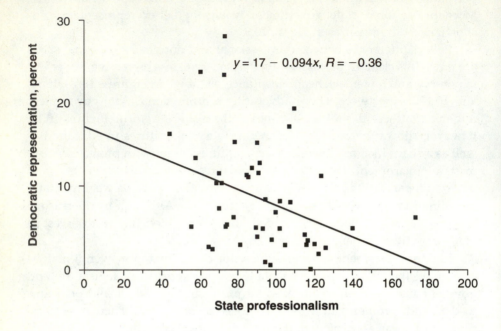

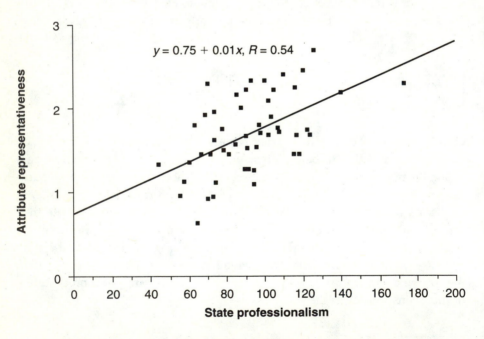

Figure 10.9 (a) Democratic representation and (b) attribute representativeness, as related to state professionalism.

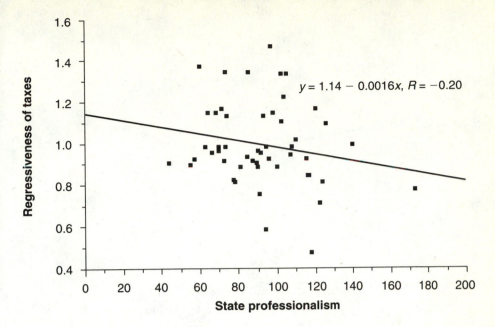

Figure 10.10 Relationship between regressiveness of taxes and state professionalism.

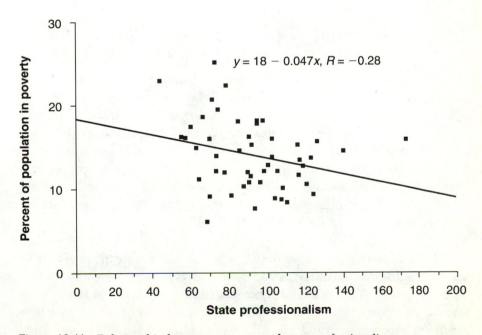

Figure 10.11 Relationship between poverty and state professionalism.

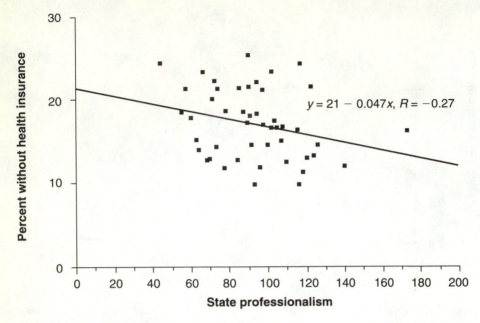

Figure 10.12   Relationship between percentage without health insurance and state professionalism.

Compensation.   As noted earlier, governors in the 50 states vary greatly in the salary they receive. The governor of Arkansas is the most poorly paid at $35,000 per year and Montana at $50,452 is next. By contrast, the figures are $130,000 for New York, $105,000 for North Carolina, and $100,077 for Michigan. There are other attractions to being governor. Housing is free at the governor's mansion. Automobiles, airplanes, and often a helicopter, and travel and expense allowances are included. The status of being called governor, not only while in office but also after retiring from the office, probably is of great importance to those seeking the office.

Leaving the Office.   As we noted earlier, 26 states force the governor to leave the office after either one or two terms. Governors can be removed from office by impeachment in all states except Oregon or by recall in 13 states. In impeachment the lower house passes the charges against the governor (the articles of impeachment) and the senate serves as a jury. Recalling a governor requires a certain number of registered voters to sign a petition for recall. The governor is recalled if a majority support this action in the resulting election.

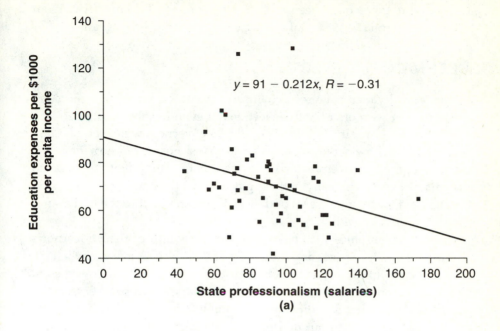

$y = 91 - 0.212x, R = -0.31$

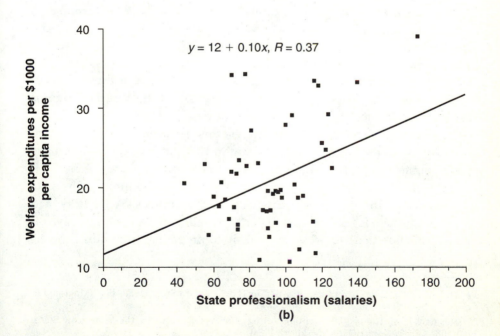

$y = 12 + 0.10x, R = 0.37$

Figure 10.13 (a) Education expenses and (b) welfare expenditures, as related to state professionalism.

There have been 19 instances in which the lower house voted to impeach the governor, and there have been eight convictions.[19] The latest was Evan Mecham of Arizona in 1988. Only a single governor has been recalled.

GUBERNATORIAL ELECTIONS

The past two decades have seen changes in how and when governors are elected. Most governors now face elections in even-number years between presidential elections. In 1990, for example, 36 governors were elected. Only three governors now serve two-year terms. Most governors now have the luxury of acting as governor for three years before they have to begin to worry about reelection. Many of these governors, of course, can be reelected only one time, so their entire second term can be devoted to the office since reelection is not allowed.

Thirteen states since 1960 have changed the length of their governor's term from two to four years and the timing of this election to years when the president is not up for election, such as 1990. This practice is followed so as to concentrate on the issues involved in gubernatorial races rather than the national concerns that so dominate presidential election years. The result, however, has been a turnout decline of nearly 4 percent, since the hoopla associated with presidential elections attracts more voters to the polls.[20]

In the 1986 and 1987 gubernatorial elections, 13 of the 39 governorships up for reelection had governors who were constitutionally proscribed from running for another term. Additionally, seven governors chose not to run again, many of whom had served for 12 years or longer. Some ran for president.[21] Nineteen governors sought reelection (73 percent of those eligible) and 15 succeeded, a 79 percent incumbency advantage. Both of these figures are somewhat higher than was the case in the past.[22] Compared with incumbency advantages in the state legislatures, this performance could be considered poor. These results are surprising in that governors certainly have greater name familiarity and can provide services that obligate voters.

The career path to becoming a governor seems to be through the state legislature and through lesser statewide elective offices. A majority had served in the state legislature and better than half held statewide elective offices, even some that would seem unlikely to prepare an individual for the

---

19 Thad L. Beyle, "The Governors, 1986–87," in The *Book of the States, 1988–89* (Lexington, KY: Council of State Governments, 1989), pp. 24–46.

20 Norman R. Luttbeg, "Differential Voting Turnout Decline in the American States 1960–1982," *Social Science Quarterly* (March 1984).

21 Beyle, "The Governors," pp. 24–25.

22 Beyle, "Governors," p. 243.

governorship, such as treasurer or secretary of state.[23] About 10 percent were members of Congress before becoming governor.[24] Local officeholders seldom become governor, although recently many large city mayors have had success. Recently, California chose between the onetime mayors of San Francisco and of San Diego. Governors seldom hold that position as their first public office, although there are such instances. Few successful businessmen "volunteer" to become governor to repay the state for their success, but again some candidates for governor in effect offer their business skills for use in the governor's office.

On leaving the governorship, most merely retire. Only 10 of 67 governors leaving the office in the 1980s won another public office, six of these in the U.S. Senate.[25] Two 1970s governors, Carter and Reagan, of course became presidents. Usually governors come from within the ranks of state-elected officials and retire to private life on leaving the office. There has been much research to suggest that governors who are responsible for introducing taxes lose their reelection efforts afterward. Certainly, over the period from 1951 to 1989 some 20 percent of gubernatorial defeats could be attributed to raising taxes.[26]

Campaigning for the Office. Many people are interested in becoming governor. In the 1986–1987 elections in 39 states, 287 candidates sought the offices.[27] With the weakening of political parties' ability to get their chosen candidates into office, these seekers of the governorship had to create their own campaign organizations and provide their own campaign funds. In these contests the combined campaign expense was nearly $7.5 million, with the winner typically spending nearly $3 million. There are many who spent much more, often only to lose. Mark White in Texas, for example, spent nearly $16 million in his losing effort to be reelected. His opponent, spending $11 million, won.

With the bulk of these funds going to purchase television time and the services of experts on using the media in campaigns, not surprisingly campaign expenses for gubernatorial candidates are rapidly increasing. In 1978 the 36 gubernatorial contests averaged $2.8 million, soaring to $7.1 million in 1986, a 254 percent increase. In 1986–1987 this cost amounted to more than $5 per vote in 23 states. Between 1978 and 1987 there were 27 gubernatorial contests in which at least $10 million each was spent by gubernatorial candidates.[28] Even states

---

23   Beyle, "Governors," pp. 204–205.

24   Schlesinger, Joseph A., *Ambition and Politics: Political Careers in the United States* (Chicago: Rand McNally, 1966); Larry Sabato, *Goodbye to Good-Time Charlie: The American Governor Transformed*, 2nd ed. (Washington, DC: CQ Press, 1983), p. 40; and Beyle, "Governors," p. 205.

25   Thad L. Beyle, "Introduction," Chapter V in Thad L. Beyle, *State Government* (Washington, DC: CQ Press, 1989) p. 100.

26   Beyle, "Governors," p. 244.

27   Beyle, "The Governors," p. 26.

28   Beyle, "Governors," p. 209.

with "inexpensive" contests typically see nearly a million dollars spent.[29] As with the increasing campaign expenditures in congressional elections, no end is in sight for less-expensive gubernatorial elections.

OTHER STATEWIDE ELECTED EXECUTIVES

Apart from the governor, there are many other statewide elected executives in most states. Although the *lieutenant governor* perhaps comes most quickly to mind as another executive, this office not unlike the vice presidency is generally quite unimportant. Only 42 states have lieutenant governors. This individual succeeds the governor in the uncommon event that the position becomes vacant. Additionally the lieutenant governor may cast a tie-breaking vote in the state senate, and fairly commonly (31 states) become acting governor when the governor is out of the state. Since the lieutenant governor is generally not elected on the same ticket as the governor, this last provision often leads to partisan mischief, unless the governor carefully times such absences. As acting governor, the lieutenant governor may veto legislation passed by the legislature in the governor's absence.

Texas seems to be the exception to the rule that lieutenant governors are quite weak politically. Under the newly retired William Hobby, the lieutenant governor assumed powers in the senate not unlike those of the speaker of the lower house. He could grant committee memberships and assign bills to committees. With the Texas governor being one of the weakest institutionally, it is rumored that Hobby when asked if he would run for governor asked why, after holding the strongest executive position in Texas, that of lieutenant governor, he would be interested in running for the number two office, that of governor.

The *attorney general* is the second most often elected executive (in 43 states). Responsibilities include giving legal advice and dealing with statewide corrupt practices. Even before a bill is passed, the attorney general will often issue an opinion concerning its constitutionality and, after passage, opinions on interpretations of the meaning of the legislation. Although these opinions can easily be overridden by the courts, the attorney general's statements carry great weight. Consumer protection matters, such as misstated product claims, bad insurance practices, poorly run and maintained health facilities, and corrupt officials, are also among the concerns of attorney generals.

---

29   Beyle, "Governors," p. 213.

The *secretary of state* (elected in 36 states) is the chief clerk of the state, to whom legally required reports, such as who won local elections, are made. The archives of the state typically are among the responsibilities of this office. The *treasurer* deposits state money in banks. The *auditor* sees that state funds are properly and legitimately spent. Other executives include the public utilities commissioners, who set rates on public utilities, such as electricity, natural gas, and telephones; the regents of public higher education institutions, who set policies and tuition for those schools; and various commissioners of agriculture, education, labor, and land. Although some of these positions may face election challenges at least when no incumbent is running, most are faceless and holders serve a lifelong career.

A FINAL NOTE ON THE BUREAUCRACY

The numerous workers in the various agencies of government are frequently called the bureaucracy. The bureaucracy is the part of the executive branch of government called upon to administer and implement the many laws and programs passed by state government. What we typically have in mind when we hear this word is hundreds of clerical workers laboring in a large room. About 13 percent of U.S. workers are employed by state and local governments, but very few of these are clerical workers. About 30 percent of all state and local employees are teachers or professors. The second biggest category of state and local employees (about 10 percent) includes health care and hospital workers, many of whom are nurses.[30] Police and those involved in fire protection constitute about 7 percent of all state and local employees. Many government employees hardly match our ideas of a bureaucracy.

One thing we do expect of all government employees is that no one else receive better treatment than what we receive. We expect such employees to understand our personal circumstances. When we buy something from a private enterprise, we feel we can go elsewhere if dissatisfied. Government typically does not provide this option. Thus generally if we are treated impartially by the bureaucracy we feel slighted; but if others are treated preferentially by the bureaucracy, we are offended. The forms used in administering programs we view as burdensome "red tape." On the other hand, generally little of the information on these forms goes unused in impartially

---

30   U.S. Bureau of the Census, *Statistical Abstract of the United States, 1989* (Washington, DC: U.S. Government Printing Office), p. 294.

evaluating our particular circumstances and eligibility for government services.

Efficiency.   Everyone would benefit were it possible to get more services out of the bureaucracy for the same dollars. Thus we could have additional services with no additional taxes. Unfortunately, no one has found a method for doing so. It is not for the lack of making the effort that we have failed. Various novel attempts to achieve efficiencies have swept through state and local governments, all with singularly few results. Actually, were you to consider a broad range of services by government and how much each individual's service costs, you would find that larger governments are more efficient. This is because there are fixed costs to providing government services—such as schools, police protection, and highways—that must be paid even for a very small population. We could facetiously suggest that the solution to inefficiency is merely to increase the population of the state.

The Political Significance of State and Local Employees.   State and local employees are much more likely to vote than others. Even in state contests, upwards of 80 percent vote.[31] Often their votes constitute more than 20 percent of the vote in local and state elections, which of course could easily shape the outcome. School teachers especially are organized enough to affect election outcomes with their involvement. Unlike the legislative branch, statewide executives, and, as we shall see, the judicial branch, state and local employees more accurately reflect the percentage of women and minorities within the state.[32] Thus the bureaucracy's participation would seem to influence state and local government toward the views of the general public.

Hatch Acts.   The Hatch Act of 1939 made partisan involvement by public employees illegal. Most states have copied this act in prohibiting much political activity among state and local government employees. Such acts have been upheld by the Supreme Court. Thus although state and local employees have great impact on elections by way of their heavy voting, they are relatively insignificant as sources of voluntary campaign activity, in running themselves or in contributing money.

---

31   Raymond E. Wolfinger and Steven J. Rosenstone, *Who Votes?* (New Haven: Yale University Press, 1980).

32   Richard C. Elling, "State Bureaucracies," in *Politics in the American States*, 4th ed. Virginia Gray, Herbert Jacob, and Ken Vines (eds.) (Boston: Little, Brown, 1983).

Affirmative Action and Collective Bargaining. *Affirmative action* is the federally inspired program that was instituted to discourage discrimination against women and minorities. As we have noted, there is little such problem in general among state and local employees, but that is not the case in higher-level positions. There few women and minorities can be found.[33] Moreover, the progress of affirmative action is "very gradual."[34] When white men and either minorities or women in equivalent positions are compared, the salaries of the white men are typically 15 or 20 percent higher.[35] This issue is related to the question of *comparable worth.*

Many state and local employees are forbidden by law from joining labor unions or going on strike. But some states—mainly California, Florida, Massachusetts, New Jersey, New York, and Pennsylvania—have most state employees engaged in collective negotiations or bargaining concerning wages to be paid by the state.[36] Collective bargaining grew during the 1960s and 1970s, but its thrust is gone, at least for now. Although there was great concern about what collective bargaining would mean to efficiency and the quality of public service, as is so often the case, careful consideration reveals few benefits or negative consequences.[37]

Unresponsiveness. As noted earlier, the merit system of employment has all but eliminated the latitude of politicians to have a say in who is employed by government. The old patronage system perhaps gave them too much say. Now that this change has been made, we can no longer expect to ask politicians to be of aid in getting government employees who are unresponsive to public opinion out of government. As we noted in our discussion of how a bill becomes a law, even legislators may have difficulty ensuring that the law as administered corresponds with the actions they had intended.

A Better Bureaucracy. Consolidation of the many agencies of state government has been a goal of many. Between 1965 and 1987, for example, 22 states reorganized, combining many agencies into broader agencies, such

33 Patrick Haas and Deal Wright, "The Changing Profile of State Administrators," *Journal of State Government* 60 (1987), pp. 270–278; Anne H. Hopkins, "Perceptions of Employment Discrimination in the Public Sector," *Public Administration Review* 40 (1980), pp. 131–137.

34 Richard C. Elling, "Bureaucracy," in *Politics in the American States*, 5th ed. Virginia Gray, Herbert Jacob, and Robert B. Albritton (eds.) (Glenview, IL: Scott Foresman, 1990).

35 Elling, "Bureaucracy," p. 206.

36 H.S. Tanimoto and G. F. Inaba, "State Employee Bargaining: Policy and Organization," *Monthly Labor Review* 108 (1985), pp. 51–55. Cited in Elling, "Bureaucracy," p. 308.

37 Elling, "Bureaucracy," p. 310.

as environment, transportation, or human services agencies, each usually administered by a gubernatorial appointee.[38] These reorganizations had little effect. There is little evidence that any effort to produce a better bureaucracy has been successful, although many within the agencies will claim that they believe the innovations have been successful. Unfortunately, there is little comparison of the quality of state bureaucracies. Certainly no particular state bureaucracy has been the envy of other states.

CONCLUSION

The elected state executive, especially the governor, has seen an ebb and flow in public support throughout U.S. history. At the time of the Declaration of Independence, few wanted any political strength for governors. Then, after being strengthened to check and balance the legislative branch, governors like legislators were distrusted by southerners. With modern complex state economies many now demand that the leadership of the governor be strengthened. Although many governors have seen their powers improved, this strengthening is largely in length of term and in salary. Certainly, the presence or absence of other statewide elected executives has never been shown to matter much to the quality of political life or of public policy. Similarly, strengthening the powers of the governor seems to follow a state's movement into a more complex economy and to matter very little.

SUMMARY

1. At various times in our history we have sought to weaken or even to discard governors and the executive, and at other times we have attempted to strengthen this office to help cope with problems faced by the states.
2. Governors vary in their formal powers to influence the policies adopted by their states. Budgetary, appointment, and veto powers are prime examples.
3. As was the case in strengthening the role of the legislative branch, a more metropolitan state is more likely to have a stronger or more professional governor.

---

38   Elling, "Bureaucracy," p. 298.

4. Increasingly, governors are elected for four-year terms with substantial salaries and other benefits, but it costs millions of dollars to win the office.
5. Most states have other statewide elected executives charged to deal with limited aspects of state services, such as controlling the investment of state surplus funds, acting as governor in the governor's absence, or having one's signature on state checks. Although these offices may serve as training grounds for governors, they have little other significance.
6. The growth of state and local employees has raised concerns about efficiency. Although there have been many innovations introduced to push bureaucracies toward more efficiency, there is little evidence of success.

SELECTED READINGS

Beyle, Thad L. "Governors," in *Politics in the American States*, 5th ed., Virginia Gray, Herbert Jacob, and Robert B. Albritton (eds.) (Glenview, IL: Scott, Foresman, 1990).

Rosenthal, Alan. *Governors & Legislatures: Contending Powers* (Washington, DC: CQ Press, 1990). This book considers changes in some states that have affected the interaction between the executive and legislative branches.

Sabato, Larry. *Goodbye to Good-Time Charlie: The American Governorship Transformed*, 2nd ed. (Washington, DC: CQ Press, 1983). This book first suggested the changes experienced by governors in the 1970s and 1980s.

Chapter 11

Adjudicating the Law: Policy and the Courts

*O*ther than giving coverage to sensational trials, the mass media (newspapers, magazines, television, and radio), limit their coverage to actions by the U.S. Supreme Court. Thus one might get the impression that only the federal courts are important in our society. Apart from the U.S. Supreme Court, the reality is just the opposite: only the state courts are very important. Nearly all trials and other court activities are in the state and local court systems, not in our federal courts. Even most of the caseload in the U.S. Supreme Court deals with cases from the state courts.

The reason is that nearly all laws that people can violate and, if caught, face a trial in court are state laws. Laws that prohibit certain behaviors, from murder to jaywalking, are crimes against the state or its local governments and are called *criminal cases*. The more serious violations, which carry substantial fines and imprisonment penalties, are called felonies. Less serious crimes are misdemeanors. With very few exceptions, criminal trials are state court trials.

Similarly, *civil cases* are overwhelmingly resolved in the state and local courts rather than in the federal courts. These cases involve disputes between two or more individuals concerning contracts, slander, and the like, in which the state and local courts resolve the dispute. Frequently, they also set the

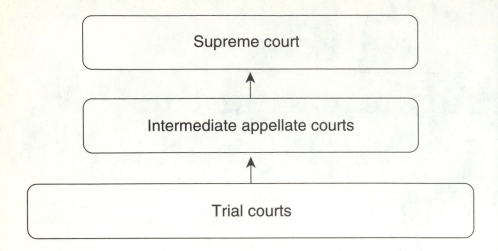

Figure 11.1   Basic structure of state courts.

damages to be awarded to the winner. Across the United States today, there will be millions of court trials, mostly in state and local courts. If we just consider only trial court cases in 1985, there were 312,200 cases considered by the federal district trial courts and more than 78 million state and local cases (about 1 case for every three Americans each year).[1] Federal court considered less than a half of a percent as many cases. You probably will be asked to serve on a jury in a state or local court, and you may be involved in a criminal or civil case. In any event you will no doubt be in a state and local court, not a federal court.

ORGANIZING THE COURTS

The state court systems and our federal court system share one basic organization. Thus in every state we have two court systems, one state and one federal, although as noted above the state system is much larger. This double court system is called a *dual court system*. At the bottom of this basic system, as shown in Figure 11.1, are the *trial courts*. They have various names, but "district" court is

---

[1]   The federal data are from U.S. Bureau of the Census: *Statistical Abstract of the United States, 1989* (Washington, DC: U.S. Government Printing Office), p. 179; the state data are from *State Court Caseload Statistics: Annual Report 1985* (Washington, DC: National Center for State Courts, 1987), pp. 214–224.

most common. This is the name also used for trial courts in the federal system.

It is these courts that we typically have in mind when we mention courts of law. In criminal cases the state's attorney argues for the conviction of the accused, based on evidence presented in court; the defense attorney presents evidence of the defendant's innocence; a jury of peers judges his or her guilt or innocence by typically unanimous agreement among the 12 of them; and a judge in robes assures fair procedures.

It is also in the trial courts that you have the "bill of rights" protections from the U.S. Constitution. Rights for the criminally accused in the individual state constitutions also apply. In the years after World War II the Supreme Court has extended the same rights in criminal procedures in federal courts to you if you are charged in state courts. But if the state constitution offers additional protection, those rights are accorded to you as well. You have the following Constitutional rights in a criminal case in state or federal courts (emphasis added):

> **Amendment V** [rights of accused persons in criminal trials]
> No person shall be held to answer for a capital, or otherwise infamous crime, unless on a presentation or *indictment of a Grand Jury*, except in cases arising in the land or naval forces, or in the Militia, when in actual service in time of War or in public danger; nor shall any person be subject *for the same offense to be twice put in jeopardy of life or limb*; nor shall be compelled in any criminal case *to be a witness against himself*, nor be deprived of life, liberty, or property, without due process of law; nor shall private property be taken for public use without just compensation.

> **Amendment VI** [right to speedy trial and more criminal trial protections]
> In all criminal prosecutions, the accused shall enjoy the right to a *speedy and public trial, by an impartial jury* of the State and district wherein the crime shall have been committed, which district shall have been previously ascertained by law, and to be *informed of the nature and cause of accusation;* to be *confronted with the witnesses against him;* to have compulsory process for obtaining Witnesses in his favor, and to have the *Assistance of Counsel for his defense.*

> **Amendment VIII** [bails and punishments]
> *Excessive bail* shall not be required, nor excessive fines imposed, nor *cruel and unusual punishments* inflicted.

In addition, Amendment VII assures, in civil cases, a trial by jury and compliance with common law. Most of these provisions now apply in state courts regardless of whether they are also in the state's constitution. Notice that a 12–person jury of one's peers and a unanimous verdict are not mentioned, although they are "required" in federal court by tradition.

Once the jury or, where permitted, the judge has decided the guilt or innocence of the accused in a criminal trial or for the plaintiff in a civil trial and punishment or a declaratory judgment has been made, the trial is complete. The loser may then "appeal" to an *intermediate appellate court*. If this level of courts accepts the appeal, which it is *not* obligated to do, it does not retry the case. Instead, typically, multiple judges in such courts examine the court record from the trial and ask questions of the attorneys representing those involved for "errors in procedures," and for "consistency with other court decisions." Incompatibility with the state or national constitutions, what is called "unconstitutionality" also is a major consideration by these courts. These courts have many options for their decisions, but "innocence of the criminal" is not one. They can conclude that a new trial is called for; that the old verdict stands or is reversed; or, in a criminal trial, that the convicted is to be released. The last two might be the result of so grievous an error that a new fair trial cannot be assured. Or the law for which the individual was found guilty is held unconstitutional and thus null and void. There is no need therefore to have tried the individual as he or she could not have violated a null-and-void law.

Lacking satisfaction with this decision, those affected can further appeal to what is usually called the state *supreme court*. This court is the final appellate court, the *court of last resorts*, unless one wishes to take the case into the federal court system, if the latter is willing to accept it. As with the intermediate appellate court, the state supreme court need not consider cases appealed to it, with the exception of cases involving capital punishment (death). State supreme courts consider all capital punishment verdicts. Cases are not retried if accepted by the supreme courts. Rather, they review the court records and previous appellate court considerations for the case. The justices may ask additional questions of the attorneys in the case and may consider the opinions of others wanting to submit statements to the court concerning their preferences; such an advisory is referred to as an *amicus curiae* ("friend of the court"). Again, all the options available to the intermediate appellate courts are available here too. In Texas and Oklahoma the situation is further complicated because they have two supreme courts: one for civil cases, called the supreme court; and one for criminal cases, called the court of criminal appeals.

As you might expect, few trial court cases are accepted by the intermediate appellate courts, and far fewer yet get to the supreme courts. About 0.2 percent of all cases—civil, criminal, traffic, and so on—reach the intermediate courts, and 0.08 percent reach the state supreme courts.[2] Since much

---

2 *State Court Caseload Statistics: Annual Report 1985* (Washington, DC: National Center for State Courts, 1987), pp. 214–224.

time and expense for attorney fees are involved in appealing cases to higher courts, only the most serious cases are likely to be appealed. You are unlikely to appeal a traffic court decision against you just because you are innocent.

There are greater variations in the state court systems than suggested here. Seventeen do not have intermediate courts of appeal, instead relying on their small population to make the caseload of the supreme court, as the only court of appeals, manageable. Many states divide their trial court levels into a tangle of courts, often with limited jurisdiction. This means they can deal only with juvenile cases, only with cases involving penalties of less than $1000, or only with cases involving no jail terms. Local courts, such as small claims, traffic courts, and "justice of the peace" courts, also further complicate this level of courts. The latter is being phased out as outdated and subject to fraud. At one time such courts received pay as a percentage of fines imposed, and therefore more fines meant more pay. The fabled "speed traps" in rural areas typically involved cooperation between local police seeking to gain revenue for their cities and justices of the peace eager to earn more money. The confusion of a large number of different trial courts has resulted in a call for a *unified court system*. Such a system would have a single type of trial court as well as intermediate appellate courts.

Appeals to the Federal Court System.   Although it is uncommon, state cases can be further appealed to the U.S. Supreme Court, if the issue involves the national Constitution. But this is an easy standard to satisfy. Most of the cases considered by the Supreme Court come from appeals from state court systems to the federal court system as involving some national constitutional issue. Usually cases have first worked their way up the state court system, but not always. Cases cannot go the other way, from federal district courts to the state appellate courts.

Judicial Activism.   As noted above, the appellate courts can accept or reject individual cases on appeal. Once accepted, the courts can judge the constitutionality of the laws involved. Such behavior is called *judicial activism*. Judicial activism was once the nearly exclusive province of the U.S. Supreme Court, especially when Earl Warren was chief justice. Some state supreme courts have entered into the void, resulting from the inactivity of the Supreme Court under chief justices Burger and Rehnquist. They have declared limitations on personal rights unconstitutional with respect to their state constitutions' bills of rights.[3] California and New Jersey led the way in

---

3   John Kincaid, "The New Judicial Federalism," in *State Government: CQ's Guide to Current Issues and Activities: 1989–90*, Thad. L. Beyle (ed.) (Washington, DC: CQ Press, 1989), pp. 152–158.

such activism. Alaska, Colorado, Hawaii, Massachusetts, Michigan, Montana, New Hampshire, New York, Oregon, Pennsylvania, Texas, Utah, Washington, and West Virginia have joined them.[4] Apart from a cluster of northeastern states, these states are mainly in the West.

Critics see this activism as lawmaking or perhaps "law unmaking" on the part of the courts and view it as not a legitimate activity by that branch of government. They prefer a more limited role for the courts as interpreters of the law rather than makers of the law, which they call *judicial restraint*. Although it is doubtful that the distinction can be drawn between making and interpreting the law, the point is probably moot, inasmuch as increasing judicial activism can be seen, even in Texas. Again, judicial activism is probably another example of changes in government resulting from more complex economies and societies.[5] As a state faces more substantial problems associated with concentrating people in urban areas, its supreme court tends to become more active in judging the constitutionality of new state laws.[6]

THE U.S. SUPREME COURT'S IMPACT ON THE STATES

Beginning in the 1950s the Supreme Court has, in a large number of its decisions, imposed the federal minimum standard of justice in our national Constitution to state criminal procedures. There are a number of exceptions, since some states do not use grand jury indictments as a check to ensure that the state has sufficient evidence even to schedule a trial. They substitute a hearing before a judge to give this protection, and the Supreme Court has yet to take exception to this provision. Similarly, some states do not use the 12-member juries traditional in federal and most state courts. Some states use

---

4 Henry R. Glick, *Supreme Courts in State Politics* (New York: Basic Books, 1971); Gregory A. Caldeira, "The Transmission of Legal Precedent: A Study of State Supreme Courts," *American Political Science Review* 79 (March 1985), pp. 178–184; and Kincaid, p. 154.

5 Since state constitutions are amendable by simple majority vote, the state supreme courts may find their efforts to protect unpopular individual rights undone by constitutional amendment (see Kincaid, p. 157). Similarly, the U.S. Supreme Court might insist that its awarded rights for individuals are the maximum rights rather than the minimum rights. Perhaps this view would mean that state judicial activism would be disabled if the Supreme Court's decisions were followed.

6 Interestingly, some state supreme courts are more often cited by other state supreme courts, suggesting some response to decisions in other states. See Gregory A. Caldeira, "Legal Precedent Structures of Communication Between State Supreme Courts," *Social Networks* 10 (1988), pp. 29–55; and Peter Harris, "Ecology and Culture in the Communication of Precedent Among State Supreme Courts, 1887–1970," *Law and Society Review* 19 (1985), pp. 449–486.

six-member juries in trials for lesser offenses. Finally, some states do not re-quire the unanimous verdict traditional in federal courts. Again, in the case of lesser offenses and civil suits, one or two jurors may take exception to the others' decision, and yet a verdict can nevertheless be reached.

Three Supreme Court decisions stand out in their importance to state criminal procedures. The first came in 1961 and is the basis of the "exclusion-ary rule," which excludes illegally seized evidence from being presented in trials. The case is *Mapp* v. *Ohio*. When Ms. Mapp refused to allow police to search her home, they ignored her and did so anyway. They found no evidence connecting her to a bombing for which she was suspected but rather found pornographic materials that were unlawful. She was arrested and con-victed. The Supreme Court overturned her conviction because, without a search warrant, the evidence was unlawfully obtained. Such evidence is to be excluded from the courts. Although the initial standard was clearly drawn, the Court has weakened it with more recent decisions.[7]

The second case is *Gideon* v. *Wainwright* (1963). Earl Gideon was found guilty of stealing from a pool hall. He was unable to afford an attorney and defended himself unsuccessfully. While in prison, he studied law and suc-cessfully appealed his case to the Supreme Court. He argued that it was un-constitutional for him not to have had an attorney provided at state expense if he could not afford to pay for one. The Court agreed. His case involved a felony, a serious crime, but this principle has since been extended to even lesser crimes, misdemeanors, involving a prison term. The time at which the assistance of an attorney is to be provided has been extended to when one becomes the prime suspect. This principle leads to the next decision.

The Court decided *Miranda* v. *Arizona* in 1966. Miranda confessed to a crime, but was not told he could speak to an attorney and remain silent. The Supreme Court said the police had violated his rights to be informed. They had not told him that he had the right to remain silent, that anything he said might be used against him, and that he had a right to an attorney. This pro-cedure of the police enumerating these rights has become called "Mirandis-ing" the accused.

SELECTING STATE JUDGES

Federal judges are appointed for life by the president with the advice and consent of the Senate, but most state judges are elected for a limited term of

---

7   This area is one in which the state supreme courts have been active in retaining a more absolute exclusionary view; see Kincaid, p. 157.

office. There are five methods used in the states for selecting judges. The oldest is probably that of having the *governor appoint judges with the consent of a majority of the state senate,* often from a listing of qualified judges from others. Delaware, Maine, Massachusetts, New Jersey, and Vermont are examples. Three states have most of their judges selected by a *majority vote of the state legislature.* They are Connecticut, South Carolina, and Virginia. At least in South Carolina, most judges so selected are former state legislators, probably as a reward for legislative service.[8] *Partisan elections* are another old method. Under this system Democrat and Republican candidates contest all judgeships. Many states use this method nearly exclusively. They are Alabama, Arkansas, Illinois, Mississippi, New Mexico, North Carolina, Tennessee, Texas, and West Virginia. *Nonpartisan selection* became popular with the early reforms of state government. Although several candidates can compete for the judgeship, they carry no political party label. This form of election, of course, is quite common in local municipality and school board elections. Thirteen states select the judges using this method, running from Ohio in the East to Washington and Oregon in the West, with most midwestern states included.

The newest method of selecting judges is called the *merit system* or the *Missouri plan,* because it was first used in Missouri. Under this system a judicial selection or nomination committee with representation of attorneys or the state bar association submits a listing of three to six "qualified" candidates to the governor, who fills the vacant judgeship from this list. After serving one to three years, the appointee must stand for a retention election, which is merely a yes or no vote. If the majority vote is yes, the judge serves a full term before again standing for a retention election. If a majority vote is no, a vacancy is declared and the procedure begins anew. This procedure is supposed to get better people to be judges and to relieve the judge from needing to make promises to defeat a challenger in an election. Alaska, Colorado, Iowa, Maryland, Nebraska, Utah, and Wyoming use this plan to select most of their judges regardless of whether the judge is to serve in the appellate courts or trial level courts. Many other states—Arizona, California, Florida, Indiana, Kansas, Oklahoma, and South Dakota—use the merit plan for appellate judges and nonpartisan elections for trial level judges. Interestingly Missouri selects some lower level judges by partisan ballot. There is also little evidence that in Missouri the quality of justice has been improved as a result of the adoption of the merit system for selecting judges.[9]

---

8   Herbert Jacob, "The Effect of Institutional Differences in the Recruitment Process: The Case of State Judges," *Journal of Public Law* 33 (1964), pp. 104–119.

9   Richard A. Watson and Rondal G. Downing, *The Politics of the Bench and Bar: Judicial Selection Under the Missouri Nonpartisan Court Plan* (New York: Wiley, 1969).

In summary, the selection of state judges follows many patterns. Often appellate level judges and trial level judges are selected by a different procedure. Reformers would advocate the merit plan or at least nonpartisan elections. One state, Rhode Island, selects judges exactly as it is done on the federal level; and two others, Massachusetts and New Hampshire, follow the federal procedures except that appointments are until the age of 70. There is little evidence that the method of selecting judges has much impact on the quality of those judges.[10] Regardless of the method of electoral selection, incumbency advantage is very common for the judicial branch.[11] Very few incumbents lose elections.

The Term of Office. States limit the terms of their judges—with the exception of all appellate and trial court judges in Massachusetts, New Hampshire, and Rhode Island, which as noted above closely follow federal procedures. Again, this limitation differs between the lower trial courts and the higher appellate courts. Supreme court judges serve an average term of just over eight years.[12] Trial level judges serve an average of six years before needing to stand for reelection. All states provide for impeaching judges, and a few provide for recall votes to remove them from the bench.

Qualifications for Judgeships. Again with the exceptions of Massachusetts, New Hampshire, and Rhode Island, all states require that judges be at least members of the state bar association, often for at least five years. Many states also set age limits above those of being a voter, with 30 being most common. Judges share the biases of their counterparts in the executive and legislative branches; they are overwhelmingly male, white, middle class, better educated, and wealthier. In Alaska and Delaware alone, more than 20 percent of the trial court judges are women.[13] Many, mainly southern and nonmetropolitan northern states, have fewer than 4 percent women trial judges. The pattern among the states for having black judges is much worse.

---

10 Bradley C. Cannon, "The Impact of Formal Selection Processes on the Characteristics of Judges," *Law and Society Review* 6 (1972), pp. 579–594; Erik Wasmann, Nicholas P. Lovrich, Jr., and Charles H. Sheldon, "Perceptions of State and Local Courts: A Comparison Across Selection Systems," *Justice System Journal* 11 (1986), pp. 168–185; Henry R. Glick and Craig F. Emmert, "Selection Systems and Judicial Characteristics: The Recruitment of State Supreme Court Judges," *Judicature* 70 (1987), pp. 228–235.

11 Susan Carbon, "Judicial Retention Elections: Are They Serving Their Intended Purpose?" *Judicature* 64 (November 1980), pp. 210–233.

12 The most common terms are as follows: 17 states have six-year terms, 12 have eight-year terms, and 12 have ten-year terms.

13 Herbert Jacob, "Courts: The Least Visible Branch," in *Politics in the American States*, 5th ed., Virginia Gray, Herbert Jacob, and Robert B. Albritton (eds.) (Glenview, IL: Scott, Foresman, 1990).

Although several, mainly southern, states have more than 10 percent black appellate judges, no state has even 10 percent of its trial judges who are black. Judges seem little representative of those they judge, and there is little variation among the states on these measures that might be expected to affect the quality of justice given in state courts.

Since, like legislators, elected judges enjoy overwhelming incumbency advantage in winning reelection,[14] this suggests that, although they are viewed as desirably held accountable to the public, judges are largely out of the public view. State supreme court judges, however, may be an exception to this custom, as judged by Californians' willingness to vote against three state supreme court judges, including the chief justice.

There is some evidence that an ethnic or partisan bias among judges may influence justice. If you are a "have-not," such as being the defendant in a criminal case, the wife in a divorce, a debtor, the victim of an employee injury case, or a government agency in business regulation cases, you will get more favorable justice from judges who are from minority backgrounds.[15] Not unexpectedly, Democratic judges, at least in appellate courts, also tend to side with "have-nots."[16] Although more current confirmations of the impact of these biases are necessary, the findings are not surprising and probably still hold true.

Compensation. Not unexpectedly, supreme court judges receive the highest salary of state judges, with those in New York being paid the highest at $115,000 and those in Montana the lowest at $50,452. Intermediate appellate courts are next best paid, with New York's $102,500 the highest and Utah's $55,100 the lowest. (It should be noted that Montana has no intermediate appellate courts.) Finally at the trial court level, New York judges again are the best paid at $95,000 and Montana the least at $49,178. Clearly, these are very livable wages, but probably they are low relative to what these individuals could make as private attorneys.

THE LOAD OF COURT CASES

The United States is often depicted as a litigious society, one in which being sued is increasingly common. Crimes against individuals and property,

---

14 Lawrence Baum, "The Electoral Fates of Incumbent Judges in the Ohio Court of Common Pleas," *Judicature* 66 (1983), pp. 420–430; and Jacob, p. 266.

15 Stuart Nagel, "Ethnic Affiliation and Judicial Propensities," *Journal of Politics* 24 (1962), pp. 92–110.

16 Stuart Nagel, "Political Party Affiliation and Judges' Decisions," *American Political Science Review*, 55 (December 1961), pp. 843–851.

moreover, are seemingly increasingly widespread and threatening. The reality, however, is somewhat different. Civil cases seem to be increasing only at a rate slightly above our increase in population.[17] Additionally, Figures 11.2 and 11.3 show little pattern of increase since 1975 in crime. This is not to say that crime and court adjudicating of those accused is not extensive and expensive in the United States or that civil cases do not choke our judicial system. As stated earlier, it is the state courts that primarily must deal with both the civil and criminal cases. And not all states are equally affected by the accumulation of cases to be brought to the courts.

Criminal Caseloads. Not every state's courts have equal numbers of cases to adjudicate or process—even if we control for the size of a state's population, as shown in Table 11.1 and Figure 11.4. Delaware and Louisiana have nearly ten times as many criminal cases per 100,000 population as do Iowa and Kansas. Although many southern states have the highest criminal case rates per 100,000 population, some do not. It should be noted, however, that five southern states have not made data available and, were it available, might be in the top category. With the exception of New York, the bottom ten states are upper midwestern states. Although we might expect that the amount of crime influences the number of criminal cases, this assumption proves to be only partially correct, as shown in Figure 11.5. Our measure of crime here is the FBI's index crimes, which are serious crimes against both individuals and property. So there is a possibility that lesser crimes do not take place where serious crimes happen, but this theory seems improbable. Factors other than the incidence of crime in a state must affect criminal caseloads.

An exploration of what does account for a large number of criminal cases per 100,000 population found only one relationship of note, which is shown in Figure 11.6. As the percentage of a state's population that is black increases, the number of criminal cases per 100,000 increases. This finding might suggest that many white criminal offenses are ignored. Alternatively, it might be suggested that since the states with high percentages of blacks are southern states that have a large number of criminal cases, then they have many criminal cases both black and white. We have already noted both the incomplete data for many southern states and the possibly high number of criminal cases for these states. We noted in Chapter 2 that persons in jails and prisons

---

17 Marc Galanter, "Reading the Landscape of Disputes: What We Know and Don't Know (and Think We Know) About Our Allegedly Contentious and Litigious Society," *UCLA Law Review* 31 (1983), pp. 1–71; Thomas B. Marvell, "Caseload Growth—Past and Future Trends," *Judicature* 71 (1987), pp. 162–168.

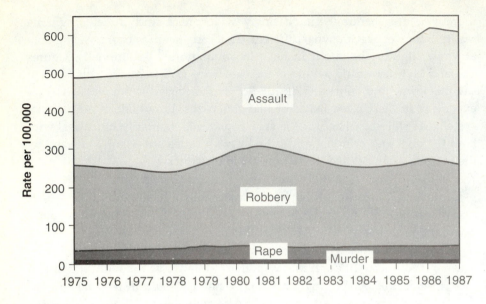

Figure 11.2 National serious crimes against people since 1975.

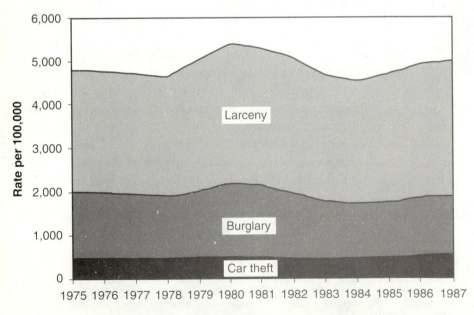

Figure 11.3 National serious crimes against property since 1975.

Table 11.1   Criminal Cases in State Courts per 100,000

Top ten			Bottom ten		
Rank	State	Criminal Cases per 100,000	Rank	State	Criminal Cases per 100,000
1	Delaware	15677	41	Indiana	4443
2	Louisiana	15518	42	Minnesota	4328
3	New Mexico	11472	43	New York	3864
4	Arizona	10392	44	South Dakota	3830
5	Arkansas	10236	45	Michigan	3757
6	Virginia	9967	46	North Dakota	3338
7	North Carolina	9696	47	Oklahoma	3071
8	Utah	8884	48	Missouri	2990
9	Alaska	8401	49	Iowa	1948
10	Idaho	7808	50	Kansas	1769

Source: State Court Caseload Statistics: Annual Report 1985 (Washington, DC: National Center for State Courts, 1987), pp. 214–224.

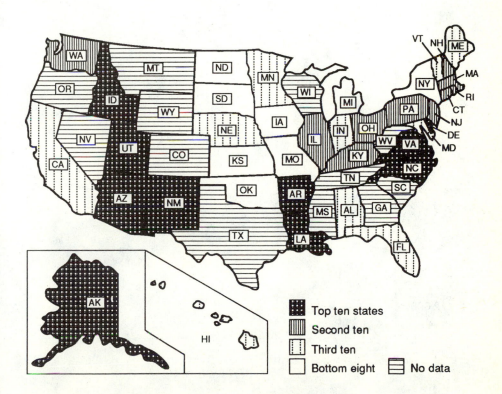

Figure 11.4   Criminal caseload per 100,000 population.

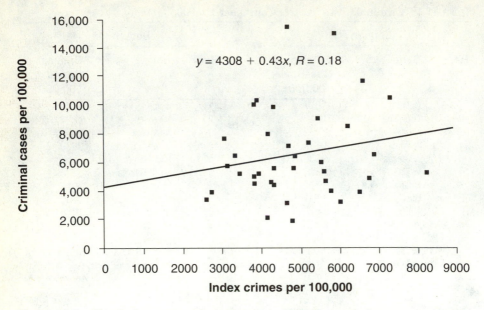

Figure 11.5   Criminal cases vs. criminal acts per 100,000 population.

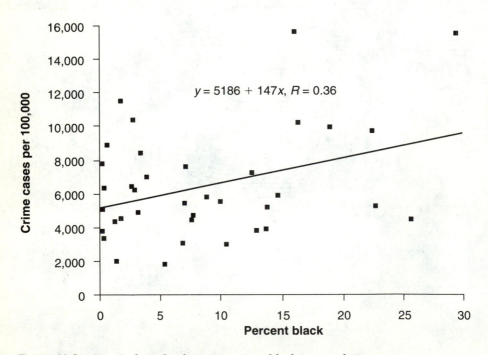

Figure 11.6   Criminal caseload vs. percentage black in population.

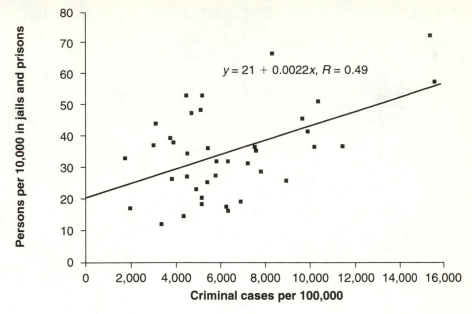

Figure 11.7   Persons in jails and prisons vs. criminal cases.

are high in the South. Figure 11.7 notes the strong relationship between criminal cases and persons in jails and prisons. This discussion tends to suggest that once again the South is different. Only further research can resolve whether criminal caseloads are driven by discrimination against blacks or by some unique characteristic of the South.

Civil Caseloads in the States.   Civil cases also burden the states (see Table 11.2). Again, on the basis of civil cases per 100,000 population, there is great variation. Virginia and Maryland have more than 15,000 cases per year per 100,000 population, whereas Tennessee has just over 2000. A glance at the map in Figure 11.8 suggests that the Northeast and the Great Lakes states have unusually high civil caseloads. The origins of this load, however, are not clear. Our measure of modern industrial economies, percentage of the population living in metropolitan areas, does not relate much to civil caseload. Some states have populations who seem more eager to sue. As shown in Figure 11.9, these states seem to be those with higher per capita income.

Dealing with Caseloads.   We certainly would expect that the court systems in states with many criminal or civil cases per 100,000 have a great burden and that the system might adapt to that burden. Fortunately, there is only a moderate

Table 11.2   Civil Cases in State Courts per 100,000

	Top ten			Bottom ten	
Rank	State	Civil Cases per 100,000	Rank	State	Civil Cases per 100,000
1	Virginia	15127	41	Pennsylvania	5052
2	Maryland	15098	42	Washington	5044
3	Delaware	9438	43	North Dakota	4944
4	Alaska	8131	44	Kentucky	4901
5	New Jersey	7900	45	Minnesota	4895
6	Massachusetts	7763	46	Maine	4847
7	New Hampshire	7398	47	Rhode Island	4839
8	Wisconsin	7335	48	Missouri	4467
9	Oklahoma	6692	49	Hawaii	4450
10	Indiana	6679	50	Tennessee	2193

Source: *State Court Caseload Statistics: Annual Report 1985* (Washington, DC: National Center for State Courts, 1987), pp. 214–224.

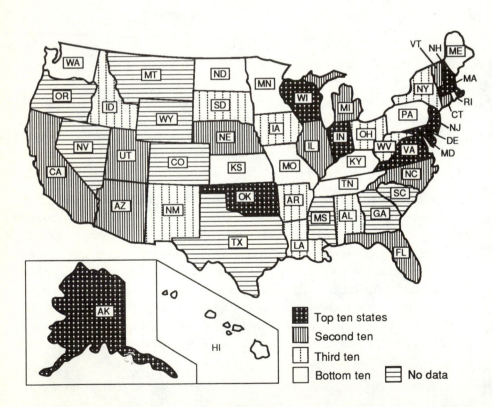

Figure 11.8   States with heavy civil caseloads.

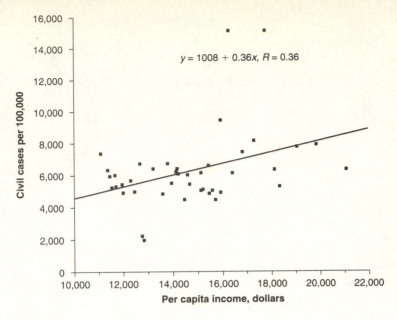

Figure 11.9   Civil cases per 100,000 vs. per capita income.

relationship between the two burdens, civil and criminal caseloads as shown in Figure 11.10. Since reform in our state court systems centers on gaining the adoption of the merit or Missouri plan or at least nonpartisan elections of judges, Figure 11.11 considers the relationship between method of judicial selection and criminal caseload. Surprisingly, those states with low criminal caseloads are somewhat more likely to have reformed, whereas those with high criminal caseloads retain the older partisan selection of judges. Again, however, this finding may just reflect the South's unwillingness to give up partisan elections to their courts.

FURTHER PROBLEMS WITH THE STATE COURT SYSTEM

To be certain, those states with substantial criminal or civil caseloads must face the question of underwriting the costs of providing the courts and judges necessary to deal with the burden of cases. Both the trial and possible appeals can be avoided by *plea bargaining*. If someone accused of a criminal offense agrees to pleading "guilty," no trial needs to be held. Usually, however, the

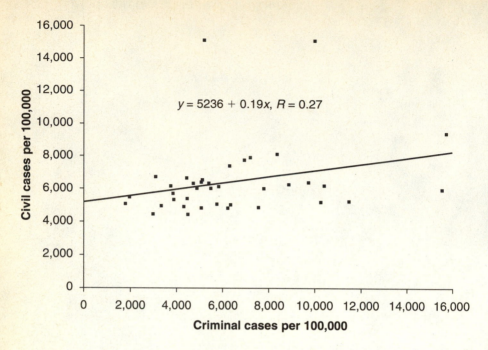

Figure 11.10   Civil and criminal caseloads compared.

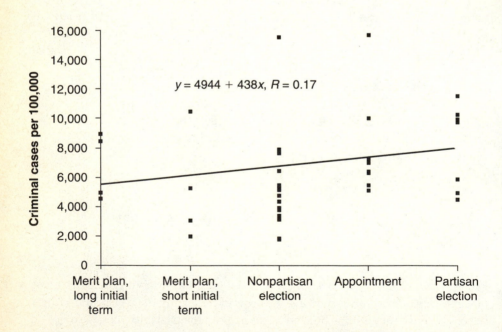

Figure 11.11   Criminal caseloads vs. method of judicial selection.

accused have to be encouraged somehow into such a plea, with the more serious offense being dropped in return for a guilty plea on a lesser offense. Certainly, plea bargaining relieves an overburdened court system. Critics, however, note that the criminal does not pay the prescribed penalty for the offense committed, which may mean that he or she will more rapidly be again out in society to commit another crime. It may be that only about one accused criminal in five goes to trial, and the others engage in some form of plea bargaining.[18] This practice would suggest that only a fivefold increase in state criminal court systems' capability to process criminal cases could relieve the pressure to use plea bargaining.

Despite the *Gideon* v. *Wainwright* decision's assurance of legal counsel provided at state expense for those who cannot afford to hire their own, there is no provision that such an attorney will be a good one. Despite Hollywood's romantic characterizations of public defenders, free justice is probably inferior justice. Even among those who can afford to hire an attorney, few can afford the best. They may—and I emphasize, may—not get as good a defense as they would with a more expensive attorney. All justice in the United States is expensive, and the *wealthy probably get better justice.*

Finally, *justice is not uniform across the country.* In some areas, acts that are criminal behaviors elsewhere are perfectly legal—and, more commonly, the severity of the penalty for a criminal act varies greatly from state to state. The probability of being found guilty as well as the severity of the penalty varies greatly not only between states but also within states. There is some evidence, furthermore, to suggest that the mass media's emphasis on crime rather than the crime rate results in more numerous guilty verdicts and more severe punishments.[19] There is also the use of grand juries by prosecutors largely for their own political careers. They may gain notoriety by using the grand jury's inquiry into possible crimes as a springboard to higher office.

Finally, the Constitution guarantees only a trial by an impartial jury, not one by ones' peers. Regardless, there is good reason to believe that the typical trial jury is neither. Most states call jurors from the rolls of those registered to vote, which makes even the initial draw biased against those who are unregistered. Additionally states typically excuse students,

---

18 H. Ted Rubin, *The Courts: Fulcrum of the Justice System* (Pacific Palisades, CA: Goodyear, 1976).

19 P. R. Wilson, *Crime and the Community* (St. Lucia, Australia: Queens University Press, 1973); George Gerbner, Larry Gross, Michael F. Elley, Marily Jackson-Beeck, Suzanne Jeffries-Fox, and Nancy Signorielli, "TV Violence Profile No. 8: The Highlights," *Journal of Communications* (Spring 1977), pp. 171–180.

mothers of small children, and small businessmen whose livelihood might be affected by serving on a jury. Thus, additional bias is added to prospective juries. Furthermore, attorneys for the two sides in criminal and civil cases may excuse prospective jurors because they seem unlikely to vote for their clients. Many persons are employed to assist attorneys in "tailoring" juries into being the most favorable possible jury for their clients. Given all of these biasing influences on our trial juries, it is thus improbable that anyone has been judged by an impartial jury of his or her peers.

SUMMARY

1. In the United States we have a dual court system with both state and federal courts. Each system has trial courts where cases are tried as well as appellate courts that may hear cases on appeal.

2. The Constitution affords those accused of crimes many protections in federal courts. Most of these protections have been extended to those accused in state courts, whether or not they were also included in state constitutions. Several Supreme Court decisions, such as *Mapp* v. *Ohio*, *Gideon* v. *Wainwright*, and *Miranda* v. *Arizona* have also structured how the courts, in particular state courts, deal with crime in the courtroom.

3. Many states have a large variety of trial courts, and some have only one appellate court, typically called the state supreme court. Reformers advocate a unified court system with a single type of trial court and an intermediate appellate court to reduce the burden on the supreme court.

4. Several state supreme courts are active in reviewing trial court decisions as based on unconstitutional laws. This procedure is called "judicial activism."

5. Although state judges are selected in many ways, many states urge selection by the merit system. In this method, a knowledgeable committee selects applicants with merit for final selection by the governor. Voters later get to approve or disapprove of the individual selected.

6. Although civil and criminal caseloads are generally heavy across the states, there is substantial variations in caseloads among the states. Reducing the heavy caseloads of the courts either entails greatly increasing the number of courts or using "plea bargaining."

SELECTED READINGS

Baum, Lawrence. "State Supreme Courts: Activism and Accountability," in *The State of the States*, Carl E. Van Horn (ed.) (Washington, DC: CQ Press, 1989). A good review of what we know specifically about state supreme courts.

Jacob, Herbert. "Courts: The Least Visible Branch," in *Politics in the American States*, 5th ed., Virginia Gray, Herbert Jacob, and Robert B. Albritton (eds.) (Glenview, IL: Scott, Foresman, 1990). A good summary of research literature on the courts.

Stumpf, Harry P. *American Judicial Politics* (San Diego: Harcourt Brace Jovanovich, 1988). A discussion of all levels of judicial politics in the United States.

Chapter
12
The Political Economies of the States and Communities

*T*he range of policies adopted by our state and local governments have enormous implications on the economic aspects of our lives. These policies may affect whether we have jobs, how high our taxes are, how much it will cost taxpayers to correct bad decisions by business and government—such as the excesses of the nation's savings and loan institutions during the 1980s. There are few decisions made at any level of U.S. government in which concerns about the impact on the economy are not raised. Those supporting a new policy will see benefits to the economy in adopting it. Opponents will see it hurting the economy. The arguments are common. Only if the city attracts new businesses by refurbishing its downtown retail area will it avoid decline. With that decline property will lose value, property taxes will decline, and government services will need to be reduced. Only if the state underwrites the education costs of poorer community schools will federal grants to schools continue, and industry will not be attracted to a poorly educated state. And if the new federally sponsored scientific facility or the new Japanese automobile manufacturing facility is located in our state, we shall see many new jobs to staff these facilities, as well as other jobs to serve those directly employed, and the economy will grow.

By implication, such growth in the economy will mean more tax money available to fund services with no increase in the tax rate. Without growth, the argument goes, new and higher services mean new and higher taxes.

There probably was a time in which the decisions of a municipality or even of a state had little, if any, impact on any economy other than its own. Such is no longer the case. As the public became more mobile and willing to relocate for a better job if not for better schools or other governmental services, local decisions could be endorsed or refuted by people moving into or out of the area. Bad decisions could result in people leaving. This is called voting with your feet. Similarly, as businesses, even those overseas, grew larger and more international, many of their policies, at least to some degree, were reactions to governmental decisions. The taxes they would have to pay, the availability of desirable labor, especially better-educated workers, and other costs of doing business, which government could shape, affected their choice of where to locate their plants.

COMPETITION IN THREE ECONOMIES

There are three substantial sources of new investment in states and communities that are sought by all who wish to see their city or state grow. The first is new investment from the *domestic private economy*, the nation's businesses and corporations. How successful are the states in attracting a larger share of the new investment by U.S. businesses? How do some become more successful? The second economy is the *international economy*. Inasmuch as many corporations now have production facilities or provide services in many countries, another source of investment in a state or community is from abroad. How successful are the states in attracting a larger share of such foreign investment in the United States? How do some become more successful?

Finally, there are *federal government dollars* to seek. This money may go directly to individuals living in the state or community as a supplement to income, such as social security payments. It may be dollars paid to civilian or military employees or dollars to build or maintain facilities, such as post offices or military bases. Finally, it may go directly to governments as grants to encourage some governmental services or to encourage certain standards for such services, such as affirmative action or a 21-year-old drinking age. Again are some states more successful in attracting such investments and how do they do so?

DOMESTIC PRIVATE ECONOMY

Each year through all of our efforts to produce goods and services we create a substantial economy, worth trillions of dollars. The sum total, called the gross national product, includes earnings made by Americans in other countries. Excluding the latter earnings, we have the gross domestic product, which amounted to $4,497,200,000,000 (about $4.5 trillion) in 1987.[1] Some of this is reinvested by Americans into new plants and equipment to increase new production. A survey in 1987 suggests that $388,600,000,000 was so invested, about 8.6 percent of the gross domestic product.[2] This sum is, of course, a good deal of money; and if one state were to get a disproportionate share, it could assure the full employment of all of its citizens. With such full employment, revenues to the state would greatly increase, thereby allowing an easy expansion of all governmental services, including a greater investment in public education. Do some states get a disproportionate share of these dollars?

Before we can consider this question we need to consider certain realities of available data. The investment dollar figure, for example, comes from asking a random sample of U.S. businesses about their investments in new plants and equipment. Too few are surveyed in each state to say much about that state. Fortunately, the fact that a very large number of manufacturers were asked about their capital investments in such equipment allows a state-by-state comparison. In the 1986 survey, U.S. manufacturers invested $76,330,800,000 or about 2 percent of the gross domestic product.[3] These are the best available data on capital investment in the states. Another uncertainty remains, however: Would a billion-dollar investment in California, for example, have the same effect on the state's economy as a similar investment in Montana? Since the fact that California's economy and population is many times as great as Montana's, the answer obviously is no. Thus in our comparisons, investment is divided by the size of the state's economy, thereby somewhat accounting for the importance of such an investment in a small economy. The measure of the size of the state's economy used is the gross state product.[4] This figure is merely the total value of goods and services produced within each of the states for a given year.

---

1   U. S. Bureau of the Census, *Statistical Abstract of the United States, 1989* (Washington, DC: U.S. Government Printing Office), p.422.

2   *Statistical Abstract*, p. 533.

3   U.S. Bureau of the Census, *Annual Survey of Manufacturers: Geographic Areas, 1986* (Washington, DC: U.S. Government Printing Office), pp. 3–5 to 3–11.

4   Vernon Renshaw, Edward A. Trott, Jr., and Howard L. Friedenberg, "Gross State Product by Industry, 1963–86," *Survey of Current Business* (May 1988), pp. 30–46.

California received more than $8 billion of capital investment from manufacturers in 1986 (the highest) versus Alaska's $46 million (the lowest). However, because of California's GSP of more than $500 billion, the investment is not considered very high. The darker states on the map in Figure 12.1 have the greatest private-economy capital investment on a percentage basis. Evidently the states vary greatly in their success in getting investment from the private sector.

FOREIGN DIRECT INVESTMENT

Foreign capital investment, though much smaller, can be quite important to the growth of a state's economy. Foreign direct investment is thoroughly reported, but for a given state it varies greatly from one year to another. The measure used here therefore is an average across three years, 1986–1988, again as a percentage of the state's gross state product. Idaho got no direct foreign investment over this period, but New York got nearly 36 billion dollars in such investment over these three years or an average of about 12 bil-

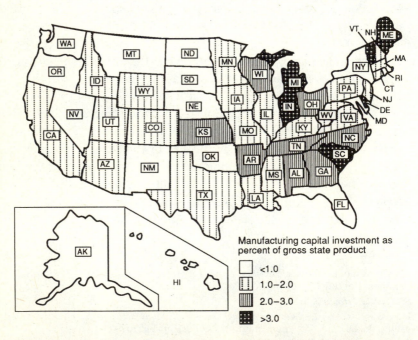

Figure 12.1   Success of states in attracting manufacturing capital investment.

lion each year. Even dividing by the gross state product, New York remains quite high.

Over the same period, 1986–1988, Delaware managed direct foreign investment at 5.9 percent of its gross state product. The other top five states were Hawaii, Ohio, Connecticut, and New York. The bottom five are Idaho (at 0 percent), South Dakota, New Mexico, Nebraska and Vermont. Overall the states that are successful in attracting foreign investment differ from those attracting domestic investment. Since all capital means jobs and probably increased revenues, the two percentages are added in Figure 12.2.

With few exceptions, the states gathering the greatest investments, as a percentage of their gross state products, are in the northeastern portion of the country, east of the Mississippi River and from the Carolinas and Tennessee north. The differences are great. Delaware is highest with an investment total of more than 9 percent of its economy. New Mexico with 0.5 percent is lowest. The two Dakotas are also at the bottom.

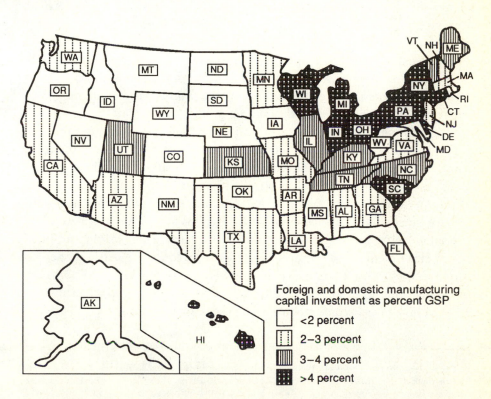

Foreign and domestic manufacturing capital investment as percent GSP

☐ <2 percent
▥ 2–3 percent
▥▥ 3–4 percent
▦ >4 percent

Figure 12.2   Combined direct foreign investment and domestic manufacturing investment as percentage of gross state product, 1986.

STATE-GRANTED INCENTIVES FOR INVESTMENT

Many of the states have been quite active in seeking to attract a more sub-stantial share of investment. The states have become rivals in passing incentives and tax breaks to attract these capital investments.[5] There is a very broad range of policy innovations that have been tried by various states to make themselves attractive both to foreign and domestic capital investment. Most of these efforts are "quick fixes" in which a decision by the state is expected to have nearly immediate results. Most at best are only of moderate cost, such as allowing a relocated business to forgo some or all taxes for the cost of the relocation. Critics, nevertheless, challenge even these as unlikely to be repaid in improved revenues after a short time as claimed by their proponents. Furthermore, the critics argue that the lost immediate tax revenues hurt the very infrastructure, such as the quality of the state's educational system, that would attract new businesses.

These incentives are of two basic forms: tax incentives and financial incentives.[6] Tax incentives range broadly from excluding earnings from abroad from state taxes—the "water's edge method"—to excluding all taxes for a short time. Some states exempt taxes if businesses settle in certain locations within the state where they might be expected to have the greatest benefits, such as in very poor areas—what are called "enterprise zones." On rare occasions the voters are asked to ratify such concessions; not infrequently they refuse, defeating the tax concession at the polls.

Incentives of another type, financial incentives, have more recently become popular. Often the state will make low-interest loans available from bonds backed by the state. Communities have also offered such loans. These loans are mainly for new construction and are often administered by state industrial development agencies. Small amounts of federal money are available for such efforts. Finally, there are incentives to relocate to a new state, but some states have passed disincentives for businesses leaving an area. "Plant-closing laws" are one example. They require an early notice to employees as well as severance pay. Another is allowing cities to encourage and assist "employee stock ownership plans" that would keep the facility by having employees become its owners. These efforts fall far short of those the

---

5   Coincidentally three books in 1988 dealt with this topic. See Peter K. Eisinger, *The Rise of the Entrepreneurial State* (Madison: University of Wisconsin Press, 1988); R. Scott Fosler, *The New Economic Role of the American States* (New York: Oxford University Press, 1988); and David Osborne, *Laboratories of Democracy* (Boston: Harvard Business School Press, 1988).

6   Keon S. Chi, *The States and Business Incentives: An Inventory of Tax and Financial Incentive Programs* (Lexington, KY: Council of State Governments, 1989).

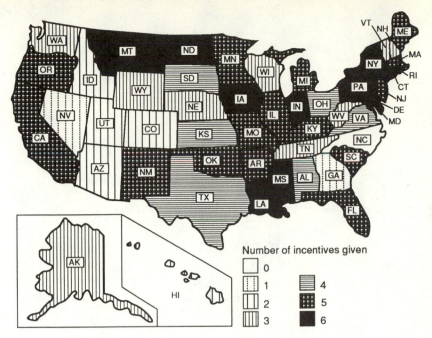

Figure 12.3   Number of tax incentives granted by each state.

states might make to discourage relocations. There is broad acceptance at least among legislators that relocations are motivated by old, inefficient plants being closed to move to new, more-efficient ones, which at least on a national basis will improve our international competitiveness.

The most popular of these incentives are: exempting goods in transit from taxes (48 states); exempting taxes on raw materials used in manufacturing (45 states); exempting manufacturers' inventories from taxes (44 states); charging no sales taxes on new equipment (44 states); having a state revenue bond agency finance new expansions (44 states); and having similar financing for existing plants (42 states).[7] Several other incentives have been widely adopted recently by the states. The states are indexed by how many of the six incentives showing the greatest growth they have adopted, as shown in Figure 12.3.[8] With exception of the mountain West being less likely to adopt

---

7   Chi, pp. 5, 10.

8   The increasingly common incentives are tax exemption or moratorium on land and capital improvements a similar exemption on equipment and machinery; exemptions in taxes for research and development; the state revenue bond agency mentioned above; and state loans for building construction and for equipment.

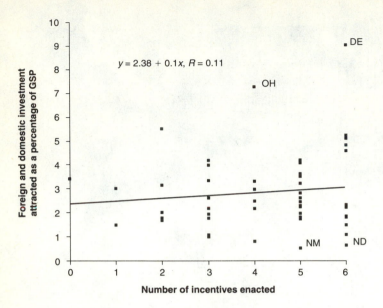

Figure 12.4   Foreign and domestic investment vs. tax incentives.

these incentives, no clear pattern is evident. However, the states offering the most incentives do not appear to be those with the most investment.

ACTIVIST BUSINESS POLICY AND SUCCESSFULLY ATTRACTING INVESTMENT

Despite the enthusiasm of governors and legislators for passing what are perceived as incentives for business to locate in their state, research has found the efforts only occasionally successful in attracting new business.[9] Although Figure 12.4 considers only whether states with the most incentives have more investment, there is a modest relationship. Each incentive enacted attracts 0.1 percent of a state's gross state product as investment, which is not much of a

---

9   Thomas R. Dye, "Taxing, Spending and Economic Growth in the American States," *Journal of Politics* 42 (Winter 1980), pp. 1085–1107; and Bryan Jones, "Public Policies and Economic Growth in the American States," *Journal of Politics* 52 (February 1990) and Paul Brace, "Party and Economic Performance in the American States," a paper presented at the annual meeting of the Midwest Political Science Association, Chicago, 1990. All of these studies find that such policies influence capital investment or at least growth in employment. Virginia Gray and David Lowery, "Interest Group Politics and Economic Growth in the U. S. States," *American Political Science Review* 82 (March 1988), pp. 109–131, and Chi, p. v, show no impact, however.

result and is certainly not assured, as evidenced by the low correlation. The great success of Delaware with better than 9 percent capital investment after enacting six incentives and of Ohio with better than 7 percent after only four enacted incentives are probably known to all legislators concerned. The failures of North Dakota with six and New Mexico with five enacted incentives to gain much capital investment are probably ignored. Perhaps this tendency to ignore failure suggests why legislatures are often eager to enact incentives despite so little success.

POLITICS AND ECONOMIC DEVELOPMENT

Politics can play a role in a state's economic development in a multitude of ways. At the simplest level, pressing a state to grant tax incentives could be simply motivated by businesses' desire to avoid paying taxes. Economic growth may just be rhetoric to get lower taxes. Thus we might expect states where business has more influence to undertake such incentives. Presumably where business is strong the Republican party would be strong as would business interest groups. There is little support for this assumption. Only 36 percent of Republican-controlled states have passed at least five incentives as compared with 63 percent of those states under the Democratic control.[10] This result is, of course, contrary to our expectations. Similarly, 50 percent of strong interest group states have passed at least five incentives, whereas 80 percent of those with weak interest groups have passed at least that many.[11] Again, this finding is unexpected. Self-interest of those most immediately affected, the states' businesses, guided through the institutions associated with them, the Republican party and pressure groups, little accounts for why states rush to adopt tax incentives.

Another theory is that coalitions develop in any society among certain industries to gain benefits from government.[12] They succeed over time; then, as means of production change, government cannot encourage the more productive segments of society. As a result, government and society decline. Olson's data confirming this theory are that more recently admitted states have shown greater growth in the 1960s and 1970s than do older states that presumably have become dominated by older coalitions. We have not been looking at growth, but rather at what is presumably a driving force in en-

---

10 Chi-square = 10.177, statistical significance = 0.60.

11 Chi-square = 11.7, statistical significance = 0.07.

12 Mancur Olson, *The Rise and Decline of Nations* (New Haven: Yale University Press, 1982).

couraging growth—namely, capital investment. Figure 12.1, however, showed earlier that investment tends to be greatest in the older rather than the newer states as suggested by Olson.

As Brace points out, there is a similar argument common in political science. The work of V.O. Key suggests that a second, successfully competing political party, not dominated by the "haves," can represent the "have-nots" and win change in government policy.[13] The data show both incentives as well as investments increase weakly where the two political parties are more evenly balanced in the state legislature. When there are more marginal (closely contested) seats in the lower house, there are slightly fewer incentives offered and slightly less investment. In short, no characteristic of a state's political parties much affects either state policy on encouraging growth or success in attracting capital investment.

As we saw in Chapter 9, state legislatures have been experiencing rapid "professionalization" as they face contemporary problems. In this regard they are following the "professionalization" of Congress. This trend seems adequately captured by the salaries granted state legislators who often have no time for an occupation other than that of a legislator. Much is seen as desirable about more "professional" legislatures. The caliber of persons attracted to such offices would seem to be related to passing policies likely to encourage growth. The arguments are made that such legislators have the time to research and to develop programs to encourage growth. If so, as we have seen, they evidently waste their time enacting incentives, which do little to encourage capital investment. Another argument is that professional legislators can better resist the entreaties of pressure groups.[14] But as we noted above, more incentives are passed in states with weak pressure groups. There seems little benefit in a more professional legislature for this reason.

Nevertheless, professional legislatures, with high legislative salaries, are both more likely to allow incentives for capital investment and to enjoy more capital investment, as shown in Figures 12.5 and 12.6. A $25,000 increase in legislative salaries is likely to result in one additional incentive being passed and about a 1.5 percent increase in total capital investment.

Such professionalization is most evident in more metropolitan states, which also have more complex and developed economies. Thus professionalization as well as economic growth may develop from such complex economies, with professionalization spuriously related to economic growth. At any rate, we cannot be certain why professional legislative states are more

13   Brace, p. 3 (see note 9); V.O. Key, Jr., *Southern Politics* (New York: Knopf, 1949).

14   L. Harmon Zeigler, "Interest Groups in the States," in *Politics in the American States*, 4th ed., Virginia Gray, Herbert Jacobs, and Kenneth Vines (eds.) (Boston: Little, Brown, 1983).

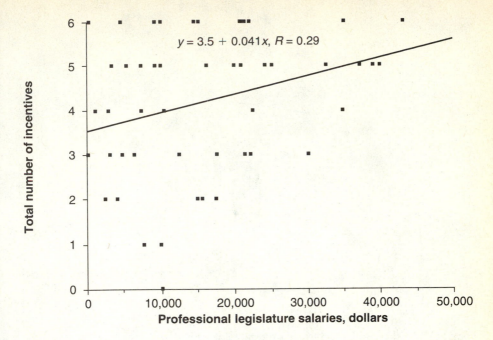

Figure 12.5   Investment incentives vs. professionalism of state legislatures.

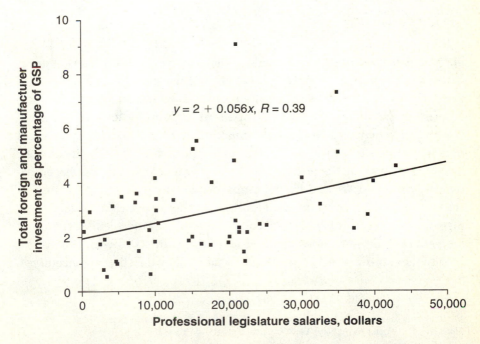

Figure 12.6   Foreign and manufacturing investment vs. professionalism of state legislatures.

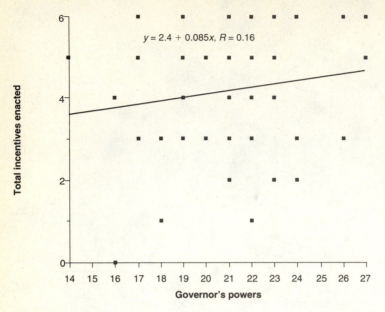

$$y = 2.4 + 0.085x, R = 0.16$$

Figure 12.7   Enacted incentives vs. governors' powers.

Source: The 1981 Development Report Card for the States, Washington, DC: Corporation for Enterprise Development, p. 26.

likely to enact tax incentives. It is not the legislature but rather the governor that is most expected to influence a state's economic growth.[15] However, Figure 12.7 shows only a very weak pattern of states with more powerful governors as having more incentives.[16] No pattern is found for total investment.

Finally, it may well be that states that do not have the capital investment of neighboring states seek to compensate or catch up by enacting incentives. Figure 12.8, showing the percentage of employment growth experienced between 1979 and 1987 and the total number of incentives enacted, finds a strong negative relationship—the less employment growth, the more enacted incentives. It is possible that incentives adversely affect employment. It seems more plausible, however, that legislatures in states with little or no employment growth seek to get the state moving by enacting tax incentives.

15   Osborne (see note 5); John E. Jackson, "Michigan," in *The New Economic Role of American States*, R. Scott Fosler (ed.) (New York: Oxford University Press, 1988).

16   Thad L. Beyle, "The Institutionalized Powers of the Governorship: 1965–1985," *Comparative State Politics Newsletter* 9 (February 1988), pp. 23–29.

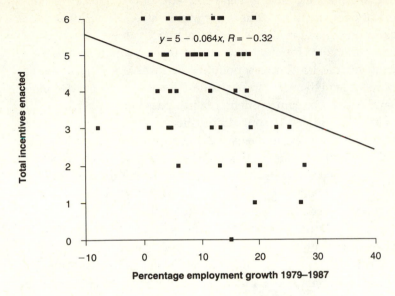

Figure 12.8   Enacted incentives vs. employment growth.

CONCLUSIONS ON BUSINESS INVESTMENTS

We find the influence of state governments on their economies to be extremely modest. There are several possible explanations. The first is that we have focused on capital investment incentives and the investment of capital without controlling for other influences. Other factors might attract investment and employable workers as well. A private organization, the Corporation for Enterprise Development, yearly publishes a "report card" on the states concerning development.[17] Their policy index includes actions by state governments that from their point of view encourage development. This measure considers not only the tax and fiscal environment, which we have considered above. In the long run, however, a state can invest in education, fairer taxes, assistance to businesses seeking to export, and many other policies to improve its economic circumstances. This index then is broadly inclusive even if some of the included measures are less than obviously encouraging of economic development. The index also includes many expen-

---

17   *The 1989 Development Report Card for the States* (Washington, DC: Corporation for Enterprise Development, 1989).

sive programs, such as increasing per-pupil education spending, early childhood (prekindergarten) education programs, state hazardous waste cleanup funds, and welfare benefits levels. Also, many valued incentives for encouraging economic development would take many years to be achieved and to bear fruit, such as tax fairness, pollution controls, and housing assistance. In short, to score high on the "policy index" a state would need to make a substantial and expensive commitment, not just pass tax incentives.

As can be seen in Figure 12.9, our simple measure of the number of incentives offered relates strongly to the overall policy index. Tax incentives are apparently fundamental to a state's effort to compete economically. The passage of a single tax incentive tends to improve a state's ranking by three places. Thus we are not missing the manner in which states compete by focusing simply on the tax incentives adopted by each state.

The broader focus of the "policy index" does, however, more strongly relate to total capital investment, as shown in Figure 12.10. Thus there would appear to be a quite broad range of investment efforts that a state must undertake to attract investment successfully. The simply provision of tax incentives has little influence on capital investment; it is merely a part of such efforts.

There still remains the possibility that the range of actions taken by the states to attract investment is insufficient to have much of an effect. In fact, as we have seen, such actions as tax incentives sweep through the states. A state cannot wait to see whether the incentives work for fear that a competing state may, by early enactment, gain a short-term benefit that would take years to overcome. The policies that do matter may be much more expensive and may take years to have much impact.

Related to this thought is the possibility that the wealthy states just get wealthier because their public has money to reinvest. This theory would suggest that the relationship is spurious, since wealthy states attract much capital and can afford to invest heavily in education. Although it is true that states with high per capita income attract more capital investment, the relationship is not strong. Furthermore, other research that has attempted more in-depth analysis controlling for the differences in wealth among the states has found much the same minimal effect of state governmental actions on influencing their economies.[18]

It is also possible that legislators do not really expect a policy to succeed or care whether it does. Their successful political careers may have little relationship to successful policies enacted. Furthermore, by passing legisla-

---

18   Brace, p. 18 (see note 9).

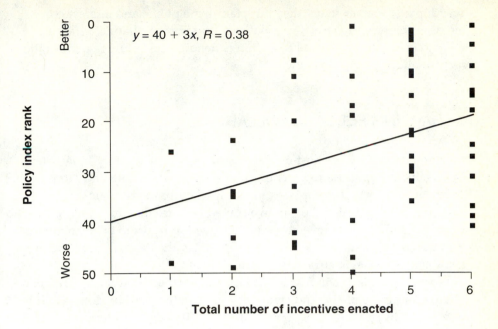

$y = 40 + 3x, R = 0.38$

Policy index rank — Better / Worse

Total number of incentives enacted

Figure 12.9   Tax incentives as an element in an overall measure of developmental policy-making by the states.

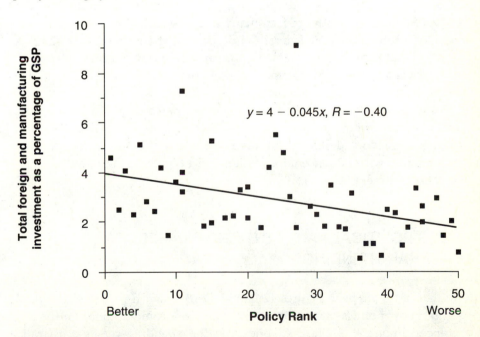

$y = 4 - 0.045x, R = -0.40$

Total foreign and manufacturing investment as a percentage of GSP

Policy Rank — Better / Worse

Figure 12.10   Total foreign and manufacturing capital investment and ranking on the "policy index."

tion adopted by other states, they can placate the public and interest groups that urge the enactment of these policies. In short, perhaps the failure of policy to influence events and happenings denotes the failure of democratic representation in policy-making.

ATTRACTING FEDERAL DOLLARS

Even large U.S. cities are hurt by the closing of nearby military bases. State officials, including those representing the state in the Senate and House of Representatives, will therefore seek to exempt their bases from such cutbacks. Of course, new federal dollars are welcomed because they mean more jobs, more state and local tax revenues, and less need to resort to tax increases to cover the costs of state and local services. We turn then to consider how successful the states are in attracting federal dollars to their states.

Normally, what is considered in state and local textbooks is the ratio of federal spending, military and civilian, in each state to the tax dollars that it sends to Washington. As shown in Figure 12.11, little or no pattern is evident, because states that are quite successful in attracting back the federal dollars they send are often adjacent to states that are unsuccessful in this regard. Clearly, federal taxation and spending do not redistribute wealth in the United States. As a matter of fact, many of the wealthier states actually get more of a return on their federal tax dollars, as shown in Figure 12.12. A criterion that is more comparable to our capital investment measure above, however, is federal tax dollars spent divided by the gross state product. This percentage is shown in Figure 12.13.

These federal dollars constitute a far larger percentage of a state's gross product than do foreign direct and manufacturers' capital investments. On average, the federal dollars amount to 19.8 percent of a state's gross product as compared with 1.3 percent for foreign and 1.8 percent for manufacturers' capital investment per year.

DOES POLITICAL PARTY STRENGTH AFFECT FEDERAL SPENDING?

Neither of the maps in Figures 12.11 and 12.13 shows a pattern that would suggest how politics, presumably in Washington, could account for the differences among the states. At one time the spending-versus-taxes ratio favored the southern tier of states, or the "Sunbelt," at the expense of the remaining states, the "Snowbelt." No such pattern is now evident. We can

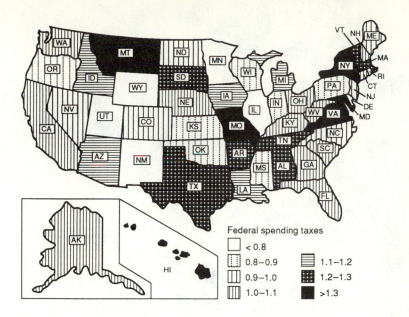

Figure 12.11   The ratio of federal spending to federal taxes among the states.

resort to plausible hypotheses to account for the differences, beginning with the idea of shared partisanship between state and national elected officials as being advantageous to a particular state. Where a state's officials are of the other political party, we might expect federal dollars to be reduced. There are several difficulties in assessing this hypothesis because state and local governments have both legislative and executive branches that can be con-

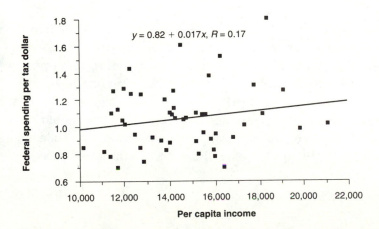

Figure 12.12   Federal spending per tax dollar vs. per capita income.

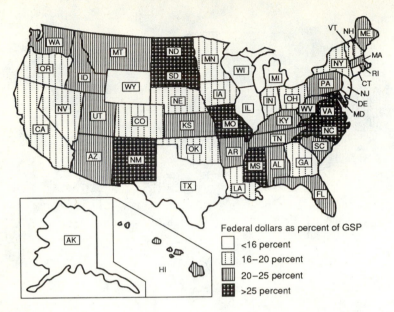

Figure 12.13   Federal spending as a percentage of gross state product.

trolled by different political parties. During the 1980s such has always been the case at the national level. Furthermore, as we have seen earlier, this division of partisan control of the legislative and executive branches is quite common at the state level as well. Additionally, the programs are ongoing. Therefore it would take some time for the conscious acts of the party in control of the federal government to begin to influence the amount of money going to a state.

If we concede the basic greater influence of the executive branch, however, we can see whether states with Republican governors when the president is a Republican are advantaged. In Figure 12.14 we can see, however, that as the percentage of the vote won by 1984 and 1986 Democratic gubernatorial candidates increased, the federal share of the state's gross product also increased. Since this is a very weak relationship, it probably should be interpreted as no relationship. The political party in control of the state as compared with that of the White House has little effect on the state's success in attracting federal dollars.[19]

19   The percentage of Democrats in the state's lower house relates more strongly to federal dollars. The correlation is 0.30.

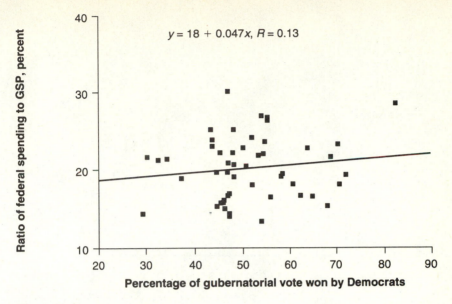

Figure 12.14   Federal spending as a percentage of GSP vs. percentage of the vote won by Democratic gubernatorial candidates in elections between 1984 and 1986.

CONCLUSION ON ATTRACTING FEDERAL DOLLARS

We can see more about what the distribution among the states of federal government funds does not reflect rather than what it does reflect. Of course, federal funds are not *evenly* distributed among the states. Also, these funds are neither distributed back to the states in *direct proportion to the tax dollars* each sends to Washington nor are they distributed to the poorer states to *redistribute* the overall wealth of the country, as evidenced by Figure 12.15. *Regional patterns* are not apparent. No region, such as the Northeast, is advantaged, nor is the South disadvantaged in terms of the distribution of federal funds. Finally, no *partisan bias* in the distribution of federal dollars can be found. Republican presidents do not benefit Republican states. A Democratic Congress gives only a modest advantage to states with disproportionately more Democrats in their legislature.

It is difficult to say how federal funds are distributed, because there are three basic elements to these funds, which in turn are distributed using different criteria. Military and defense funds go to where there are defense contractors and military bases, many of which are located where they are for reasons of geography and climate. Social security funds go to where social security recipients are concentrated. Finally, all other funds go to the states on the basis of various criteria, including need. No clear overall pattern is

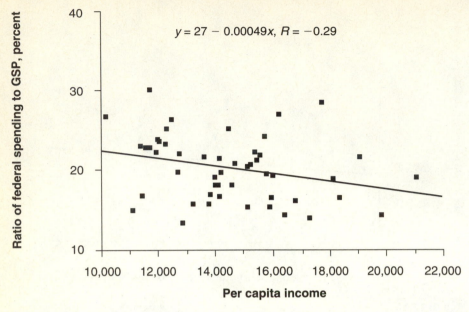

Figure 12.15   Federal spending as a percentage of GSP vs. per capita income.

evident. No attribute of states and probably no effort by the states will greatly affect the infusion of total tax dollars.

SUCCESS IN ALL THREE ECONOMIES

Although no further political explanations of success in attracting federal spending were considered, the overall assessment of success in attracting dollars in all three economies—international capital, manufacturer's capital, and federal— yielded surprising results. What is evident in Figure 12.16 is that states succeeding in attracting investment capital fail to do well in getting dollars out of Washington, and vice versa. Perhaps what is happening is, again, compensation. Since federal dollars are more substantial, perhaps those states that fail to attract these dollars resort to other means to improve their economies, seeking private capital investment both domestically and internationally.

As we have seen, the policies thought to attract such investment most directly, tax incentives, fail to be very successful. Since we are dealing with actual invested dollars in Figure 12.16 rather than such incentives, the compensation argument fails. Some states seek private investment and others federal dollars, perhaps out of ideological conviction. This argument too fails, at least if we assume that conservatives would favor seeking private rather than federal dollars.

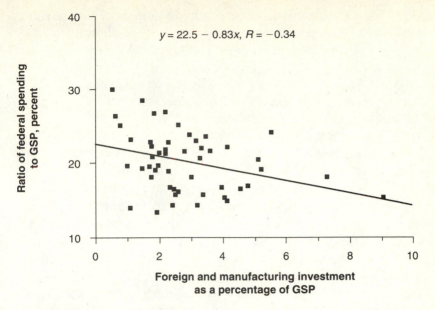

Figure 12.16 Federal spending as a percentage of GSP vs. foreign and manufacturing investment as a percentage of GSP.

As the percentage of liberals within the public increases, the federal investment decreases.[20] If the representatives of these publics reflect these opinions, our hypothesis is refuted.

CONCLUSION

The states and communities can no longer ignore happenings of economic importance within their borders. Even if they were to ignore the impact of such events on tax revenues and thus on tax rates or governmental services, those affected would no doubt turn to local elected officials to help. But other than offering rhetoric, such as "I Love New York" or "Virginia Is for Lovers," or appealing to morals or patriotism, anything government might do entails making some actions lawful or unlawful or committing tax revenues to a program. Only the costs of enforcement are involved in making some actions lawful or unlawful, so passing laws is cheap. Plant-closing laws are an example. States cannot pass a law stating that a business has to open a new plant in the states or that existing businesses have to reinvest additional

---

20   The relationship is as follows: $y = 26.5 - 0.32x$, $R = 0.32$.

funds in their businesses. Furthermore, the latitude allowed to local governments is restricted by state government; and the latitude allowed to state governments is restricted by their being subject to federal law and constitutional interpretations.

Although great latitude is allowed in making tax concessions to attract investment, anticipating actual improvement in revenues as a result of growth is very uncertain. If concessions are too extensive, the city or state may lose revenues as a result of any new investment. Also, such incentives may be disregarded by those decisions on how to invest their funds in preference for factors beyond the control of elected officials. We have seen what other researchers have long seen—that some states are more successful at attracting investments, but government actions in attracting investment seem of little importance.

Similarly, the potential impact on a community or a state cannot be ignored by elected officials. The "pork" or federal funds brought to congressional districts and senatorial districts (states) is lovingly announced by representatives and senators in the belief that constituents will reward them with reelection to office. You see few instances in which state or local elected officials are credited for attracting such funds. But the loss of such funds with a military base closing or other curtailing of federal funds coming to an area seldom has anyone claiming responsibility, although it must be equally there. No doubt there are examples of federal, state, or local officials having their reelection chances hurt by such losses of federal funds.

At any rate, here also state and local officials seek new investments of federal money and seek to discourage any loss of federal funds. Often this task involves following up on federal grants available by proposal or seeking major science investments, such as the superaccelerator. Mayors of major cities may pressure the federal government to underwrite a greater share of the costs of their drug and pollution problems. We have not considered the states' successes in such individual areas as attracting military expenditures or social security recipients. In the overall pursuit of federal dollars, however, states again differ in the results of their efforts, which are more obscure than their efforts in seeking capital investment. Again, however, we certainly have again been unable to identify the source or sources of their ability to do so. Probably state officials should not be credited for success in attracting either investment or federal dollars, nor should they be held accountable for failure to attract such dollars or for their loss.

SUMMARY

1. The economies of the states greatly influence the funds that state governments have available to provide services and, presumably,

public satisfaction with the jobs being done by governors and the state legislators.

2. States compete to attract investments in their economies by domestic businesses, by foreign businesses, and by the federal government. Some states are quite successful and others fail.

3. Although states give "incentives," such as lowered taxes or construction loans, to attract business investment, there is little evidence that they work. In fact, low growth in employment seems to motivate legislatures to enact such incentives.

4. Federal dollars invested in the state can also contribute greatly to both jobs and the wealth of the state's public. Federal dollars are not given equally to all the states, nor are they given to the poorer states to redistribute income.

5. Although we can scarcely predict which states will be more successful in attracting federal dollars, those with less success in attracting business investments seem more likely to get federal dollars.

6. Actions by state officials seem irrelevant to each state's success in attracting either business or federal dollars.

SELECTED READINGS

Eisinger, Peter K. *The Rise of the Entrepreneurial State* (Madison: University of Wisconsin Press, 1988). One of several books, along with Fosler, appearing in 1988 dealing with the role of state government in state economies.

Fosler, R. Scott. *The New Economic Role of the American States* (New York: Oxford University Press, 1988).

Williams, Bruce A. "Regulation and Economic Development," in *Politics in the American States*, 5th ed., Virginia Gray, Herbert Jacob, and Robert B. Albritton (Glenview, IL: Scott, Foresman, 1990). A good summary of this topic.

Chapter
13

Education, Poverty, and Crime: State and Local Efforts

*L*iberals and conservatives take opposite positions on many controversial issues. Policies dealing with education, poverty, and crime find perhaps the greatest consistency of such positions across policy areas.[1] Dealing with these in reverse order, conservatives view criminal behavior as evidence of a character fault of the individual. Some are drawn to crime, and society is safe only after such individuals are incarcerated. The liberal, by contrast, notes that criminals are overwhelmingly uneducated and poor. For this reason, crime is the result of society's failure to meet the needs of certain individuals, in effect forcing the poorly educated and poor into a life of crime. Liberals share with conservatives the belief that some crimes must be punished as offenses against society, including murder, rape, and most violent crimes. The liberal, however, is likely to forgive individuals who have repaid society for criminal acts. The conservative, seeing a faulty individual, is unlikely to do so.

---

1 Robert S. Erikson, Norman R. Luttbeg, and Kent L. Tedin, *American Public Opinion*, 3rd ed. (New York: Macmillan, 1988).

Conservatives are likely to see those living in poverty having failed to make the effort necessary to have a job and pay their own way. If society provides a minimum amount of money for food and housing, conservatives view this practice as removing the incentive for those on such welfare to get a job. Again, from the conservative perspective, most people on welfare have a character fault. As implied above, the liberal views poverty as a failure of society to provide some people with the skills needed to get a job paying above minimum wages. Both liberals and conservatives share the belief that some are poor through no fault of their own and believe society should show compassion towards such individuals. Children, the severely handicapped, and the elderly are among these individuals.

Finally, the liberal is likely to see public education as the one point in which society has the leverage to change individuals. By giving each a good education, society grants them an equal opportunity for a good life. If public education fails to educate children, it dooms them to difficulties in finding employment. Poverty and the lack of either self-respect or respect for property, which might lead to criminal behavior, may follow. Poor success in educating students is society's failure. The conservative accepts the need for public educational opportunities as a benefit to society. If an individual fails to use educational opportunities, however, the individual, not the educational system, is at fault.

State and local governments devote nearly half of their expenditures to providing education and welfare and to providing protection against crime. Despite great investment of taxpayer money, public education has not resulted in all students being of top quality. Furthermore, this expense has not seen poverty decrease to being nearly nonexistent, and it has not stopped or even reduced crime. As we have seen, many view our educational system as falling short of what it once was and certainly as no match for our economic rivals, such as Japan.[2] Figure 13.1 shows this decline, which is a decrease of 2.79 points per year. It is not as dramatic as is suggested in the press, but it is worrisome nevertheless.

Poverty remains a major problem in our society, although it has shown an erratic decline over time.[3] As revealed in Figure 13.2, there appears to be a long-term decrease of 0.22 percent per year. At this rate, in approximately 63 years we would have no one living in poverty. It should be noted, how-

---

2 National Commission on Excellence in Education, *A Nation at Risk* (Washington, DC: Government Printing Office, 1983).

3 Robert Albritton, "Social Services: Welfare and Health" in *Politics in the American States*, 5th ed., Virginia Gray, Herbert Jacob, and Robert B. Albritton (eds.) (Glenview, IL: Scott, Foresman, 1990).

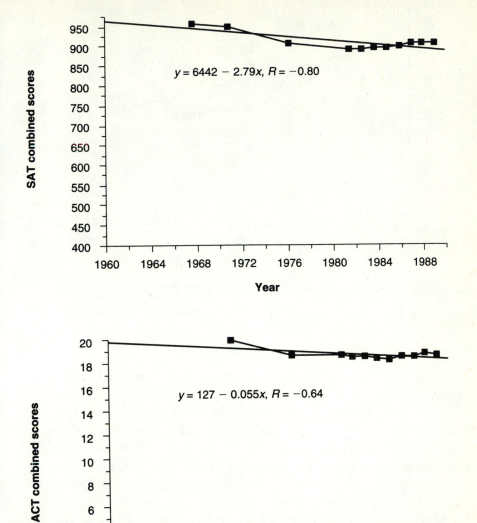

Figure 13.1   The trend in SAT and ACT scores over time. The minimum SAT score is 400; the minimum ACT score is 1.

Source: U.S. Bureau of the Census, *Statistical Abstract of the United States, 1988.* Washington, DC: U.S. Government Printing Office, p. 452.

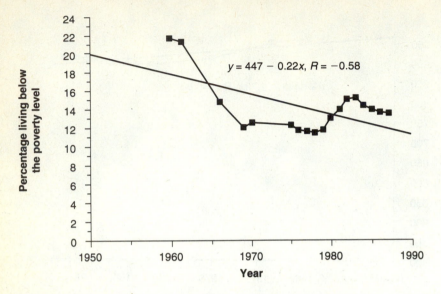

Figure 13.2   The trend in percentage living in poverty over time.

Source: U.S. Bureau of the Census, *Statistical Abstract of the United States, 1988.* Washington, DC: U.S. Government Printing Office, p. 452.

ever, that the 13.5 percent living in poverty in 1987 represents 32.5 million people.

As shown in Figure 13.3, crime continues to ebb and flow over time in the United States, but the long-term trend is slightly upward.[4] The increase is 8.4 crimes per 100,000 per year, a modest figure. With a population of 250 million, however, it represents 21,000 additional serious crimes each year. Although crime appears to be highly cyclical, no explanations for these variations are to be found in the research on crime.

None of these problems shows any prospect of going away. In fact, only poverty is even going in the desired direction. Our efforts then are either unsuccessful or at most modestly successful. Not surprisingly, liberals and conservatives react predictably to these failures. The conservative sees the need of more efficiency and better performance, less gentle treatment for criminals, and less welfare fraud. The reader may question whether, if these failures are attributable to character faults, we have more faulty individuals today than in the past. And is the American character inferior to that of the Japanese?

---

4   Wesley G. Skogan, in "Crime and Punishment," in *Politics in the American States,* 5th ed., Virginia Gray, Herbert Jacob, and Robert B. Albritton (eds.) (Glenview, IL.: Scott, Foresman, 1990).

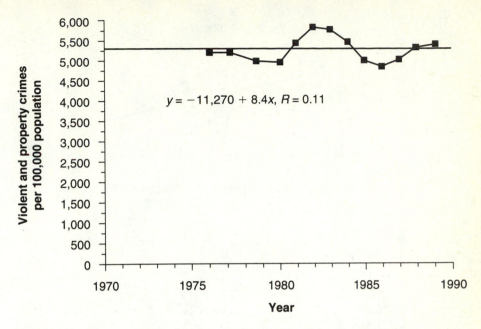

Figure 13.3   The trend in total violent and property crimes over time.

Source: U.S. Bureau of the Census, *Statistical Abstract of the United States, 1988*. Washington, DC: U.S. Government Printing Office, p. 167.

The liberal merely sees the need for greater investment by society. But if more money has failed in the past, why will it work in the future?

Since society has been devoting money to these areas for some time, this difference of opinion probably was heard in government before the turn of the century. Furthermore, it will no doubt continue into the future. Neither perspective, however, shows much interest in the possibility of learning from noting differences among the states.

DIFFERENCES AMONG THE STATES ON THESE POLICIES

We have previously noted that some states have more living in poverty, that some have more crime, and that some have better educated publics. There is a pattern to these differences. Although we might expect, given both the liberal and the conservative perspectives, that poor education, poverty, and crime go together, such is not the case among the states. Figure 13.4 demonstrates that

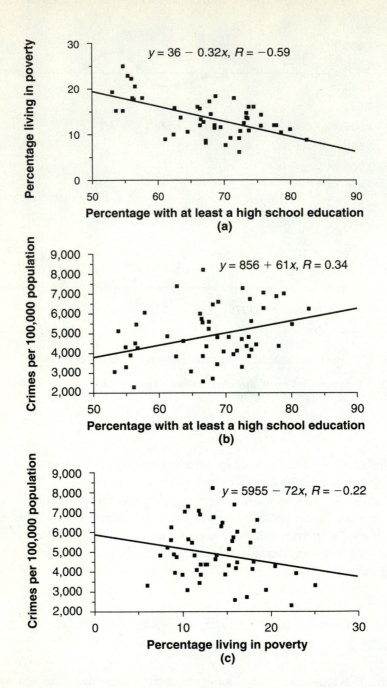

Figure 13.4 Interrelationships between (a) percentage in poverty and percentage with a high school education or better, (b) crimes per 100,000 population and percentage with a high school education, and (c) crimes per 100,000 population and percentage in poverty.

poorly educated states have more living in poverty, but they have less rather than more crime.

At the individual level, such findings make little sense. At the state level, however, they should not be too surprising. Basically, it is those states that are more metropolitan, have more complex economies, and find many wealthy living in proximity to the very poor that are at the root of these relationships. Figure 13.5 shows that the more-metropolitan states have somewhat better educated publics, fewer living in poverty, and more crime. This result would suggest that expectations based on individuals and the arguments between liberals and conservatives need not be relevant in discussing patterns among the states. Rather than seeking to deal with any of these policy areas as though we were dealing with just a large number of individuals, we need to consider how such relationships can be understood for states or communities.

It is also suggested that the dynamics between these variables may not be as simple as liberals and conservatives suggest. Thus a legislature seeking to reduce crime in its state would not be able to anticipate a reduction in the crime rate if more money were invested in public education. Similarly, if the quality of life of those on welfare were to be improved, crime would not necessarily be reduced. Although it is ridiculous to suggest such a thing, becoming less metropolitan would be all that we might require given what we know thus far.

COPING WITH EDUCATION, POVERTY, AND CRIME

Education.   At various times in our history, there has been great concern with the quality of U.S. education. When the Soviet Union put its sputnik into orbit before the United States was successful in orbiting its own satellite, many sought educational reform with a stress on science and mathematics to help America catch up and keep up. Those who were better in mathematics and the sciences were encouraged to continue their studies, and national funds were dedicated to underwriting science education. Our present concern is with competing with the educational system of Japan, although few Americans probably would endorse a Japanese-style university admissions examination.

Reforms have been quite numerous, usually with state governments forcing these reforms on local school districts.[5] Not surprisingly, these reforms have little basis in research and the actual impact of none has been assessed. The slight improvement in SAT scores, however, has been claimed by those

---

5   Frederick Wirt and Samuel Gove, "Education," in *Politics in the American States*, 5th ed., Virginia Gray, Herbert Jacob, and Robert B. Albritton (eds.) (Glenview, IL: Scott, Foresman, 1990).

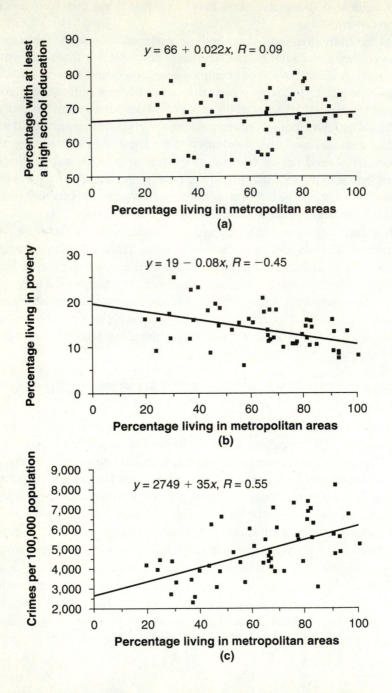

Figure 13.5   (a) Education, (b) poverty level, and (c) crime rate, as related to percentage living in metropolitan areas.

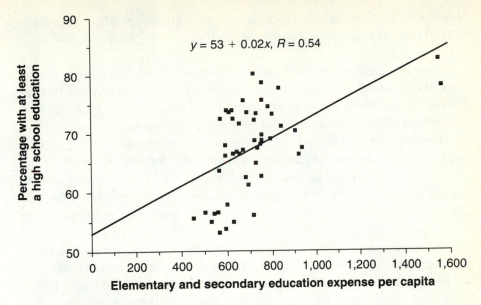

Figure 13.6   Education level vs. education expenditures.

advocating these reforms as demonstrating their desirable impact. This conclusion is probably invalid.

The most common reforms have been raising teacher preparation and certification standards (49 states), higher requirements for high school graduation (46 states), student tests for different grade levels (43 states), enrichment programs (41 states), and professional development programs (43 states).[6] Additionally, many states have increased time in the classroom, set conditions on extracurricular participation, improved disciplinary programs, and raised college admission standards. Notably, most of these reforms do not cost much; they are efficiency-improving efforts.

As Figure 13.6 demonstrates, states with better or (since our measure is the percentage with at least a high school education) more complete educational systems spend more. Each $100 increase in per capita elementary and secondary education expenditures results in a 2 percent increase in the number with at least a high school education. Apart from the two outliers, Alaska and Wyoming, with nearly $1600 per capita expenditures, the relationship is a good deal stronger. The reader should note the possibility that wealthy

---

6   Wirt and Gove, p. 466.

states with well-educated publics may have more to spend on education. Wealth may be causing educational expenditures.

Poverty. Reforms in coping with poverty are much like those in education. Many federal government programs seek to deal with poverty, thereby greatly complicating the analysis inasmuch as federal funds typically set a baseline to which the state can make further contributions.

Programs for dealing with poverty are numerous. Some welfare programs, such as those included in Supplemental Security Income (SSI) and food stamps, are largely administered by and funded by the federal government.[7] Aid for families with dependent children (AFDC) provides money to the poor with the hope of making poor children live better and hopefully to break out of the cycle of poverty. The states administer this program, but federal government covers a minimum monthly payment for each dependent child. The states define who is eligible, and many states exclude such payments to families with able-bodied unemployed males. The thought here is that they could get a job. State-funded general assistance programs lack funds, and many poor are ineligible. In our assessment of state efforts to deal with poverty, all state and local funds dedicated to welfare per capita are used.

Figure 13.7 again shows a relationship between spending in a policy area and success or failure to deal with the problem. More money spent on welfare reduces the percentage living in poverty. The relationship shown suggests that poverty sharply decreases with increasing per capita welfare expenditures from $200 to $300. The overall pattern, however, is that a $100 per capita increase results in a 1.4 percent decrease in those living in poverty.

The reader should note that poor states may be unable to find funds for welfare, whereas rich states can. Here too, the causality might be just the opposite of what we expect. It may be that states with few living in poverty can afford higher per capita expenditures on welfare. This situation, of course, would make life difficult for the policymaker seeking to reduce the number of people living in poverty. Moving the poor to a wealthy state might be the limit of how they can cope. We shall have more to say about this subject shortly.

Crime. Even more than the resentment among taxpayers for payments to those in poverty, few want to devote money to criminals. Taxpayers even resent money for law enforcement. Money for the criminal court systems is

---

7   Albritton, pp. 412–420.

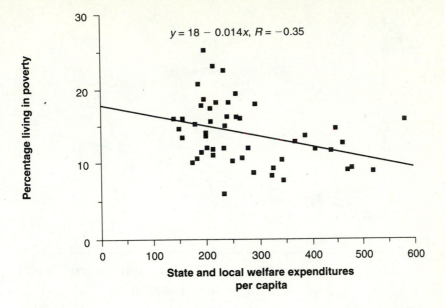

Figure 13.7   Percentage living in poverty vs. per capita welfare expenditures.

limited. Greater efficiency is called for rather than more money. Reforms in prison systems, such as limiting the number of prisoners to each cell, tend to be undertaken only under federal court order.[8] States house the majority of those imprisoned, and the number of prisoners is increasing, with little additional space being funded. Excessively crowded prisons are relieved by releasing those prisoners who are least threatening or those soon to be released anyway. This practice is expedient but is not a reform.

The courts also are overloaded with little in the way of additional resources. They use plea bargaining to get pleas of guilty from those criminally accused so as to reduce the backlog of cases before the courts. As mentioned previously, in plea bargaining the accused and the state negotiate over how reduced a charge the accused will plead guilty to rather than face a trial on a more substantial charge. The joke is that the criminal pleas guilty to a charge of double parking rather than being tried for murder. Plea bargaining is also an expedient but not a reform.

There has been uncertainty concerning the direction of causality in our consideration of educational and welfare expenditures and their impact on

---

8   Skogan, p. 404 (see note 4).

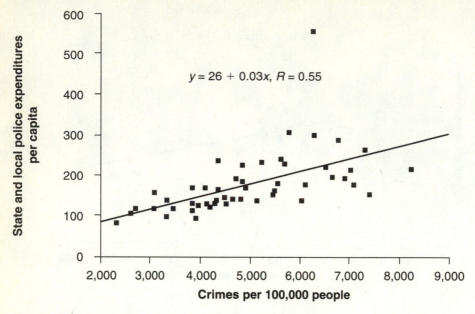

Figure 13.8   Per capita police expenditures vs. crime rate.

education and poverty, respectively. Such is not the case in Figure 13.8, which could be presented as an argument that expenditures cause crime. Here, however, we present the data as though increased crime causes greater expenditures. Each hundred crimes per 100,000 people results in a three-dollar per capita increase in police expenditures. "Results" may be too strong a word. Wealthy states may have more crime and may be able to spend more to combat it.

RESOURCES AND SPENDING

We noted in Chapter 2 that resources available to a state derive from the wealth of its public. Moreover, wealthy states spend more on government services, as shown again in Figure 13.9. In each case there is a quite strong pattern for per capita income to relate to state per capita expenditures. Also in each case the southern states, each shown as an "s," tend to be at one corner of the distribution of states. They increase the relationship. They tend to be low in per capita income and low in expenditures for all programs. Additionally, the seven states in which more than 90 percent live in metropolitan areas, shown by an "m," are in the diagonally opposite corner.[9] They have the

---

9   Florida falls in both categories but is shown only as a southern state.

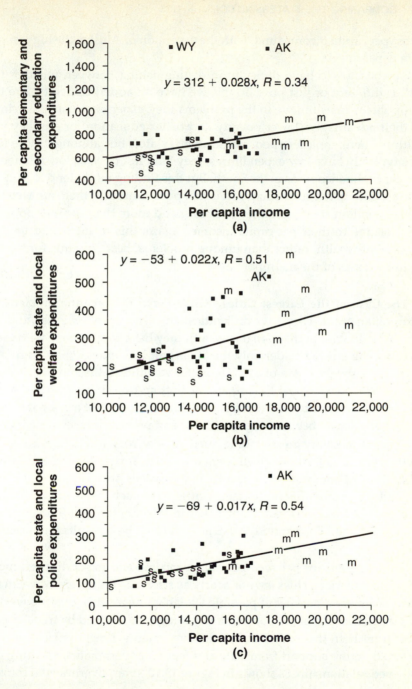

Figure 13.9 (a) Education, (b) welfare, and (c) police expenditures, as related to income, all on a per capita basis.

Source: U.S. Bureau of the Census, *Statistical Abstract of the United States*, Washington, DC: U.S. Government Printing Office, pp. 177, 140, and 274.

highest per capita incomes and, with the exception of Alaska, the highest per capita expenditures.

We continue to have difficulty in distinguishing between whether the South is different or just poor. To this we have an added difficulty. Are the metropolitan states unique in the problems they experience (such as crime) and their advantages (lower poverty and better education) or are they just wealthy? There are a few poor nonsouthern states; but although these few states typically have low expenditures, they tend not to be as low relative to their per capita income as in the South. But this finding might tend to suggest that the South is not truly unique, it is just poor. Similarly, there are wealthy nonmetropolitan states, and they tend to spend more than the metropolitan states relative to their per capita income. Again, this result would tend to suggest that wealth, rather than unique problems, best accounts for the expenditure levels of the metropolitan states.

The Case of the Largest Cities.   Cities certainly have the problems of metropolitan areas. They have difficulties with crime, the homeless, and the poor. They do vary in the available wealth they have to help cope with these problems. We shall consider only the 50 largest U.S. cities.[10] San Francisco, with a per capita income of $13,575, is the wealthiest. Washington is next, with $13,530. Newark and El Paso are the bottom two cities, with $6494 and $7670, respectively. So the range from the highest to lowest among the cities is about as great as between the wealthiest and poorest states.

City services vary greatly; some, such as New York and Baltimore, spend much on education. Although all spend on police, fire protection, and streets and highways, some spend on health and hospitals and welfare. Education is excluded because only northeastern cities have such responsibilities. Total per capita expenditures vary from $2164 in Washington and $1486 in New York to $162 in El Paso and $172 in San Antonio. These results are shown in Figure 13.10.

The relationships between per capita income and expenditures among the top 50 American cities are not nearly as strong as they were between the states. There are a number of possible explanations for this. First, as we saw much earlier, a substantial portion of city budgets is covered by transfer payments from both the federal and state governments. It is possible that poor cities enjoy more support from state and federal governments, resulting in a weakened relationship, as shown in Figure 13.10. Intergovernmental transfer

---

10 For a very thorough consideration of how a limited number of cities spend their revenues see Terry N. Clark and Lorna C. Ferguson, *City Money* (New York: Columbia University Press, 1983).

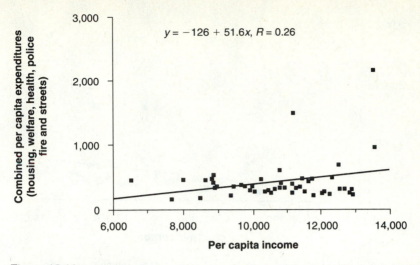

Figure 13.10   Combined per capita expenditures vs. per capita income for the 50 largest U.S. cities.

Source: U.S. Bureau of the Census, *Statistical Abstract of the United States, 1989,* Washington, DC: U.S. Government Printing Office, pp. 35, 289, 451.

of funds to these cities, however, is unrelated to the per capita wealth. The hypothesis is unsupported.

Second, the magnitude of a given problem in a city may force its expenditures higher despite its low wealth. Crime may be a severe problem forcing unusually high spending on police. Spending on police, however, is little related to how much crime a city experiences. Again there seems little support for this hypothesis. Finally, property taxes may be at the root of the lack of relationship. Such taxes may increase little with increasing public wealth. Services therefore cannot be provided as the wealth of a city's public little relates to revenues. Actually, however, tax revenues do increase with the per capita wealth of cities' publics, as indicated in Figure 13.11. The rate of increase is not as fast as in the case of the states. So a revised version of this hypothesis—to the effect that the restrictive increase in taxes with increased wealth dampens expansion of services—does seem to be upheld.

Finally, we have two hypotheses for which we lack data for evaluation. First, public tastes for what they would like city governments to do, if there were sufficient money, may differ greatly across the country. The public in some cities may want greater investment in amenities, such as parks and recreation if the city can afford it. Others may want the city to help the poor and unhealthy. Others may want lower taxes. As a result, expenditures in a

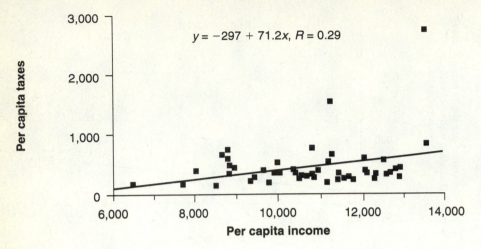

Figure 13.11   Per capita taxes relative to per capita income for the 50 largest U.S. cities.

given area may be unrelated to wealth, and even combined expenditures may be unrelated to wealth. Second, state government may mandate city services without providing funds, resulting in little relationship between being able to afford the services and providing the services.

Although public education, welfare, and highway expenditures are the big three in terms of how state and local governments spend their revenues, there are many other problems confronted by the states. These issues may not entail the expenditures evident in the programs above, but many rouse strong emotions in their proponents and opponents.

ABORTION

The Supreme Court's ruling in the *Webster* case (1989) allows the states to regulate the availability of abortion more extensively than under *Roe* v. *Wade* (1972). Opponents of abortion relish the chance to get state governments to be much more restrictive than the Court's standard—abortion on demand during the first trimester of pregnancy. Few politicians welcome the attention paid by antiabortion activists or by their more recently organized opponents who refer to their position as pro-choice. Many legislatures have since considered bills to restrict abortions.

Abortions are not readily available in many parts of the United States. Local hospitals and doctors decline to offer them either because of personal views or anxieties about community reactions were abortions available. Certainly this situation also applies to the states. As we saw in Chapter 2, legal abortions per 1000 women of ages between 15 and 44 range from highs of

47.9 and 47.4 in California and New York to lows of 7.9 and 9.7 in Wyoming and Mississippi. Interestingly, two states that have been at the forefront of efforts to restrict abortions, Pennsylvania and Louisiana, are states where legal abortion is fairly uncommon. Pennsylvania's rate is 21.3 and Louisiana's is 17.4.

Figure 13.12 shows that legal abortions are far more common in more metropolitan states, perhaps because of life-style differences or the anonymity of doctors and hospitals providing this service in big cities. Legal abortion is also more common in states with high per capita incomes. Since the relationship is stronger than that for how metropolitan the state is, it seems less likely that this higher rate is merely related to the fact that metropolitan states have higher per capita incomes. Well-to-do women may be more likely to get abortions, leaving in question what poorer women do. Those with pro-choice opinions suggest that the real alternative to legal abortion is illegal abortion. Figure 13.13 suggests that infant mortality is one of the costs of restricting abortions.

Not unexpectedly, legal abortions are less common in states with large percentages of people identifying themselves as "Christians," as shown in Figure 13.14. This finding would suggest that the political process is responsive to a state's public opinion in facilitating or discouraging, even outlawing, abortion. Alternatively, the extent of legal abortions may be unrelated to the laws passed by legislatures. To be more precise, abortion may be uncommon in some states despite little legal restriction. We turn next to the question of the political process and abortion.

Very little about the political process relates to the prevalence of abortion among the states. More participant states, more Democratic states, and more competitive states differ little in the prevalence of abortion. One measure, however, proves strongly related (see Figure 13.15). States whose legislatures more accurately reflect the demographic attributes of their citizens, such as having more women and black legislators, have a much higher abortion rate. This result need not imply causality, however. Metropolitan states have both more abortions and more accurate demographic sharing between their legislators and the public.

The *Roe* v. *Wade* decision declared most state laws restricting abortion to be unconstitutional, but many laws remain among state statutes, just unenforced. The coding of state abortion laws seeks to capture the potential restrictiveness of each state's abortion laws were *Roe* v. *Wade* overturned. For example, if a state retains an outright ban on abortion that predates this decision but does not enforce it, we might expect enforcement to resume quickly if such restrictions were judged constitutional. A state with no restrictions can hardly be expected to enact them swiftly.

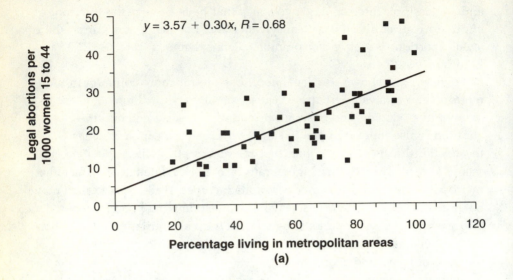

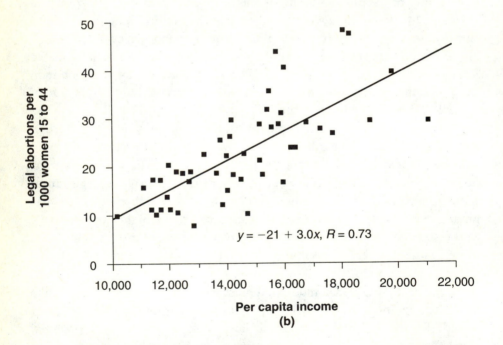

Figure 13.12 Rate of legal abortions relative to (a) percentage living in metropolitan areas and (b) per capita income.

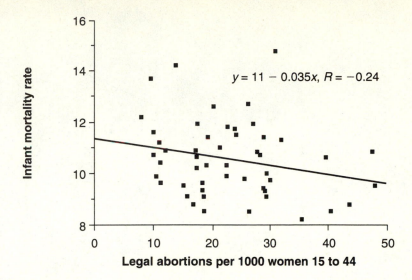

Figure 13.13   Infant mortality rate vs. abortion rate.

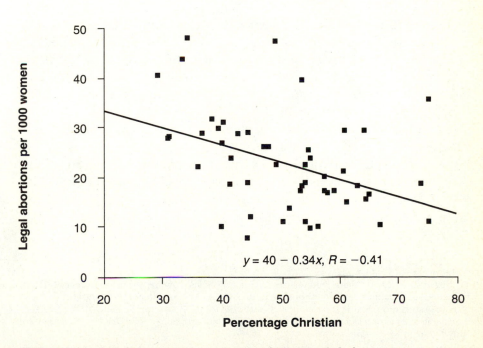

Figure 13.14   Legal abortion vs. percentage of Christian belief.

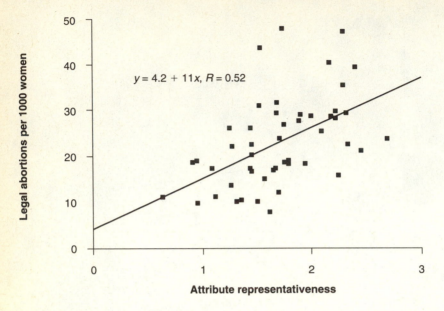

Figure 13.15   The relationship between legal abortions and attribute representativeness.

Figure 13.16 shows no apparent pattern of southern or metropolitan states to have been more restrictive on abortion. We have, however, noted a strong relationship between the number of abortions and how metropolitan a state is. The abortion rate relates to whether a state is urban or southern, but restrictive abortion laws do not. We might therefore expect little relationship between the earlier restrictiveness of the law and the actual number of abortions. Such is indeed the case, as shown in Figure 13.17. It has also been observed by others.[11] Classifications of the states' abortion laws by Halva-Neubauer (see Figure 13.18) show a very similar pattern.[12] If we can use the past and future restrictiveness of laws on abortion as a guide for how restrictive a state might be were the Supreme Court to allow states further latitude in restricting abortion, we can expect a clash between the law and the be-

---

11   Susan B. Hansen, "State Differences in Public Policies Toward Women: A Test of Three Hypotheses," a paper prepared for presentation at the annual meeting of the American Political Science Association, San Francisco, 1990; Charles A. Johnson and Jon R. Bond, "Coercive and Noncoercive Abortion Deterrence Policies," in *Policy Implementation*, John Brigham and Don W. Brown (eds.) (Beverly Hills: Sage, 1980), pp. 185–207.

12   Glen Halva-Neubauer, "Abortion Policy in the Post-*Webster* Age," *Publius* (Summer 1990), p. 32 (corrected).

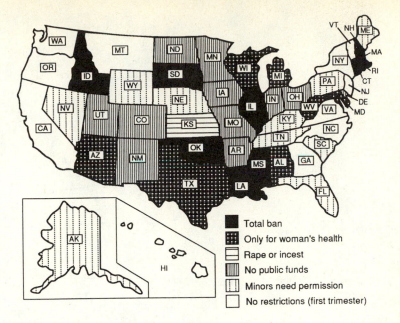

Total ban

Only for woman's health

Rape or incest

No public funds

Minors need permission

No restrictions (first trimester)

Figure 13.16 The pattern of abortion laws prior to 1973.

Source: New York Times (June 25, 1989), pp. 20–21.

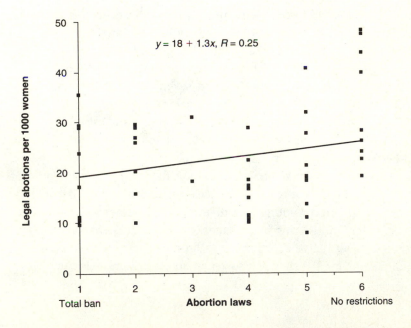

Figure 13.17 Relationship between legal abortions and abortion laws (before 1973).

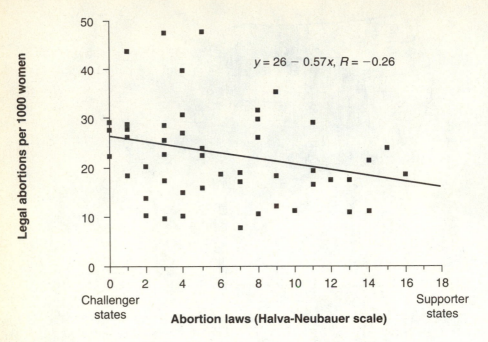

Figure 13.18 Rate of legal abortion vs. abortion policies of states.

havior. The fact that the earlier restrictiveness little manifests itself in present behavior suggests that future laws will have very limited impact.

Restrictive abortion laws may be predictable given the compositions of states. The number of women in the legislature, the number in the work force, the number of women's lobbying groups, and several other measures of the mobilization of women do not prove useful in making such predictions, however.[13] Rather, it is historic support that best predicts present and future support.

What is more important is that we have yet another example of the efforts of state legislators to pass laws to reshape behavior but fail to have much impact. In this case in particular, we may well conclude that there are two public opinions. One public opinion affects, or at least elected officials expect it to affect, the reelection chances of those voting the public policy. The other public opinion shares the behavior of those living in the state. Legislators in Pennsylvania may feel pressed to pass restrictive abortion laws. But the women of Pennsylvania feel little guilt in crossing the state line to get an abortion in more lenient New York.

---

13 Hansen, p. 13.

CONCLUSIONS

All modern industrial democracies face continuing problems with providing affordable public education. The underemployment of many, which leaves them unable to provide for themselves the quality of life enjoyed by many in the society, including health care, also continues to be a problem. Crimes against both property and persons, of course, are yet another continuing problem. The United States seems unique only in the amount of crime we experience. None of these problems is evenly spread across the land. Since geographic boundaries often leave some areas with many problems and few resources, some regional governments or local governments are worse off than others.

In coping with problems, nothing is better than having excellent resources. Often we have found that resources are spent in the problem areas by the state governments on which we have focused. However, there are other means for coping with problems rather than spending on them. Certainly, many such programs have been attempted. Often these programs are intended to improve the efficiency of providing government services. Schools will be more efficient, or the courts will be more efficient in dealing with those accused of crimes. Other efforts have sought to outlaw the problem and then to provide enforcement for those ignoring the law. At least in these policy areas, no great success can be claimed by any such low-expenditure innovations. Perhaps we have not been sufficiently innovative, or more likely we have just not taken strong enough actions to alter human behavior.

This discussion may sound as though only money can influence behavior. As noted above for education and poverty, increased per capita expenditures do relate to improved education and fewer living in poverty. Does this indicate that higher expenditures do solve problems? We cannot really be certain. But expenditures in fighting crime increase crime, or at least this would be the implication if we were to follow the arguments for education and poverty. So it seems that perhaps expenditures do not solve problems either. In recommending new policies for poor states, we cannot even say that squeezing more dollars per capita to spend in problem areas will result in improvements there.

SUMMARY

1. The consistent belief among liberals is that poor education leads to poverty and crime, whereas conservatives see those not benefiting

from education, victimized by poverty, and engaging in criminal behavior as having character faults.

2. Educational quality (SAT and ACT scores) has declined since the 1960s, as has poverty. But crime has slightly increased. States differ on each of these measures. Some are quite poorly educated, some are poor, and some have much crime. However, although those states that are poorly educated have much poverty, it is those with better education and fewer in poverty that have the most crime.

3. Metropolitan states have fewer living in poverty but much greater crime rates.

4. States that spend more on education have better education. Similarly, those that spend more on welfare have fewer living in poverty. But those spending more on crime have *more* crime. Wealthy and metropolitan states spend more on all programs.

5. Abortions are more common in some states, especially more metropolitan states. Abortions are somewhat more common when the state is less restrictive.

6. Overall, those states with the wealth of their publics allowing investment in seeking to improve education and to reduce poverty and crime do so. These tend to be metropolitan states, which face more serious problems with education, poverty, and crime.

SELECTED READINGS

Albritton, Robert. "Social Services: Welfare and Health," in *Politics in the American States*, 5th ed., Virginia Gray, Herbert Jacob, and Robert B. Albritton (eds.) (Glenview, IL: Scott, Foresman, 1990).

Skogan, Wesley G. "Crime and Punishment," in *Politics in the American States*, 5th ed., Virginia Gray, Herbert Jacob, and Robert B. Albritton (eds.) (Glenview, IL: Scott, Foresman, 1990).

Wirt, Frederick, and Samuel Gove. "Education," in *Politics in the American States*, 5th ed., Virginia Gray, Herbert Jacob, and Robert B. Albritton (eds.) (Glenview, IL: Scott, Foresman, 1990).

Chapter
14

State Policy-Making: Do They Do Only What They Have to Do?

*W*e have seen that states differ in many ways. California has more than 27 million people living within its borders, whereas Wyoming has only 490,000. Some have many residents with quite substantial incomes and others have few such persons. Connecticut has a per capita personal income of over $21,000 while Arkansas has just over $11,000. Politically the states also differ. Voters in Montana turn out at a 64 percent rate in gubernatorial contests, but Georgians at only a 26 percent rate. Without going over the material presented in Chapter 2 again, we can say that states vary geographically, climatically, socially, economically, politically, and perhaps even democratically.

If one were interested in living in a state with few people, in a rich state where even a low tax rate would generate millions of dollars in revenues, or a more politically active state, the data can identify exemplary states. But were we to be interested in moving to a state that provides a superior public education, or one that has successfully coped with crime, or one in which representatives closely reflect the general public, analysis such as that in this text cannot be of much help. No such state or states stand out.

As we saw in Chapter 13, states do make more and less expensive efforts in problem areas, such as in education, poverty, and crime. There is, however, little evidence that these investments result in improvements; for example, investing in police "results" in increased crime. What is more important, we noted a strong pattern of more wealthy states to expend more in all problem areas. Even if they have a much better educated populace, wealthy states spend more for the education of each of their students. One plausible explanation of this pattern is that there is a continual demand in all states for new and improved government services to improve education, reduce crime, and the like. Usually legislators can simply state that, "We just cannot afford it." As resources improve, this argument rings less true; and the service is undertaken.

It should be noted that the states do not just provide services. They also set conditions for doing business in the state, select among various taxes that might be imposed, license some occupations, and make some actions unlawful. Although some of these cost money, all are inexpensive when compared with the costs of education, welfare, and highways. Nevertheless, a state's resources seem an unlikely explanation for why it undertakes a policy to license landscape architects or civil engineers, or why it passes "no-fault" automobile insurance.

We have seen throughout this text that the South on nearly every dimension stands apart from the rest of the states. It is poor, has a large minority population, is less educated, has many in prison, is politically uncompetitive, and votes at a very low rate. Wealth may not be alone in explaining the differences there are in policies among the states. Certainly, however, the South differs in many acts of government that involve little expense. We saw that the South has very restrictive and long constitutions and imposed many restrictions on voter eligibility in the past, to give but two examples. States would behave much more similarly if there were none in the South.

Heavily metropolitan states have many benefits and liabilities. Their complex economies allow many to earn substantial salaries and to pay substantial dollars in taxes. Additionally, they are well educated and have lower percentages living in poverty. They also have high crime rates, many environmental problems, and costly decaying older central cities. The South and metropolitan states stand on opposite ends with regard to our relationships between per capita income and per capita expenditures.

Metropolitan states do not only differ in wealth. As we have seen, their metropolitan areas first pressed for government services to cope with their problems. They continue to experience problems with which only government can cope, or at least seek to solve. The poor are disproportionately concentrated in the older "core" cities in metropolitan areas. These areas also are where crime is most prevalent. They also have what is called "decaying physical plant." These core cities, such as St. Louis, Chicago, Boston, and Philadelphia, have old sewer and water systems. Their jails, police buildings, schools, highways, parks, court buildings, and even city halls tend to be so old that they need to be replaced totally, at an expense beyond local property tax resources. They tend to turn to the state and federal government for such money. States would also behave more similarly were they all heavily urbanized in metropolitan areas with aging center cities.

Were all states to be wealthy, metropolitan, and nonsouthern, we would expect their policies and certainly their expenditures to vary little. Although one might seek a state for its climate, proximity to an ocean, or because one grew up there, little else would recommend a particular state. Taxes would be much the same, as would be services. Education would be nearly identical, as would crime rates, the extent of competition between the two major political parties, and turnout rate in elections.

DIFFERENCES APART FROM WEALTH

To suggest what this situation might look like, in Table 14.1 we find the dollars spent by each state for each thousand dollars of personal income of its residents. For example, Alabama spent just over $2 billion on elementary and secondary education and had a total personal income of nearly $48.5 billion. Dividing the first by the second figure and moving the decimal three places gives $42.52 expenditure for every $1000 in income. This division removes the ease with which more wealthy states can devote more resources per individual to education and other programs.

In effect, the table shows what states invest in education independent of how wealthy they are. With some notable exceptions, the states with high educational expenditures are smaller and poorer states where the effort is a heavy burden on residents. The states investing little relative to their wealth are quite wealthy. In fact, each $1000 increase in per capita wealth reduces by $1.28 the per $1000 expenditures for education. Overall, as might be expected, holding wealth constant sharply decreases the variation among the states.

Police expenditures per $1000 income narrow even more. West Virginia expends $7.56 for every $1000 in personal income. Next lowest is New Hampshire at $8.11. The highest states are Nevada at $18.69 and Arizona at $18.55. More than any of the other measures considered in Chapter 13, police expenditures seem to feel the impact of urbanization. The states most heavily

Table 14.1 Elementary and Secondary Educational Expenditures per $1000 Personal Income (Alaska and Wyoming Excluded)

Top ten			Bottom ten		
Rank	State	Revenue	Rank	State	Revenue
1	New Mexico	68.58	48	Massachusetts	37.95
2	West Virginia	63.87	47	Illinois	38.29
3	Utah	63.36	46	New Hampshire	38.42
4	Montana	63.31	45	Hawaii	38.64
5	Vermont	60.41	44	California	38.76
6	Maine	56.25	43	Missouri	39.43
7	Texas	54.81	42	Arkansas	39.76
8	Oregon	54.41	41	Georgia	40.36
9	Washington	54.22	40	Arizona	41.59
10	Idaho	53.05	39	Maryland	41.92

Source: U.S. Bureau of the Census, *Statistical Abstract of the United States, 1989* (Washington, DC: U.S. Government Printing Office), p. 140.

expending for police are more metropolitan.[1] This may suggest the severity of the crime problems in such states. Crime is higher in metropolitan states but some have more serious problems. Figure 14.1 shows the pattern between police expenditures and crime for the 20 most metropolitan states. Regardless of their wealth, when a metropolitan state such as Florida, Arizona, and Texas experiences much crime, it spends heavily.

Welfare expenditures do vary, even in studies that attempt to control for wealth. Nevada spends the least, $9.41 per $1000 of personal wealth. Florida and Texas are next lowest at $10.14 and $10.20. On the whole, southern states spend least on welfare. The top states are New York ($31.71), Rhode Island ($30.39), and Wisconsin ($29.84). If all states were unaffected by whatever affects southern states, differences would probably be far smaller.

CONCLUSION ON DIFFERENCES

Actually the states do vary in the public policies that they adopt. The variations, however, are caused by factors beyond the control of state government. The wealth of a state or its taxpaying public strongly relates to its expenditures in different policy areas. Apart from efforts to attract new industry and high-paying jobs to the state and improving the education of the public, state government

---

1 The equation is: ($7.73/ $1000 personal income) + 0.059 times percentage metropolitan, $R = 0.47$.

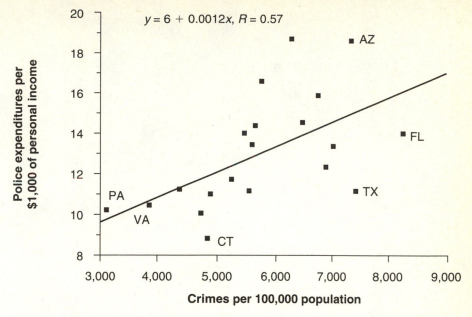

Figure 14.1 Police expenditures vs. crime rates in the 20 most metropolitan states.

can do little to influence the wealth of the state. A law saying that all residents will have double their personal income next year obviously will not work.

Similarly, more metropolitan states differ from those that are more rural. We noted the impact of such urbanization, but the state government cannot do much either to encourage or discourage where people live. Finally, state policy in the South differs from that in the remainder of the country. Certainly southern leaders in the past tried to make public policy in the South different. Actions now to make policy in the South like that in the North cannot be expected to change greatly how the South acts. It cannot easily overcome its poverty.

A final example concerning the environment can perhaps bring home the major point here. There has been increasing concern evident in the mass media as well as in public opinion polls concerning global warming, the depletion of ozone in the stratosphere, and other environmental concerns. The federal government, through the Environmental Protection Agency and a multitude of national laws mandating actions by state and local governments, scrutinizes the actions of these governments. We might expect that the wealth of a state would little affect how ardently it undertook various environment programs, such as reduction of air pollution, recycling, and developing renewable resources. Such is not the case, however.

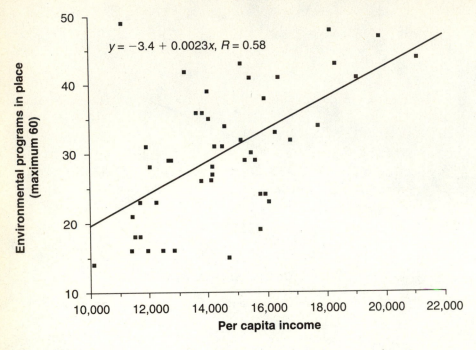

Figure 14.2   Extent of environmental policies vs. per capita personal income.

Figure 14.2 shows that environmental policies also proceed as the wealth of the state increases. The states getting the most points for their various environmental programs are the wealthy states.[2] Apparently the affordability of the programs, not the severity of the problem, the support of the public, or the activism of environmentalist determines whether a state is environmentally active.

POSSIBLE EXPLANATIONS FOR THE LITTLE DIFFERENCE AMONG THE STATES

One of the justifications for federalism is that the regional governments can experiment or innovate without the entire nation being at risk of any failures.

---

2   *The State of the States 1987* (Washington, DC: Fund for Renewable Energy and the Environment).

If the states' policy decisions predominantly reflect their wealth, region, and urban concentrations, they cannot be praised for being innovative. There is little research to help us sort through a multitude of possible explanations for the lack of difference. Where possible for each of these hypotheses, we will bring to bear relevant information; but we have much to learn.

The Dominance of the National Constitution and the Supremacy Clause. Since ratification, the Constitution has limited the actions available to the states. Federal law is the supreme law of the land. When it conflicts with any state law, it takes precedence, with the state law becoming null and void. Certainly our history is one of increasing centralization of government, with powers first taken from city governments, then by the states, and later from state governments by actions in Washington, D.C. Perhaps so little latitude is left as to straitjacket state governments. They have no latitude on the drinking age or on the maximum highway speed limit, except the right to declare rural interstate highways to have a higher, 65-mph limit.

The federal courts too have forced policies on the states in such areas as the conditions of state prisons and local schools' dependence on the property tax. Even residency for in-state tuition has been defined by some federal courts as immediate and not after one year of residency prior to entering college, as most states prefer. The federal courts seem more than willing to apply national constitutional rights in judging the constitutionality of state laws. Were a state to make castration the penalty for conviction for rape, it would be innovative and perhaps would sharply reduce this crime. The federal courts, however, probably would rule it "cruel and unusual punishment" in violation of the Eighth Amendment.

There would seem to be a good deal of truth to the central or federal government's restricting the states. Service and tax levels, however, vary greatly from state to state, as we have much discussed. Furthermore, many innovative solutions to problems would probably not conflict with the Bill of Rights as viewed by the federal courts. Some people advocate granting parents the right to take state and local support for the education of their children to any school of their choice. Presumably, schools that are successful at the task of education, whether public or private, would attract students.

Although it is questionable whether we know how to educate students better, this approach might prove superior. If any were excluded from the school of their choice, however, the due process and equal protection clause of the Fourteenth Amendment might make the program unconstitutional. While their involvement in a federal system no doubt constricts the latitude of policy actions available to the states, they have a substantial range of choice.

Resource Limitations. We have seen that both revenues and expenditures expand in states with more wealthy publics. It is certainly plausible that a poor state can expand governmental services and expenditures only by placing a greater tax burden on its citizens, but why do wealthy states expand services? We have seen that many wealthy states are metropolitan; with such urban concentrations go many problems, not the least of which is increased crime. Perhaps improved resources coming with more living in metropolitan areas barely precedes the need to commit those resources to alleviating the problem. We saw in Figure 14.1, however, that where crime is less pressing, states commit less of their wealth to coping with it. There may be other equally pressing demands for these resources.

If there are resources, many equally worthy uses for them may be ever present. Texas, for example, again in Figure 14.1, while having a serious crime problem even for a metropolitan state, underinvests its wealth in police expenditures. Two other metropolitan and crime-troubled states, Florida and Arizona, by contrast, fail to match Texas's commitment to education. Texas spends $54.81 on elementary and secondary education for every $1000 in personal income. Arizona's figure is $41.59 and Florida's $42.75.

As suggested earlier, the legislature may argue to proponents for state support of pet programs that the state cannot afford them. If resources improve, the argument is less persuasive. Apparently, the legislature has little ability in such a circumstance of saying no to anyone. All services increase with improved resources, although Figure 14.1 would suggest that high crime may encourage committing resources to fight it. This hypothesis says little to exonerate state governments from the charge of making no hard decisions. They either say no to increases requested by everyone because the state is too poor, or yes to everyone.

Have a Problem? Pass a Law. Prohibition is a classic case of the American conviction that problems can be solved simply and relatively inexpensively by making the problem behavior illegal. The solution to drunkenness is making it unlawful. When most people agree, it is easy to gain compliance with such laws. Of course if most agree on a desirable behavior, there is seldom a reason to enact the law. In the case of prohibition, most did not agree; and enforcement became quite expensive. Entrepreneurs soon provided alcohol at a high price to offset the risks they withstood.

The temptation of laws prohibiting a behavior is that, apart from costs of enforcement, they are cheap. Sometimes enforcement too is cheap, such as laws proscribing behaviors by students, public school teachers, or other state and local employees. Often, however, enforcement is costly. Often legislators, while eager to appear to be seeking a solution to a problem, are hesitant to commit resources to enforcement.

This hypothesis thus becomes a variant of that above. Passing a law may not solve anything if the vast majority do not support it, but committing resources to enforcement may only come with improved resources. Like talk, laws are cheap. Furthermore, those strongly advocating the law may not notice that it is ineffective.

Unchanging Human Behavior. Social scientists have been studying human behavior for about 60 years. We know much about factors that contribute to how people behave, as well as people's substantial capabilities to resist anything that changes that behavior. The studies of when and from whom children learn about politics and government (called socialization studies) would certainly suggest that our political behavior can best be shaped early in our lives. It is probable that other behaviors are also shaped early and from then on resist change.

Governments also must face the difficulty in changing undesirable behaviors. Unless the desired behavior is instilled early, it will take massive efforts to change behavior. Since early socialization varies little from one state to another, no state legislature has an easier or a harder task to change behavior in some desired direction. We can take efforts to improve education again as an example. It would be easy to pass a law requiring schools to function throughout the year. But students and their parents are accustomed to a summer vacation. Only if it was the norm to have no such break would enforcement be easy. Probably only by starting with the youngest students and yearly moving up one grade would this practice be at all acceptable. The same problems face other solutions, such as having learning rather than age define which grade a student is in, or emulating Japan's early college admission examinations. Parents learned that this was not the norm when they were in school, and therefore they do not expect it for their children.

This discussion is not meant to suggest that it is impossible to change human behavior. The success resulting from the availability of billions of dollars to children for selling drugs strongly suggests that if the enticements are great enough, the behavior can be changed. These billions are not tax dollars, but those willingly paid by people to get the drugs. An equal effort by a state government may not be supportable given the fact that it must come from taxes. Perhaps our efforts to buy solutions have failed because we are willing to pay too little.

Except for Interest Groups, States May Not Be Salient Most laws that affect our lives are passed by state legislatures. Additionally, nearly all governmental services that we use are provided by state governments or their local creations: municipalities, counties, and school boards. Nevertheless, the general public may not think of states as the government to help solve their problems. If the local government cannot solve a problem, Congress rather than the legislature is turned to for a solution. Often, of course, this approach makes sense. Crime, pollution, a decaying highway system, toxic wastes, and health care are examples of problems beyond local resources where Congress rather than the states are turned to for solutions. Congress may be approached because it is a national problem, because only the federal government has sufficient resources, or because only a national standard makes much sense. The states may not be innovative because no one thinks of them as problem solvers.

Many in a state, however, may know that the state's laws can protect or threaten them. Although they may gain favorable actions by the state legislature, these acts may little affect most of us. If the focus is on major policies, substantial state-by-state differences on laws that little affect most of us are ignored. It was not lobbying success by political scientists that resulted in the requirement for two political science courses in Texas, but certainly few residents are much affected by the law.

Everyone Wants the Same Things.   Were the public opinions in the 50 states identical in terms of what they wanted of state government, we could explain few differences, especially if we were to add a corollary to the effect that all public opinions favor "doing what we can afford," which has already been discussed above. In the "resource limitations" hypothesis, only the opinion of legislators across the states needs to be shared. The "everyone wants the same things" hypothesis includes the general public.

This hypothesis rests on the assumption that decision makers, presumably legislators and the governor, represent public opinion when they enact laws and provide services. Furthermore, this representativeness would have to hold across all states. Such equal representativeness seems improbable, but then again so does shared public opinions across all states. From our discussions of the South and the traditional political culture, we would scarcely expect this region to share opinions with those in the north central part of the country, such as Wisconsin and Minnesota. It is equally implausible that a farm-oriented state, such as Iowa, would share opinions with those living in Massachusetts. Similarly, the life-style of California seems unlikely to result in the same opinions as in South Carolina.

States React to Forces Not Easily Resisted by the Public.   We have seen that urbanization with its increasingly dependent population, an underclass of immigrants living in ghettos, the Civil War and its aftermath, the needs for intercity transportation and statewide health and building codes, the Great Depression and U.S. involvement in the world, the civil rights movement, and probably the waste products of technologically advanced economies have all driven changes in government. Compared with such forces for change, a state government's acts seeking to make the state more efficient, to have a better educational system, and so on, seem insignificant. State governments have been changed by each of the events enumerated above, but not by the actions of a single legislator, a given legislature, a dominant political party, or even the complex of interest groups in a state. This situation may be related to the relative resistance to change of humans. All the listed events that changed government have had great impacts on people's lives.

Competition Among the States. We saw in Chapter 12 that modern states economically compete with each other. There would be an advantage to having a better education system, having lower taxes, or having a low crime rate. To innovate in seeking such goals, however, could result in failure and a great disadvantage. Rather than risk being disadvantaged by a failed effort, a competitor merely matches the opponent. Certainly, one frequently hears appeals for a new program because most states have such a program. When new taxes must be considered, the consensus seems to be that sales taxes cannot be raised above the highest level found among the states. Competitively, states cringe at the thought of being called Taxachusetts, as Massachusetts is often called, referring to its high taxes.

A Successful Political Career and Innovative Policies Are Independent. Average citizens, legislators, and statewide elected executives all have their own concerns with life. Few of these concerns hinge on whether public education improves or remains about the same, whether sales taxes are at 7.75 percent or 8.00 percent, or even whether oil spills continue or are stopped. We all have our priorities, and quality public policy is seldom among them. Legislators, even if they wish to serve longer, can probably accept the advice of professionals running their campaigns that policies are unimportant to voters. What matters is how you appear to the voters. Voters can probably rest assured that if the person they opposed wins, little policy difference can be expected.

Policies are passed in a complex interplay between many actors. What the public will accept and what it expects are factors. What representatives think they need to win the support of groups who will contribute the hundreds of thousands of dollars necessary for political campaigns will shape their actions. Lobbyists will seek not only the support of those whose campaigns they supported, but also that of those they unwisely opposed. Governors may aspire to run for the presidency or the U.S. Senate and may seek national attention, as a "take charge" and "do something" governor, or they may be satisfied merely with the title of governor and have no policy interests. Even the communications media may believe that their audience share or the number of newspapers sold will increase with coverage of sleeping legislators rather than with trying to cover complex issues. In short, the policies enacted may be intended by no one.

Democracy Is a Sham.   Representatives in all state legislature and in governor's offices share little with residents of their state. We have seen that they are predominantly white, middle-class, middle-aged males. However, they differ more substantially in the extent of their involvement in politics. This political activism may be motivated by altruism, by the need to make a living, especially in the case of more high-paying legislatures, by psychological needs to be important as evidenced by having the title, senator or governor, or by more sinister reasons. Certainly most representatives gain their public office by spending in their campaign more than their potential salary. Why would anyone spend more to get a job than it pays?

Few representatives pay for their campaigns out of their own pockets. Others pay for the campaign with their contributions. But why would anyone pay for you to get a job for which they will not be paid? The answer, of course, is that they expect your vote to support their positions. We have seen that few can now win elected office without substantial campaign expenditures. We have also seen that voters are poorly equipped to select the candidate other than the well-financed incumbent or the candidate of the political party to which they are loyal. This means that nearly all representatives have substantial obligations to those responsible for their having a job, and those responsible are certainly not the voters.

Public officeholders are in effect bought; but even were they not, they probably share few of the concerns of their constituents. Public policies are not a reflection of public opinion. They reflect at best the middle-class, white, male biases of legislators, or at worst the upper-middle-class values of those with money to contribute to campaigns. States may therefore differ little in their public policies, because the middle or upper middle class across the nation shares an expectation of what government should do. Since the reforms that destroyed the city machines of the late 1800s, democracy has been a sham.

CONCLUSION ON LACK OF DIFFERENCES

Most of these hypotheses at least partially explain why no state is renowned for successfully dealing with crime, for having the best educational system, for being most representative, or for being most efficient in the operation of its government. The issue then becomes one of whether we want state governments to change and how such changes could be accomplished. I seriously doubt that if the public were informed on this very complex question, there would be public endorsement for change. Certainly change would be difficult to accomplish. We might have to draft a new national Constitution, substantially alter the process for selecting legislators and governors, somehow dampen competition between the states, commit additional resources to government, or somehow get the public to monitor government much more closely, including holding those responsible for dumb decisions accountable.

Until such changes are successfully undertaken, citizens should have certain expectations of the state and local governments. You probably cannot vote with your feet, save to move to a wealthy state if you expect much in the way of government services. The state grasses are not greener on the other side of the state line. As a state becomes more urban, state government will become more active in coping with the problems associated with urbanization. Fortunately, personal wealth will improve, allowing resources for such efforts. Campaign calls for greater efficiency in government, even if they result in the election of the candidate, will see no change in efficiency. For that matter, even if a candidate violates the advice of those running his or her campaign and takes a position on an important issue and wins election, along with sufficient numbers of likeminded legislators, the law or laws they pass will be unlikely to change behavior in the intended direction to any significant degree.

There are a number of forces foreseeable in the future that might be sufficient to change government as some did in our past. A true AIDS epidemic with tens of millions dying, an enduring oil shortage where Middle East oil resources are destroyed, a technological breakthrough for an alternative energy source, an obvious environmental threat endangering humanity, or a nuclear war would be such forces. It is doubtful, however, whether state governments in any of these cases would be turned to for governmental actions.

SUMMARY

1. There are clear patterns of differences among the states that center on (a) their wealth or more accurately the wealth of their residents; (b) how metropolitan they are, which provides a measure of both the problems faced and the resources available; (c) their political culture; and (d) the uniqueness of the South.

2. Most of these differences greatly overlap; for example, the South tends to be traditional, poor, and nonmetropolitan.

3. Both institutional innovations or improvements in politics—such as having a more professional legislature, a stronger governor, or more competition between the political parties—and most measures of better public policies—such as more investment in education, or more extensive governmental services—also show these patterns of differences.

4. It thus appears that it is not possible to say that one state or one group of states enacts better policies because it has better institutions or better politics.

5. If you want less-extensive governmental services, you need to move away from metropolitan states and endure less competition between political parties. Optimally, you will need to move to the South.

6. All of the possible factors that cause states to differ little other than in wealth, culture, metropolitan concentration, and region are not readily changed by actions taken by government.

SELECTED READINGS

Dahl, Robert A. *Dilemmas of Pluralist Democracy* (New Haven, CT: Yale University Press, 1982). Dahl considers difficulties in the contemporary U.S. expression of democracy.

Pateman, Carole. *Participation and Democratic Theory* (New York: Cambridge University Press, 1970). This work is critical of pluralism or what is called "contemporary theory of democracy." Perhaps if the public in some states were given more of a role than is even the case in California, the states would differ.

Name Index

Subject Index